Family Religion

Matthew Henry

Family Religion

PRINCIPLES FOR RAISING A GODLY FAMILY

Matthew Henry

Copyright © Christian Focus Publications 2008

ISBN 1-84550-2096-4
ISBN 978-1-84550-2096-6

This edition published in 2008
in the
Christian Heritage Imprint
by
Christian Focus Publications,
Geanies House, Fearn, Ross-shire,
Scotland, IV20 ITW, UK

www.christianfocus.com

Cover design by Moose77.com

Printed and bound by
CPD, Wales

CONTENTS

Treatise on Baptism

THIS VOLUME

Apart from in the *Miscellaneous Works of Matthew Henry,* the contents of this book have not been published together before. They represent a collection of his writings on the practice and foundation of religion in the family. The text is unchanged from that found in his *Works* except where the following features, designed to make the book more user-friendly, required minor changes:

1. We have inserted subheadings, sometimes extending to four levels and largely based on the original numeric structure. The contents pages include primary and secondary subheadings to aid navigation.
2. Sentences enumerating more than five or six items, lists of more than one sentence, selected notes, and some 'short digressions' are broken off from the main text and displayed.
3. We have made the style and placement of biblical references consistent with modern practice and changed Roman numerals to Arabic.

INTRODUCTION

Matthew Henry's Life and His Family Devotions

Matthew Henry is well known throughout the world because of his Bible commentary. Nearly all of his other works are accessible in the two-volume set of his complete works, but despite the fact that some of them have been reprinted in recent times, they are not quoted nearly so often. This present book contains four of his publications that all relate to religious life within the family. To appreciate these writings fully we must see them in the particular context of Matthew Henry's own life and practice.

Matthew Henry was born in 1662, a momentous year in English religious history. Over 2,000 pastors were ejected from their livings in the Church of England because they refused to conform to the requirements laid upon them by the Act of Uniformity. This meant that these non-conformists who became Presbyterian or Congregationalist or Baptist pastors were deprived of opportunities to minister publicly, and non-conformist students were excluded from Oxford and Cambridge Universities. One of the ejected pastors was Matthew Henry's own father, Philip Henry. After schooling in London, Philip Henry proceeded for tertiary study at Christ's College, Oxford. This was the period in which the great Puritan leaders John Owen and Thomas Goodwin were exercising their most persuasive influence there. After finishing at Oxford, Philip Henry was settled as the Anglican pastor in the small village of Worthenbury in Flintshire, near the Welsh border, and it was from that parish that he was ejected in 1662. He married Katherine Matthews, the only child of a wealthy couple, and though driven out from his parish and thus losing his stipend, because of his wife's wealth and inheritance the family were able to live without any income from the church. They moved and took up residence at the Matthews' family home at Broad Oak, Flintshire, and remained there for the rest of their lives.

Being brought up in the home of such a godly father and pastor meant that Matthew Henry was from his earliest years exposed to deep religious commitment and training in the things of God. The parents took very seriously their role in the spiritual life of the children. On the occasion of his mother's death, Matthew Henry commented that his parents 'taught us the good knowledge of the Lord, of the Lord Jesus, and led us into an acquaintance with Jesus Christ, and him crucified'. At the age of twenty, he numbered some of the blessings he had received from God. One of them was: 'That I had a Religious Education, the Principles of Religion instill'd into me with my very milk, and from a Child have been taught the good Knowledge of God'.

Sunday was kept as the Lord's Day, and it was a special, joyful day for the family. Philip Henry often greeted his family with the words used in the early church: 'The Lord is risen; he is risen indeed.' Family worship, both morning and evening, was longer than on other days of the week. In addition, the children and servants were catechised, as he wanted to ensure that they were not just memorising by rote. At the end he prayed for the entire household, and for the ministry at Broad Oak and in neighbouring towns such as Chester, Nantwich, Wrexham and Whitechurch.

Worship on the Lord's Day, both in the home and in public, was not the only religious practice in the Henry household. The parents followed the regular Puritan habit of worship in the family circle. After prayer asking for help in understanding the Scripture reading, a biblical passage was read, often accompanied by some appropriate comments by the father. The Scripture reading followed the biblical order, and normally a practical exposition of it was given. A Psalm was sung as well, usually from Barton's edition, singing quickly with the use of a good variety of tunes. The children were briefly questioned as to what they remembered of the reading and exposition, before the family knelt in prayer. Philip Henry prayed, confessing family sins but also giving thanks for family mercies. Evening worship followed much the same pattern, sometimes with a longer explanation of the passage and perhaps catechising of the children.

In writing the life of his father, Matthew Henry documented something of the religious practice of the family home. While the father had the main responsibility of leading the family worship, Philip Henry recommended that the wife should sometimes pray with the husband, so that she would be familiar with leading worship in his absence, or carry it on if he died. He wanted others to follow similar practices in their homes, and encouraged them to make their home a little church. Philip Henry set a pattern that was followed by others, and John Wesley commended it as a model.

After a thorough education from his father, Matthew Henry studied in London at the dissenting academy run by Dr Thomas Doolittle. He caught some sort of fever while there, and when recovered returned home for a time. He later went back to London and studied law for a time, as dissenting students were still not able to study at the universities. His parents kept a watchful eye on him from a distance. His mother once wrote to him: 'I write a line or two to you to mind you keep in touch with God, as I hope you do, by solemn, secret, daily prayer; watching therein with perseverance; not forgetting what you have been taught.'

His sense of call to the Christian ministry gradually deepened, and though he seems to have considered entering into the ministry of the Church of England, by 1687 he had decided to accept a call to a non-conformist congregation. Henry chose to go to Chester in the west of England, entering into the pastorate of a congregation that did not have its own building. The opening in 1690 of its own chapel rectified this lack. His ministry was not confined to Chester, but he moved widely around the local area, preaching in many localities. Various attempts were made to induce him to leave Chester, but it was not until 1712 that he accepted a call to the congregation in Hackney, London.

His growing literary work was a factor in this move, as he was producing many other works quite apart from his commentary. He was not spared to exercise a long-term ministry there, for he died in 1714, at the age of fifty-two.

In his first year of ministry in Chester, he married. He had already heard about Katharine Hardware, and on coming to Chester, desired to marry her. However, Mrs Hardware was not at all willing for this to happen, and considered that a dissenting pastor did not have enough of this world's goods to care for her daughter, who had already received proposals from gentlemen with much larger estates. Later she admitted that she had been governed by 'covetousness and pride' when she tried to prevent the marriage. She regretted her initial stand about the marriage, but recognized that God had overruled for good.

In the end true love prevailed, and the marriage took place in July 1687. For four months the young couple stayed in the house of one of the prominent members of the congregation, and then moved in October to premises in the Friery. This was to be home for Matthew Henry for the next twenty-two years. Philip Henry gave excellent advice to his son and new daughter-in-law by penning some poetry for them. This was advice 'from a pious aged father to his son, a minister newly married'.

> Dear Pair, whom God hath now of two made One
> Suffer a Father's exhortation.
> In the first Place see that with joynt indeavor—
> You set yourselves to serve the Lord together,
> You are yoakt to work but for work Wages write,
> His Yoak is easie, & his burden light,
> Love one another, Pray oft together, and see,
> You never both together Angry bee—
> If one speak fire t'other with water come,
> Is one provok'd be tother soft or dumb—
> Walk low, but aim high, spotless be your life
> You are a Minister, and a Minister's Wife
> Therefore as Beacons set upon a Hill—
> To angels and to men a spectacle—
> Your slips will falls be calld, your falls each one
> Will be a blemish to Religion—
> Do good to all, bee affable and meek
> Your converse must be Preaching all the week—
> Your Garb and Dress must not be vain or Gay,

Reckon good works your richest, best array—
Your House must be a Bethel, and your Door
Always stand open to relieve the Poor
Call your estate God's, not your own, ingrave
Holiness to the Lord on all you have,
Count upon suffering, or you count amis,
Sufficient to each day its evil is,
All are born once to trouble, but saints twice,
And as experience shews Min[iste]rs thrice,
But if you suffer with and for your Lord,
You'l reign with him according to his Word.

The marriage was an extremely happy one, but only lasted eighteen months. Katharine contracted smallpox and died on 14 February 1689 after giving birth to a daughter. She was only twenty-five years of age. Katharine's mother bore the tragedy well and acknowledged that it was the Lord's will. His friend William Tong came to console Matthew who, after shedding tears, was able to say: 'I know nothing that could support me under such a loss as this, but the good hope that she is gone to heaven, and that, in a little time, I shall follow her thither.' She was buried in Trinity Church, Chester on Saturday, 16 February 1689, with a service at Matthew Henry's chapel afterwards, when Mr Lawrence preached on Philippians 1: 21: 'To die is gain.'

Philip Henry also came to console his son, whose grief was tempered by the fact that the life of his first-born was spared. She was called Katharine after her mother, and baptized by her grandfather. Her father made the usual confession of faith in Christ, but then added:

Although my house be not now so with God, yet he hath made with me an everlasting covenant, ordered in all things and sure, and this is all my salvation, and all my desire, although he make me not to grow; and according to the tenor of this covenant, I offer up this child to the Great God, a plant out of a dry ground, desiring that it may be implanted into Christ.

The large congregation present was deeply touched by this and burst into tears.

Matthew Henry continued with his normal ministerial work and also remained living with his deceased wife's parents. After some time, Mrs Hardware recommended that he marry again, and even suggested a relative of her own, Mary Warburton, as his future wife. She had godly parents. Her father and grandfather were both devout Christian men. In his later years her father spent much of his time in reading and prayer. His Bible and a copy of Richard Baxter's *The Saints' Everlasting Rest*, was always on the parlour table. Her mother was a Londoner and shared both her husband's faith and his commitment to the non-conformist cause. Ejected ministers, who were silenced by their expulsion from their parishes, found a ready welcome at the Warburton home, and dissenting believers often gathered there.

The wedding took place on 8 July 1690 at the bride's home at Grange in Cheshire. Philip and Katharine Henry were present, and a few days later accompanied their son and their new daughter-in-law to Chester. When they had settled in, the Hardwares left Chester and went back to live in their own estate at Bromborough Court in Wirral. Matthew and Mary were blessed by the arrival of a daughter, Elizabeth, on 12 April 1691, who was baptized by her grandfather Philip on the normal lecture day in his son's congregation.

The household joy was not to last long, for Elizabeth took ill when about three months old. She had whooping cough and a fever. From 9 November 1690, Matthew Henry kept a diary, and so we can read his reaction to this illness. Just three days before Elizabeth died he wrote:

> The child has been ill all night; she is very weak, and in all appearance worse; but I am much comforted by her baptism. I desire to leave her in the arms of Him who gave her to me. The will of the Lord be done. I have said, if the Lord will spare her, I will endeavour to bring her up for him. I am now sitting by her, thinking of the mischievous nature of original sin, by which death reigns over poor infants.

On the day of her death he penned these words:

> In the morning I had the child in my arms, endeavouring solemnly to give her up to God, and to bring my heart to his will: and presently there seemed some reviving. But while I was writing this, I was suddenly called out of my closet. I went for the doctor, and brought him with me; but, as soon as we came in, the sweet babe quietly departed between the

> mother's arms and mine, without any struggle, for nature
> was spent by its long illness; and now my house is a house
> of mourning.

He endeavoured to comfort his wife as they prepared for the funeral. When it was over he wrote: 'I have been this Day doing a Work that I never did, burying a Child, a sad Day's Work.' Friends came and showed their kindness to the bereaved family, and attended the afternoon lecture at which his good friend Mr Lawrence preached from Psalm 39: 9: 'I was dumb, I opened not my mouth, because thou didest it.'

Another daughter, Mary, was born the following year, on 3 April 1693. The grandfather came from Broad Oak and baptized both her and her cousin, Katharine Hulton, and in his diary he recorded the prayer: 'The Lord write their Names in the Book of the Living.' But this baby only lived for three weeks, dying the same month, on 22 April. In his diary, he expressed his grief, and then wrote: 'The Lord is righteous, he takes and gives, gives and takes again; I desire to submit, but, O Lord, shew me wherefore thou contendest with me.' On the following Lord's Day he expounded Job 38, a passage dealing with the assertion of God's sovereignty, while he preached on Romans 5: 14: 'Nevertheless death reigned from Adam to Moses, even over them that had not sinned, after the similitude of Adam's transgression, who is the figure of him who was to come.' Even when noting that within the year two of his children and two of his brother's had been buried in Trinity Church, he could still say: 'The Lord is gracious.'

Joy came to the Henrys in the following year when a daughter, Esther, was born on 27 September 1694. Despite various illnesses, especially one when she was three years old, she survived. At that time Matthew Henry referred to her as 'the Delight of my Eyes'.

Within the home circle Matthew Henry followed the same pattern of worship as his father had adopted. This included singing. As in the church services, the singing was a cappella, as no musical instrument was used in dissenting services at that period. In 1694 he published a volume entitled, *Family Hymns, Gathered Mostly out of the Translations of David's Psalms*. He preferred singing songs taken from Scripture, though in the third edition he included three paraphrases of passages — from

Isaiah, Luke 1–2, and the book of Revelation — and Ambrose's *Te Deum*. He explained his action by saying that the inclusion of 'some of the New Testament Hymns, which being calculated for gospel times, I doubt not, be very agreeable to every good Christian.' While the translations are very close to the Hebrew text, at times there is interpretation that intrudes a distinctly New Testament idea into the text. Thus, for example, in Psalm 51, after very accurate translation of the opening verses, verse 7 is given in this form:

> With hyssop sprinkle me, and then
>   I shall be clean, I know;
> And make me with my Saviour's blood
>   Whiter than driven snow.

In this respect he was moving in the way that Isaac Watts would shortly afterwards, as he sought to bring out the Christian application of the Psalms.

In a preface to the reader he explained that his concern was to promote singing at family worship. He pointed out that it was the ancient practice of Christians to sing in the home, and he quotes from a variety of sources—from the New Testament, from writers such as Pliny, Clement of Alexandria, Cyprian, Tertullian and on to those of the more recent times in England. According to him, it did not matter if neighbours heard the singing as Christians serve a master of whom they have no reason to be ashamed. As to the manner of singing, he insisted that with only a small degree of skill a family could manage to sing the Psalms, and 'in private families the quickest way of singing seems to be the most agreeable'.

'Family Hymns' consists of ninety hymns, though often a hymn is made up of selections from several different psalms or biblical passages. Here is an example of one set out for the Lord's Day morning.

HYMN XXVII Ps. xxvii.4

> This is my great request, O God,
> Which here I do present,
> That all the days I have to live
> May in thy house be spent.

There to contemplate and behold
The beauty of the Lord,
And in his temple to inquire
Into his holy word.

8–9

When as thou saidst, My face seek ye,
Instructed by thy grace,
My ready heart with joy replied,
Lord, I will seek thy face.
Hide not thy face from me in wrath;
Lord turn me not away:
My Saviour, thou hast been my help,
Be still my strength and stay.

____xliii. 3, 4

O send out light and truth divine,
To lead and bring me near
Unto that holy hill of thine,
And tabernacles there.
Then to God's altar I will go,
The gladness of my joy,
O God, my God thy praise to show,
My harp I will employ.

____cxix. 32

And I will run with full consent
The way thou givest in charge,
When with thy sweet encouragement
Thou shalt my heart enlarge.

No music was printed, but sometimes a note is given indicating that the Psalm was to be sung to the tune of Ps. 67, or that the hymns of praise (comprising hymns 67 to 90) were to be sung to the tune of the 100th Psalm and the 148th Psalm. This means that the first section of this group were long metre (and could be sung to the tune *The Old 100th*), while the later ones were in 6.6.6.6.8.8 metre.

One practice that Matthew Henry sought to discourage was giving out each line before it was sung. This was an English custom to enable those who could not read to join in the singing. This practice of 'lining-out' meant that the singing took much longer, and in general resulted in a very slow pace. In the discussions at the Westminster Assembly, the Scottish commissioners argued against the practice, but *The Directory of Public Worship* includes reference to it. What Matthew Henry suggested was that each member of the family have a book so that the psalm or hymn 'may be sung without reading out each line, which is the general practice of the reformed churches abroad, renders the duty more pleasant and profitable, takes up less time, and is practicable enough in a family, if not in large congregations.'

Acknowledgement was given that the work of others had been used. His ultimate aim was beautifully expressed in the closing sentences of the preface:

> The performance indeed is but very small, yet the design is honest; and it will be fruit abounding to a good account, if it do but help forward the work of singing psalms in which the will of God is done on earth, somewhat like it is in heaven, where singing hallelujahs to him that sits upon the throne, and unto the Lamb, is both the everlasting work, and the everlasting felicity, of those glorified beings that wear the crown of perfection within the vail.

On the second Saturday he was in Chester, he started to catechise the children in the congregation on Saturday afternoons. He heard them repeat answers from the *Shorter Catechism* and expounded to them one at a time. When his own catechism was published, he examined them on that. He chose Saturday afternoon as it gave him greater time and freedom with the children than if he had to do it on the Lord's Day. In alternate years, when he had finished the catechism, he preached a special sermon for the children at their usual meeting time. No record remains of these sermons, but presumably they were adapted to suit the needs of the children. When his own children were born, similar catechising of them took place within the family circle.

In addition to his own family, Matthew and Mary Henry had to care for other relatives. Two of his sisters died within a few weeks of each other in 1697. Eleanor (Mrs Samuel Radford) died on 13 August, while Ann (Mrs John Hulton) died on

6 September. When Samuel Radford died two years later, the Henrys took into their home the four orphan children. They cared for them as their own, and the children were later to testify to the love and care they received in the Henry home.

BACKGROUND TO MATTHEW HENRY'S WRITING

Before briefly introducing the four works printed in this volume, I need to say something about three other aspects of background information. The first concerns the heritage of biblical study and commentary that influenced Matthew Henry. His work is the fruit of developments that go back to the Renaissance and Reformation periods. Much of the exposition of the Bible in the medieval period was not through the application of careful grammatical study. Rather it was a superimposed allegorical method that made nonsense of the literal understanding. While some resisted the common method, it was only in the Renaissance and Reformation period that significant change came. The Renaissance movement paved the way by insisting on the need to get back to the sources, and helped by providing the tools that were needed for biblical research (texts, grammars, lexicons). In the case, of Martin Luther and John Calvin, their humanist training was certainly applied very productively to their work, and this helps to explain the enduring nature of their biblical exegesis. While it is not true to say that there would never have been a reformation without the Renaissance, it is true that the Reformation took the precise form it did because its approach to the biblical text was one which was developed from principles set out by the humanist scholars in their return to the sources.

Matthew Henry's work was produced at the very end of the Puritan movement. The method of biblical exposition used by the Puritans and that of the Reformers carried on the approach to the Bible established by Luther and Calvin and their fellow reformers, and so approached Scripture seeking to interpret it literally and grammatically. Though Matthew Henry did not personally sit at the feet of the great Puritans, his father Philip had, and so he was influenced by their approach.

The second aspect of Matthew Henry's writing on which comment is needed is its orderliness. In this respect the Puritans were influenced by the work of a French Huguenot scholar, Peter Ramus, who taught that analysis is the key to understanding. This resulted in them setting out their material logically, so that they had headings, sub-headings, and sub-sub-headings! Behind this method was the understanding that there is an intellectual element in presenting the Gospel. The mind must be informed before the emotions and the will are affected.

Matthew Henry's systematic and logical approach is evident both in his commentary and his sermons. He followed the Puritans in stressing the intellectual character of ministry, both spoken and written. Preaching in the Reformed tradition 'was the product of arduous mental exercise, and it was designed to provoke an exercise of mind in those to whom it was addressed. These men were concerned with truth. Their view of the Gospel was that it is the truth "as it is in Jesus", and it is therefore as truth that it must be declared. Truth demands understanding in the preacher, and is addressed to the understanding of the hearer'.

The third thing to note is that Matthew Henry had a remarkable knowledge of the Bible, first of all in the form of the Authorised Version of 1611. He knew it intimately, and also its marginal readings. The AV translators say in their preface: 'If you ask what they had before them, truly it was the Hebrew text of the Old Testament, the Greek of the New.... If truth be to be tried by these tongues, then whence should a translation be made, but out of them.' There are 6,637 marginal readings in the Old Testament, of which 4,034 give the literal meaning of the Hebrew and Aramaic; 2,156 offer alternative readings; 63 give the meaning of proper names; and 31 give the manuscript differences as noted by the Jewish massoretic scholars. Matthew Henry from an early age was a scholar of Hebrew and Greek, and without parading his learning, he draws upon it in his exegesis both in his sermons and his other writings.

Matthew must have been very aware himself of advice his father regularly gave to prospective pastors. Students who had gone through their studies at private academies wanted to spend some time with Philip Henry and his family before they entered into the ministry. When they came to stay, what he did was to impress on them the need above all else to be familiar with the text of the Bible. He reminded them of the maxim, *bonus textarius est bonus theologus*, 'the good textual student is a good theologian'.

NOTES ON THE WRITINGS IN THIS COLLECTION

The first of the writings in this volume is a sermon that Matthew Henry preached in London on 7 April 1713 to a group of people undergoing instruction at the church ministered to by Mr Harris. It is entitled 'A Sermon concerning the Catechising of Youth', and it is based on 2 Timothy 1: 13: 'Hold fast the form of sound words which thou hast heard of me, in faith and love which is in Christ Jesus.' It is a sermon in typical Matthew Henry style, in which he develops the thought that home teaching and public exposition by ministers must work hand in hand. Also in his usual style he applies the teaching to his audience, encouraging them to treasure the teaching they have received, to pray over it so that it may touch their hearts, and to live out the teaching in a way that adorns the doctrine of God our Saviour. Later, Dr Isaac Watts, in his *Discourses on Instruction by Catechisms*, mentions with approval this excellent sermon.

The second piece is another sermon, this time one preached on 6 March 1713. It is entitled 'Christ's Favour to Little Children Displayed', and is based on the words in Mark 10: 16: 'And he took them up in his arms, put his hands upon them and blessed them.' It was preached on the occasion of the baptism of Eleanor, daughter of the Revd. Jeremiah Smith. In it he encourages parents to bring their children to Christ's feet, impressing upon them their need to be taught by him and to believe his truths. Though written from a paedobaptist viewpoint, Matthew Henry indicates to parents that their children might receive the water of baptism and yet remain strangers to God's grace. When he comes to application he first of all addresses the 'little children', 'the lambs of the flock'. He asks them the questions: 'Has [Christ] thus loved you, and will not you love him?' 'Does he invite you to him, and will not you accept of his invitation?' He points them to books, but especially the Holy Scriptures that are able to make them wise unto salvation.

The third piece, 'A Church in the House', was again a sermon, this time preached in London on 16 April 1704 when Matthew Henry was there on a visit while he was still a pastor in Chester. The idea comes from the words in 1 Corinthians 16: 19: '...with the church that is in their house'. This is a concept that will challenge many parents in our day, as readers are encouraged to dedicate their homes to the Lord and to view the religious life of the home as virtually a mini-church.

The fourth and longest section is 'A Treatise on Baptism.' It is uncertain when Matthew Henry started to think about the subject of baptism and to write on it. In his diary he wrote: '1707, August 15. I had a letter from a meeting of ministers in Buckinghamshire, to urge me to publish something of the baptismal covenant; the Lord direct my studies, and incline me to that in which he will own me.' However, during his lifetime this piece of writing remained unpublished. Ultimately it was published in an abridged form in 1783 by Thomas Robins. The Revd. S. Palmer, in his account of Matthew Henry's life prefixed to the 1811 edition of his commentary, said that he had compared it with the original and that the aim had been 'to retain everything important, and omit what was redundant'.

We know that Philip Henry prepared a short baptismal covenant for his children which they repeated every Lord's Day evening. The position that his son Matthew takes in this treatise is fully consistent with his father's position and typical of evangelical Anglicanism and Presbyterianism. He wrote against promiscuous baptism of children, insisting that at least one parent be a believer. Also, he specifically notes that baptism does not operate automatically.

These four pieces of Matthew Henry's writings fit together well. They show the emphasis he placed on religion in the home, and the responsibility that parents have for bringing up their children in the fear and instruction of the Lord. In his typical organised way he sets out both the obligations and blessings that belong to the church in the home.

Allan M. Harman

1

A CHURCH IN THE HOUSE

'With the church that is in their house' (1 Cor. 16: 19).

Some very good interpreters I know understand this as a settled, stated, solemn meeting of Christians at the house of Aquila and Priscilla, for public worship; and they were glad of houses to meet in, where they wanted those better conveniences, which the church was afterwards in her prosperous days, accommodated with. When they had not such places as they could wish, they thankfully made use of such as they could get.

But others think it is meant only of their own family, and the strangers within their gates, among whom there was so much piety and devotion, that it might well be called a church, or religious house. Thus the ancients generally understood it. Nor was it only Aquila and Priscilla whose house was thus celebrated for religion here (Rom. 16: 5) but Nymphas also had a 'church in his house' (Col. 4: 15) and Philemon (v. 2). Not but that others, to whom and from whom salutations are sent in St. Paul's Epistles, made conscience of keeping up religion in their families; but these are mentioned, probably because their families were more numerous than most of those other families were, which made their family devotions more solemn, and consequently more taken notice of.

In this sense I shall choose to take it; from hence to recommend family religion to you, under the notion of a church in the house. When we see your public assemblies so well filled, so well frequented, we cannot but thank God, and take courage; your diligent attendance on the ministry of the word and prayers, is your praise, and I trust, through grace, it redounds to your spiritual comfort and benefit. But my subject at this time will lead me to inquire into the state of religion in your private houses, whether it flourish or wither there? Whether it be upon the throne, or under foot there? Herein I desire to deal plainly and faithfully with your consciences, and I beg you will give them leave to deal so with you.

The pious and zealous endeavours both of magistrates and ministers for the reformation of manners, and the suppression of vice and profaneness, are the joy and encouragement of all good people in the land, and a happy indication that God has yet mercy in store for us: 'If the Lord were pleased to kill us, he would not have told us such things as these' (Judg. 13: 23). Now I know not any thing that will contribute more to the furtherance of this good work than the bringing of family religion more into practice and reputation. Here the reformation must begin. Other methods may check the disease we complain of, but this, if it might universally obtain, would cure it. Salt must be cast into these springs, and then the waters would be healed.

Many a time, no doubt, you have been urged to this part of your duty; many a good sermon perhaps you have heard, and many a good book hath been put into your hands with this design, to persuade you to keep up religion in your families and to assist you therein: but I hope a further attempt to advance this good work, by one who is a hearty wellwisher to it, and to the prosperity of your souls and families, will not be thought altogether needless, and that by the grace of God it will not be wholly fruitless; at least it will serve to remind you of what you have received and heard to this purpose, that you may hold fast what is good, and repent of what is amiss (Rev. 3: 3). The lesson then which I would recommend to you from this text, is this:

'That the families of Christians should be little churches', or thus, 'That wherever we have a house, God should have a church in it.'

Unhappy contests there have been, and still are, among wise and good men about the constitution, order, and government of churches; God by his grace heal these breaches, lead us into all truth, and dispose our minds to love and peace; that while we endeavour herein to 'walk according to the light God hath given us,' we may 'charitably believe that others do so too', longing to be there where we shall be all of a mind.

But I am now speaking of churches, concerning which there is no controversy. All agree that masters of families who profess religion, and the fear of God themselves, should, according to the talents they are entrusted with, maintain and keep up religion and the fear of God in their families, 'as those who must give account', and that families as such should contribute to the support of Christianity in a nation whose honour and happiness it is to be a Christian nation. As nature makes families little kingdoms, and perhaps economics were the first and most ancient politics, so grace makes families little churches; and those were the primitive churches of the Old Testament, before 'men began to call upon the name of the Lord' in solemn assemblies, and 'the sons of God came together to present themselves' before him.

Not that I would have these family churches set up and kept up in competition with, much less in contradiction to, public religious assemblies, which ought always to have the preference: 'The Lord loves the gates of Sion more than all the dwellings of Jacob' (Ps. 87: 2), and so must we; and must not forsake the assembling of ourselves together, under colour of exhorting one another daily at home. Far be it from us to offer anything that may countenance the invading of the office of the ministry, or laying it in common, and the usurping or superseding of the administration of sacraments. No, but these family churches (which are but figuratively so) must be erected and maintained in subordination to those more sacred and solemn establishments.

Now, that I may the more distinctly open to you, and press upon you, this great duty of family religion, from the example of this and other texts of a church in the house, I shall endeavour:

1. To show what this church in the house is, and when our families may be called churches.
2. To persuade you by some motives thus to turn your families into churches.
3. To address you upon the whole matter by way of application.

WHAT IS A CHURCH IN THE HOUSE?

I am in the first place to tell you what that family religion is which will be as a church in the house, and wherein it consists, that you may see what it is we are persuading you to.

Churches are sacred societies, incorporated for the honour and service of God in Christ, devoted to God, and employed for him; so should our families be.

A FAMILY DEVOTED TO GOD

Churches are societies devoted to God, called out of the world, taken in out of the common to be enclosures for God: he hath set them apart for himself; and because he hath chosen them, they also have chosen him, and set themselves apart for him. The Jewish church was separated to God for a peculiar people, a kingdom of priests.

Thus our houses must be churches; with ourselves we must give up our houses to the Lord, to be to him for a name and a people. All the interest we have, both in our relations, and in our possessions, must be consecrated to God; as under the law all that the servant had was his master's for ever, after he had consented to have his ear bored to the doorpost. When God effectually called Abram out of Ur of the Chaldees, his family assumed the appearance of a particular church; for in obedience to God's precept, and in dependence on God's promise, they took all the substance they had gathered, and the souls they had gotten, and put themselves and their all under a divine conduct and government (Gen. 12: 5). His was a great family, not only numerous, but very considerable; the father of it was the father of all them that believe; but even little families, jointly and entirely given up to God, so become churches. When all the members of the family yield themselves to God, subscribe with their hands to be the Lord's, and surname themselves by the name of Israel; and the master of the family, with himself, gives up all his right, title, and interest, in his house, and all that belongs to it, unto God, to be used for him, and disposed of by him, here is a church in the house.

Baptism was ordained for the discipling of nations (Matt. 28: 19), that the kingdoms of the world, as such, might, by the conversion of their people to the faith of Christ, and the consecration of their powers and governments to the honour of Christ, become his kingdoms (Rev. 11: 15). Thus, by baptism households likewise are discipled, as Lydia's and the jailer's (Acts 16: 15, 33), and in their family capacity are given up to him, who is in a particular manner the God of all the families of Israel (Jer. 31: 1). Circumcision was at first a family ordinance, and in that particular, as well as others, baptism somewhat symbolizes with it. When the children of Christian parents are by baptism admitted as members of the universal church, as their right to baptism is grounded upon, so their communion with the universal church is, during their infancy, maintained and kept up chiefly by, their immediate relation to these churches in the house; to them therefore, they are first given back, and in them they are deposited, under their tuition, to be trained up till they become capable of a place and a name in particular churches of larger figure and extent. So that baptized families, that own their baptism, and adhere to it, and in their joint and relative capacity make profession of the Christian faith, may so far be called little churches.

More than once in the Old Testament we read of the dedication of private houses. It is spoken of as common practice: 'What man is there that hath built a new house, and hath not dedicated it?' (Deut. 20: 5), that is, taken possession of it; in the doing of which it was usual to dedicate it to God by some solemn acts of religious worship. The thirtieth Psalm is entitled, 'A Psalm or Song at the dedication of the house of David.' It is a good thing when a man has a house of his own, thus to convert it into a church, by dedicating it to the service and honour of God, that it may be a Bethel, a house of God, and not a Bethaven, a house of vanity and iniquity. Every good Christian who is a householder, no doubt doth this habitually and virtually; having first

It is a good thing when a man has a house of his own, thus to convert it into a church, by dedicating it to the service and honour of God...

given his own self to the Lord, he freely surrenders all he has to him: but it may be of good use to do it actually and expressly, and often to repeat this act of resignation; 'This stone which I have set for a pillar shall be God's house' (Gen. 28: 22). Let all I have in my house, and all I do in it, be for the glory of God; I own him to be my great Landlord, and I hold all from under him: to him I promise to pay the rents—the quit-rents—of daily praises and thanksgivings; and to do the services—the easy services—of gospel obedience. Let holiness to the Lord be written upon the house, and all the furniture of it, according to the word which God has spoken (Zech. 14: 20–1), that every pot in Jerusalem and Judah 'shall be Holiness to the Lord of hosts'. Let God by his providence dispose of the affairs of my family, and by his grace dispose the affections of all in my family, according to his will, to his own praise. Let me and mine be only, wholly, and for ever his.

Be persuaded brethren, thus to dedicate your houses to God, and beg of him to come and take possession of them. If you never did it, do it tonight with all possible seriousness and sincerity. 'Lift up your heads, O ye gates, and be ye lifted up, ye everlasting doors, and the King of glory shall come in' (Ps. 24: 7). Bring the ark of the Lord into the tent you have pitched, and oblige yourselves, and all yours, to attend it. Look upon your houses as temples for God, places for worship, and all your possessions as dedicated things, to be used for God's honour, and not to be alienated or profaned.

A SOCIETY EMPLOYED FOR GOD

Churches are societies employed for God, pursuant to the true intent and meaning of this dedication.

There are three things necessary to the well-being of a church, and which are most considerable in the constitution of it.

Those are doctrine, worship and discipline; where the truths of Christ are professed and taught, the ordinances of Christ administered and observed, and due care taken to put the laws of Christ in execution among all who profess themselves his subjects, and this under the conduct and inspection of a gospel ministry; there is a church. And something answerable to this there must be in our families, to denominate them 'little churches'.

Masters of families, who preside in the other affairs of the house, must go before their households in the things of God. They must be as prophets, priests and kings in their own families; and as such they must keep up family doctrine, family worship and family discipline; then is there a church in the house, and this is the family religion that I am persuading you to.

Keep Up Family Doctrine

It is not enough that you and yours are baptized into the Christian faith, and profess to own the truth as it is in Jesus, but care must be taken, and means used, that you and yours be well acquainted with that truth, and that you grow in that acquaintance, to the honour of Christ and his holy religion, and the improvement of your own minds, and theirs who are under your charge. You must deal with your families as men of knowledge (1 Pet. 3: 7) that is, as men who desire to grow in knowledge yourselves, and to communicate your knowledge for the benefit of others, which are the two good properties of those who deserve to be called men of knowledge.

READ THE SCRIPTURES TO YOUR FAMILIES, in a solemn manner, requiring their attendance on your reading, and their attention to it; and inquiring sometimes whether they understand what you read. I hope you are none of you without Bibles in your houses, store of Bibles, every one a Bible. Thanks be to God, we have them cheap and common in a language that we understand. The book of the law is not such a rarity with us as it was in Josiah's time. We need not fetch this knowledge from afar, nor send from sea to sea, and from the river to the ends of the earth, to seek the word of God; no, the Word is near us. When popery reigned in our land, English Bibles were scarce things; a load of hay (it is said) was once given for one torn leaf of a Bible. But now Bibles are every one's money. You know where to buy them; or if not able to do that, perhaps in this charitable city you may know where to beg them. It is better to be without bread in your houses than without Bibles, for the words of God's mouth are and should be to you more than your necessary food.

But what will it avail you to have Bibles in your houses, if you do not use them? To have the great things of God's law and gospel written to you, if you count them as a strange thing? You look daily into your shop-books, and perhaps converse much with the news-books, and shall your Bibles be thrown by as an almanac out of date? It is not now penal to read the Scriptures in your families, as it was in the dawning of the day of reformation from popery, when there were those who were accused and prosecuted mid-prose for reading in a certain great heretical book, called an English Bible. The Philistines do not now 'stop up these wells' (as Gen. 26: 18), nor do the 'shepherds drive away' your flocks from them (as Exod. 2: 17), nor are they as a spring shut up, or a fountain sealed; but the gifts given to men have been happily employed in rolling away the stone from the mouth of these wells. You have great encouragements to read the Scripture; for notwithstanding the malicious endeavours of atheists to vilify sacred things, the knowledge of the Scripture is still in reputation with all wise and good men. You have also a variety of excellent helps to understand the Scripture, and to improve your reading of it; so that if you or yours perish for lack of this knowledge, as you certainly will if you persist in the neglect of it, you may thank yourselves, the guilt will lie wholly at your own doors.

Let me therefore, with all earnestness press it upon you to make the solemn reading of the Scripture a part of your daily worship in your families. When you speak to God by prayer, be willing to hear him speak to you in his word, that there may be a complete communion between you and God. This will add much to the solemnity of your family worship, and will make the transaction the more awful and serious, if it be done in a right manner; which will conduce much to the honour of God, and your own and your family's edification. It will help to make the word of God familiar to yourselves, and your children and servants, that you may be ready and mighty in the Scriptures, and may from thence be thoroughly furnished for every good word and work. It will likewise furnish you with matter and words for prayer, and so be helpful to you in other parts of the service. If some parts of Scripture seem less edifying, let those be most frequently read that are most so. David's Psalms are of daily use in devotion, and Solomon's proverbs in conversation: it will be greatly to your advantage to be well versed in them. And I hope I need not press any Christian to the study of the New Testament, nor any Christian parents to the frequent instructing of their children in the pleasant and profitable histories of the Old Testament. When you only hear your children read the Bible, they are tempted to look upon it as no more than a school-book; but when they hear you read it to them in a solemn, religious manner, it comes as it ought, with more authority. Those masters of families who make conscience of doing this daily, morning and evening, reckoning it part of that which the duty of every day requires, I am sure they have comfort and satisfaction in so doing, and find it contributes much to their own improvement in Christian knowledge, and the edification of those who dwell under their shadow; and the more, if those who are ministers expound themselves, and other masters of families read some plain and profitable exposition of what is read, or of some part of it.

It is easy to add under this head, that the seasonable reading of other good books will contribute very much to family instruction. In helps of this kind we are as happy as any people under the sun, if we have but hearts to use the helps we have, as those who must give an account shortly of them among other talents which we are entrusted with.

YOU MUST ALSO CATECHISE YOUR CHILDREN and servants, so long as they continue in that age of life which needs this milk. Oblige them to learn some good catechism by heart, and to keep it in remembrance; and by familiar discourse with them help them to understand it, as they become capable. It is an excellent method of catechising, which God himself directs us to (Deut. 6: 7), to teach our children the things of God, by talking of them as we sit in the house, and go by the way, when we lie down, and when we rise up. It is good to keep up stated times for this service, and be constant to them, as those who know how industrious the enemy is to sow tares while men sleep. If this good work be not kept going forward, it will of itself go backward. Wisdom also will direct you to manage your catechising, as well as the other branches of family religion, so as not to make it a task and burden, but as much as may be a pleasure to those under your charge, that the blame may lie wholly upon their own impiety, and not at all upon your imprudence, if they should say 'Behold what a weariness it is!'

This way of instruction by catechising does in a special manner belong to the church in the house; for that is the nursery in which the trees of righteousness are reared, that afterwards are planted in the courts of our God. Public catechising will turn to little account without family catechising. The labour of ministers in instructing youth and feeding the lambs of the flock therefore proves to many labour in vain, because masters of families do not do their duty in preparing them for public instruction and examining their improvement by it. As mothers are children's best nurses, so parents are, or should be, their best teachers. Solomon's father was his tutor (Prov. 4: 3–4), and he never forgot the lessons his mother taught him (Prov. 31: 1).

The baptism of your children, as it laid a strong and lasting obligation upon them to live in the fear of God, so it brought you under the most powerful engagements imaginable to bring them up in that fear. The child you gave up to God to be dedicated to him, and admitted as a member of Christ's visible church, was in God's name given back to you, with the same charge that Pharaoh's daughter gave to Moses' mother, 'Take this child and nurse it for me;' and in nursing it for God, you nurse it for better preferment than that of being called the son of Pharaoh's daughter. It is worth observing, that he to whom God first did the honour of entailing the seal of the covenant upon his seed, was eminent for this part of family religion: I know Abraham, says God, that he will 'command his children and his household after him, and they shall keep the way of the Lord' (Gen. 18: 19). Those, therefore, who would have the comfort of God's covenant with them and their seed, and would share in that blessing of Abraham which comes upon the Gentiles, must herein follow the example of faithful Abraham. The entail of the covenant of grace is forfeited and cut off, if care be not taken, with it, to transmit the means of grace. To what purpose were they discipled if they be not taught? Why did you give them a Christian name, if you will not give them the knowledge of Christ and Christianity? God has owned them as his children, born to him (Ezek. 16: 20), and therefore he expects that they should be brought up for him; you are unjust to your God, unkind to your children, and unfaithful to your trust, if having by baptism entered your children in Christ's school, and listed them under his banner, you do not make conscience of training them up in the learning of Christ's scholars, and under the discipline of his soldiers.

Consider what your children are now capable of, even in the days of their childhood. They are capable of receiving impressions now which may abide upon them while they live; they are turned as clay to the seal, and now is the time to apply to them the 'seal of the living God'. They are capable of honouring God now, if they be well taught: and by their joining, as they can, in religious services with so much reverence and application as their age will admit, God is honoured, and you in them present to him 'living sacrifices, holy and acceptable'. The hosannas even of children well taught will be the perfecting of praise, and highly pleasing to the Lord Jesus.

Consider what your children are designed for, we hope, in this world; they must be a 'seed to serve the Lord', which shall be 'accounted to him for a generation'. They are to bear up the name of Christ in their day, and into their hands must be transmitted that good thing which is committed to us. They are to be praising God on earth, when we are praising him in heaven. Let them then be brought up accordingly, that they may answer the end of their birth and being. They are designed for the service of their generation, and to do good in their day. Consult the public welfare then, and let nothing be wanting on your parts to qualify them for usefulness, according as their place and capacity is.

Consider especially what they are designed for in another world: they are made for eternity. Every child you have has a precious and immortal soul, that must be forever either in heaven or hell, according as it is prepared in this present state; and perhaps it must remove to that world of spirits very shortly: and will it not be very sad, if through your carelessness and neglect, your children should learn the ways of sin, and perish eternally in those ways? Give them warning, that, if possible, you may deliver their souls; at least, that you may deliver your own, and may not bring their curse and God's too, their blood and your own too, upon your heads.

I know you cannot give grace to your children, nor is a religious conversation the constant consequence of a religious education; 'the race is not always to the swift, nor the battle to the strong' (Eccles. 9: 11), but if you make conscience of doing your duty, by keeping up family doctrine; if you teach them the good and the right way, and warn them of by-paths; if you reprove, exhort and encourage them as there is occasion; if you pray with them, and for them, and set them a good example, and at last consult their soul's welfare in the disposal of them, you have done your part, and may comfortably leave the issue and success with God.

Keep Up Family Worship

You must not only as prophets teach your families, but as priests must go before them, in offering the spiritual sacrifices of prayer and praise. Herein likewise you must tread in the steps of faithful Abraham, whose sons you are while thus you do well; you must not only like him instruct your household, but like him you must with them 'call on the name of the Lord, the everlasting God' (Gen. 21: 33). Wherever he pitched his tent, 'there he built an altar unto the Lord' (Gen. 12: 7, 8; 13: 4, 18) though he was yet in an unsettled state, but a stranger and a sojourner; though he was among jealous and envious neighbours, for the Canaanite and the Perizzite 'dwelled then in the land', yet, wherever Abraham had a tent, God had an altar in it, and he himself served at that altar. Herein he has left us an example.

Families, as such, have many errands at the throne of grace, which furnish them with matter and occasion for family prayer every day; errands which cannot be done so well in secret or public, but are fittest to be done by the family in consort, and apart from other families. And it is good for those who go before the rest in family devotions, ordinarily to dwell most upon the concerns of those who join in their family capacity, that it may be indeed a family prayer, not only offered up in and by the family, but suited to it. In this and other services we should endeavour not only to say something, but something to the purpose.

Five things especially you should have upon your heart in your family prayer, and should endeavour to bring something of each, more or less, into every prayer with your families.

ACKNOWLEDGE YOUR DEPENDENCE UPON GOD and his providence, as you are a family. Our great business in all acts of religious worship, is to 'give unto the Lord the glory due unto his name', and this we must do in our family worship. Give honour to God as the founder of families by his ordinance, because 'it was not good for man to be alone', as the founder of your families by his providence, for he it is that 'buildeth the house, and setteth the solitary in families' (Ps. 68: 6). Give honour to him as the Owner and Ruler of families; acknowledge that you and yours are his, under his government, and at his disposal, as 'the sheep of his pasture'. Especially adore him as the God of all the families of Israel, in covenant relation to them, and having a particular concern for them above others (Jer. 31: 1). Give honour to the great Redeemer as the head of all the churches, even those in your houses; call him the Master of the family, and the great upholder and benefactor of it; for he it is 'in whom all the families of the earth are blessed' (Gen. 12: 3). All family blessings are owing to Christ, and come to us through his hand, by his blood. Own your dependence upon God, and your obligations to Christ, for all good things 'pertaining both to life and godliness'; make conscience of paying homage to your chief Lord, and never set up a title to any of your enjoyments in competition with his.

CONFESS YOUR SINS AGAINST GOD; those sins you have contracted the guilt of in your family capacity. We read in Scripture of the iniquity of the house, as of Eli's (1 Sam. 3: 13–14). Iniquity visited upon the children; sins that bring wrath upon families, and a curse that enters into the house to consume it, with the 'timber thereof, and the stones thereof' (Zech. 5: 4). How sad is the condition of those families that sin together, and never pray together! That by concurring in frauds, quarrels and excesses, by strengthening one another's hands in impiety and profaneness, fill the measure of family guilt, and never agree together to do anything to empty it!

And even religious families, that are not polluted with gross and scandalous sins, yet have need to join every day in solemn acts and expressions of repentance before God for their sins of daily infirmity: their vain words and unprofitable conversation among themselves; their manifold defects in relative duties, provoking one another's lusts and passions, instead of provoking one another to love and to good works; these ought to be confessed and bewailed by the family together, that God may be glorified, and what has been amiss may be amended for the future. It was not only in a time of great and extraordinary repentance that families mourned apart (Zech. 12: 12), but in the stated returns of the day of expiation the priest was particularly to make 'atonement for his household' (Lev. 16: 17). In many things we all offend God, and one another; and a penitent confession of it in prayer together will be the most effectual way of reconciling ourselves both to God, and to one another. The best families, and those in which piety and love prevail most, yet in many things come short, and do enough every day to bring them upon their knees at night.

> *In many things we all offend God, and one another; and a penitent confession of it in prayer together, will be the most effectual way of reconciling ourselves both to God, and to one another.*

OFFER UP FAMILY THANKSGIVINGS for the blessings which you, with your families, receive from God. Many are the mercies which you enjoy the sweetness and benefit of in common; which, if wanting to one, all the family would be sensible of it. Has not God made a hedge of protection about you and your houses, and all that you have? (Job 1: 10). Has he not created a defence upon 'every dwelling place of Mount Zion, as well us upon her assemblies?' (Isa. 4: 5). The dreadful alarms of a storm, and the desolations made, as by a fire, once in an age, should make us sensible of our obligations to the Divine Providence for our preservation from tempests and fire every day and every night. 'It is of the Lord's mercies that we are not consumed', and buried in the ruins of our houses. When the whole family comes together safe in the morning from their respective retirements, and when they return safe at night from their respective employments, there having been no disaster, no adversary, no evil occurrence, it is so reasonable, and (as I may say) so natural, for them to join together in solemn thanksgivings to their great Protector, that I wonder how any who believe in a God, and a providence, can omit it. Have you not health in your family, sickness kept or taken from the midst of you? Does not God bring plentifully into your hands, and increase your substance? Have you not your table spread, and your cup running over, and manna rained about your tents? And does not the whole family share in the comfort of all this? Shall not then the voice of thanksgiving be in those tabernacles where the voice of rejoicing is? (Ps. 118: 15). Is the vine by the house-side fruitful and flourishing, and the olive plants round the table green and growing? Are family relations comfortable and agreeable, not broken nor embittered, and shall not that God be acknowledged herein who makes every creature to be that to us that it is? Shall not the God of your mercies, your family mercies, be the God of your praises, your family praises, and that daily?

The benefit and honour of your being Christian families, your having in God's house, and within his walls, a place and a name better than that of sons and daughters, and the salvation this brings to your house, furnishes you with abundant matter for joint thanksgivings. 'You hath he known above all the families of the earth', and therefore, he expects in a special manner to be owned by you. Of all houses, the house of Israel, the house of Aaron, and the house of Levi have most reason to bless the Lord, and to say that 'his mercy endures for ever'.

PRESENT YOUR FAMILY PETITIONS for the mercy and grace which your families stand in need of. Daily bread is received by families together, and we are taught not only to pray for it every day, but to pray together for it, saying, 'Our Father, give it us.' There are affairs and employments which the family is jointly concerned in the success of, and therefore, should jointly ask of God wisdom for the management of them, and prosperity therein. There are family cares to be cast upon God by prayer, family comforts to be sought for, and family crosses which they should together beg for the sanctification and removal of. Hereby your children will be more effectually possessed with a belief of, and regard to, the Divine Providence, than by all the instructions you can give them; which will look best in their eye, when thus reduced to practice by your daily acknowledging God in all your ways.

You desire that God will give wisdom and grace to your children, you 'travel in birth again till you see Christ formed in them', you pray for them; it is well, but it is not enough; you must pray with them. Let them hear you pray to God for a blessing upon the good instructions and counsels you give them; it may perhaps put them upon praying for themselves, and increase their esteem both of you, and of the good lessons you teach them. You would have your servants diligent and faithful, and this perhaps would help to make them so. Masters do not give to their servants that which is just and equal if they do not continue in prayer with them. They are put together (Col. 4: 1–2).

There are some temptations which families, as such, lie open to. Busy families are in temptation to worldliness and neglect of religious duties; mixed families are in temptation to discord, and mutual jealousies; decaying families are in temptation to distrust, discontent, and indirect courses to help themselves; they should therefore not only watch, but pray together, that they be not overcome by the temptations they are exposed to.

There are family blessings which God has promised, and for which he will be sought unto, such as those on the house of Obed-edom for the ark's sake; or the mercy which St. Paul begs for the house of Onesiphorus (2 Tim. 1: 16). These joint blessings must be sued out by joint prayers. There is a special blessing which God commands upon families that dwell together in unity (Ps. 133: 1–3), which they must seek for by prayer, and come together to seek for it, in token of that unity which qualifies for it. Where God commands the blessing, we must beg the blessing. God by promise blesses David's house, and therefore, David by prayer blesses it too (2 Sam. 6: 20).

MAKE FAMILY INTERCESSIONS FOR OTHERS ALSO. There are families you stand related to, or which by neighbourhood, friendship, or acquaintance, you become interested in and concerned for; and these you should recommend in your prayers to the grace of God, and your family that are joined with you in the alliances should join with you in those prayers. Evil tidings perhaps are received from relations at a distance, which are the grief of the family; God must then be sought unto by the family for succour and deliverance. Some of the branches of the family are, perhaps, in distant countries, and in dangerous circumstances, and you are solicitous about them; it will be a comfort to yourselves, and perhaps of advantage to them, to make mention of them daily in your family prayers. The benefit of prayer will reach far, because he who hears prayer can extend his hand of power and mercy to the utmost corners of the earth, and to them that are afar off upon the sea.

In the public peace likewise we and our families have peace; and therefore, if we forget thee, O Jerusalem, we are unworthy ever to stand in thy courts, or dwell within thy walls. Our families should be witnesses for us that we pray daily for the land of our nativity, and the prosperity of all its interests; that praying everywhere we make supplication for the Queen, and all in authority (1 Tim. 2: 2, 8); and that we bear upon our hearts the concerns of God's church abroad, especially the suffering parts of it, thus keeping up a spiritual communion with all the families that 'in every place call on the name of the Lord Jesus'.

In a word, let us go by this rule in our family devotions; whatever is the matter of our care, let it be the matter of our prayer; and let us allow no care which we cannot in faith spread before God. And whatever is the matter of our rejoicing, let it be the matter of our thanksgiving; and let us withhold our hearts from all those joys which do not dispose us for the duty of praise.

Under this head of family worship, I must not omit to recommend to you the singing of psalms in your families, as a part of daily worship, especially Sabbath worship. This is a part of religious worship, which participates both of the word and prayer; for therein we are not only to give glory to God, but to teach and admonish one another; it is therefore very proper to make it a transition from the one to the other. It will warm and quicken you, refresh and comfort you; and perhaps, if you have little children in your houses, they will sooner take notice of it than

I must not omit to recommend to you the singing of psalms in your families, as a part of daily worship... it will warm and quicken you, refresh and comfort you.

43

of any other part of your family devotion: and some good impressions may thereby be fastened upon them insensibly.

Keep Up Family Discipline

Keep up family discipline, that so you may have a complete church in your house, though in little. Reason teaches us that 'every man should bear rule in his own house' (Esther 1: 22). And since that as well as other power is of God, it ought to be employed for God; and they who so rule must be just, ruling in his fear. Joshua looked further than the acts of religious worship when he made that pious resolution, 'As for me and my house, we will serve the Lord' (Josh. 24: 15). For we do not 'serve him in sincerity and truth', which is the service he there speaks of (v. 14), if we and ours serve him only on our knees, and do not take care to serve him in all the instances of a religious conversation. Those only who have clean hands, and a pure heart, are accounted 'the generation of them that seek God' (Ps. 24: 4, 6). And without this those who pretend to 'seek God daily' do but mock him (Isa. 58: 2).

The authority God has given you over your children and servants is principally designed for this end, that you may thereby engage them for God and godliness. If you use it only to oblige them to do your will, and so to serve your pride; and to do your business, and so to serve your worldliness, you do not answer the great end of your being invested with it; you must use it for God's honour, by it to engage them as far as you can, to do the will of God, and mind the business of religion. Holy David not only blessed his household, but took care to keep good order in it, as appears by that plan of his family discipline which we have in the 101st Psalm, a psalm which Mr Fox tells us that blessed martyr Bishop Ridley often read to his family, as the rule by which he resolved to govern it. You are made keepers of the vineyard; be faithful to your trust, and carefully watch over those who are under your charge, knowing that you must give account.

COUNTENANCE EVERY THING THAT IS GOOD and praise-worthy in your children and servants. It is as much your duty to commend and encourage those in your family who do well, as to reprove and admonish those who do amiss; and if you take delight only in blaming that which is culpable, and are backward to praise that which is laudable, you give occasion to suspect something of an ill nature, not becoming a good man, much less a good Christian. It should be a trouble to us when we have a reproof to give, but a pleasure to us to say with the apostle, 'Now I praise you' (1 Cor. 11: 2). Most people will be easier led than driven, and we all love to be spoken to fairly: when you see anything that is hopeful and promising in your inferiors, anything of a towardly and tractable disposition, much more anything of a pious affection to the things of God, you should contrive to encourage it. Smile upon them when you see them set their faces heavenwards, and take the first opportunity to let them know you observe it, and are well pleased with it, and do not despise the day of small things. This will quicken them to continue and abound in that which is good, it will hearten them against the difficulties they see in their way; and, perhaps, may turn the wavering, trembling scale the right way, and effectually determine their resolutions to cleave to the Lord. When you see them forward to come to family worship, attentive to the word, devout in prayer, industrious to get knowledge, afraid of sin, and careful to do their duty, let them have the praise of it, for you have the comfort of it, and God must have all the glory. Draw them with the cords of a man, hold them with the bands of love; so shall your rebukes, when they are necessary, be the more acceptable and effectual. The great Shepherd (Isa. 40: 11) 'gathers the lambs in his arms, and carries them in his bosom, and gently leads them', and so should you.

DISCOUNTENANCE EVERY THING THAT IS EVIL in your children and servants. Use your authority for the preventing of sin, and the suppressing of every root of bitterness, lest 'it spring up, and trouble you, and thereby many be defiled' (Heb. 12: 15). Frown upon everything that brings sin into your families, and introduces any ill words, or ill practices. Pride and passion, strife and contention, idleness and intemperance, lying and slandering, these are sins which you must not connive at, nor suffer to go without a rebuke. If you return to the Almighty, this among other things is required of you, that you put away iniquity, all iniquity, these and other the like iniquities, 'far from thy tabernacle' (Job 22: 23). Make it to appear, that in the government of your families you are more jealous for God's honour than for your own authority and interest; and show yourselves more displeased at that which is an offence to God, than at that which is only an affront or damage to yourselves.

You must indeed be careful not to provoke your children to wrath, lest they be discouraged; and as to your servants, it is your duty to forbear or moderate threatening: yet you must also, with holy zeal and resolution, and the meekness of wisdom, keep good order in your families, and set no wicked thing before their eyes, but witness against it. 'A little leaven leavens the whole lump.' Be afraid of having wicked servants in your houses, lest your children learn their ways, and get a snare to their souls. Drive away with an angry countenance all that evil communication which corrupts good manners, that your houses may be habitations of righteousness, and sin may never find shelter in them.

WHY HAVE A CHURCH IN YOUR HOUSE?

I come now to offer some motives to persuade you thus to turn your families into little churches. And, O that I could find out acceptable words, with which to reason with you, so as to prevail! Suffer me a little and I will show you what is to be said on God's behalf, which is worth your consideration.

GOD WILL COME TO DWELL WITH YOU

If your families be little churches, God will come to you, and dwell with you in them; for he has said concerning the church, 'This is my rest for ever, here will I dwell.' It is a very desirable thing to have the gracious presence of God with us in our families, that presence which is promised where 'two or three are gathered together in his name.' This was it that David was so desirous of: 'O when wilt thou come unto me!' (Ps. 101: 2). His palace, his court, would be as a prison, as a dungeon to him, if God did not come to him, and dwell with him in it; and cannot your hearts witness to this desire? You who have houses of your own, would you not have God come to you, and dwell with you in them? Invite him then, beg his presence, court his stay. Nay, he invites himself to your houses by the offers of his favour and grace: 'Behold, he stands at your door and knocks.' It is the voice of your beloved; open to him, and bid him welcome: meet him with your Hosannas, 'Blessed is he that cometh.' He comes peaceably, he brings a blessing with him, a blessing which he will cause to rest upon the habitations of the righteous (Ezek. 44: 30). He will command a blessing, which shall amount to no less than life for evermore (Ps. 133: 3). This presence and blessing of God will make your relations comfortable, your affairs successful, your enjoyments sweet; and behold, by it all things are made clean to you. This will make your family comforts double comforts, and your family crosses but half crosses; it will turn a tent into a temple, a cottage into a palace; 'Beautiful for situation, the joy of the whole earth' (Ps. 48: 2) are the houses in which God dwells.

Now the way to have God's presence with you in your houses, is to furnish them for his entertainment. Thus the good Shunamite invited the prophet Elisha to the chamber she had prepared for him, by accommodating him there with 'a bed and a table, a stool and a candlestick' (2 Kings 4: 10). Would you furnish your houses for the presence of God, it is not expected that you furnish them as his tabernacle was of old furnished, with 'blue, and purple, and scarlet, and fine linen,' but set up and keep up for him a throne and an altar, that from the altar you and yours may 'give glory to him', and from the throne he may give law to you and yours; and then you may be sure of his presence and blessing, and may solace yourselves from day to day in the comfort of it. God will be with you in a way of mercy while you are with him in a way of duty; 'If you seek him he will be found of you.' The secret of God shall be in your tabernacle, as it was in Job's (29: 4); as it is with the righteous (Ps. 25: 14; Prov. 3: 32–3).

GOD WILL BE YOUR SANCTUARY

If you make your houses little churches, 'God will make them little sanctuaries'; nay, he will himself be to you as a 'little sanctuary' (Ezek. 11: 16). The way to be safe in your houses, is to keep up religion and the fear of God in your houses; so shall you dwell on high, and the place of your defence 'shall be the munition of rocks' (Isa. 33: 16). The law looks upon a man's house as his castle, religion makes it truly so. If God's grace be the 'glory in the midst' of the house, his providence will 'make a wall of fire round about it' (Zech. 2: 5). Satan found it to his confusion, that God made a hedge about pious Job, about his house, and about all that he had on every side, so that he could not find one gap by which to break in upon him (Job 1: 10). Every dwelling place of mount Sion shall be protected as the tabernacle was in the wilderness, for God has promised to 'create upon it a cloud and smoke by day, and the shining of a flaming fire by night', which shall be a defence upon all the glory (Isa. 4: 5). If we thus 'dwell in the house of the Lord all the days of our life', by making our houses his houses, we shall be hid in his pavilion, 'in the secret of his tabernacle shall he hide us' (Ps. 27: 4, 5).

Wherever we encamp, 'under the banner of Christ', the angels of God will 'encamp round about us,' and pitch their tents where we pitch ours; and we little think how much we owe to the ministration of the good angels, that we and ours are preserved from the malice of evil angels, who are continually seeking to do mischief to good people. There are terrors that fly by night and by day, which they only who 'abide under the shadow of the Almighty' can promise themselves to be safe from (Ps. 91: 1, 5). Would you insure your houses by the best policy of insurance, turn them into churches, and then they shall be taken under the special protection of him who keeps Israel, 'and neither slumbers nor sleeps'; and if any damage come to them, it shall be made up in grace and glory. The way of duty is without doubt the way of safety.

Praying families are kept from more mischiefs than they themselves are aware of. They are not always sensible of the distinction which a kind providence makes between them and others; though God is pleased sometimes to make it

> *Praying families are kept from more mischiefs than they themselves are aware of.*

remarkable, as in the story which is credibly related of a certain village in the Canton of Bern in Switzerland, consisting of ninety houses, which in the year 1584, were all destroyed by an earthquake, except one house, in which the good man and his family were at that time together praying. That promise is sure to all the seed of faithful Abraham, 'Fear not, I am thy shield'

(Gen. 15: 1). Wisdom herself has past her word for it (Prov. 1: 33). 'Whoso harkeneth to me,' wherever he dwells, he 'shall dwell safely, and shall be quiet from' all real evil itself, and from the amazing, tormenting fear of evil. Nothing can hurt, nothing needs frighten, those whom God protects.

To Keep Satan Out

If you have not a church in your house, it is to be feared that Satan will have a seat there. If religion does not rule in your families, sin and wickedness will rule there. 'I know where thou dwellest,' says Christ to the angel of the church of Pergamos (Rev. 2: 13), 'even where Satan's seat is'; that was his affliction: but there are many whose sin it is; by their irreligion and immorality they allow Satan a seat in their houses, and that seat a throne. They are very willing that the 'strong man armed should keep his palace' there, and that his goods should be at peace; and the surest way to prevent this, is by setting up a church in the house. It is commonly said, that where God has a church, the devil will have his chapel; but it may more truly be said in this case, where God has not a church, the devil will have his chapel. If the unclean spirit find the house in this sense empty, empty of good, though it be 'swept and garnished, he takes to himself seven other spirits more wicked than himself and they enter in and dwell there' (Matt. 12: 44–5).

Terrible stories have been told of houses haunted by the devil, and of the fear people have had of dwelling in such houses; verily those houses in which rioting and drunkenness reign, in which swearing and cursing are the language of the house, or in which the more spiritual wickednesses of pride, malice, covetousness, and deceit have the ascendant, may truly be said to be haunted by the devil, and they are most uncomfortable houses for any man to live in; they are 'holds of foul spirits, and cages of unclean and hateful birds', even as Babylon the great will be when it is fallen (Rev. 18: 2).

Now the way to keep sin out of the house, is to keep up religion in the house, which will be the most effectual antidote against Satan's poison. When Abraham thought concerning Abimelech's house, 'Surely the fear of God is not in this place', he concluded no less but 'they will slay me for my wife's sake' (Gen. 20: 11).

Where no fear of God is, no reading, no praying, no devotion, what can one expect but all that is bad? Where there is impiety there will be immorality; they who 'restrain prayer, cast off fear' (Job 15: 4). But if religious worship has its place in the house, it may be hoped that vice will not have a place there. There is much of truth in that saying of good Mr Dodd, 'Either praying will make a man give over sinning, or sinning will make a man give over praying.' There remains some hope concerning those who are otherwise bad, as long as they keep up prayer. Though there be a struggle between Christ and Belial in your houses, and the insults of sin and Satan are daring and threatening, yet as long as religion keeps the field, and the weapons of its warfare are made use of, we may hope the enemy will lose ground.

FOR THE ENJOYMENT OF YOUR FAMILY

A church in the house will make it very comfortable to yourselves. Nothing more agreeable to a gracious soul than constant communion with a gracious God; it is the one thing it desires, to dwell in the home of the Lord; here it is as in its element, it is its rest for ever. If, therefore our houses be houses of the Lord, we shall for that reason love home, reckoning our daily devotion the sweetest of our daily delights, and our family worship the most valuable of our family comforts. This will sanctify to us all the conveniences of our houses, and reconcile us to the inconveniences of it. What are 'Solomon's gardens, and orchards, and pools of water,' and the other 'delights of the sons of men' (Eccles. 2: 5–6, 8) in comparison with these delights of the children of God?

Family religion will help to make our family relations comfortable to us, by promoting love, preventing quarrels, and extinguishing heats that may at any time happen. A family living in the fear of God, and joining daily in religious worship, truly enjoys itself; 'Behold how good and how pleasant a thing it is for brethren thus to dwell together!' It is not only like ointment and perfume which rejoice the heart, but like the holy ointment, the holy perfume, wherewith Aaron the saint of the Lord was consecrated; not only like the common dew to the grass, but like the dew which descends upon the mountains of Sion, the holy mountains (Ps. 133: 1-3). The communion of saints in that which is the work of saints, is without doubt the most pleasant communion here on earth, and the liveliest representation and surest pledge of those everlasting joys which are the happiness of 'the spirits of just men made perfect', and the hopes of holy souls in this imperfect state.

Family religion will make the affairs of the family successful; and though they may not in everything issue to our mind, yet we may by faith foresee that they will at last issue to our good. If this 'beauty of the Lord our God be upon us' and our families, it will 'prosper the work of our hands unto us, yea, the work of our hands' it will establish; or however, it will establish our hearts in that comfort which makes everything that occurs easy (Ps. 90: 17; 112: 8).

We cannot suppose our mountain to stand so strong but that it will be moved; trouble in the flesh we must expect, and affliction in that from which we promise ourselves most comfort; and when the Divine Providence makes our houses, houses of mourning, then it will be comfortable to have them houses of prayer, and to have had them so before. When sickness, and sorrow, and death come into our families (and sooner or later they will come) it is good that they should find the wheels of prayer a-going, and the family accustomed to seek God; for if we are then to begin this good work when distress forces us to it, we shall drive heavily in it. They that pray constantly when they are well, may pray comfortably when they are sick.

So That You Leave a Good Legacy

A church in the house will be a good legacy, nay, it will be a good inheritance, to be left to your children after you. Reason directs us to consult the welfare of posterity, and to lay up in store a good foundation for those that shall come after us to build upon: and we cannot do this better than by keeping up religion in our houses. A family altar will be the best entail; your children will for this rise up and call you blessed, and it may be hoped they will be praising God for you, and praising God like you, here on earth, when you are praising him in heaven.

It may be hoped they will be praising God for you, and praising God like you, here on earth, when you are praising him in heaven.

You will hereby leave your children the benefit of many prayers put up to heaven for them, which will be kept (as it were) upon the file there, to be answered to their comfort, when you are silent in the dust. It is true of prayer, what we say of winter, 'It never rots in the skies.' The seed of Jacob know they do not seek in vain, though perhaps they live not to see their prayers answered. Some good Christians that have made conscience of praying daily with and for their children, have been encouraged to hope that the children of so many prayers should not miscarry at last; and thus encouraged, Joseph's dying word has been the language of many a dying Christian's faith, 'I die, but God will surely visit you' (Gen. 50: 24). I have heard of a hopeful son, who said he valued his interest in his pious father's prayer far more than his interest in his estate, though a considerable one.

You will likewise hereby leave your children a good example, which you may hope they will follow when they come into houses of their own. The usage and practice of your families is commonly transmitted from one generation to another; bad customs are many times thus entailed. They who burnt incense to the queen of heaven learnt it of their fathers (Jer. 44: 17). And a vain conversation was thus 'received by tradition' (1 Pet. 1: 18). And why may not good customs be in like manner handed down to posterity? Thus we should make known the ways of God to our children, that they may arise and declare them to their children (Ps. 78: 6) and religion may become an heirloom in our families. Let your children be able to say, when they are tempted to sit loose to religion, that it was the way of their family, the good old way, in which their fathers walked, and in which they themselves were educated and trained up; and with this they may answer him who reproaches them. Let family worship, besides all its other pleas for itself, be able in your houses to plead prescription. And though to the acceptableness of the service, it is requisite that it be done from a higher and better principle than purely to keep up the custom of the family, yet better so than not at all: and the form of godliness may by the grace of God at length prove the happy vehicle of its power; and dry bones, whilst unburied, may be made to live. Thus a good man leaves an inheritance to his children; and the generation of the upright shall be blessed.

FOR THE PROSPERITY OF THE CHURCH

A church in the house will contribute very much to the prosperity of the church of God in the nation. Family religion, if that prevail, will put a face of religion upon the land, and very much advance the beauty and peace of our English Jerusalem. This is that which I hope we are all hearty well-wishers to; setting aside the consideration of parties, and separate interests, and burying all names of distinction in the grave of Christian charity, we earnestly desire to see true catholic Christianity, and serious godliness in the power of it, prevailing and flourishing in our land; to see knowledge filling the land, as the waters cover the sea; to see holiness and love giving law, and triumphing over sin and strife: we would see cause to call your city, a city of righteousness, a faithful city, its 'walls salvation, and its gates praise'. Now all this would be effected, if family religion were generally set up and kept up.

When the wall was to be built about Jerusalem, it was presently done by this expedient, every one undertook to repair over against his own house (see Neh. 3: 10 ff). And if ever the decayed walls of the gospel Jerusalem be built up, it must be by the same method. Every one must sweep before his own door, and then the street will be clean. If there were a church in every house, there would be such a church in our land as would make it a praise throughout the whole earth. We cannot better serve our country than by keeping up religion in our families.

Let families be well catechised, and then the public preaching of the word will be the more profitable, and the more successful. For want of this, when we speak ever so plainly of the things pertaining to the kingdom of God, to the most we do but speak parables. The book of the Lord is delivered to those who are not catechised, saying, 'Read this' and they say, 'We are not learned'; learned enough in other things, but not in the one thing needful (Isa. 29: 12). But our work is easy with those who from their childhood have known the Holy Scriptures.

If every family were a praying family, public prayers would be the better joined in, more intelligently, and more affectionately; for the more we are used to prayer, the more expert we shall be in that holy and divine art of 'entering into the holiest' in that duty. And public reproofs and admonitions would be as a nail in a sure place, if masters of families would second them with their family discipline, and so clench those nails.

Religious families are blessings to the neighbourhood they live in, at least by their prayers. A good man thus becomes a public good, and it is his ambition to be so. Though he sees his children's children, he has small joy of that if he does not see peace upon Israel (Ps. 128: 5–6). And therefore postponing all his own interests, and satisfactions, he sets himself to seek the good of Jerusalem all the days of his life. Happy were we if we had many such.

HOW TO HAVE A CHURCH IN YOUR HOUSE

That which now remains is to address myself to you upon the whole matter by way of exhortation; and I pray you let my counsel be acceptable to you; and while I endeavour to give every one his portion, let your consciences assist me herein, and take to yourselves that which belongs to you.

BEGIN A GOOD WORK

Let those masters of families that have hitherto lived in the neglect of family religion be persuaded now to set it up, and from henceforward to make conscience of it. I know it is hard to persuade people to begin even a good work that they have not been used to, yet, if God by his grace set in with this word, who can tell but some may be wrought upon to comply with the design of it? We have no ill design in urging you to this part of your duty: we aim not at the advantage of a party, but purely at the prosperity of your families. We are sure we have reason on our side, and if you will but suffer that to rule you, we shall gain our point; and you will all go home firmly resolved, as Joshua was, and whatever others do themselves, and whatever they say of you, 'You and your houses will serve the Lord.' God put it into you, and 'keep it in the imagination of the thought of your heart, and establish your way therein before him!'

Proceed in the right method; first set up Christ upon the throne in your hearts, and then set up a church for Christ in your house. Let Christ dwell in your hearts by faith, and then let him dwell in your houses; you do not begin at the right end of your work, if you do not 'first give your own selves unto the Lord'; God had respect first to Abel, and then to his offering. Let the fear and love of God rule in your hearts, and have a commanding sway and empire there, and then set up an altar for God in your tents; for you cannot do that acceptably till you have first consecrated yourselves as spiritual priests to God, to serve at that altar.

And when your hearts, like Lydia's, are opened to Christ, let your house, like hers, be opened to him too (Acts 16: 14–15). Let there be churches in all your houses; let those who have the stateliest, richest, and best furnished houses, reckon a church in them to be their best ornament; let those who have houses of the greatest care and business, reckon family religion their best employment, and not neglect the one thing needful, while they are careful and cumbered about many things: nor let those that have close and mean habitations be discouraged; the ark of God long dwelt in curtains. Your dwelling is not so strait, but you may find room for a church in it. Church work uses to be chargeable, but you may do this church work cheap: you need not make silver shrines, as they did for Diana, nor lavish gold out of the bag, as idolaters did in the service of their gods (Isa. 46: 6). No: an altar of earth shall you make to your God (Exod. 20: 24) and he will accept it. Church work uses to be slow work, but you may do this quickly. Put on resolution, and you may set up this tabernacle tonight, before tomorrow.

Would you keep up your authority in your family? You cannot do it better than by keeping up religion in your family. If ever a master of a family looks great, truly great, it is when he is going before his house in the service of God, and presiding among them in holy things. Then he shows himself worthy of double honour, when he teaches them the good knowledge of the Lord, and is their mouth to God in prayer, blessing them in the name of God.

Would you have your family relations comfortable, your affairs successful, and give an evidence of your professed subjection to the gospel of Christ? Would you live in God's fear, and die in his favour, and escape that curse which is entailed upon prayerless families? Let religion in the power of it have its due place, that is, the uppermost place in your houses.

Many objections your own corrupt hearts will make against building these churches, but they will all appear frivolous and trifling to a pious mind that is steadfastly resolved for God and godliness: you will never go on in your way to heaven, if you will be frightened by lions in the street. Whatever is the difficulty you dread, the discouragement you apprehend in it, I am confident it is not insuperable, it is not unanswerable. But 'he that observes the wind shall not sow, and he that regards the clouds shall not reap' (Eccles. 11: 4).

Be not loath to begin a new custom, if it be a good custom, especially if it be a duty (as certainly this is) which while you continue in the neglect of, you live in sin: for omissions are sins, and must come into judgment. It may be that you have been convinced that you ought to worship God in your families, and that it is a good thing to do so; but you have put it off to some more convenient season. Will you now at last take occasion from this sermon to begin it! And do not defer so good a work any longer. The present season is without doubt the most convenient season. Begin this day; let this be the day of your laying the foundation of the Lord's temple in your house; and then consider, from this day onwards, as God by the prophet reasons with the people who neglected to 'build the temple' (Hag. 2: 18–19). Take notice whether God does not from this day remarkably bless you in all that you have and do.

Plead not your own weakness and inability to perform family worship; make use of the helps that are provided for you; do as well as you can when you cannot do so well as you would, and God will accept of you. You willingly write what is necessary for the carrying on of your trade, though you cannot write so fine a hand as some others can; and will you not be as wise in the work of your Christian calling, to do your best, though it be far short of the best, rather than not do it at all? To him who has but one talent, and trades with that, more shall be given; but from him that buries it, it shall be taken away. Be at some pains to make the Scriptures familiar to you, especially David's Psalms, and then you cannot be to seek for a variety of apt expressions proper to be used in prayer, for they will lie always at your right hand. Take with you those words, words which the Holy Ghost teaches, for you cannot find more acceptable words.

And now shall I prevail with you in this matter! I am loath to leave you unresolved, or but almost persuaded; I beg of you, for God's sake, for Christ's sake, for your own precious soul's sake, and for the children's sake of your own bodies, that you will live no longer in the neglect of so great, and necessary, and comfortable a duty as this of family worship. When we press upon you the more inward duties of faith and love, and the fear of God, it cannot be so evident that we succeed in our errand as it may be in this. It is certain that you get no good by this sermon, but it is wholly lost upon you, if, after you have heard it, or read it, you continue in the neglect of family religion; and if still you cast off fear, and restrain prayer before God. Your families will be witnesses against you that this work was undone; and this sermon will witness against you, that it was not for want of being called to do it, but for want of a heart to do it when you were called. But I hope better things of you, my brethren, and things that accompany salvation, though I thus speak.

Revive a Good Work

Let those who have kept up family worship formerly, but of late have left it off, be persuaded to revive it. This perhaps, is the case of some of you; you remember the kindness of your youth, and the love of your espousals; time was when you sought God daily, and delighted to know his ways, as families that did righteousness, and forsook not the ordinances of your God; but now it is otherwise. The altar of the Lord is broken down and neglected, the daily sacrifice is ceased; and God has kept an account of how many days it has ceased, whether you have or not (Dan. 8: 13–14). Now God comes into your houses seeking fruit, but he finds none, or next to none: you are so eager in your worldly pursuits, that you have neither hearts nor time for religious exercises. You began at first frequently to omit the service, and a small matter served for an excuse to put it by, and so by degrees it came to nothing.

O that those who have thus left their first love would now remember whence they are fallen, and repent, and do their first works. Inquire how this good work came to be neglected; was it not because your love to God cooled, and the love of the world prevailed? Have you not found a manifest decay in the prosperity of your souls since you let fall this good work? Has not sin got ground in your hearts and in your houses? And though, when you dropped your family worship, you promised yourselves that you would make it up in secret worship, because you were not willing to allow yourselves time for both, yet have you not declined in that also? Are you not grown less frequent, and less fervent, in your closet devotions too? Where is now the blessedness of which you have formerly spoken? I beseech you to lay out yourselves to retrieve it in time. Say, as that penitent adulteress, 'I will go and return to my first husband, for then was it better with me than now' (Hos. 2: 7). Cleanse the sanctuary, and put away the strange gods. Is money the god, or the belly the god that has gained possession of your heart and house? Whatever it is, cast it out. Repair the altar of the Lord, and begin again the daily sacrifice and oblation. Light the lamps again, and burn the incense. Rear up the tabernacle of David which is fallen down, lengthen its cords, and strengthen its stakes, and resolve it shall never be neglected again as it has been. Perhaps you and your families have been manifestly under the rebukes of providence since you left off your duty—as Jacob was, while he neglected to pay his vow; I beseech you, hear at length the voice of the rod, and of him who has appointed it, for it reminds you of your forgotten vows, saying, 'Arise, go up to Bethel, and dwell there' (Gen. 35: 1). Let the place you dwell in ever be a Bethel, so shall God dwell with you there.

MAINTAIN A GOOD WORK

Let those who are remiss and negligent in their family worship be awakened to more zeal and constancy. Some of you perhaps have a church in your house, but it is not a flourishing church; it is like the church of Laodicea, neither cold nor hot; or like the church of Sardis, in which 'the things that remain are ready to die', so that it hath little more than a name to live. Something of this work of the Lord is done for fashion's sake, but it is done deceitfully: you have (Mal. 1: 14) 'in your flock a male', but you 'vow and sacrifice unto the Lord a corrupt thing'; you grow customary in your accustomed services, and bring the 'torn and the blind, the lame and the sick', for sacrifice; and you offer that to your God which you would scorn to offer to your governor; and though it is but little you do for the church in your house, you think that too much, and say, 'Behold what a weariness it is!' You put it off with a small and inconsiderable scantling of your day, and that the dregs and refuse of it. You can spare no time at all for it in the morning, nor any in the evening, till you are half asleep. It is thrust into a corner, and almost lost in a crowd of worldly business and carnal converse. When it is done, it is done so slightly, in so much haste, and with so little reverence, that it makes no impression upon yourselves or your families. The Bible lies ready, but you have no time to read; your servants are otherwise employed, and you think it is no matter for calling them in: you yourselves can take up with a word or two of prayer, or rest in a lifeless, heartless tale of words. Thus it is every day, and perhaps little better on the Lord's day; no repetition, no catechising, no singing of psalms, or none to any purpose.

Is it thus with any of your families? Is this the present state of the church in your house? My brethren, 'these things ought not' to be so. It is not enough that you do that which is good, but you must do it well. God and religion have in effect no place in your hearts or houses, if they have not the innermost and uppermost place. Christ will come no whither to be an underling; he is not a guest to be set behind the door. What comfort, what benefit can you promise to yourselves from such trifling services as these; from an empty form of godliness without the power of it?

I beseech you, sirs, make a business of your family religion, and not a by-business. Let it be your pleasure and delight, and not a task and drudgery. Contrive your affairs so that the most convenient time may be allotted both morning and evening for your family worship, so that you may not be unfit for it, or disturbed and straitened in it; herein 'wisdom is profitable to direct'. Address yourselves to it with reverence and seriousness, and a solemn pause; that those who join with you may see and say, that 'God is with you of it truth,' and may be struck thereby into a like holy awe. You need not be long in the service, but you ought to be lively in it; 'not slothful in this business', because it is business for God and your souls, 'but fervent in spirit, serving the Lord'.

ADORN YOUR PRACTICE

Let those who have a church in their house be very careful to adorn and beautify it in their conversation. If you pray in your families, and read the Scriptures, and sing psalms, and yet are passionate and froward with your relations, quarrelsome and contentious with your neighbours, unjust and deceitful in your dealings, intemperate and given to tippling, or allow yourselves in any other sinful way, you pull down with one hand what you build up with the other. Your prayers will be an abomination to God, and to good men too, if they be thus polluted. 'Be not deceived, God is not mocked.'

See that you be universal in your religion, that it may appear that you are sincere in it. Show that you believe a reality in it, by acting always under the commanding power and influence of it. Be not Christians upon your knees, and unbelievers in your shops. While you seem saints in your devotions, prove not yourselves sinners in your conversations. Having begun the day in the fear of God, be in that fear all the day long. Let the example you set your families be throughout good, and by it teach them not only to read and pray, for that is but half their work, but by it teach them to be meek and humble, sober and temperate, loving and peaceable, just and honest; so shall you adorn the doctrine of God our Saviour; and those who will not be won by the word, shall be won by your conversation. Your family worship is an honour to you, see to it that neither you nor yours be in anything a disgrace to it.

DO NOT PROCRASTINATE

Let those who are setting out in the world set up a church in their house at first, and not defer it. Plead not youth and bashfulness; if you have confidence enough to rule a family, I hope you have confidence enough to pray with a family. Say not, 'the time is not come, the time that the Lord's house should be built', as they did that dwelt in their ceiled houses, while God's house lay waste (Hag. 1: 2, 4). It ought to be built presently; and the longer you put it off, the more difficulty there will be in the doing of it, and the more danger that it will never be done.

Now you are beginning the world (as you call it) is it not your wisdom as well as your duty to begin with God? Can you begin better? Or can you expect to prosper if you do not begin thus? The fuller your heads are of care about setting up house, and setting up shop, and settling in both, the more need you have of daily prayer, that by it you may cast your care on God, and fetch in wisdom and direction from on high.

Always Take the Church With You

In all your removes be sure you take the church in your house along with you. Abraham often removed his tent, but wherever he pitched it, there the first thing he did was to build an altar. It is observable concerning Aquila and Priscilla, of whose pious family my text speaks, that when St. Paul wrote his epistle to the Romans they were at Rome: for he sends salutations to them thither, and there it is said they had 'a church in their house' (Rom. 16: 5). But now, when he wrote this epistle to the Corinthians, they were at Ephesus, for thence it should seem this epistle bore date, and here he sends salutations from them; and at Ephesus also they had a church in their house. As wherever we go ourselves we must take our religion with us; so wherever we take our families, or part of them, we must take our family religion with us; for in all places we need divine protection, and experience divine goodness. 'I will therefore that men pray everywhere.'

When you are in your city houses, let not the business of them crowd out your family religion: nor let the diversions of your country houses indispose your minds to these serious exercises. That care and that pleasure are unseasonable and inordinate, which leave you not both heart and time to attend the service of the church in your house.

Let me here be an advocate also for those families whose masters are often absent from them, for their health or pleasure, especially on the Lord's day, or long absent upon business. And let me beg these absent masters to consider with whom they leave those few 'sheep in the wilderness' (1 Sam. 17: 28), and whether they do not leave them neglected and exposed. Perhaps there is not a just cause for your absence so much, nor can you give a good answer to that question, 'What dost thou here, Elijah?' But if there be a just cause, you ought to take care that the church in your house be not neglected when you are abroad, but that the work be done when you are not at home to do it.

BE WHOLE-HEARTED

Let inferior relations help to promote religion in the families where they are. If family worship be not kept up in the houses where you live, let so much the more be done in your closets for God and your souls: if it be, yet think not that will excuse you from secret worship. All is little enough to keep up the life of religion in your hearts, and help you forward toward heaven.

Let the children of praying parents, and the servants of praying masters, account it a great privilege to live in houses that have churches in them, and be careful to improve that privilege. Be you also ready to every good work; make the religious exercises of your family easy and pleasant to those that perform them, by showing yourselves forward to attend on them, and careful to attend to them; for your backwardness and mindlessness will be their greatest discouragement. Let your lives also be credit to good education, and make it appear to all with whom you converse, that you are in every way the better for living in religious families.

REMEMBER YOU ARE NEVER ALONE

Let solitary people, that are not set in families, have churches in their chambers, churches in their closets. When every man repaired the wall of Jerusalem over against his own house, we read of one that repaired over against his chamber (Neh. 3: 30). Those that live alone, out of the way of family worship, ought to take so much the more time for their secret worship, and, if possible, add the more solemnity to it. You have not families to read the Scriptures to, read them so much the more to yourselves. You have not children and servants to catechise, nor parents or masters to be catechised by; catechise yourselves then, that you may hold fast the form of sound words, which you have received. 'Exhort one another'; so we read it (Heb. 3: 13). Exhort yourselves so it might as well be read. You are not made keepers of the vineyards, and therefore the greater is your shame if your own vineyard you do not keep. When you are alone, yet you are not alone, for the Father is with you, to observe what you do, and to own and accept you, if you do well.

Let Spiritual Concerns Govern Family Choices

Let those who are to choose a settlement consult the welfare of their souls in the choice. If a church in the house be so necessary, so comfortable, then be ye not unequally yoked with unbelievers, who will have no kindness for the church in the house, nor assist in the support of it, but instead of building this house, pluck it down with their hands (Prov. 14: 1). Let apprenticeships and other services be chosen by this rule, that that is best for us which is best for our souls; and therefore it is our interest to go with those, and be with those, with whom God is (Zech. 8: 23). When Lot was to choose a habitation, he was determined therein purely by secular advantages (Gen. 13: 11, 13), and God justly corrected his sensual choice, for he never had a quiet day in the Sodom he chose, till he was fired out of it. The Jewish writers tell of one of their devout Rabbis, who being courted to dwell in a place which was otherwise well accommodated, but had no synagogue near, utterly refused to accept the invitation, and gave that text for this reason, 'The law of thy mouth is better to me than thousands of pieces of gold and silver' (Ps. 119: 72).

Let Christian Families Uphold One Another

Let religious families keep up friendship and fellowship with each other, and as they have opportunity, assist one another in doing good. The communion of churches has always been accounted their beauty, strength, and comfort, and so is the communion of these domestic churches. We find here, and in other of St. Paul's epistles, kind salutations sent to and from the houses that had churches in them. Religious families should greet one another, visit one another, love one another, pray for one another, and as becomes households of faith, do all the good they can one to another; forasmuch as they all meet daily at the same throne of grace, and hope to meet shortly at the same throne of glory, to be no more, as they are now divided in Jacob, and scattered in Israel.

ENJOY GOD

Let those houses that have churches in them, flourishing churches, have comfort in them. Is religion in the power of it uppermost in your houses? And are you and yours serving the Lord, serving him daily? Go on and prosper, for the Lord is with you while you be with him. See your houses under the protection and blessing of heaven, and be assured that all things shall work together for good to you. Make it to appear by your holy cheerfulness that you find God a good master; wisdom's ways pleasantness, and her paths peace; and that you see no reason to envy those who spend their days in carnal mirth, for you are acquainted with better pleasures than to which they can pretend.

Are your houses on earth God's houses? Are they dedicated to him, and employed for him? Be of good comfort, his house in heaven shall be yours shortly: 'In my Father's house there are many mansions'; and one, you may be sure, for each of you that 'by a patient continuance in well-doing, seek for glory, honour, and immortality' (Rom. 2: 7).

2

THE CATECHISING OF YOUTH

Hold fast the form of sound words which thou hast heard of me, in
faith and love which is in Christ Jesus (2 Tim. 1: 13).

Blessed Paul in this, as in the former epistle, is giving wholesome
advice and instruction to Timothy; for the enforcing of it,
among other things, puts him in mind of his education, and
the advantages of it; the good principles which by it had been
instilled in him, and the good practices he had been trained up
in: and upon trial, now he came to years of understanding, he
could not but see that they were good.

Let him therefore adhere to them, and abide by them, and
now build upon the foundation then laid.

He particularly mentions the two great advantages he was
blessed with in his child hood: that he was bred up, both
under the tuition of godly parents and under the direction and
instruction of an able faithful ministry; and both these are
requisite to complete the blessings of a religious education.

He had been well taught by his godly parents (v. 5–6), his
grandmother Lois and his mother Eunice, whose unfeigned

faith the Apostle would have him frequently to think of, and thereby be minded to stir up the gift of God that was in him. His father was a Greek, one that had little religion in him, but left it to his mother to bring him up as she thought fit; and she and his grandmother were not wanting to season the vessel betimes with a good savour; so that from a child he knew the holy scriptures, and was made wise to salvation by them (2 Tim. 3: 15). It is a great opportunity which mothers have, and which prudent pious mothers will improve, to fill the minds of their children when they are young with good knowledge, and to form them to a good disposition. If the tree must be bent, it must be done when it is young and tender, and with a very gentle, easy hand, for the spirit is not to be broken but bowed.

He had been well taught by St. Paul too. His mother and grandmother had taught him the Scriptures, and made him ready in them, as a child of God; then Paul expounded the Scriptures more fully to him, and by the grace of God made him mighty in them, so that he became a man of God, thoroughly furnished to all good works. The text speaks of the form of sound words, which he had heard of Paul, either in private lectures read to him as his pupil, or in his public teaching and catechising, on which Timothy was constantly and diligently attending.

Now those two methods of instruction, both by parents in their families, and by ministers in more public assemblies, are necessary, and do mutually assist each other, and neither will excuse the want of the other. Let not parents think to leave it wholly to ministers; as if because their children are well taught in public they need not take any pains with them at home. No, there the foundation must be laid, and there the improvement by public catechising must be examined, and there a more particular application must be made according to the children's capacities and dispositions, than it is possible for ministers to make in public. The people of Israel had the Levites dispersed among them, whose office it was to teach them the good knowledge of the Lord; and yet it is required of parents that they not only receive God's words into their own hearts, but that they teach them diligently to their children, and talk of them in their families, and tell those under their charge the meaning of the testimonies and judgments which he had commanded them (Deut. 6: 7, 20). If father or mother, or both, do not teach their children first, and teach them last too, they will not be fit for, nor much the better by, public catechising.

And on the other hand, let not ministers think to leave it wholly to parents, as if because the children were well taught at home, they needed not to contribute any help of theirs to their instruction. The great Shepherd of the sheep has charged them to feed his lambs with food proper for them (John 21: 15). Besides the natural authority and affection of parents, it is fit that the spiritual authority and affection of ministers likewise, should be improved for the advantage of the rising generation. And it may be presumed, that according to the gift given to them, they have greater abilities for instruction than the parents have. In teaching your children other arts and sciences, though you may have some insight into them yourselves, yet you make use of those who particularly profess those arts and sciences, and make it their business to teach them; and will you not do so in that which is the one thing needful for them to learn well? You are to feed your kids, but you must do it beside the shepherds' tents (S. of S. 1: 8), under the conduct of a gospel ministry.

Now Timothy having had this double advantage, Paul urges him still to proceed in that good way wherein he had so well set out; to hold fast that form of sound words which he had received.

This implies that he had a form of sound words delivered to him by Paul; a brief summary of the Christian doctrine, and of all those things which are most surely believed among Christians, as St. Luke expresses it: ὑποτύπωσιν—a delineation, a scheme, or rough draught of the gospel institutes. It is a metaphor taken from painters; in drawing a face, they first draw the shape and lines of it, and then fill it up with proper colours. Such a model or plan of the truths and law of Christ Timothy had, as he might afterwards, in his meditation and preaching, enlarge upon. Whether this form of sound words was a creed, or confession of faith, I cannot say: I rather think it was in the way of a catechism, because that method of instruction was used in the early ages of the church: for we find it alluded to in St. Peter's ἐπερώτημα—the answer of a good conscience (1 Pet. 3: 21), or rather the interrogation; so that I think if we apply it, especially to our catechisms, to the forms of sound words so formed, we shall offer no violence at all in the text.

Here is the charge to him to hold it fast, εχε—have it. Have it by you, have it with you, have it in line, have it always ready for use; do not part with it, nor in any instance depart from it. Have it, that is, make it to appear that you have it; as to have grace is to have it in action and exercise, and to him who so has, has and uses what he has, shall be given. Or, as we read it, 'Hold it fast'; it was delivered to us, to have and to hold; and we have it in vain, if we do not hold it.

Accordingly, we may hence learn two doctrines.

1. That good catechisms, containing the grounds and principles of the Christian religion, are useful forms of sound words; and it is a great mercy to have heard and learned those forms.
2. Those who have heard and learned the good forms of sound words must hold them fast in faith and love.

A GREAT MERCY TO BE TAUGHT

It is a very great advantage to young people to hear and learn the Christian forms of sound words in the days of their youth: to have been well taught some good catechism or confession of faith.

THE WORDS OF THE GOSPEL

Observe here, the words of the gospel are ὑγιαινόντων—sound words, or as some render it, healthful, wholesome, healing words.

Valuable and Valid

There is value and validity in the words of the gospel; as there is in that which is sound and firm, and in good condition. They are what they seem, and there is no cheat in them. Try them and you will find you may trust them, as you may that which is sound, and will never be made ashamed of your confidence in them. Men speak with flattering lips and with a double heart (Ps. 12: 2); but the words of the Lord are pure words, and have no mixture of falsehood in them. The law was written in stone, to intimate its stability and perpetuity; and the gospel is no less firm; every iota and tittle of both shall survive heaven and earth (Matt. 5: 18).

Assure yourselves, brethren, the words of the gospel which we preach to you, and which you are trained up in the knowledge of, are unchangeable and inviolable. Holy Job's creed concerning his Redeemer was graven with an iron pen and lead in the rock for ever (Job 19: 24–5); much more is ours so; it is what you may venture your souls and your everlasting welfare upon. That is a sound word. That Jesus Christ came into the world to save sinners; even the chief (1 Tim. 1: 15). And that is a sound word. That God has given to us eternal life and this life is in his Son (1 John 5: 11). It is sound speech that cannot be condemned: for it has been more than a thousand times tried, and it stands firm as the everlasting mountains. These are the true sayings of God (Rev. 19: 9), and if we compare the traditions of the elders, or the speculations of the philosophers, with them, we shall say, with the prophet, 'What is the chaff to the wheat?' (Jer. 23: 28).

Virtuous

There is virtue to be drawn from them for healing and health to us. They are not only clear from everything that is hurtful and unwholesome, but there is that, in them, which is medicinal and restorative, not only of health and strength, but of life itself. These waters of the sanctuary (Ezek. 47: 8–9), these leaves of the trees of life, are healing to the nations (Rev. 22: 2). These words, if duly applied and mixed with faith, restore the soul, and put it in frame, heal its maladies, and reduce to a just temper its distempered and disordered powers. It was said of old concerning those who were sick, that God sent his word and healed them (Ps. 107: 20). And when Christ was here upon earth, it was by the power of his word that he healed all who had need of healing, and in a sense of their need applied themselves to him for it. And this was a figure of the efficacy of the word of the gospel for the healing of diseased souls, a divine power going along with it; and in it the Sun of Righteousness arises in the soul, as it did in the world, with healing under his wings (Mal. 4: 2).

Let this therefore recommend to you the words we teach you, that they are not only of inestimable value in themselves, but will be of unspeakable advantage to you. They are healing words indeed, for they are regenerating and recreating words, whereby you may be saved (Acts 11: 14). Mix faith with them, and you will experience the power of them, setting you to rights, and giving you a new life and vigour. They are therefore not only faithful sayings, but well worthy of all acceptation, of your acceptation. Accept them therefore, and receive the benefit of them, that you receive not God's grace in vain: and if they be in vain, and you be not healed by them, the fault is in yourselves.

A PATHWAY INTO SCRIPTURE

It is good to have forms of these sound words drawn up for the use of those who are to learn the first principles of the oracles of God (Heb. 5: 12; 6: 1); not to be imposed as of equal authority with the Scriptures, but to be proposed in order to the further study of the Scriptures.

Bear us witness, we set up no other rule of faith and practice, no other oracle, no other touchstone or test of orthodoxy, but the Holy Scriptures of the Old and New Testament: these only are the fountains whence we fetch our knowledge; these only the foundations on which we build our faith and hope; these the *dernier* resort of all our inquiries and appeals in the things of God, for they only are given by divine inspiration. This is the principle we abide by. To the law and to the testimony (Isa. 8: 20): that is the *regula regulans*—the paramount rule, and far be it from us that we should set up any form of words in competition with it, much less in contradiction to it; or admit any rival with it in the conduct and guardianship of our souls, as some do the traditions of the church, and others, I know not what light within. Every other help we have for our souls we make use of a *regula regulata*—a rule controlled, in subordination and subserviency to the Scriptures; and among the rest our catechisms and confessions of faith.

Give me leave to illustrate this by an appeal to the gentlemen of the long robe. They know very well that the common law of England lies in the Year Book, and books of report, in the records of immemorial customs, and in cases occasionally adjudged: which are not an artificial system drawn up by the rules of method, but rather historical collections of what was solemnly discussed, and judiciously delivered, in several reigns, *pro re nata*—as occasions have arisen, and always taken for law; and according to which the practice has always been; (with which, if I may be allowed to compare that which, infinitely more sacred and inviolable, cannot be altered or amended by any wisdom or power on earth): such are the books of the Scripture, histories of the several ages of the church (as those of the several reigns of the kings) and of the discoveries of God's mind and will in every age, as there was occasion; and these, too, built upon ancient principles, received and submitted to before these divine annals began to be written.

But though those are the fountains and foundations of the law, those gentlemen know that institutes and abridgements, collection of, and references to, the cases adjudged in the books, are of great use to them, to prepare them for the study of the originals, and to assist them in the application of them, but are not thought to derogate from the authority and honour of them. Such we reckon our forms of sound words to be; if in anything they mistake the sense of the text, or misapply it, they must be corrected by it; but as far as they agree with it, they are of great use to make it more easy and ready to us.

That which is intended in these forms of sound words is not, like the council of Trent, to make new creed, and add it to what we have in the Scriptures; but to collect and arrange the truths and laws of God, and to make them familiar.

Key Doctrines Defined

By these forms of sound words, the main principles of Christianity, which lie scattered in the Scriptures, are collected and brought together. We know that all Scripture is given by inspiration of God, and is profitable, and that there is no idle word in God's book, nothing that is unnecessary; but we know that all is not alike profitable, or alike necessary. Every line in a well-drawn picture is of use, and answers some end; but every line is not alike serviceable to the main design of the picture, which is to represent the face of the person whose picture it is; yet we must not say, therefore, that it might as well have been spared. The Scriptures give us the things of God in their native purity and plainness, yet not without their proper illustrations. It is naked truth, that is, without disguise or the ambiguity which Apollo's oracles were noted for, but not naked truth, without dress and ornament.

Now our catechisms and confessions of faith pick up from the several parts of holy writ those passages which, though perhaps occasionally delivered, contain the essentials of religion, the foundations and main pillars upon which Christianity is built; which we are concerned rightly to understand, and firmly to believe, in the first place, and, then, to go on to perfection. We cannot contain all the Scriptures: but there are some more weighty and comprehensive sayings, which (like those which the Jews wrote in their phylacteries) we should bind, for a sign, upon our hand, and which should be as frontlets between our eyes (Deut. 6: 8). And our forms of sound words furnish us with these.

God's Truth Mapped Out

By these, the truths of God are arranged and put in order. The several books of Scripture are written in an excellent method, according to their particular nature and intention, and they are put together in an admirably good order: but when out of them the main principles of religion are to be gathered, it is necessary that they be put into some method proper to serve the design of representing them at one view, that we may understand them the more distinctly, by observing their mutual references to each other, their connection with, and dependence upon, each other; and thereby they appear in their truer light, and fuller lustre.

These forms of sound words show us the order that is in God's words, as well as in his works; the harmony of divine truths, how one thing tends to another, and all centre in Christ, and the glory of God in Christ: and thus, like the stones in an arch, they mutually support, and strengthen, and fix one another. They are as a map of the land of promise, by the help of which we may travel it over with our eye in a little time, and know the true situation of every tribe, though we cannot give a particular description of every part of its inheritance.

God's Truths in an Accessible Form

By these, the truths of God are brought down to the capacity of young ones, and those who are as yet but weak in understanding. Not that God has spoken in secret, in a dark place of the earth (Isa. 45: 19); no the words of wisdom's mouth are all plain to him that understands (Prov. 8: 9). But to those who are yet babes they need to be explained; to them we must give the sense, and cause them to understand the reading (Neh. 8: 8); and this is in part done by those forms of sound words, which lead us by the hand, as it were, into the knowledge of the truth as it is in Jesus. Not that we need to seek other words than those which the Holy Ghost teaches: they are the most proper vehicle of the limits which are given us of God to know (1 Cor. 2: 13), and it is unsafe to depart from them. Many, under pretence of refining upon the Scriptures, and expressing the things contained in them more philosophically, have but darkened counsel by words without knowledge (Job 38: 2): the faithful servant will deliver his message as near as he can in his master's own words; Go (says God to Ezekiel) get thee to the house of Israel; and do not only speak my words, but speak with my words to them (Ezek. 3: 4).

But spiritual things must be compared with spiritual, and by the plainer parts of Scripture, those must be explained that are more dark and hard to be understood; and this is done by our forms of sound words, which make the principles of religion to be as milk for babes, who as yet cannot bear strong meat (Heb. 5: 12). The Ten Commandments are a divine form of sound words to direct our practice, but they are short and exceedingly comprehensive; it is therefore necessary that we be taught from other Scriptures what each commandment requires and forbids. The Lord's prayer is another divine form of sound words to direct our petition; but that also is short and comprehensive, and it is requisite that we should be taught from other Scriptures what we pray for in each petition. The form of baptism is another divine form of sound words, peculiar to the Christian dispensation; but that also needs to be explained by other Scriptures, as it is excellently well in the ancient creeds, which we receive and embrace, and greatly rejoice in, as standing, lasting testimonies to the faith once delivered to the saints (Jude 3), which, by the grace of God, we will not only adhere to, but earnestly contend for, and live and die by. And all these divine forms of sound words you have fully and faithfully set before you, and opened to you, in the Assembly's Larger and Shorter Catechism; as, blessed be God, they are in many other both in our own and other reformed churches.

A Privilege to Learn in Childhood

Those are happy who are well taught, and have well learned, those forms of sound words when they are young. It is a great privilege, and a very improving one, to be betimes instructed in the principles of religion, and to have the truths of Christ instilled into us in the days of our youth, and to be trained up in an acquaintance and converse with them from the first; by the care of godly parents especially, who have many advantages in dealing with children which ministers cannot have, to be put betimes upon reading the Scriptures, and getting portions of it by heart; remembering and repeating sermons; to be taught the catechism, and examined in it, and not only made to say it, but made, as we are capable, to understand it, and taught to prove it by Scripture, and give a reason for it; to be directed to pray, and obliged to do it; and to a strict observation of the Lord's day, in order to do all this. And if to all this be added ministerial catechising, the more copious and accurate explication of the mysteries of God by the appointed stewards of those mysteries, it consummates the happiness of a religious education, from which abundant advantages may be reaped, if it be wisely and faithfully improved.

I know I speak to those who enjoy this privilege, to whom the doctrine of Christ not only comes down in showers, in the preaching of the word, but on whom it distils more slowly and softly, as the dew, and as the small rain upon the tender herb (Deut. 32: 2), in catechising. And I commend your pious zeal in coveting and seeking instruction this way. Go on, and prosper, the Lord is with you while you be with him: and I hope it is a token for good, and will prove so, that God has mercy in store for the next generation—that there are so many young people among us who are asking their way to Zion, and desire to be told it, with their faces thitherward. Who hath begotten us these?

I know also that there are many, and many there have been, who were blest with a religious education when they were young, and were then trained up in the way in which they should go, who have afterwards turned aside from the holy commandment; who though they were not born of fornication, but were the seed of the faithful, yet have proved an unfaithful seed, and have themselves gone away from their God. This should not discourage parents and ministers from doing their duty, in catechising youth, but should direct them to look up to God for his grace, without which all our care and pains is fruitless, and we do but beat the air: and should engage you who are catechised to be jealous over yourselves, with a godly jealousy, that you may not be conceited of yourselves, or confident in yourselves, may not be high-minded, but may always fear lest you seem to come short of that which is expected from you, or seem to fall off to any evil work or way, and though now you think you stand, may always take heed lest you fall.

But I know that your being thus catechised, if you improve it aright, and be not wanting to yourselves, will be of unspeakable advantage to you; and I hope to be of use, both to direct you and to encourage you, if I tell you how and which way it may be made so.

A Good Use of Time

Hereby you are, for some time, well employed now you are young. Childhood and youth, upon this account (among others) are vanity (Eccles. 11: 10), that so much of the time is then spent to so little purpose, and yet better than, as it is afterwards spent by many, to evil purposes. But your being catechised obliges you to spend at least some part of your time well, and so as you may afterwards reflect upon it with comfort and satisfaction above many other, perhaps above any other, of your precious moments. If the time which children and young people would otherwise spend in sport and recreation (they call it PAS(S)TIME., when we have more need of STAY-times than pastimes, for it passes away fast enough of itself) is thus happily retrieved, and is spent in good exercises; in conversing with the word of God (which we should be meditating on day and night), in reviewing and relating to ourselves the things of God; we cannot but say that it is a kindness to us, and much greater than it would be, to keep man from spending an estate wastefully, and put him into a way of getting an estate easily and honourably. Whatever goes with the rest of your time here is a portion of it spent so as to turn to a good account, and so as you may meet it again with comfort on the other side of death and the grave.

Those who are catechised either by their parents or ministers on the evening of the Lord's day have a particular advantage therein: that those precious minutes (and one minute of Sabbath time is worth three of any other day), which so many young people idle away in foreign, foolish talk, either in the fields, or at the doors of their houses (which corrupts the mind and manners, and dispels what they had gained, if they had gained anything, in and by the duties of the day), they spend in that which serves such good purposes, and will help to clench the nail that has been driven, that it may be a nail in a sure place. I know not how young people can be trained up to a better piece of good husbandry, than to a good husbandry of time, especially Sabbath time.

Makes Preaching Profitable

Hereby you will become better able to understand the word preached, and more capable of profiting by it, and so it will be a great advantage to you. I am sure it is the duty of ministers to preach the word, and therein to be constant, to be instant in season and out of season; they have (2 Tim. 4: 1–2) received a solemn charge to do so, and if so either you must hear, or they must preach to the walls. And I am sure you are concerned to hear, so that your souls may live; and therefore to take heed how you hear, and, in order to your profiting, to hear with understanding. The highway ground in our Saviour's parable represents those who hear the words of the kingdom, and understand it not (Matt. 13: 19); for it is not ploughed up and prepared to receive it; they are not instructed in the things that are spoken of, and therefore such as speak to them of those things are barbarians. They who are not catechised, not taught the forms of sound words, apprehend not what we mean when we speak of their misery by nature, the sinfulness of sin, the mediation of Christ, the operations of the Spirit, and the great things of the other world; we had as good talk Greek to them; they are ready to say of us, as the people did of Ezekiel's preaching, 'Doth he not speak parables?' (Ezek. 20: 49).

They who are not cate-chised...apprehend not what we mean when we speak of their misery by nature, the sinfulness of sin, the mediation of Christ, the operations of the Spirit, and the great things of the other world; we had as good talk Greek to them.

But you who are catechised understand our dialect, are acquainted with Scripture language; you are accustomed to it, and can say, 'This good word is the confirmation, and that the illustration, and the other the application, of what we have many a time heard, and knew before, but thus are made to know better.' And therefore though those who have not been catechized do most need instruction, by the preaching of the word (and for their sakes we must many a time stay to explain things which are most plain, wherein they who are strong ought to bear with us, in compassion to the infirmities of the weak), yet those who have been well catechised do most desire it, and delight in it, and are edified by it, because they understand it. Catechising does to the preaching of the word the same good office that John the Baptist did to our Saviour; it prepares its way, and makes its paths straight, and yet like him does but say the same things: 'Repent with an eye to the kingdom of heaven.'

Lays the Foundation for a Work of Grace

Hereby you will have a foundation laid for a good work of grace in your souls. It is true, that God in his favours to us, and his operations on us, acts as a God, with an incontestable sovereignty, and an irresistible power; but it is as true that he deals with men as men, as reasonable creatures, in a way suited to their nature, he draws with the cords of a man (Hos. 11: 4), he gains possession of the will and affections by opening the understanding, informing the judgment, and rectifying its mistakes. And this is entering into the soul, as the good

Shepherd, whose own the sheep are, enters into the sheepfold by the door (John 10: 1–2); whereas Satan debauches the affections, and so perverts the will, and bribes and blinds the understanding, which is climbing up another way, for he is a thief and a robber. Christ opens the understanding, and so makes the heart to burn; opens men's eyes, and causes the scales to fall from them; and so turns men from Satan to God.

Now though Christ can give an understanding immediately, as to Paul, yet ordinarily he enlightens it, in the use of means, and gives a knowledge of divine things, by the instructions of parents and ministers; and afterwards by his Spirit and grace brings them home to the mind and conscience, delivers the soul into the mould of them, and by them works a saving change in it. It was the prerogative of an apostle to come to the knowledge of the gospel, not by man, nor to be taught it, but by the revelation of Jesus Christ (Gal. 1: 12); we must come to the knowledge of it, in the way of instituted ordinances; and none more likely to prepare for the particular applications of divine grace than this particular application of good instruction by catechizing.

Arms Against False Teachers

You will be armed against the assaults and insinuations of seducers, and such as lie in wait to deceive, and draw you aside into the paths of error. Satan is a roaring lion, who seeks in this way to devour souls; and none are such an easy prey to him as those who are ignorant and unskilful in the word of righteousness. But those who are well instructed in the forms of sound words, and understand the evidence of divine truths, are aware of the fallacies with which others are beguiled, and know how to detect and escape them, for surely in vain is the net spread in the sight of any bird. They who grow in the knowledge of Christ will not be visibly led away by the error of the wicked, so as to fall from their own steadfastness (2 Pet. 3: 17); those who are thus established when they are children will not be always children, tossed about with every wind of doctrine (Eph. 4: 14).

Those who are well catechised, are well fortified against temptations to atheism and infidelity, which, under pretence of free-thinking, invite men to false and foolish thinking;

and by debauching their principles, corrupt their morals: and which, under pretence of a free conversation, allure to vice and immorality, enslave the soul to the most brutish lusts, and by corrupting the morals, debauch the principles. It will likewise be an excellent antidote against the poison of popery: a national zeal against which is, then, likely to be an effectual defence of the protestant religion, when it is a zeal according to knowledge. A right understanding of the offices and ordinances of Christ, the former of which are daringly usurped, and the latter wickedly corrupted and profaned, in the church of Rome, will, by the blessing of God, preserve us from going in with those strong delusions, though the temptation should be ever so strong, and prepare us to suffer, rather than to sin, if we should be called out to it.

Equips to Help Others

You will be furnished for doing good to others, in the places where God has set you. Your being well instructed in the forms of sound words will qualify you to be useful in your generation, for the glory of God, and the edification of many; which will be your honour and comfort now, and will add to your crown hereafter. Out of a good treasure of Christian knowledge well laid up when you are young, you will be able, like the good householder, to bring forth things new and old (Matt. 13: 52), as there is occasion, for the entertainment and benefit of others. Out of the abundance of the heart the mouth will speak. Hereby you will be able to resist and oppose that evil communication which corrupts good manners, and to put to silence the ignorance of foolish men; and not only so, but to advance and keep up that communication which is good, and to the use of edifying (Eph. 4: 29), which may manifest grace in your hearts, and minister grace to the hearer. These forms of sound words will teach you that sound spirit which cannot be condemned (Titus 2: 8). And thus your lips will feed many.

It will be likewise of great use to you in prayer; both in secret, and with your families, when God calls you to the charge of families. With what solid judgment, exact method, aptness, and great variety of expression, have I heard private Christians, who have been well instructed in the things of God, and are conversant with the Scripture, offer up their prayers and supplications to God, without the help of any other forms, but those forms of sound words: and this with such undissembled indications of pious affection, as has been very proper to kindle and excite, to raise and carry on, the devotions of those who joined with them. I believe some who are pleased to be severe, in their reflections upon all extemporary prayer, as we call it, would not be so, if they knew this so well as I have done.

Assists Growth in Grace

Those that have a good work of grace begun in them, will be greatly assisted in the progress of it. Timothy, by the help of these forms of sound words, is nourished up in faith and good doctrine, whereunto he has attained (1 Tim. 4: 6). They who have pure hearts and clean hands, hereby shall become stronger and stronger (Job 17: 9) in judgment, in affection, and in resolution. The more firmly the foundation is laid, the broader and the higher the building may be carried. And the better we understand the road we are to travel, the better we shall get forward in our journey. Affectionate Christians who are weak in knowledge, have but the wings of a dove that flies low; but knowing Christians are carried on as upon eagles' wings, with which they mount up for the prize of the high calling—they run and are not weary.

And those who have themselves some good measures of knowledge and grace, may be greatly improved in both, by attending upon public catechising; and if young, by bearing a part in it. Apollos was an eloquent man, and mighty in the Scriptures; and he was instructed in the way of the Lord (Acts 18: 24–6), κατηχημένος—he was catechised, so the word is, and he was fervent in spirit, yet he was still willing to learn, and found advantage by it; for there were those who took him, and expounded to him the way of God more perfectly. Those who think they understand the way of God pretty well, yet should still be increasing with the increase of God, should not think they have already attained, or are already perfect, but should be pressing forward, and covet to understand the way of God more perfectly.

Food for Thought

You will have your memories well stored for your own use, and will have always good matter ready at hand for pious thoughts and meditations. It is certainly as much the benefit, as it is the duty, of Christians, to converse much in their hearts with the things of God. It is the character of the blessed man, and an evidence of his delighting in the law of God after the inner man, that in that law he meditates day and night (Ps. 1: 2). O how do I love it! says David, it is my meditation all the day (Ps. 119: 97); it is the subject not only of my frequent, but of my fixed, thoughts: not now and then, upon an occasion, but constantly. And if David could find such employment and entertainment for his thoughts from morning till night in the law of God, much more may we find satisfaction in it, and the gospel of Christ too, which so far excels it.

Now one reason why this duty of meditation is so much neglected, is because people want matter for their thoughts to enlarge and expatiate upon; and the reason for that is because they were never enriched, as they should have been, in all knowledge (1 Cor. 1: 5); their stock is soon exhausted, and they know not what to think of next. But if you get an abundance of good knowledge, you will never hate to seek for something proper and useful to entertain yourselves with. You soon forget the sermons you hear; but if your catechism was well learned, and the proofs of it, you can never forget them; so that you may at any time take an answer of your catechism, and dwell upon that in your thoughts, till your hearts burn within you.

Passes on a Sacred Deposit

You will be enabled to transmit, pure and entire, to those who come after you that good thing which is committed to you. The truths and ordinances of Christ are a sacred deposit, a truth handed down to us by our believing predecessors, and lodged in our hands, to be carefully kept in our day, and faithfully transferred to the generations to come: but how can we do that, if we be not ourselves both rightly and fully apprized of it? We are false to this trust, not only if we betray it, by the admission of heresy and idolatry; but if we lose it, and let it drop, by ignorance and carelessness, and unacquaintedness with, and indifference to, the interests of Christianity.

We of this age cannot otherwise repay what we received from those who went before us, than by consigning the value received to those who come after us; nor make any other requital to our parents, for giving us a good education, but by giving the like to our children; which, therefore, with the utmost care and pains we should qualify ourselves to do, and then make conscience of doing. And those who have not children of their own, ought to do it for the children of their relations, and the children of the poor, and to promote public catechisings and charity schools; and thus contribute what they can to the raising up of a seed to serve Christ, which shall be accounted to him for a generation, that thus the name of Christ may endure for ever, and his throne as the days of heaven. What has been told to us of the wondrous works of God, we must tell to our children, that they may tell them to their children, that those who shall be created may praise the Lord (Ps. 78: 5–6).

A CHARGE TO KEEP

Those who have the privilege to hear and learn the forms of sound words, with it have a charge—to hold them fast in faith and love, which is in Christ Jesus.

This implies that you are in danger of losing them, and being robbed of them, through your own negligence of having them snatched out of your hands by your spiritual enemies, or drop through your fingers if you do not hold them fast. Satan is that wicked one who steals the word of God out of the hearts of the careless hearers and learners; as the fowls of the air do the seed from the highway ground (Matt. 13: 19), that it could not have any root in. Many have had the form of sound words, and with it a form of godliness, and a name to live; but have let them go, and lost them; have made shipwreck of the faith, and of their own souls. Let their falls be warnings to us, and let us therefore fear lest we also come short, or so much as seem to come short.

I know I speak to those who have the form of sound words, who have hold of it. In God's name therefore I charge you to hold it fast, to keep your hold of it, in faith and love which is in Christ Jesus.

KEEP IT IN MIND

You must hold it fast, that is, you must retain the remembrance of it; keep it in mind and memory; you have it, see that you always have it, that you have it ready for your use upon all occasions. Great stress is laid upon this: the gospel is that by which we are saved, if we keep in memory what has been preached unto us (1 Cor. 15: 1–2). Not as if the bare remembering and being able to recite these sound words, and the forms of them, were sufficient to save us; they do not heal as charms and spells pretend to do, merely by the repeating or writing of them; a man may be able to say all the Bible over by heart, and yet come short of grace and glory; but the remembering of these things is necessary to our due improvement of them, and to the other duties required of us: if we so remember the covenant as to be ever mindful of it; if we remember his commandments to do them (Ps. 103: 18), we remember them aright.

For Your Own Good

It will be of good use to you, to retain the words you now learn and hear; and in order to do that, frequently to review them, to catechise yourselves, and repeat them over to yourselves. What you said to your parents perhaps by rote, when you were children, and not yet capable of knowing the intent and extent of, you should now say to yourselves with understanding, and judgment, and affection. Let not the wisest and best be ashamed to repeat the words of their catechism, as they have occasion to quote them; but let them rather be ashamed who cannot do it; who can remember, all their days, the idle foolish stories and songs they learned when they were young, but forget the forms of those words whereby they must be saved, and must be judged.

An Absolute Necessity

It is of absolute necessity that you retain the remembrance of these things, so as to have them ready for use, though it be in your own words. It is necessary that you should be well acquainted with the mystery of the gospel; with your need of a Saviour; with the method in which the salvation was wrought out by the Son of God, and is applied by the Spirit of God; with the breadth of the commandment, and with the strictness and spiritual nature of it; with the tenor of the new covenant, and the precious privileges of it; and with the great truths concerning the upper and future world: in these things you have been instructed, and are concerned to give the more earnest heed to the things you have heard, lest at any time you let them slip (Heb. 2: 1–3).

OUR LIVES DEPEND ON IT. They are things worth remembering; of inestimable value in themselves, and of vast importance and concern to us; in comparison with which, an abundance of other things with which we fill our memories, are but toys and trash. How many things do we retain the remembrance of, which tend to defile our minds, or to disquiet them, which we would willingly forget if we could? And how many more are we industrious to keep in memory, which serve only to the carrying on of our business in the world: whilst that is seldom or never seriously thought of, and so comes by degrees to be in a manner forgotten, which belongs to our peace, our everlasting peace; and justly may that be hid from our eyes (Luke 19: 41), which we thus hide our eyes from. The reason Moses gives to Israel, why they should set their hearts to all the words he testified to them, will hold more strongly, why we should treasure up Christ's word in our heart, and let it dwell in us richly, that it is not a vain thing for us, but it is our life (Deut. 32: 46–7), and the lives of our souls depend upon it.

TO FORTIFY US AGAINST EVIL. The remembrance of them will be of very great and good use to us daily; both to fortify us against every evil word and work, by suggesting to us the most powerful arguments against sin, and the most pertinent answers to the temptations of Satan; and to furnish us for every good word and work, by suggesting to us the wisest directions, and the sweetest encouragements, in doing our duty. If we hold fast these forms of sound words as we ought, our mouths, like those of the righteous, shall speak wisdom, and our tongues shall be able to talk of judgment. And if thus the law of our God be in our heart, none of our steps shall slide. Solomon for this reason writes to us excellent things in counsel and knowledge, that we may answer the words of truth to those that send to us (Prov. 22: 20–1), or as the margin reads it to those that send us, to God, who sent us into the world to do all the good we can in it.

A SOUND INVESTMENT. It was for this end that we have heard and learned them, that we might lay them up in our hearts, in order to their being of use to us after; so that we receive the grace of God therein in vain, if we do not retain them. They are not intended merely for your present exercise and entertainment, as a task upon you to keep you employed, much less as an amusement to keep up in you a reverence for your parents and teachers; but they were intended to fit you for the service of God in this world, and the vision and fruition of him in a better world. You learn your catechism, not as you who were designed for tradesmen learned Latin and Greek, when you went to school, it may be; with design to forget it, because you had a notion you should never have occasion for it in your business; but as you learned to write and cast accounts, with design to retain it, because you were told you would have use for it daily in carrying on your trade. You are taught now, that you may, as long as you live, live according to what you are taught.

YOU WILL BE CALLED TO ACCOUNT. You will be called to an account shortly for these, as well as other of your advantages; and therefore are concerned to improve them, so that you may give up your account with joy, such joy as shall be an earnest of that joy of our Lord, into which good and faithful servants, who have diligently and faithfully improved their talents, shall enter, and in which they shall be forever happy. For your having heard and learned these things, will but aggravate your condemnation if you do not hold them fast. You know what was Chorazin's doom, and Bethsaida's, and Capernaum's; tremble lest it should be yours. It is an awful thought which I have somewhere met with, 'That the professors of this age, in which there is such plenty of the means of knowledge and grace, whether they go to heaven or hell, will be the greatest debtors in either of these places: if to heaven, the greatest debtors to divine mercy and grace for those improved means that helped to bring them thither; if to hell, the greatest debtors to divine justice for those abused means that would have helped to keep them thence.'

Let not what I have said of the necessity of remembering the sound words we hear be a discouragement to any serious, conscientious Christians, who have honest and good hearts, but weak and treacherous memories; nor make the righteous sad, who ought not to be made sad. You who tremble at God's word, do really get good by it, though you cannot recollect the method and language in which it is delivered to you. If you live in the fear of God, and in a course of holy watchfulness against sin, and diligence in duty, you retain the impressions of the word, though you cannot retain the expressions of it. I have been told of a good man, who was much affected with a sermon he heard concerning, as it would appear, the vanity of the world; and commending it afterwards to a friend, was desired to give some account of the sermon: 'Truly,' says he, 'I cannot remember any thing of it, but I am resolved, by the grace of God, I will never set my heart so much upon this world as I have done.' 'Why then' (says his friend) 'thou rememberest all.' David will never forget God's precepts, for (says he) by them thou hast quickened me (Ps. 119: 93). If we find our hearts quickened by the word, we do not forget it; and it is to be hoped we

> *Though we cannot repeat the good sermons we have heard; yet if, through grace, our hearts and ways are purified by them, they are not lost.*

will not, we shall not, forget it. Put a sieve that is dirty into the water, and though when you take it out it carries away little or nothing of the water with it, yet it is washed and made clean. Though we cannot repeat the good sermons we have heard; yet if, through grace, our hearts and ways are purified by them, they are not lost.

But let what I have said engage you who hear and learn the forms of sound words, to hold them fast, to imprint them in your minds and memories, that you may have them ready to you at all times, as occasion requires. In order to do this, labour to understand them; and let your knowledge be clear and distinct, and then you will be likely to retain it; set every truth in its proper place, and then you will know where to find it; set it in its true light, and then you will know what use to make of it. Get your hearts duly affected with divine things, and abide and act under the power and influence of them; and then you will remember them. Be often repeating them to yourselves: the Virgin Mary kept the sayings of Christ, by pondering them in her heart (Luke 2: 19).

MIX IT WITH FAITH

You must hold it fast in faith. It is not enough to remember the good truths that are taught you; but you must mix them with faith (Heb. 4: 2), or they will not profit you. You let them go, though you remember them ever so well, if you let go the belief of them, and the profession of your faith concerning them: it is by a hand of faith that you take hold of them, and keep hold.

Give a Firm Assent

You must hold them fast in faith, that is, you must give a firm assent to them as faithful sayings; must set to your seal that God is true. And every word of his is so, even that which you cannot comprehend the mystery of, as the eternity of God, the immensity of all his perfections, the Trinity, the incarnation of the Son of God, the operations of the Spirit upon the soul of man, and the like; yet because they are things which God has revealed, you must subscribe to the truth of them: if you do not, you make God a liar; and do in effect make yourselves wiser than God, when you say, How can this be? Whereas you should say, Lord, I believe, help thou mine unbelief.

Know Why You Believe

You must grow up to a full assurance of the undeniable truth, and incontestable evidence, of these sound words. Pass on toward perfection; acquaint yourselves with the Confirming Catechism; know not only what it is we believe, but why we believe it; and be ready always to give a reason for the hope that is in you (1 Pet. 3: 15). Solomon had this view in instructing his son; That I might make thee know the certainty of the words of truth (Prov. 22: 21); that thou mayst be convinced that they are words of truth, and receive them accordingly. And Luke the evangelist had the same design in writing his gospel, and inscribing it to his friend Theophilus, who, probably, had been his pupil: That thou mightest know the certainty of those things wherein thou hast been instructed (Luke 1: 4); this is holding it fast in faith.

Take it to Heart

You must make a faithful application of these sound and healing words to yourselves; else they will not answer the end, or be healing to you, any more than food not eaten, physic not taken, or a plaster not applied. Of the word of Christ you must say, not only, 'This is true,' but, 'This is true concerning me': He loved me, and gave himself for me; to save me, not in my sins, but from them; and to purify me to himself, and make me zealous of good works. Hear it, and know it, for thy good (Job 5: 27), says Eliphaz to Job, for thyself, so it is in the margin. Then only we know it for our good, when we know it for ourselves.

HOLD IT IN LOVE

You must hold it fast in love; that is the other arm with which these forms of sound words must be embraced, and held, that we may not let them go.

Delight in the Truth

You must take delight in them, and in the knowledge of them: that which we love we will hold fast, and not easily part with. It is not enough for us to know the truth, but we must love it; not enough that we receive it as a faithful saying, but also as well worthy of all acceptation; we must not only give it credit as true news, but bid it welcome as good news, and rejoice in it; and when Christ says, 'Surely, I come quickly', we must not only say, 'Even so, so IT is, he WILL come,' but 'Amen, so BE IT; COME, Lord Jesus' (Rev. 22: 20). This wisdom, this knowledge, must so enter into thy heart, as to become pleasant to thy soul (Prov. 2: 10). They say it was a ceremony used of old by the Jews, when they sent their children to school, they gave them a piece of a honeycomb to eat, repeating those words of Solomon, 'My son, eat thou honey because it is good, and the honeycomb, which is sweet to thy taste; so shall the knowledge of wisdom be unto thy soul, when thou hast found it' (Prov. 24: 13–14). And that which is not thus delighted in, will not be long held fast.

Let Them Shape Your Attitudes

You must be affected with them, and lay them to heart, as things that concern you to the last degree. Love is the leading affection, and rules the rest; as that goes, all the rest move. Be affected with love to the good word of God; and then you will conceive a high value and veneration for Christ, and a rooted antipathy to sin; a holy contempt of the world, a deep concern for your own souls, and a care about your everlasting state; and all other good affections, that will be the principles of a steady and regular motion of the soul heaven-wards. And then you will hold fast this form of sound words, when it makes such impressions as those upon you, and (as Christ's sayings ought to do) sinks down into your hearts (Luke 9: 44), and impresses a weight and stamp upon them.

Let Them Determine Your Actions

You must be influenced by them, and act under the commanding power of them. That love in which the sound words must be held fast, is here put for all that evangelical obedience of which holy love is the principle; for, as faith works by love, so love works by keeping the commandments of God; for this is the love of God, that we keep his commandments, and his commandments are not grievous (1 John 5: 3). We then hold fast the sayings of Christ, when we hold to them, in the constant temper of our minds, and tenor of our lives, and govern ourselves by them in all we say or do, that we may thus adorn the doctrine of God our Saviour.

Focus on Jesus

There is one word more in the text to be touched upon, and it is the centre and crown of all: this faith and love must be in Christ

Jesus. Blessed Paul, full of blessed Jesus, breathes nothing so much as Christ; he is his Alpha and Omega, and must be ours; it is the token in every epistle. We must hold fast the sound words of the gospel, in that faith and love which has Christ for its author, its object, and its end.

THE AUTHOR OF OUR FAITH. Which has Christ for its author; that faith and love which is wrought in us, not by the strength of any natural reasonings or resolutions of our own, but by the Spirit and grace of Christ, darting rays of divine light into the understanding, and striking sparks of divine fire into the affections, for these are not of ourselves, they are the gift of God. Thou therefore, my son, be strong in the grace that is in Christ Jesus (2 Tim. 2: 1); for on him is our help laid, and in him only is our help found. Depend not upon any ability of your own, lean not to your own understanding, but go forth and go on, take hold and keep hold, in Christ's strength.

THE OBJECT OF OUR FAITH. Which has Christ for its object; that faith and love in which the truths of the gospel must be held fast, as it must flow from Christ, so it must fasten on him. It is Christ in the gospel that we must embrace, and hold fast; who is the true treasure hid in that field, which we must think it worthwhile to part with all we have to purchase. It is by faith in Christ, and love to Christ, that we must hold fast what we have received. For this reason we must embrace these sound words, because we find so much of Christ in them. He is that golden thread that runs through the web of the whole gospel. St. Augustine somewhere says of himself, that before his conversion he took great delight in reading the writings of Tully, the Roman orator, but now (says he) I cannot relish them at all, as I used to do, because I find nothing of Christ in them.

THE END OF OUR FAITH. Which has Christ for its end. It must be that faith and love which has an eye to Christ; which has this always in view, to glorify Christ, and to be glorified with Christ: that faith which presses toward its own perfection, in the immediate sight of Christ, and that love which presses toward its own perfection, in the everlasting enjoyment of him.

Exhortations and Obligations

Let me now close with a few words of exhortation, in reference to the form of sound words.

Bless God for National Privileges

Let us bless God, that our lot is cast in a land of light; that he who determines the times before appointed, and the bounds of men's habitations, has determined ours so well, and so much to our advantage; that those statutes and judgments, which the heathen have not known, are revealed to us. We can never be thankful enough to God for this distinguishing favour, his manifesting himself to us, so as not unto the world. Blessed are our eyes for they see the joyful light, and our ears, for they hear the joyful sound, which many prophets and kings desired to see, desired to hear, and might not (Matt. 13: 16–17). We can never be thankful enough to God for it, that living in a Christian nation we have Bibles; in a protestant nation, we have them in a language we understand; that to us are committed the oracles of God (Rom. 3: 2), the lively oracles, with more advantage than to the Jews of old; that with us are the priests, the Lord's ministers, sounding with his trumpets (2 Chr. 13: 12). So many and so great are our privileges, above most other nations, that it may justly be expected, I wish it could lie as justly said, 'Surely this great nation is a wise and understanding people' (Deut. 4: 6).

Thank God for Catechisms and Confessions

Let us particularly be thankful to God, for the forms of sound words, both ancient and modern, which we have among us; for our catechisms and confessions of faith; that we have plenty of them, and a variety of them, not clashing and contradicting each other, but rather confirming and illustrating each other; for to Christ they all with one consent bear witness, and to the law and to the testimony they all appeal: though the methods be different, they meet in the same centre; and tend to direct those of different tastes and capacities to it likewise.

PARENTS INSTRUCT YOUR CHILDREN

Let parents and governors of families make conscience of instructing their children, and servants, in the forms of sound words. Here this work must begin, for it must begin betimes. Whom shall he teach knowledge? Whom shalt he make to understand doctrine? The prophet there answers. Them that are weaned from the milk, and drawn from the breasts when they are very young (Isa. 28: 9), under the immediate care of their mothers or grandmothers, as Timothy was: they are the teachers of babes (Rom. 2: 20). When Solomon was tender, and only-beloved in the sight of his mother (Prov. 4: 3), she taught him (Prov. 31: 1). The history of the Scripture is most proper to acquaint your children with in the first place; we see how soon they apprehend, and are affected, with other stories, and why may not impressions be made upon them as soon by the Scripture stories? Pleasant and profitable instructions may also be given to children by the Psalms for singing, and by divine poems and verses suited to their capacity.

It will be of great use likewise to your children to be told betimes, what it is supposed natural for them to ask, 'What we mean by this and the other religious service' (Exod. 12: 26). Tell them why you read the Bible with so much veneration: because it is the book of God, and holy men wrote the several parts of it, as they were moved by the Holy Ghost. Tell them why you make conscience of praying to God so solemnly every day: because you have a necessary and constant dependence upon God, and upon his providence and grace, that you are daily receiving mercy from him, and daily need his favour. Tell them why you observe the Lord's day, and make such a difference between that and other days; that it is in remembrance of the creation of the world, the resurrection of Christ, and the pouring out of the Spirit. Especially tell them of their baptism; take all opportunities to let them see children baptized (in order to which it is very good to have it done publicly) and tell them, thus they were baptized in their infancy, and by that solemnity dedicated and devoted to God the Father, Son, and Holy Ghost; and what was done for them then, they must now do for themselves. Tell them of the corruption of their nature, which needed cleansing; and of the grace of God in Christ, in which there is a cleansing virtue.

Set them to learn their catechism; let them commit some portions of Scripture to memory, as you find they are able to do it; and examine them, what they can remember of the sermons they hear. You will meet with some difficulty herein from the corruption of their nature, which you must endeavour to get over as much as may be by a gentle hand; give them instruction with all possible freedom and familiarity, with compassion and condescension to their capacity. Those teach these things most diligently to their children, not who are the most dictatorial in doing it, and make the greatest noise, but who talk of them frequently; when they sit in the house, and walk by the way, when they lie down, and when they rise up (Deut. 6: 7), frequently dropping good instructions among their children: and if but one in ten insensibly slip into their minds, and fasten there, what good proficients may we hope they will be in time. Contrive how to make this work, as much as may be, a pleasure and delight to your children and servants, and not a task, or a terror, or a drudgery. Teach them as Christ teaches, who is meek and lowly in heart.

MINISTERS—FEED CHRIST'S LAMBS

Let the ministers of Christ look upon themselves as under a charge to feed the lambs of Christ's flock. All the reformed churches make this a part of their work; to be done either publicly or privately; either in their solemn religious assemblies, or in meetings on purpose for this work; or in visiting their families, either by themselves, or, as in some churches abroad, by some other proper persons qualified for, and deputed to, this service particularly. Private catechising has the advantage of a more particular application to the persons catechised: public catechising has the advantage of a more general edification; and therefore both should be used in their season, or that which, all circumstances considered, may turn to the best account.

O that we who are ministers were filled with a zeal for the spiritual welfare and eternal salvation of young people, and a concern for the rising generation; and were to do our utmost as our ability and opportunity is, to fill the minds of young ones, in their early days, with the knowledge of Christ, and to fix them for Christ, that the next generation may be better than this. And O that those who are employed in public catechising may see of the travail of their souls to their satisfaction, and not labour in vain!

TEACH UNCHURCHED CHILDREN

Let us look with pity upon the great numbers of children, even in our own land, who are not taught these forms of sound words, but are bred up in ignorance and profaneness; strangers and enemies to Christ and true Christianity. They are poor, they are foolish, they know not the way of the Lord, nor the judgement of their God (Jer. 5: 4). They sit in darkness in a land of light, and walk on in darkness, and if infinite mercy do not interpose to prevent, they are hastening into utter darkness. If you can do anything, sirs, have compassion upon them and help them, pick up some of those neglected, abandoned young ones, you who have ability, and rescue them from ruin, by putting them into a way of receiving instruction. We have charity schools set up in the city and country; which, if managed by the rules of catholic Christianity, have a direct tendency to the bettering of the world, and the reforming of the next age, if the reforming of this should be despaired of. What is given to the support and encouragment of them, is charity, both to soul and body, and will be fruit abounding to your account.

RETAIN WHAT YOU HAVE LEARNED

Let those who have heard and learned the forms of sound words long ago, retain them still, and improve more and more. I have reason to think I speak to many who were blessed with a good education, were trained up in the way wherein they should go: I beseech you to examine yourselves, not only whether you have not departed from it, I hope you have not quite deserted it, but what progress have you made in it? What have you built upon that foundation? Has it been wood, hay, and stubble (1 Cor. 3: 12): airy notions, nice speculations, perverse disputings, and strifes of words; or has it been gold, silver, and precious stones: advances in serious godliness, in holiness, and heavenly mindedness, and the power of that kingdom of God, which is not meat or drink, but righteousness, and peace, and joy in the

Holy Ghost? (Rom. 14: 17). Go on and prosper, for the Lord is with you. But if you have in any degree let go that good thing which was committed to your trust, I beseech you to bethink yourselves whence you have fallen, and remember again what you have received and heard, and hold fast, and repent. Be watchful, and strengthen the things which remain, that are ready to die (Rev. 3: 2–3).

GROW IN KNOWLEDGE OF CHRIST

I must not part without a word to you, whose request brought me to this service here to-day, you who are catechised in the principles of religion, that you may grow yet more and more in the knowledge of Christ and Christianity.

Pay Careful Attention

Carefully attend to the instructions that are given you; and treasure them up, with sincerity, and all the marks of reverence and seriousness. Give attendance on, and attention to, what is taught you, and set your heart to it. You must take pains, else you cannot expect to reap advantage; for it is in labour that there is profit. Be careful to mark what is said, not critical to make remarks upon it; and give account of it with affection, but without affectation; and attend here not for ostentation, because you think yourselves better than others, but for your edification, because you would be better than you are.

Pray

Pray over what is taught you, and beg of God to bless it to you. Man can but teach the outward ear, it is God only that can bring it to the heart, and in that respect none teach like him. It is he who teaches with a strong hand (Isa. 8: 11), and then the teaching is effectual; who seals the instruction (Job 33: 16), and then it is abiding; who gives the understanding, and opens the heart. Look up to him therefore by faithful and fervent prayer, for that grace of his which is necessary to your profiting by the means of grace. You crave his blessing upon the food for your body, that it may be nourishing to you; and can you expect your spiritual food should nourish you without that blessing, or that you should have that blessing, if you do not pray for it? That good thing which is by the word committed to you to keep for God, do you by prayer commit to God to keep for you, and bring it to your minds when you should use it.

Adorn the Doctrine of God Our Saviour

Live as those who by attendance on such an exercise as this, make a profession of religion above many others. Hereby you seem to be more solicitous about your souls, and more inquisitive concerning the way to heaven, than your neighbours; but what will it avail you that you seem to be so, unless you be really so? The tree will be known by its fruits. Evidence that you receive not so much instruction in vain, by the exemplary purity and piety, seriousness and strictness, of your whole conversation. By your justice and charity, and unshaken veracity and fidelity; your sobriety and temperance; your humility and meekness; your conscientious obedience to your parents and masters, and a steady course of godliness and honesty; you ought to adorn the doctrine of God our Saviour. I remember Epictetus— pressing his pupil to show by his practice of virtue, his profiting by the instructions given him—illustrates it by this similitude: 'The sheep,' says he, 'do not come to their shepherd, and show him how much meat they have eaten, but they make it to appear by their growing fatter and fitter for use.' Thus, therefore, do you make it appear, that you improve in Christian knowledge, by the agreeableness and evenness of your Christian practice, and your perseverance in it to the end, that you and we may rejoice, in the day of the Lord, that we have not run in vain, nor laboured in vain.

CHRIST'S FAVOUR TO LITTLE CHILDREN

And he took them up in his arms,
and put his hands upon them,
and blessed them (Mark 10: 16).

Application was made to our Lord Jesus, when he was here upon earth, on a great variety of occasions: some we find imploring his favour upon one account, and some upon another; some for themselves, and some for their relations; some for the body, and some for the soul: thus was fulfilled the prediction of the dying patriarch concerning Shiloh, that to him shall the gathering of the people be (Gen. 49: 10). And be it observed, for the encouragement of all who humbly, and in faith, apply themselves to him: of the multitudes that spread their complaints before him, he never sent any away from him, ashamed of their hope in him: he gave them all an answer of peace; and they had what they came for.

But here in this paragraph, of which my text is the close, we have application made to Christ, upon an errand different from any other, but such a one as those who knew the heart of a parent, of a Christian parent, will be glad to be encouraged and directed to come to him upon, and will therefore bless God that it is here upon record. There were those who brought young children to him, that he should touch them (v. 13). In St. Matthew's gospel it is said, they desired that he would put his hands upon them, and pray (Matt. 19: 13).

Who they were that brought these children, we are not told; whether their parents, or no: it is most likely they were, for who should show so much concern for them as they! Nor are we told what number of children were brought; nor whether they were all of one family; nor just of what age they were, but as to that, St. Luke tells us they were infants, τα βρεφη (Luke 18: 15), it is the word which in the story of Christ's birth we translate 'the babe', in swaddling clothes, and in the manger (Luke 2: 12); and it is put for new-born babes, that desire the breast (1 Pet. 2:2). The critics say it signifies a child being nursed; they are said to be brought to Christ, which intimates that they could not go themselves; and it is plain that they were very little, for he took them up in his arms; so little, that he could easily hold them in one arm, for so he did when he put his hands upon them to bless them.

Christ came to teach, and heal, and bless; to teach a world that sat in darkness, to heal a world that was sick and dying, and to bless a world that lay under the curse.

1. These children were not brought to Christ to be taught, for they were not yet capable of receiving instruction; nor could they profit by his preaching, or put any questions to him. Those who are grown up to years of understanding have need to be busy in getting knowledge now, that they may redeem the time they lost through the invincible incapacities of their infancy.

2. Were they brought to Christ to be cured, for it does not appear that they needed it? Little children are indeed liable to many distempers, painful, mortal ones. The physicians have a book among them, *De Morbis Infantum*—on the death of infants. Death and its harbingers reign even over them who have not sinned after the similitude of Adam's transgression (Rom. 5: 14), but these children were strong and healthful, and we do not find that anything ailed them.

3. But, they were brought to Christ to be blessed, so they

meant when they desired that he would touch them: the sign is put for the thing signified. The laying on of hands was a ceremony anciently used in blessing. When Joseph brought his two sons to Israel, and put one to his left hand, and the other to his right, that he might touch them, that which he desired was, that he would bless them (Gen. 48: 13). So these here brought their children to Christ, not that he might touch and heal them, but that he might touch and bless them, with the saving strength of his right hand.

They looked upon Christ as a prophet, as a great prophet, as that Prophet which should come into the world, as one that had a great interest in heaven, and consequently a great influence upon this earth; if he be a prophet he shall pray for you (Gen. 20: 7); but then you must pay him so much respect as to desire his prayers. This honour they here give to Christ (as it is fit those should do, who expect to receive favour from him) in their humble request that he would lift up a prayer for their children; which they believe will avail much, as the effectual fervent prayer of a righteous man (Jas. 5: 16).

It is good to have an interest in the prayers of those who are of the spiritual seed of Jacob, that seek God and know how to wrestle with him, and to improve that interest for ourselves and our children. We should not only pray with, and for our families ourselves, but engage the prayers of our friends for them, that we may hereby not only put an honour upon our brethren, and upon the communion of saints; not only the communion of churches, but the communion of religious families, who all meet in him, in whom all the families, all the praying families, of the earth are blessed (Gen. 12: 3). A treasury of prayers laid up for our children may stand them in better stead than thousands of pieces of gold and silver laid up for them. But if we desire this kindness of our friends, and brethren, and ministers, we must remember that one good turn requires another, and must, therefore, make conscience of praying for them and their families, as for ourselves and for our own. St. Paul, who prays so earnestly for his friends, did as earnestly desire their prayers for him (Rom. 15: 30). The Lord give mercy to the households (2 Tim. 1: 16) of our acquaintance, is a petition which (or something like it) should have a place in our daily prayers.

Now the text tells us, how they succeeded, who brought their little children to Christ to be blessed, and prayed for, how well they succeeded. And it is recorded by three of the evangelists, because it was a manifest indication of the design of Christ, to continue to the children of believers, under the New Testament dispensation, the same covenant right, and visible church membership, which they had under the Old Testament dispensation, by virtue of God's promise to Abraham, and his seed; that blessing of Abraham (Gal. 3: 14) which comes upon the Gentiles through Jesus Christ; and because it gives us great encouragement when we come to Christ ourselves, to bring our children with us, and present them also to him.

They who brought these infants to Christ were frowned upon and discountenanced by the disciples; they rebuked them, because they would not have such a needless trouble (so they thought it) given to their Master, who had other work enough upon his hands. If this be encouraged, they shall see no end of it. Was it not enough that he cured the sick, which none but he could do, but he must bless the well too, which others might do? How well is it for us, that our Master has more tenderness and compassion than the best of his ministers have; and is touched more nearly than they are or can be with the blessing of our infirmities (Heb. 4: 15), and an inclination to gratify those innocent desires of humble and believing supplicants, which those who think themselves polite and refined look upon with a slight, as not worth taking notice of. In grace and goodness he is God and not man (Hos. 11: 9). Nay he is both God and man: as man, he has himself suffered being tempted, and is therefore able with the greater sympathy, to succour them who are tempted (Heb. 2: 18); and as God, in doing good his thoughts and ways are infinitely above ours, the best of ours, above those of the best of us (Isa. 55: 9).

As, when God promised to show Moses his glory he proclaimed all his goodness, and caused that to pass before him (Exod. 33: 18, 19); so our Lord Jesus, when he would let his chosen ones see his glory, the glory as of the only begotten of the Father, he showed himself upon all occasions full of grace. Among men it is looked upon to be the symptom of a sweet and loving disposition, to take notice of little children, and to be familiar with them. By this among many other instances, our

Lord Jesus showed himself to be kind and benign, meek and lowly in heart; that, upon all occasions, he discovered a particular kindness for little children, and never more than upon this occasion, when he gave a severe reprimand to his disciples for prohibiting those that brought their children to him: he was much displeased at it; he was both sorry and angry that his own disciples did not better know his mind, and that they should be adversaries to those for whom they ought to have been advocates. And he gave orders immediately that they should be called to him, who brought the children (who perhaps, upon the disciples check, were going off) and that room should be made for them to come to him: By all means suffer the little children to come to me, and do not forbid them, for they belong to the church still as much as ever: The Kingdom of God which I come to set up includes them; they are within the Allegiance of Messiah the Prince, and he will own them as his subjects.

And not only for the satisfaction of those who brought them, and to please them, but for the benefit and advantage of the children, he took them up, with a great deal of endearing tenderness in his arms, put his hands upon them, and blessed them; did not only pray for a blessing, as they desired, but commanded the blessing, as one having authority, even life for evermore (Ps. 133: 3), which is inclusive of all blessings.

But what encouragement (you will say) does this give to us? Christ is not now among us as he was then; and we cannot either make such addresses to him, or receive such favours from him, as they then might. It is true we cannot in such a sensible manner, but we may as really in a spiritual way, make our applications to him, and expect communications from him; for in him all fullness dwells, to him all judgment is committed, and the knee of every supplicant must bow to him: and we are sure he has blessings as much at command now as ever he had. And, therefore, from the kind entertainment he gave to these children who were brought to him, we are warranted to infer his readiness to receive our children that are offered up to him, for it is certain never anyone was the worse for going to heaven.

From hence observe then, that our Lord Jesus has given us great encouragement to hope that he will favourably accept our little children, when, in a right manner, we bring them to him for a blessing.

I shall endeavour to show how we must now bring our little children to Christ, what entertainment we may promise ourselves they shall find with him according to this instance in the text, and then make application.

HOW WE MUST BRING OUR CHILDREN TO CHRIST

Those who are truly ambitious of this honour for their children, and covetous of this wealth for them, to have them blessed of Christ, cannot but wish to know how they may bring their children to him, so that they may hope to obtain his favour. Say not in your heart, 'Who shall ascend into heaven (Rom. 10: 6, 8), where Christ sits at God's right hand, and take my children with him thither to receive his blessing?' No: the word of God is near to you; and Christ in the word, and his blessings, to be received by faith, applying the word to ourselves. The tabernacle of God is among us; the priests, the spiritual sacrifices, the Israel of God; where two or three of them are gathered in his name, he will be in the midst of them (Matt. 18: 20), both to receive their homage, and to give out his favours. Where his ordinances are administered according to his institution, and those things which he has commanded, observed and taught, there will he be all the days, even to the end of the world (Matt. 28: 19, 20). There he records his name, and there will meet his people, and bless them. Nay, wherever a true Christian is, there is a living temple, in which God is served and honoured, and his blessings and favours communicated, by his Spirit dwelling in the heart. There is still a way of access to Christ, a new and living way, by which we may not only come to Christ ourselves, but bring others to him, bring ours to him, our children, who are pieces of ourselves.

SURRENDER THEM TO HIM

When by a deliberate and solemn act of our souls, we resign and give up, with ourselves, the children also which God has graciously given us, to the Lord Jesus, to be to him for a people, and for a name, and for a praise, and for a glory (Jer. 13: 11); to be Christians, devoted to his honour, and employed in his service; to be members of that body whereof he is the head, servants in that family whereof he is the Master, and subjects in that kingdom of his among men, which is incorporated by that great gospel charter, 'Disciple all nations into the name of the Father, Son, and Holy Ghost' (Matt. 28: 19); then we may bring our children to Christ: we present them to him (Rom. 12: 1), (a poor present to him who has a world of angels at command, yet such as he requires and will accept of) as living sacrifices, which we desire may be holy and acceptable; it is our reasonable service.

Parents are invested by nature in a right to their children, and an authority over them for their good. A daughter in her father's house was accounted by the law not *sui juris*; he could disannul her vows (Num. 30: 5). Now this right in our children we must not only acknowledge to be subordinate to that prior superior title God has to them; for we are only the fathers of their flesh, he is the Father of their spirits (Heb. 12: 9); but we must also transfer to our Lord Jesus, whom the Father has constituted the great trustee, both of all the powers with which he intended mankind should be ruled, and of all the favours with which he intended mankind should be blessed.

Our children are God's children; they are my sons and my daughters, saith God, which thou hast born unto me (Ezek. 16: 20); and therefore it is sacrilege to alienate them from him, and to devote them to the service of the world and the flesh; it is profaning the holy things of the *It is sacrilege to alienate them from him, and to devote them to the service of the world and the flesh.* Lord our God. And it is our duty to dedicate them and dispose of them as he directs. Now he directs us to give them up to Christ; to enrol them among his disciples; to enter their names among his servants (Ps. 116: 16), who being born in his house, belong to his family, and are entitled to the protection and provisions of it, and taken under the order and discipline of it.

That is a great word, and speaks much of the dignity and power of our Lord Jesus: 'The Father loves the Son, and hath given all things into his hand' (John 3: 35), all the things that concern his honour and government, all his part of the matters in variance between himself and fallen man, he has put into the hands of the Mediator, as referee of the controversy, the blessed Day's man, who has laid his hand upon us both. Now that which he requires of us (and with reason) is that we love the Son, and give all things into his hand; all our interests and concerns; and particularly our children, who were made and born for immortality, who are entered into a state of probation and preparation for eternity, whom therefore we commit to him as to their Guardian: by whose gospel, life and immortality are brought to light (2 Tim. 1: 10), and brought to hand.

Hereby we do honour to the exalted Redeemer, and recognize his authority; as one to whom the Father has therefore given power over all flesh, especially over the spirits of all flesh, that he should give eternal life to as many as he had given him (John 17: 2), as many of them. We own his dominion both in heaven and on earth, by owning his indisputable title to our children; both to their bodies, by which they are allied to the earth, and to their souls, by which they are allied to heaven and the world of spirits.

Hereby we confess, that as we ourselves, so our children, are more his than our own; and therefore we desire that both we and ours may live to him. And in thus honouring the Son, we honour the Father also; for Christ came to bring us to himself, that he might bring us to God (1 Pet. 3: 18). Our children are therefore brought to Christ, the Mediator of the covenant, that through him they may be brought to God, as their God in covenant. When Israel was taken into covenant with God, express notice is taken not only of their captains, and elders, and officers, but of their little ones, as parties to the covenant which the Lord their God made with them (Deut. 29: 10–12).

Hereby we do well for our children, the best we can do for them, for we give them up to him who is able to do that for them which we cannot do, and which must be done for them, or they are undone. We know they derive through our loins sinful and corrupt natures; we know they are shapen in iniquity, they are called, and not miscalled, transgressors from the womb (Isa. 48: 8): what therefore can we do for them, but bring them to him who came to save sinners, to save them from their sins? They are born polluted; and by presenting them to Christ, we bring them to the fountain that was opened for Judah and Jerusalem to wash in from sin, which is uncleanness (Zech. 13: 1). They are born distempered; and we thus bring them to the great Physician, to have their temperament corrected, to have their very constitution altered; to have not the mass of their blood, but of their minds, changed for the better, that as they have born the image of the earthly, they may also bear the image of the heavenly (1 Cor. 15: 49).

Now this solemn surrender of our children to God as theirs in covenant, if we ourselves be in covenant with God, I think ought to be done by the ordinance of baptism; an ordinance peculiar to the Redeemer's kingdom, and a seal, as circumcision was, of the righteousness which is by faith (Rom. 4: 11), and therefore, like it, belonging both to believers and to their infant seed. Our Saviour, when he instituted that ordinance, gave a double intimation concerning his gospel kingdom which was then to be set up. One was, that it must not be confined to the Jews, but spread to the Gentiles; therefore go and make all nations disciples. The other was, that it should not be confined to that generation, and live and die with the apostles. It must not be (as the historian faith of the Roman commonwealth) *Res unius ætatis*; no, it must continue, for Christ will continue at the head of it, and in the midst of it, always, even to the end of the world. Now, as baptism did subserve the former design, and attended the progress of the gospel to the most distant regions of the earth; so we have reason to think it was instituted equally to subserve the latter design, and to attend the propagating of the gospel to the latest ages of time; that by taking early hold of the seed of the faithful, and giving their parents, and ministers, and consciences, early hold of them, provision might be made (as was by the altar, *Erd.*) that nothing might make them cease from fearing the Lord (Josh. 22: 25, 34): that thus a seed might serve the Lord Jesus, which should be accounted to him for a generation (Ps. 22: 29, 30); and by keeping up the entail, and as it were by a continual claim, the name of Christ might endure for ever, and his throne as the days of heaven (Ps. 89: 29).

But waving this dispute; I insist upon that, in which I am sure we are all agreed, that our children are to be given up to the Lord Jesus; and of his own do we give him, for he has bought them with a price (1 Cor. 6: 20), that they may glorify him in body and spirit, and he may be honoured even by their hosannas. We lend them to the Lord, as Hannah did Samuel (1 Sam. 1: 28), that they may be his all the days of their life; and if they be so, they shall be his to the endless ages of eternity.

SEEK HIM FOR THEM

We must bring them to Christ, by seeking him for them, as those who are surrendered to him. They are to be but once baptized, but they are to be daily prayed for, and the promise sealed to them in their baptism put in suit and pleaded with God in their behalf. These here brought their children to Christ, when they begged his blessing on them, and thus we must bring ours to him; bring their case to him, the case of their souls, their precious souls, which ought to be laid nearer our hearts than anything else that concerns them.

When Christ was here upon earth, we read of many who applied themselves to him for mercy for their children: Lord, have mercy upon my son (Matt. 17: 15), said one; Lord, have mercy upon my daughter (Matt. 15: 22), said another: and the children fared the better for the faith and prayers of the parents. And we may, as easily, come to him now he is in heaven, and more easily; and with the same petition: Lord, have mercy on my son, on my daughter, who is foolish, and vain, and carnally minded, which is death (Rom. 8: 6), and much under the power of Satan. Even our little children's souls are to be prayed for; for we believe they are born in sin, and foolishness is bound in their hearts; and we see how soon corrupt nature appears and works in them, and how the tares spring up with the wheat: let us therefore be earnest with God for the operation of his grace upon their hearts betimes; that Christ be formed in their souls when they are young, and they may be sanctified from their infancy. They are thine, save them (Ps. 119: 94). Ishmael was very young when Abraham prayed so affectionately, O that Ishmael might live before thee (Gen. 17: 18)!

Our children are capable of being prayed for, and of receiving benefit by prayer, before they are capable of being taught, and of receiving benefit by instruction: and as their being baptized lays us under an engagement to teach them, so it gives us an encouragement to pray for them: and we should begin early to do it. Look up to Christ, and beg of him to bless them with all spiritual blessings in heavenly things, which will be the best provision and the best portion for them.

Be constant in praying for your children; pray for them as duly as for yourselves, as St. Paul for his friends, making mention of them always in every prayer. Be particular in praying for them; pray for each particular child, as holy Job offered burnt-offerings for his sons, according to the number of them all (Job 1: 5); that you may be able to say, as Hannah: For this child I prayed (1 Sam. 1: 27); pray for particular blessings for your children, according as you see their case requires, for that grace which you observe their natural temper (or distemper rather) calls for.

Let us take heed lest our prayers degenerate into formality, and we pray for them only from custom, and in no better manner than we can soon teach them to pray for themselves, and for us too, by rote: but let us pray for them, from a principle of concern for their precious souls; in the prosperity and welfare of which their happiness, and our comfort in them, is bound up. When a child is born, there is a candle lighted that must burn to eternity, either in heaven or hell; the consideration whereof should awaken us to pray with all possible earnestness for the salvation of their souls, next to that of our own.

> *When a child is born, there is a candle lighted that must burn to eternity, either in heaven or hell.*

When they are little, they cannot pray for themselves; and if you do not pray for them, who should? When they are grown up, it may be that they are careless, and will not pray for themselves to any purpose, and then their case is the more piteous; it may be that they are wicked and profane, and hate prayer, yet continue to pray for them, for while there is life there is hope, and while there is hope, there is room for prayer; and who knows but he who waits to be gracious, may at length be gracious to you, and your child that is dead may be alive again (2 Sam. 12: 22).

Have an eye to Christ in all your prayers for your children; let the prayer be directed to him, as it was here. It was in his name particularly that they were baptized, and therefore in his name they must be prayed for, and into his hands all our petitions to God must be put; we may with him plead their baptism: Lord, they are given up to thee to be thine; make them thine own, then own them as thine. Plead his interest in them as the children of his family, the lambs of his flock, the pets of his school, plead your dedication of them to him, and his acceptance of them; and resolve to leave them with him.

It is by prayer that we cast our care upon God; cast it upon the Lord Jesus, to whom the Father has committed all judgment, and who is entrusted with the administration of the providential kingdom, in subserviency to the mediatorial kingdom. Our children are a considerable part of our care. What they will prove, and what will become of them? We must by prayer cast this care upon Christ; and believe that the children of the greatest are not above the need of his care, nor those of the meanest beneath the cognizance of it.

Submit Them to His Providence

We must bring them to Christ, by submitting them to the disposal of his providence. When we have by prayer sought him for them, we must by a cheerful acquiescence in his wisdom and goodness, make ourselves easy concerning them; believing that Christ knows what is fit for them and us better than we do. We bring them to Christ, when we bring our will, concerning them, into an entire submission to his will; believing that he will be sanctified, and resolving that then we will be satisfied (Lev. 10: 3).

Let us make Christ guardian to our children, not only when we are dead, but while we live; trust them with him, and put them under his protection; as Jacob did his children when he was parting with them: God Almighty give you mercy (Gen. 43: 14)! And when be was parting from them: the angel that redeemed me from all evil (Gen. 48: 16) (and that can be no other than the Lord Jesus, the angel of the covenant) bless the lads!

When we can refer it to the divine will, whether our children shall be healthful or sickly, high or low, rich or poor, prosperous or crossed, thriving or declining in the world; whether they shall live to be old, or die young; provided it may but go well with their precious souls, and they may be happy to eternity; then we bring them to Christ, as a skilful, faithful Physician, willing he should take what method he pleases with them, so he will but cure them, and save them. I have read of a good man, whose son being disposed of in the world, met with great affliction, which he once very feelingly complained of to his good father, who answered (according to the principle I am now upon), 'Anything, child, to bring thee to heaven.'

SUBJECT THEM TO HIS GOVERNMENT

We must bring them to Christ, by subjecting them, as far as we can, to the government of his grace. Having laid their necks under the yoke of Christ in their baptism, we must teach them to draw in it, and use our interest in them, and authority over them, to keep them under that easy yoke, and bring them up in the nurture and admonition of our Lord Jesus (Eph. 6: 4).

Having got them enrolled among his servants, we must teach them, betimes, to know their Master, and to own his dominion over them, and their obligations to him; bring them into their Master's presence, bring them to see him, bring them to hear him, by bringing them to his word and ordinances; feed your kids beside the shepherd's tents (S. of S. 1: 8); let them have family instruction, as soon as they are capable of receiving it, and be brought to sit under the public ministry, as soon as they are capable of not being a disturbance to it.

Bring them to Christ's feet, by taking pains to impress upon their minds the indispensable necessity of their being taught and ruled by Jesus Christ, of their believing his truths, and obeying his laws, in order to their present and eternal welfare. We brought them to Christ, by an instituted sign of their being his, in their baptism; we bring them to Christ, by the instituted means of their being his, in their religious education; both those we second with prayer, that they may be his: thus far we must go, and further we cannot.

WHY CHRIST WILL RECEIVE THEM

You see how you may bring your little children to Christ. I come next to show you, for your encouragement, how you may hope he will receive those who are thus brought to him, and what entertainment they may expect; surely, something like the kind entertainment he here gave to these little ones: He took them up in his arms, put his hand upon them, and blessed them. Such visible, sensible signs of his favour we are not now to expect, but that which is more than equivalent in spiritual blessings.

Only let me premise, that we cannot be so confident of God's giving his grace to our children, if we in sincerity pray to him for it, and use the means, as we may be of his giving it to ourselves, if we do so. Many a godly parent no doubt has brought his children to Christ, as before directed, who yet have proved wicked and vile, and strangers to Christ, and come short of his blessing, but it has been through their own default. Many are sacramentally regenerated, and born again of water, by which they have been partakers of the Christian name who yet, are never really regenerated and born again of the Spirit (John 3: 5), but live and die destitute of the nature of Christians. All we can say is, that if we thus bring our children to Christ, they stand much fairer for, and nearer to, his blessing, than if they be not brought to him. There are promises and precedents which we may take encouragements from, and upon which we are caused to hope, that Christ will give them his grace, will work his good work in them, both as a token of, and as a qualification for, his good will towards them; and if he does, it will be an addition to our comfort, that it is an answer to our prayers, and the fruit of our labours; if he does not, it will be a support to us under our grief to have the testimony of our conscience that, by the grace of God, we have in some measure done our duty, and then left the event with God, whose grace is his own.

Let us now observe the instance of Christ's favour to these children; and inquire what we may expect that has some resemblance of it.

HE TOOK THEM UP IN HIS ARMS

See how Christ does more for humble believing supplicants than they can ask or think: it was only desired that he would touch them, but he did more, he embraced them; and it speaks not only his wonderful condescension, but his compassion and affection. A little while previously, when he had occasion to set a little child before his disciples as a pattern of humility, he not only set the child in the midst of them, which was sufficient to answer his intention; but he took him in his arms (Mark 9: 36), to show his tender love to those who are as little children. When Israel was a child, then I loved him (Hos. 11: 1). This spoke the kindness our Saviour (Titus 3: 3) had for the human nature and race: his φιλανθρωπια—his joy in the habitable part of the earth, and his delight in the sons of men (Prov. 8: 31).

Christ took up these children in his arms as one well pleased with them, and concerned for them; that the Scripture might be fulfilled which said concerning him, 'He shall feed his flock like a shepherd, he shall gather his lambs in his arms, and carry them in his bosom' (Isa. 40: 11). Time was, when he himself was taken up in old Simeon's arms (Luke 2: 28). And he did himself pass through the age of infancy, to make it honourable and comfortable to the children of his people; and the expressions of his favour afterwards to little children make it much more so: when their mothers and nurses carry them in their arms, and are almost tired with the load, let them refresh themselves with this thought, that the Holy Child Jesus was carried in arms, and did himself take up little children in his arms. When Moses was charged thus to bear Israel, he found himself aggrieved. Have I conceived all this people (Num. 11: 12)? Have I begotten them, that thou shouldest say unto me, carry them in my bosom as a nursing father bears the sucking child? But what Moses complained of, Christ had complacency in; he took them up in his arms: it is but one word in the original, ἐναγκαλεσαμενος—he in-armed them, he took them into his embraces; as he did his spouse, who said with satisfaction, 'His left hand is under my head, and his right hand doth embrace me' (S. of S. 2: 6).

But how may we hope he will take our children in his arms, when we bring them to him? Surely we may promise ourselves no less than what David promised himself: 'When my father and my mother forsake me, then the Lord will take me up' (Ps. 27: 10).

In the Arms of His Power and Providence

We may hope that he will take them up in the arms of his power and providence; that he will hold their souls in life, and protect them from, or carry them through, the weaknesses and perils of the infant age: that he will give his angels (Matt. 18: 10), the little ones' angels, a charge concerning them, to bear them in their arms (Ps. 91: 12); and their arms are his arms, the arms of his power. 'The name of the Lord is a strong tower' (Prov. 18: 10), into which the righteous are not only welcome to run themselves, but to bring their children; and where they and theirs may hope to be safe, so safe, as that no real evil, no only evil, shall befall them. The arm of the Lord is revealed in favour of the little ones, even of a sinful race; witness those of unbelieving murmuring Israel: But your little ones, though living in a barren wilderness, and likely to be made a prey, them will I bring into that land which I have promised, and you have despised (Num. 14: 31). Much more shall it be stretched out for the relief and preservation of the faithful seed, whose refuge the eternal God is (Deut. 33: 27), and will be, and underneath them are the everlasting arms; such are the arms of the Lord Jesus, which cannot faint or be weary, and by which all things are upheld, else they would sink.

That divine providence which supports children in their childhood, and carries them through that helpless age, which puts it into the hearts of parents to provide for them; which preserves to them their limbs and senses, of which they might, by a thousand ill accidents, be deprived in a moment; by which they grow in strength and stature; is to be mentioned to the honour of the Redeemer, to whom it is owing that the race of mankind continues in being upon the face of the earth, though guilty and obnoxious. It is in the Redeemer's arms, by whom all things consist (Col. 1: 16), that children are born up, and carried on to full age; for to him are owing all the reprieves of God's patience (2 Pet. 3: 15), and all the gifts of his common providence. This we have all experienced ourselves, and must acknowledge it with thankfulness to the Redeemer's praise, as the royal Psalmist does: Thou art he that took me out of the womb; thou didst make me hope, and kept me in safety when I was upon my mother's breast. I was cast upon thee from the womb; thou art my God from my mother's belly (Ps. 22: 9, 10). By thee have I been holden up, and therefore my praise shall be continually of thee (Ps. 71: 5, 6). And what we have experienced ourselves, we may humbly expect for our children, if we bring them to Christ, to whom we have brought ourselves.

In the Arms of His Pity and Grace

That he will take them up in the arms of his pity and grace; that he will in compassion to their precious souls, the case of which by nature is very piteous, undertake to cleanse and cure them, to sanctify and save them; that, as in his love and pity he has shed his blood to wash from sin, and so prepared the laver, he will, in love to them, and pity to them, sprinkle that purifying, healing blood upon them, that they may by it be washed from their sin, and sanctified for God, as their God.

The loveliest, sweetest babe we ever saw, though like Moses in the ark of bulrushes, exceeding fair, to admiration, yet, like him, is born in a land of Egypt, in a house of bondage; like him, marked for the sword as soon as born; nay, it is like the infant in Ezekiel's parable, polluted in its own blood, and cast out to the loathing of its person (Ezek. 16: 5–6): it is shaped in iniquity, it is born in sin and its precious soul is defiled and deformed, and an object of pity. This is a melancholy thought, and a damp to the pleasure we take in our children. But this is a comfort: that Christ has compassion on them, has arms to gather them up in, and has given us hopes that he will say unto them: Live, yea, he will say to them, live (Ezek. 16: 6), will wash them from their filth, will clothe them with his grace: and the time will be a time of love indeed, both to them and us (Ezek. 16: 8–10). That he will embrace them, as the father of the prodigal did his returning son, when he fell on his neck and kissed him (Luke 15: 20); will receive them into the arms of a covenant of grace, out of which they shall never be plucked, and in which they shall be for ever easy and happy.

HE PUT HIS HANDS UPON THEM

They desired that he would touch them (Rev. 1: 17), one touch from Christ has done wonders; but he did more, he put his hands on them, as he did on John when he said, 'Fear not'; and as he did on many whom he cured; to intimate that virtue went out of him for the purpose to which he intended it.

But how may we hope that Jesus Christ will now put his hands upon us and ours? If he set us and ours apart for himself (Psa. 4: 3), as his own peculiar people, we may say he puts his hand upon us and ours: as the buyer lays his hand on the goods he has agreed for, they are now his own. As Jacob put his hand on the head of Joseph's sons to signify not only his blessing them, but his adopting them, and taking them for his own. Let my name be named upon them (Gen. 48: 16). This we hope Christ doth for our children, when we bring them to him; he owns them for his; and we may say they do in some degree belong to Christ, are retainers to his family.

It is an honour and comfort to have our little children called Christians, called by Christ's name; to have them numbered among his peculiar ones, among the servants born in his house, distinguished from the children of heathens, who have not the knowledge of God and Christ; to have them added to the church, which is God's treasure in the world; planted in his vineyard, sown in his field, to be a holy seed, a seed for God; especially if we have good hopes, through grace, that they are not admitted to a place in the courts of God's house now, but are designed for his holy place above, for the congregation of the righteous there. If Christ will but put his hand upon them, and say, they shall be mine in that day when I make up my jewels (Mal. 3: 17), we have enough, we have all we wished for in bringing them to him.

If he give his Holy Spirit to us and ours, it truly be said, he puts his hand upon us and them. The Spirit is sometimes called the finger of God (Luke 11: 20); and sometimes the hand of God; so that Christ's putting his hand upon us (Ezek. 3: 14) not only puts us into a relation to him, but works a real change in us, lays hold on the soul for him, and puts his image, as well as superscription upon it. The laying on of hands was a ceremony used in conferring the Holy Ghost; and this we pray for, and hope for from Christ, for our children, when we bring them to him.

And there are words upon which he has encouraged us to hope for this. We find it possible that children may be sanctified from their birth (Jer. 1: 5), that they may be filled with the Holy Ghost from their mother's womb (Luke 1: 15); nay, we find it promised that God will pour his spirit upon our seed (Isa. 44: 3), and his blessing, that blessing of blessings upon our offspring (Isa. 59: 21): that his Spirit upon thee shall not depart from thy seed; that his Spirit shall be poured out upon our sons and daughters (Joel 2: 28); that our children shall all be taught of the Lord (Isa. 54: 13); and great shall be their peace. The New Testament promise is to us and to our children (Acts 2: 38–9); not only that of the forgiveness of sins, but that of the gift of the Holy Ghost. These are the true sayings of God, and we may put them in suit, and expect the performance of them for our children, when we bring them to Christ, and O that he would thus put his hand upon them.

HE BLESSED THEM

He was desired to pray for a blessing for them, but he did more, he commanded the blessing (Ps. 133: 3), blessed with authority; he pronounced them blessed, and thereby made them so; for those whom he blesses are blessed indeed. Christ is the great High Priest, whose office it is to bless the people of God, and all theirs. When he parted from his disciples at his ascension, he blessed them (Luke 24: 50); he left blessings behind him for his church on earth, and all the members of it, the little ones not excepted.

When God took Abraham into covenant, he promised to bless him; and the blessing wherewith he blessed him was, I will be a God to thee and to thy seed (Gen. 17: 7): but that was not all; he promised in the Messiah, who should descend from his loins, all the nations of the earth should be blessed (Gen. 12: 2–3); not only blessed by him, but blessed in him, in that righteousness and salvation which should be wrought out and brought in by him. The transferring of this blessing was the great care and business of the patriarchs; Jacob and Esau strove for it, and Jacob got it; the Jews sinned it away for themselves, but not for the world; and therefore, by the gospel this blessing of Abraham comes upon the Gentiles (Gal. 3: 14), that comprehensive blessing, that God will be a God to them that believe, and to their seed: this blessing Christ has the conferring of, for he is the Mediator of the covenant, and Trustee of the blessings of it. Now if we in faith bring our children to him, as Mediator, we may hope he will bestow this blessing upon them with the other children of the church: for St. Peter gives the Jews this reason why God, having raised up his Son Jesus, sent him to bless them, because they were the Children of the Prophets, and of the Covenant (Acts 3: 25, 26). Now if we and ours be the Children of the Prophets and of the Covenant, of the Prophets by our assent to gospel truths, and of the Covenant, by our consent to gospel terms, we may hope to inherit (and our seed after us) that blessing which Christ was sent to bestow.

The prayers made by the Israel of God for all its members, from the least to the greatest, are encouraging to us to hope that they shall share in the blessing: Our children are not only prayed for by us as a part of our family, but they are prayed for by all that in every place call on the name of Jesus Christ (1 Cor. 1: 2); their Lord and ours, as belonging to Christ's family, to the nursery in that family; the welfare and prosperity of which, all who are concerned for the perpetuating of Christ's name and throne cannot but have a particular and tender concern for. In bringing them to Christ, we bring them within the prayers of all good Christians: which we hope may obtain a blessing for them.

The promises made to the Israel of God are yet more encouraging: especially since Christ came to confirm the promises made to the fathers (Rom. 15: 8), that in him they might be Yea and Amen. Now it is promised that the generation of the upright shall be blessed (Ps. 112: 2); that the seed of God's servants shall be established before him (Ps. 102: 28): that they shall be so remarkably pious and prosperous, that all who see them shall acknowledge them (Isa. 61: 9), that they are the seed which the Lord has blessed. Lord, be it unto thy servants according to the word which thou hast spoken.

Children, Jesus Has Concern for You

Let me hence address myself to children, to little children, to the lambs of the flock, to the youngest that can hear with understanding (Neh. 8: 2): will not you be glad to hear this, that the Lord Jesus Christ has a tender concern and affection for you; and that he has blessings in store for you, if you apply yourselves to him, according to your capacity? Shall I speak to you in the words of David? 'Come ye children, hearken to me, and I will teach you' (Ps. 34: 11), as young as you are, the fear of the Lord. Nay, I would teach you not only the fear of God, but the faith of Christ; and therefore address myself to you, in the words of St. Paul, 'My little children, of whom I travail in birth again, until Christ be formed in you' (Gal. 4: 19), till his image be renewed upon you, and he live in you (Gal. 2: 20).

You hear, dear little ones, what Christ has done for you, what favour he has showed to those of your age: and will not you put in for an interest in his favour, and the provision he has made for the entertainment of children? Has he thus loved you, and will not you love him? Has he such kind thoughts toward you, and will not you have dutiful thoughts toward him? Does he invite you to him, and will not you accept of his invitation? He says here, Suffer little children not only to be brought to me, but to come to me; to come as they can themselves, to make it their own act and deed; and do not forbid them, for it is possible, that of those of their age may be the kingdom of God, that they may get to heaven.

You love those who take notice of you, and play with you, and give you toys; and will you not love those who pray for you, and instruct you, and would bring you to be acquainted with the best things? Will you not reckon them your friends indeed, who seek the welfare of your souls, your eternal welfare?

Be sensible betimes of the corruption of your nature, that foolishness is bound in your heart; and give all diligence to get a change wrought in you. Begin betimes to put a difference between God's name and other names, God's book and other books, God's day and other days. Be dutiful to your parents, and labour to be a comfort to them. Love prayer, learn to pray, and be much in it. Mortify your passions, keep them under, and do not indulge them. Hate and abhor lying, and make conscience of speaking truth.

There are little books, both of counsels and examples, suited to your age: 'The Token for Children', by Mr Janeway, and Mr White's 'Little Book for Little Children': which you should not be strangers to. Love your catechism, and hold fast the form of sound words, which you have heard; but above all, see to it that from your childhood you know the Holy Scriptures, which are able to make you wise to salvation.

Lay yourselves at Christ's feet, and he will take you up in his arms. Give yourselves to him, and he will give himself in his graces and comforts to you. Lie in his way, by a diligent attendance on his ordinances, and he will not pass by without putting his hand on you. And if you value his blessings aright, and be earnest with him for blessings, he will bless you with the best of blessings, such as will make you eternally blessed.

PARENTS—CHRIST WELCOMES CHILDREN

This passage affords both direction and encouragement to Christian parents: I write to you fathers, and to you mothers, who have a tender concern for your children, and desire they may do well, and would fain do well for them. Observe the entertainment Christ gave to the children who were brought to him, and see it written for your learning.

Have You Brought Them to Christ?

Let this direct us, who are parents, concerning our children. We have seen how we are to bring them to Christ; and have we thus brought them to him? We brought them to baptism; but did we thereupon bring them to Christ? Was it done as unto the Lord? If it was, let us now make it to appear. Have we brought our children to Christ, with hopes that they have been accepted of him?

By Faith and Prayer

Bring them to him, by faith and prayer, according as their case requires; be daily laying them at his feet, by resigning them to his conduct, and referring all events concerning them to his wise and gracious disposal; be daily putting them in his arms, by entreating his favour towards them, as that which is the life of their souls, and better than the life of the body.

You see here what to desire and pray for, for your children: that the Mediator's blessing may be their portion; for that is a portion for the soul and eternity, a good part that shall never be taken away from those who have it. Covet not great things in the world for them, a little will serve to bear their charges through it; but be earnest with God for them in heavenly things by Christ Jesus; let them have these, and they have enough.

When you bless your children (and it is good sometimes to do it solemnly), let your eye be to Christ, in whom alone it is that blessings are entailed on us and ours, and through whose hand are derived. The patriarchs in blessing their sons had an eye to a Christ to come; and to him now he is come, much more ought we to have an eye.

Pray daily with your children and servants; that they may hear you pray for them and may thereby be taught and quickened to pray for themselves. I hope none of you dare live in the neglect of family prayer, dare omit it, either morning or evening, when you know that, instead of the blessing of Christ, the wrath and curse of God is poured out on families that call not on his name (Jer. 10: 25). While you and your families live without prayer, you live without God; you make no joint acknowledgment of him, and can expect no joint receiving from him. It may justly be feared that those who throw aside so necessary, so comfortable, so advantageous a duty as family prayer, do not make conscience of secret prayer either, but frequently omit it, or at least do not make a business of it, but suffer it to degenerate into a formality. And how can you expect daily blessings upon your children, if you do not daily ask for them? Or to have an interest in the intercession which Jesus Christ is continually making for us in heaven, if you do not pray continually morning and evening, in the virtue of that intercession. Have you settled a correspondence between Christ and families, by devoting your children to him in their baptism? And will you not keep up that correspondence? How can you expect the benefit of it, if you do not on your part keep it up?

You who have the charge of families, remember you are Christians, and ought in that capacity to confess Christ, and to own and honour him before your families; there is such a general disuse of Christian conference, that most are ashamed of that, to acknowledge Christ before their neighbours; but they cannot have that pretence to decline it before their own children and servants. If therefore with the heart you believe unto righteousness, think how necessary it is, that thus with the mouth you make confession unto salvation (Rom. 10: 10). Remember that your family is a family of Christians, not a herd of brute beasts, and you look upon them as no better then brute beasts if you do not pray with them; nay and worse, for the ox knows his owner, and the ass his master's crib (Isa. 1: 3), but you go not before them in acknowledging their great owner, nor lead them to the footstool of their Master's throne of grace. But I hope better things of you.

Use the baptism of your children as an argument with yourselves to pray with them; and then you may use it as a plea with God, for the mercies you ask of him for them. Lord Jesus, I have presented my children to thee, and thou hast accepted them. I still present them to thee, and wilt not thou still accept them? Thou hast blessed them: wilt thou not say they shall be blessed? And then they are blessed indeed.

Bring Them Up for Him

Have we any good hope, through grace, that Christ has owned our dedication of ours to him, has taken them up in his arms, put his hands on them, and blessed them? Let us then receive each of them from him again, as it is given to us with the same charge that Pharaoh's daughter gave to Moses's mother: Take this child and nurse it for me. You are to look upon your children as given up to Christ, and to manage them accordingly.

Has Christ showed such a tender affection to your little children? Be not then hardened against them, do not rule them with rigour; provoke them not to wrath (Eph. 6: 4), lest they be discouraged. Be gentle among them, for so the nurse cherishes her children (1 Thess. 2: 7). Study to make your children love you; and then everything you enjoin them to will be easy. When you are angry at them, let it be for that only, for which you know Christ would be angry at them; and that is for their sins, which must be restrained by the rod and reproof, not for their weaknesses and childish infirmities, which time will wear off. Has Christ blessed your children, and put honour upon them? Do not you curse them, and give them such scurrilous language as Saul gave to his son Jonathan (1 Sam. 20: 30), lest you teach them to give the like to their inferiors. Bless and curse not.

Have you given up your children to Christ? Bring them up then in his nurture and admonition. It is not enough that you pray with them and for them daily, but you must daily instruct them in the things of God, and in all those things that will be profitable to them. It is observable, that immediately after the laying down of that great truth, that the Lord our God is one Lord, and of that great Law, thou shalt love the Lord thy God with all thine heart, it follows as an indispensable duty, and a means of keeping up religion in the world, thou shalt teach them diligently to thy children, and look upon it to be one of the most needful pieces of work thou hast to do; more needful to get the Knowledge of God for them, than to get estates for them, nay, than to get bread for them. Thou shalt therefore not only hear them their catechism once a week, but thou shalt talk freely and familiarly of the truths and Laws of God among them, with all gravity and seriousness, when thou sittest with them in thy house, and when thou walkest with them by the way (Deut 6: 4–7); at night when thou liest down read a portion of Scripture to them, and oblige them to take notice of it; and again in the morning when thou risest up; that thus the word of Christ might dwell in them richly. You know they cannot learn Latin, but they must go to school every day; nor learn a trade, but must go to shop every day; and ought they not to have daily instructions out of the word of God, in order to their getting the knowledge of Christ, which is infinitely more excellent?

Take particular care to make your children acquainted with Jesus Christ, the true treasure hid in the field of the Scriptures; Christ and him crucified, Christ and him glorified. You call the baptizing of your children, the christening of them. I wish you would consider it; and think, how little it will avail them to have been christened, if they do not learn Christ, if they be not taught the truth as it is in Jesus (Eph. 4: 20). Let not your children rest in a mere natural religion; that is good, it is necessary, but it is not enough. You must make them sensible of their need of Christ, of their lost and undone condition without him; must endeavour to lead them into the mysteries of our reconciliation to God, and our redemption from sin and wrath, by a Mediator; and O that they may experimentally know him, and the power of his resurrection!

In teaching children the knowledge of God, both the parents are concerned to do their part. Solomon speaks both of the instruction of the father, and the law of the mother (Prov. 1: 8); but when they are little, the mother has a greater opportunity of instilling into them that which is good, and ought to improve it. Timothy got to know the Holy Scriptures from his childhood, by being brought up under a good mother and grandmother (2 Tim. 1: 5); and King Lemuel, when he is come to the throne, forgets not the prophecy that his mother taught him (Prov. 31: 1).

And as in other accomplishments of your children, so in the business of religion, which is their best and true accomplishment, you must, as they come to be capable, put them on to advance. When they have gone through their learning, you put them into business; when they have served their apprenticeship, you set them up for themselves; and thus when you have brought them to some competent knowledge of Christ, and have some reason to hope that the Spirit of grace has begun a good work in their souls, persuade them to take the covenant of baptism upon themselves, in the use of the other seal, that of the Lord's supper, and so by their own act and deed to join themselves to the Lord. Tell them, you brought them to Christ when they were infants, you have been ever since showing them the way to him, and now they must come themselves to him. Though they be weak, if they be willing, you may assure them, they shall be welcome; for those who come unto him he will not, no, he will not cast them out (John 6: 37). If they sit down at his feet to hear his words, he will take them up in his arms, and bless them.

And there is one thing more, in which I must be a monitor particularly; else I should not be a faithful monitor to parents, who have brought their children to Christ, and who hope that he has blessed them; and that is, that they be careful how they dispose of them in the world when they are grown up, lest by an error here, they undo all that they have been doing for them. In putting them apprentices, placing them in callings, and in marrying them, let Christ be consulted about it; let the interests of the better part be consulted in it. That is best for them which is best for their souls, against which you should not be swayed by any worldly interests or regards whatsoever. If you have laid a good foundation, let it be your care and endeavour that it may be built upon.

Hope Well for Your Children

Let this encourage us, who are parents, concerning our children; and enable us to think of them with comfort and hope, in the midst of our cares about them. They are dear to us, we look with pleasure upon these olive plants round about our tables, yet not without a mixture of pain, because children are (as we commonly say) 'certain cares, but uncertain comforts'; these arrows in the hand may prove arrows in the heart (Ps. 127: 4); Absalom, whose name signifies 'the peace of his father', lived to be his greatest trouble. But when we consider that we have brought them to Christ, and he has received them, we cannot but thank God and take courage. When we wish well to them, we would willingly hope well; and this is ground the of hope, that our Lord Jesus has expressed so much favour to little children.

As Infants

This may comfort and encourage the tender careful mothers in nursing them, that they are carrying those in their arms whom Christ has taken up in his. Not only their natural affection to them, as pieces of themselves, may sweeten and ease the pains they take about them; that makes even the sea monsters draw out their breasts and give suck to their young (Lam. 4: 3). But their gracious affection to them as members of Christ, as beloved of him, and partakers of benefit by him (1 Tim. 6: 2), may much more do it. You are careful for them with all this care; they require a constant attendance, and many a time, it may be, break your sleep; but if you do it as unto the Lord, if you have an eye to Christ in it: this I do for a child that is adopted into his family, as well as born into mine; you may depend upon him to pay your wages though it be your own child (Exod. 2: 9). Your care about your little ones keeps you from church, it may be, many a time; and keeps you, that you cannot spend so much time in your closets as you used to do; but if thus it be sanctified by an eye to the Lord Jesus, and by your prayers to God for them as his, more than as your own, you are therein truly serving the Lord Christ yourselves, and not only so, but are breeding up servants for him, that you hope will be vessels of grace and glory.

When They Are Ill

This may comfort and encourage us if our children labour under any bodily weaknesses and infirmities, if they be unhealthful and often ailing, which is an allay to our comfort in them; let this serve to balance that, if they belong to Christ, and be blessed of him, they are blessed indeed; and nothing amiss of that kind shall be any prejudice to their blessedness, or diminution of it; but may, being sanctified, become rather a friend and furtherance of it. Many have been the wiser and better, the more humble and heavenly, for their having borne the yoke of affliction in their youth (Lam. 3: 27). You see what an affection Christ discovered for these children; and may conclude, by reflecting upon yourselves, that he has a particular tenderness for children in affliction; those are commonly most indulged by their parents that are sickly; and like as a father pities those children (Ps. 103: 13), so does the Lord Jesus much more, as he often evidenced when he was upon earth. As the abiding illnesses of the children are the parents continual affliction, it is a cross they are to take up daily; so the abiding compassions of Christ toward them ought to be their continual consolation, and a cordial they may have recourse to daily.

As Workers Together for Christ

This may comfort and encourage us in teaching and catechising our children, in giving them a pious education, and in praying with them and for them, that we are doing it for Christ; that we are workers together with him, and we may hope he will work together with us, and then our labour shall not be in vain. If we have given them to Christ, they shall be taught by his Spirit, and are within the reach of that precious promise, that all shall know God, from the least even to the greatest (Heb. 8: 11). It may be that they are dull and slow, and not so apt to learn as we could wish; Christ's own disciples were so, yet he bore with them, and brought them at last to a full assurance of understanding, and therefore despair not concerning your children that are but of a small capacity. It may be that your children are hopeful and forward, and very promising, and it is your joy to see it in hopes they will be ornaments to your families, but it ought to be much more so, in hopes they will be in their day faithful servants to the interests of God's kingdom among men. And what prospect can be more pleasing next to that of our own everlasting bliss, than to have good hope, through grace, that our children shall be praising God on earth, when we are praising him in heaven: and that we and they shall be together, for ever praising him. I have no greater joy, says the apostle, than to hear that my children walk in the truth.

When They Grow Up

This may comfort and encourage us in all our cares concerning our children when they grow up, in providing for them, and disposing of them. If we have in sincerity given them up to Christ, and he has accepted of them, we may hope he will dispose of everything that concerns them, for the best, and they shall in this world reap the benefit of the promises made to the faithful and their seed (Ps. 37: 25–6); and the prayers made by the faithful for their seed. If they be not feasted, yet verily they shall be fed; if we have but little to give them, yet the blessing of Christ upon that little will make it every way better to them than the riches of many wicked (Ps. 37: 3, 16). Many, no doubt, have had reason to acknowledge that their comfortable passage through this world has been very much owing to the blessing of Christ, upon their early dedication to him, and education for him. If Christ has taken up our little ones into his arms, provided they do not by their wickedness throw themselves out of his arms, we may be sure he is able to keep what we have committed to him, through all the attempts of an ensnaring world; that he will never drop them, neither shall any pluck them out of his hands (John 10: 28).

If They Die in Childhood

This may comfort and encourage us if our children be removed from us by death in their childhood; this is a common case; that which came forth like a flower, is soon cut down, and the gourd which came up one night, and which we were exceeding glad of, withers the next night, and leaves us in tears. Now it is enough to silence us in such a case, that it is the Lord that gave and the Lord that takes away and if he takes away who can hinder him? May he do what he will with his own? Let Aaron therefore hold his peace (Lev. 10: 3), for God is glorified. But this goes further, and may satisfy us that if Christ has owned them in the kingdom of his grace, he will receive them into the kingdom of his glory. We are indeed kept in the dark concerning the state of those that die in infancy; they are left to the mercy of God; but the children that are given up to Christ by their believing parents are not left to uncovenanted mercy: The Lord knows them that are his; though we do not; but we may hope it shall go well with those whom Christ has taken up in his arms, and blessed; and, that he who was so well pleased with the children's Hosannas, even in the Old Jerusalem (Matt. 21: 15–16), will reckon himself glorified by their Hallelujahs in the New Jerusalem.

If We Die When They Are Children

This may comfort and encourage us if we are taken away from our children by death while they are little; this also is a common case and mournful one; we know not how soon we may fall under the arrests of death, and may see the day, that awful day approaching, which will cut off the number of our months in the midst. In such a case, as to our own souls, we may perhaps be able to say, as our Master did, with an air of triumph: Now we are no more in this world (John 17: 11). (O that we may be able, at such a time, with cheerfulness, to say so!) But, though we should, yet, like him concerning his disciples, we must say concerning our children, but these are in the world: How shall we leave them? Where and with whom shall we leave them? With whom, but with him who has said, 'Leave thy fatherless children with me, I will preserve them alive, and let thy widows trust in me' (Jer. 49: 11); who has taken it among the titles of his honour, to be a Father of the fatherless, and a Judge of the widows (Ps. 68: 5). If we have made Christ guardian to our children, let us make it appear we are entirely well satisfied in his wisdom and faithfulness.

Should They Rebel

What may we have to comfort and encourage us if our children should prove wicked and vile; if they should forsake their God, and the God of their fathers, and walk in the paths of the destroyer, notwithstanding our utmost endeavours to engage them for Christ? It is very often a case in fact; we cannot deny it; it is possible that the best parents may have the worst children; yet if we should suppose a falling from grace and holiness adherent, which, through the divine condescension and compassion, might have availed to the salvation of such as die in infancy, that will not infer a falling from grace and holiness inherent: what Christ does herein, we know not now, but we shall know hereafter (John 13: 7). But disputes in this case are cold comforts to the poor parents whose hearts bleed and break to see the destructive courses which their children take, whom they thought they had lodged safe in the hands of the Mediator, for whom they have prayed many a prayer, and shed many a tear. They thought

Christ had taken them up in his arms, put his hands upon them, and blessed them, but it does not prove so. What shall we say to comfort such?

It may be some satisfaction to them, that however it goes with their children, Christ will be glorified; if they do not give honour to him, he will get him honour upon them. And if God be sanctified, we ought to be satisfied, and with reverence to behold both the goodness and severity of God; on them which fall, severity; but towards them who stand, goodness, if they continue in his goodness (Rom. 11: 22).

But it will be yet more satisfaction to them, if they have the testimony of their consciences for them that they have done their duty; which they did, with a resolution to leave the event with God. They knew they could not give grace to their children; but their hearts can witness for them, that to the best of their power, they digged about these barren trees, and dunged them, as the dresser of the vineyard did (Luke 13: 8–9); and if they bring forth fruit well, they shall have the comfort, and God the glory; but if not, they must be content to see them cut down, and though they cannot have comfort in that, yet God will have glory, and they acquiesce.

But the greatest comfort of all in such a case is, that the unbelief and disobedience of their children shall not make void God's promise to them, and therefore ought not to make void their comfort in God. 'Though Israel be not gathered, yet shall I be glorious' (Isa. 49: 5). Abraham is happy in heaven, though there be those in hell who can call Abraham father. It was the comfort of holy David, though he saw a great deal of sin and trouble in his family: Although my house be not so with God as I could wish it, yet I am sure of this, he has made with me an everlasting covenant, which is well ordered in all things and sure, and that is all my salvation, and therefore shall be all my desire (2 Sam. 23: 5).

TREATISE ON BAPTISM

1

THE NATURE OF BAPTISM

The apostle, among his six principles of Christianity which constitute the foundation, reckons 'the doctrine of baptisms', thus intimating that baptism is to be asserted and adhered to, as a fundamental point in our religion. He uses the plural number (probably) in reference to the different kinds of baptism mentioned in the New Testament, where we read of 'the baptism of the Holy Ghost and of fire' (Matt. 3: 11); and 'the baptism of blood' (Mark 10: 38), or suffering, as well as of 'the baptism of water'. The latter indeed alone is properly so called the others are termed baptisms only by way of analogy and resemblance. And this is the baptism concerning which we are to make further inquiry, the baptism of water, that is, in plain English, washing with water; though in our translation (and indeed in most others) the Greek word baptism is generally retained, as peculiarly significant.

Washing (or baptizing) with water was used long before our Lord's time, not only as a common action, but as a religious rite. It was so used even in some heathen countries; and still more among the professing people of God, from the earliest ages. It was prescribed by the law of Moses in almost all cases of ceremonial pollution, and on all occasions that called for peculiar purity. It was customary among the Jews to admit proselytes into their church by baptism, and even their own female children. In conformity to this sacred custom, John, the harbinger of Christ, who was sent to proclaim his approach, and prepare the way for his coming, admitted persons his disciples by the same rite, a rite which our Lord himself owned, and honoured, by submitting to it; and that as a part of righteousness.

Water baptism then, when our Lord appeared, was no new thing: it had been applied, in every age of the church, and especially under the Mosaic dispensation, to religious uses. For this reason, among others, our Lord might probably choose it as one of his institutions; thereby showing that the spirit of his gospel was not a spirit of innovation and contradiction. And this institution he bequeathed to his church at his departure, as a sacred deposit, to be preserved pure and entire, without further alteration, till his second coming.

The nature of this ordinance, then, it will be proper more particularly to consider.

Those ordinances of worship which are moral, and of natural and perpetual obligation, have no difficulty in their explication (we readily understand what praying, and praising, and reading the word of God are), but those institutions which are positive, require a fuller illustration. Concerning them, the question should be asked, 'What mean ye by this service?' (Exod. 12: 26) And the rather, because unsanctified understandings are so unapt to receive, and so prone to mistake, such institutions. It is a lamentation, and shall be for a lamentation, that in a Christian nation there are so many who bring their children readily enough to baptism, and would take it very hard if it were denied them, who yet understand no more of the ordinance than that it is the custom of their country, and the usual time of naming their children, and treating their friends. It is therefore requisite to inquire a little into the true nature of this ordinance.

A SACRAMENT

In general, it is a sacrament. This indeed is a Latin word, and therefore not to be found in the Scriptures; but it is a word which the church has long used, and therefore we willingly receive it. Among the Latins, it was used to express an oath (which has ever been accounted a sacred thing), and more particularly a military oath; the oath which soldiers took to be true to the government, obedient to their generals, and never to quit their post, or run their colours.

Waving a discussion of the several definitions of a sacrament, we may acquiesce in Paul's description of one (Rom. 4: 11), where speaking of circumcision (the initiatory sacrament of the Old Testament), he calls it 'a sign', and 'a seal of the righteousness of faith'.

The tree of life was a sacrament to Adam in innocency; a sign and seal of the covenant of works; 'Do this and live.' Since the fall (by which our intellectual faculties are sadly depraved, and the veil of flesh thickened), we have much more need of sacraments; outward and sensible representations of things spiritual, to carry them home with the greater clearness to our understandings, with the more convincing certainty to our faith, and with the stronger impression to our affections. When the sanctified soul shall be released from the body of flesh, or when reunited to it refined and made spiritual, there will be no need of sacraments. These glasses shall be laid aside, when we shall see 'eye to eye' the distant object being brought nearer, and the debility of the organ cured.

But in the mean time, we are, with a cheerful thankfulness, and a ready compliance, to acknowledge the great goodness of God, in condescending to lisp to us in our own language; and to represent, seal, and apply to our souls things spiritual, by those things which are natural and ordinary. Thus doth Christ, in the sacraments, 'tell us earthly things' (as some understand John 3: 12), that is, spiritual things clothed with earthly expressions (as there the mystery of sanctification by the metaphor of a new birth); and if we do not believe, and understand, how should we apprehend those things, if they were spoken to us in their own abstract and simple notions, and in the language of the upper world? God in the sacraments speaks to us 'after the manner of men; uses similitudes' (Hos. 12: 10); not only to our ears, as by the ministry of the prophets, but to our eyes, that, if it be possible, spiritual things may insinuate themselves into, and get possession of, our hearts.

Thus it hath pleased God to deal with men, in his covenant transactions with them. When he made a covenant with Noah and his sons, never again to drown the world, or interrupt the succession of day and night, he gave them a sacrament, the 'bow in the clouds' (Gen. 9: 12–13), which doubtless was there before (whenever there was a disposition of the air), but never till then a token of the covenant. Sacraments are instituted to be:

1. Signs. Not natural signs, as smoke is a sign of fire, but voluntary and instituted. Not purely intellectual signs, as the sign of the prophet Jonas, but sensible and visible. Not signs barely for memorials, as the heap of stones in Jordan, but signs that exhibit, and, as instruments, convey. So that the essence, or formal nature, of a sacrament, consists in a relative union between the sign and the thing signified.

2. Seals. Not bare signs, as the map of a lordship represents that lordship to every one who looks upon it: but such signs as deeds, or charters of feoffment, sealed and delivered, which convey the lordship to the feoffee, upon such conditions; and give him a right and title to the premises, to all intents and purposes, upon the performance of those conditions. Thus the rainbow, Gideon's fleece, the coal from the altar that touched Isaiah's lips, and many others, were not only signs signifying, but signs confirming, the promises to which they were annexed.

But not to expatiate in this large field, let us confine our thoughts to the sacrament of baptism, in which (as the nature of a sacrament requires) there is a sign, and the thing signified by it.

A Sign—Washing with Water

The element is water; the action, washing with that water. And here, if we inquire why this sign was appointed for the ordinance of admission, this and no other, it must be referred to the will of the Lord Jesus, who instituted it. And his will, in this as in everything else, is most certainly his wisdom. But it may be useful to observe what kind of a sign it is.

COMMON

Washing with water is a common thing; common to all persons, to all times, and therefore fitly chosen to be stamped for an ordinance, whereby to admit persons into the belief of the 'common salvation' (Jude 3). Such the gospel salvation is. Therefore, in the other sacrament, eating and drinking are the sacramental actions, which are also common actions, used by all the world; for Christ is a Saviour to all, and whoever will, may come and take of the water of life.

As long as the church was confined to one people, the sign of admission was a thing very unusual, perhaps to note the peculiarity of that dispensation: but now the veil is rent, and the partition wall taken away. Infinite wisdom hath appointed the common salvation to be sealed by a common action.

CHEAP

Washing with water is a cheap thing. It puts us to no expense: which may intimate that the poor are welcome to Christ as well as the rich. If he had intended to have taken the rich only into the bond of the covenant, he would probably have appointed some costly ordinance of admission, which would have been more agreeable to the state and spirit of the rich, and within the reach of them only: but God has called and chosen 'the poor of this world' (Jas. 2: 5). In point of acceptance with God, rich and poor stand upon the same level; and therefore, since the poor cannot reach a costly ordinance, God will have the rich stoop to a cheap one. The ceremonial institutions were many of them chargeable; and good reason, because that dispensation had more of the promise of the life that now is. When God had freely given the Israelites 'so good a land, houses full of all good things' (a very considerable grant in that covenant), they could not complain, if he required, as a chief rent by way of acknowledgment, the 'lambs out of their flocks', and the 'bullocks of their stalls'. And yet even then, in diverse cases, poverty was considered (Lev. 12: 8). But now, under the gospel, the appointments are cheap. Christ will reject none for their poverty. As in other things, so in holy ordinances, 'rich and poor meet together' (Prov. 22: 2). In Christ Jesus there is neither 'bond nor free' (Gal. 3: 28).

PLAIN

Washing with water is a plain thing. And the perfection of a gospel ordinance lies much in its simplicity. Baptism is an ordinance which will neither puzzle the understanding with the intricacy, nor burden the memory with the multitude and variety, of its circumstances. 'It is a highway, and a way' not hard to hit, 'the wayfaring men, though fools, shall not err therein' (Isa. 35: 8). The institution of the water of purification, appointed by the Levitical law, was attended with so many nice circumstances, to be religiously observed, as did not only clog it, and make it difficult, but cloud it, and make it obscure. It was so with the other ceremonial appointments. But the New Testament baptism is plain. Nothing appointed, but only, 'Go and baptize them': the necessary circumstances are left, partly to Christian prudence, and partly to the directions which the nature of the thing gives. And for additional ceremonies, the institution knows none. It should seem, that some have thought it too plain to please the luxuriant fancies of 'men of corrupt minds', and therefore have been patching and painting it, and tricking it up with their own inventions, adding I know not what significant (or rather insignificant) ceremonies of their own (witness the Roman ritual): but our great master who came to abolish the law of commandments, and to introduce a spiritual worship, I am confident, will, another day, give those no thanks who think so meanly of the comeliness he hath put upon his spouse, as thus to dress her up in the tawdry attire of a harlot; as if that would improve, which does indeed impair and spoil, her beauty.

EASY

Washing with water is an easy thing. It was not a causeless complaint that was made of the ceremonial law, that it was a 'yoke, which neither their fathers, nor they, were able to bear' (Acts 15: 10). Those who are under it are said to be 'in bondage to the rudiments of this world' (Gal. 4: 3). And some think it is this which our Lord supposes those to be 'weary of, and heavy laden with' (Matt. 11: 28), whom he invites to submit to his 'yoke (that is, his institutions) as very easy and light'. And certainly, in this ordinance there is nothing hard or uneasy; no burden of which there is the least pretence to complain. Indeed, such are the privileges which attend the ordinance, that if our Master had bid us do some great thing, would we not have done it, rather than come short of them? (2 Kings 5: 13). Much more, when he only says to us, wash and be clean; wash and be Christians.

SAFE

Washing with water is a safe thing. The ordinance of admission under the law was a painful and bloody rite, and proved fatal to the unwary Shechemites; but there is neither pain nor peril in baptism. The Lord hath made it appear that he is 'for the body', by appointing an ordinance so consistent with its ease and safety. It is so safe, that it may be applied to infants, without the least difficulty or danger; a presumptive evidence that Christ designed it for them.

EXPRESSIVE AND SIGNIFICANT

Washing with water is an expressive and significant thing. So it hath been reckoned in other cases; and so it is in this institution. How could it be otherwise, when chosen by infinite wisdom, by him 'who did all things well'? Though the significance of it arises from the institution, yet it has a peculiar aptness so to signify.

WHAT IT SIGNIFIES

But this brings us to consider the thing signified; the substance represented by this shadow. This, like the kernel in the nut, is the main thing in the ordinance, viz. the meaning of this service. Now the outward sign is such, as that we are purely passive therein; 'washed with water'; not washing ourselves; which intimates that the chief thing intended to be signified is that which God in the covenant does for us (the communications of his grace and favour, in which we are receptive), and our obligations and engagements to him, only by way of necessary consequence. The washing with water implies the doing of something for us, and upon us; whence we infer, something to be done by us.

The Blood of Christ

The water in baptism signifies the blood of Christ; and the sprinkling of that for justification. The 'washing of the body with pure water' represents 'the sprinkling of the heart from an evil conscience'. One great promise of the new covenant is 'that God will be merciful to our unrighteouness', so that the seal of the covenant, as it is a covenant of reconciliation, is principally intended to be the seal of a pardon. Hence, the Nicene Creed supposes the remission of sins to be principally intended in baptism: 'I believe in baptism for the remission of sins.' Now, for as much as sin is pardoned, only in and through the merit of Christ's death and sufferings, that pardon is signified, and sealed, by washing with water, which represents the application of Christ's blood to the soul. The blood of the legal victim was necessary to make atonement (Heb. 9: 22); therefore the benefits of redemption are often attributed to the blood of Christ, as the meritorious and procuring cause; especially remission of sin. See 1 John 1: 7: 'The blood of Christ cleanses us from all sin'; and Revelation 1: 5 : '...washed us from our sins in his own blood'. And his blood, in allusion to the legal purifications, is called 'the blood of sprinkling' (Heb. 12: 24). Compare Heb. 9: 13–14. Cyril calls baptism the antitype of Christ's sufferings. His passion, with the fruits and benefits of it, are represented and applied, in this ordinance, by washing with water. Hence Ananias's exhortation to Paul, 'Arise and wash away thy sins' (Acts 22: 16). It is generally supposed to have been in the person of the suffering Jesus that David complained, 'I am poured out like water' (Ps. 22: 14). And there is something of the same metaphor in that expression, 'He poured out his soul unto death' (Isa. 53: 12), as water was poured out, especially in sacrificing. (See 1 Kings 18: 35, compared with 1 Sam. 7: 6.) Thus was a fountain opened, the rock smitten, that thence streams of water might issue for the use of Israel. In baptism this is applied. So that therein, the forgiveness of sins, upon repentance, is sealed by the application of Christ's blood.

It is observable that the grant of remission is, in both the sacraments, signified and applied, by something that primarily represents the blood of Christ, by which that remission was procured; in baptism by water, in the Lord's supper by wine. The design of God herein, is to convey spiritual and heavenly blessings to us, in such a way as may most advance the honour of Jesus Christ, and recommend him, and his salvation, to our esteem and affection. He will have us to see all the precious privileges of the new covenant flowing to us in the blood of Jesus. In the water of baptism, we may see (*pretium sanguinis*) the price of blood, written upon all our benefits; which should engage us to prize them, and to glorify God with them. 'It is the blood of these men', says David (1 Chr. 11: 19); only blood exposed; but this is the blood of the man Christ Jesus; blood actually shed. What a value then should we put upon it!

THE SPIRIT AND GRACE OF CHRIST

The water in baptism signifies the Spirit and grace of Christ, and the sprinkling of that for sanctifiction.

It must signify this, as well as pardon by the blood of Christ, for they are inseparable in the application of them. Ye are washed (says the apostle), viz. in baptism, which signifies, both that 'ye are sanctified', and that 'ye are justified' (1 Cor. 6: 11); for they always go together. The 'water and the blood' came together out of the pierced side of the dying Redeemer (John 19: 34). Wherever Jesus Christ is 'made of God righteousness to any soul', it is certain that he is made of God, unto that soul, sanctification (1 Cor. 1: 30).

Fallen man is to be looked upon, not only as guilty, but as defiled; not only as liable to the punishment of sin, but subject to the power and dominion of sin; and therefore as standing in need, not only of a relative change, in justification, by the righteousness of Christ imputed; but of a real change, in sanctification, by the grace of Christ implanted. And this also is signified in baptism: which is therefore called 'the washing of regeneration' (Titus 3: 5). Yea, not only signified, but sealed and applied, conditionally. As is the promise, so is the sacrament; the seal operates, as it is led and directed by the words of the deed to which it is affixed. Now the promise is, 'Turn ye at my reproof:

behold, I will pour out my Spirit unto you' (Prov. 1: 23). Those who are baptized may upon their turning, therefore, plead their baptism as the seal of that promise.

Now these two, the blood of Christ, and the Spirit of Christ, include all the benefits of redemption; some are the acts of God's grace for us; others are the works of God's grace in us; and both of these are signified and sealed in baptism. If then we be not wanting to ourselves, we may from our baptism fetch a comfortable assurance, that God will not be wanting to us. That we might have strong consolation, he has instituted a sign, apt and proper, to signify these two mainsprings of our comfort and happiness, the merit and grace of Christ; and the particular application of them to us. For being baptized into Christ Jesus, we are 'baptized into his death' (Rom. 6: 3).

2

THE MEANING OF BAPTISM

Having thus opened the nature of this ordinance in general, as it is a sacrament, we come next more particularly to inquire into the meaning of this service.

Its Institution

And our best way will be, to have recourse to the institution, which gave it being as an ordinance, and put the stamp upon it. Bring the word to the element, and that makes the sacrament. As the impression of the seal upon the wax, and the solemn delivery of the instrument so sealed, puts a great value on that, which, otherwise, is but a mean, common thing. And therefore, as from the institution we must take warrant for the practice, so from the institution we must take light, touching the nature of the ordinance. When a question was put to our Lord Jesus, by the Pharisees, concerning marriage, he referred them to the institution and original law (Matt. 19: 3–4) to teach us to go by the same rule in other ordinances. Run up the stream of the observation (which in a long course sometimes contracts filth) to the spring of the institution, and see what it was from the beginning. We are taking that method, in the explication of this ordinance.

The institution of baptism was at Christ's sixth appearance after his resurrection, viz. that at the mountain in Galilee, not only to the eleven, but to many others of the disciples, probably the five hundred brethren spoken of (1 Cor. 15: 6). He had mentioned this appointed meeting both before and after his resurrection; and whereas most of his other appearances were occasional and surprising, this seems to have been solemn and expected. And here, the four evangelists explain and enlarge on each other. Matthew, who wrote first, gives the fullest account: 'Go ye therefore, and teach all nations, baptizing them in the name of the Father, and of the Son, and of the Holy Ghost; teaching them to observe all things whatsoever I have commanded you: and, lo, I am with you alway, even unto the end of the world' (Matt. 28: 19–20). Here we have not only a warrant to make baptism lawful, but an order to make it a duty.

ON CHRIST'S AUTHORITY

He premises his own authority; his commission under the broad seal of heaven: 'All power is given unto me in heaven and in earth' (Matt. 28: 18).

As a divine person, all power was originally and essentially his; but as Mediator, all power was given him. What that power more especially was, he himself tells us, 'Thou hast given him power over all flesh, that he should give eternal life to as many as thou hast given him' (John 17: 2). So that this mediatorial power was an authoritative disposition of the eternal states of the children of men, 'the keys of hell' (Rev. 1: 18), or the unseen world, including the keys of heaven too. 'The world to come was put in subjection', not to angels, but 'to Christ' (Heb. 2: 5). Jesus Christ is 'set (fixed, inaugurated, enthroned) King upon the holy hill of Zion' (Ps. 2: 6); constituted absolute sovereign in his church: invested with legislative power. As king, he has sole authority to institute and appoint ordinances which shall be binding; and it is certainly a daring, and very unjustifiable, presumption for any creature (though calling himself by ever so great and pompous a name) to assume to himself a like power in the church. To institute ordinances is Christ's prerogative, and a branch of his glory which he neither does nor will give to another. Our Lord Jesus 'glorified not himself' herein, but was 'called of God to it' (Heb. 5: 4–5), and his call was completed when he was raised from the dead. Then it was that the Father said unto him, 'Thou art my Son, this day have I begotten thee' (Acts 13: 33).

It was after his resurrection that our Lord claimed all power. We read of power given him before (Matt. 9: 6), 'power to forgive sins'; but here, 'all power'. It was by dying that he won the 'name above every name' (Phil. 2: 9). Now he was entering upon the exercise of his authority; 'was hastening to the far country, to receive for himself a kingdom' (Luke 19: 12). It was part of the glory which he claimed as the recompense of his sufferings (John 17: 4–5).

Power in heaven and in earth, that is, in all places; heaven and earth comprehend the whole universe (Gen. 1: 1). Jesus is the only universal monarch. He has power in heaven over the angels (Eph. 1: 10) and power on earth to subdue the Gentile world to his sceptre.

AN APOSTOLIC COMMISSION

He directs his commission to the apostles and their successors. (Compare John 20: 21, 'As the father hath sent me, so send I you', which speaks not equality of power, but similitude of mission.) Having showed how the Father had sent him, he here sends them. Go ye: ye apostles, primarily (for they were the master-builders who laid the foundation); including, likewise, their successors in the pastoral office to the end of the world. Ministers are the stewards of this, as well as the other mysteries of God (1 Cor. 4: 1). And much of the wisdom and goodness of our Lord Jesus Christ appears in his appointing such officers in the church. Now he was 'ascending on high, he gave gifts unto men'; and they were precious gifts; not only apostles, prophets, and evangelists (extraordinary ministers), but pastors and teachers (ordinary ministers) to continue in succession to the end of time. Though the keys are said to have been given to Peter, perhaps because he was the first who opened the door of faith to the Gentiles, yet all the apostles, and in them all Christian ministers, were invested with the same power (John 20: 23); a power of admitting into the Christian church, according to gospel terms. Nor need we contend for an uninterrupted succession, in a right line, from the apostles; for this power is not received from the ordainers, but from Christ; and ordination is only the solemn designation, approbation, and benediction of a person judged duly qualified to be the subject of this power.

To All Nations

He extends their commission to all nations. 'Go ye'; a word of command and encouragement: Go and fear not; have not I sent you? Those whom Christ sends have often need of encouragement against their fears, when those whom he sends not run with boldness. These words broke down the partition wall, which had so long kept out the Gentiles. Hitherto, in Judah only was God known; a little spot; but now the veil is rent, and the despised Gentiles admitted into the holiest. The baptism of John was only for the Jews; the morning star appeared only in that horizon; and even the Sun of Righteousness, while rising, was pleased to confine his influences to the 'lost sheep of the house of Israel'. When he first sent out his disciples, he charged them 'not to go into the way of the Gentiles' (Matt. 10: 5); but now the commission is enlarged, 'Go ye into all the world' (Mark 16: 15). The enmity between the Jews and the Gentiles had been very great; but that enmity was now slain, and 'they both became one sheepfold, under the great Shepherd and Bishop of souls'.

'Teach all nations'; that is, all whom you can reach. Exclude none out of the church who are willing to come in, that is, none who do not exclude themselves. And accordingly, their sound did go 'into all the earth, and their words to the end of the world' (Rom. 10: 18). The heathen were given to Christ for an inheritance; and therefore he sends his apostles into all the territories of his dominions. He having purchased, they must proffer, a common salvation.

Go...Teach...Baptize

The commission itself is 'Go, teach all nations, baptizing them in the name of the Father, and of the Son, and of the

Holy Ghost.' Here is our warrant, without which we would not, we dare not, baptize. The word which we translate teach is, I think, not well translated. It is a different word which is used in v. 20, 'teaching them to observe'; 'Go, disciple all nations,' I think it should be rendered. Make them my disciples, that is, admit them my scholars. I find the word used only here, and in two other places: 'every scribe discipled unto the kingdom of heaven' (that is, a Christian scribe, or such a disciple of Christ as is arrived at the standing and proficiency of a scribe, Matt. 13: 52) is like a man that is a householder: and concerning Joseph of Arimathea, 'one who had given up himself as a disciple to Jesus' (Matt. 27: 57); had discipled it, or been ranked among the disciples of Jesus; or (as some understand it) had discipled others to Jesus. So that the word here must signify, to make disciples, as the phrase is in John 4: 1; that is, to admit them into the school of Christ. Thus a Jewish ear would readily apprehend it; for, as Lightfoot observes, discipling was not of persons already taught, but to the end that they might be taught. And in their schools, a person was made תלמיד, a scholar, or disciple, when he gave himself up to be trained up by such a master. *Proselytum me fac, ut me doceas.*

I insist so much upon the right sense of the word, not only to vindicate the text from the mistake of those who will have none baptized (of whomsoever born) till they are thoroughly taught, grounding it on the words of the institution, which, if rightly Englished, would intimate no such thing; for though infants are not capable of being taught, they are capable of being disciplined; but also, from hence to explain the nature of the ordinance, which is:

1. A solemn admission into the visible church of Christ. 'Go disciple all nations'; open the door to them all; and those who are willing, admit by baptising them; let that be the sign and ceremony of admission.
2. A seal of the covenant of grace, 'Baptising them in (or into) the name of the Father, and of the Son, and of the Holy Ghost.' So that we need look no further for the meaning of this service.

ADMISSION INTO THE VISIBLE CHURCH

Baptism is an ordinance of Christ, whereby the person baptized is solemnly admitted as a member of the visible church.

It is a discipling ordinance. The professors of the Christian religion were first called disciples, till at Antioch the name was changed, and they were called Christians (Acts 11: 26). To disciple all nations then (to speak according to the change of title) is to Christianize all nations. So that baptizing is, as it is commonly called (significantly enough if it were duly considered) Christening. Not making a person a Christian, *in foro Coeli*—in the judgment of Heaven, but declaring him a Christian, *in foro ecclesica*—in the judgment of the church.

I say of the visible church, not of the invisible church (as it is called) 'the church of the firstborn whose names are written in heaven', but the visible church; comprehending all that profess faith in Christ, and obedience to him. Many are baptized, and so taken into that number, who yet remain 'in the gall of bitterness, and the bond of iniquity'; witness Simon Magus (Acts 8: 13, 23). But, *de secretis non judicat ecclesia*—the church does not judge the secrets of men. Baptism is an ordinance of the visible church members; appointed for the admission of visible church members; admission, not into the internal communion, but only into that which is visible and external, in the profession of faith, and participation of sacraments.

I say the visible church, meaning the catholic universal church. Baptism is not to be looked upon as the door of admission into any particular church. The eunuch could not be admitted into such a church, and yet was baptized. And hence appears the mistake of those who maintain, that because they were baptized into the church of England, they are therefore bound never to leave it, nor attempt any alterations in it.

He who seriously professes faith in Christ, and obedience to him, but is not yet baptized, hath a sort of church-membership, but remote, imperfect, and irregular. Many in the primitive times, upon a mistaken apprehension of the unpardonableness of sin committed after baptism, deferred it long (some even till the dying moment) who yet are not to be looked upon as outcasts. Many of the martyrs died in the state of catechumens. So that baptism does not give the title, but recognises it. Only educe the power into act, and complete that church membership, which before was only (*in fieri*) in the doing.

ADDED TO THE NUMBER

When I say that by baptism we are brought into the church, I mean that we are added to the number. Thus (Acts 2: 41) those that were baptized, are said to be 'added to the church', that is, to the number of visible believers. The number of the church militant is daily decreasing by death; baptism is appointed for filling up the vacancy, that there may not want a church to stand before the Lord on earth, while the sun and the moon endureth.

ENTITLED TO THE PRIVILEGES OF THE CHURCH

Church privileges are either such as are peculiar to true believers, even union and communion with Christ in grace and glory, and fellowship with the Father, and with his Son, by the Holy Ghost (and though baptism does not give a title to these, it seals and ratifies that title to true believers); or such as are common to visible believers. And these, baptism, duly administered, entitles us to, and invests us in.

Now the privileges of visible church-membership which baptism confers, are such as these:

Honour

To be set apart among the peculiar people, and numbered among the chosen. Is it not an honour to bear the name, and wear the livery, of the Lord Jesus? To be called Christians, a people near unto him? To be baptized, is a great preferment: it is to be enrolled in a very honourable corporation; admitted into a society upon all accounts truly great and noble.

Safety

The visible church is under God's peculiar care and government. He is 'a defence upon all its glory' (Isa. 4: 5). Those who are taken into the church (to borrow the Jews' expression) are gathered under the wings of the Divine Majesty; and so are often sheltered from those calamities to which others lie exposed. Baptism is compared to the ark (1 Pet. 3: 20–21) which sheltered even Ham from the universal deluge. It is a privilege to be on the protected side.

Communion

Baptism gives a title to the ordinances. Those who were baptized, we presently find 'in the apostles' doctrine, and fellowship, and in breaking of bread, and in prayer', (Acts 2: 41–2). The word, and prayer, and the Lord's supper, and church fellowship, are the ordinances which those who are baptized may (as they become capable) lay claim to. And is it not a privilege to be interested in the ministers of Christ 'Paul, and Apollos, and Cephas', variously gifted, but all their gifts bestowed upon the visible church, and intended for the good of its members; the labours, the sufferings, of ministers, for the church's sake? (see 1 Cor. 3: 22; Eph. 4: 11–12). Is it not a privilege to be a partaker of the prayers of all the churches? To be remembered by them at the throne of grace, as one with them? Is it not a privilege to sit down with them at the table of the Lord? To be admitted to that feast, that altar, which they have no right to eat of who serve the tabernacle? Is not the communion of saints a privilege? To have a share in the friendship and affection of all who fear God, and the right hand of fellowship in all the ordinances? To be with those among whom Jesus walks, and with whom God is of a truth? To have a nail in God's holy place?

Opportunity

The lively oracles are committed to the visible church. It is in the church that the ordinary means of salvation are; 'he hath showed his word unto Jacob: there God is known, and his name is great': there the joyful sound is heard; and blessed are they that hear it (Ps. 147: 19–20). The visible church, though it is not the fountain of truth (as the papists would have it, deriving the authority of the Scriptures from the dictates of the church), yet is the channel of conveyance. It is the pillar and ground of truth (both the body and basis of the pillar); not as the pillars of a house, on which the house is built (for in this sense, the church is built upon the truth, not the truth upon the church) but as the pillar, which hath an inscription upon it, or to which a proclamation is affixed, it holds forth to view of all what is so put upon it. Thus the church is the pillar of truth. It is a great privilege to be taken into the church, for that is the Goshen, the land of light; out of which there are no ordinary means of saving knowledge. Those who are taken into the church have gospel discoveries and gospel offers made unto them: and (which is a great advantage, and contributes to the efficacy of the word) by being admitted into the church, gospel offers have more hold of them than when they were without.

UNDER THE LAWS OF THE CHURCH

We come under the laws of the church. Not of this or that particular church, but the universal church. I mean, that being admitted to the privileges, we are engaged to the duties, of the communion of saints.

The laws of the church are; to own the ministers of it, and to esteem them highly in love for their works' sake; to adhere to its ordinances, and to receive, observe, and keep them pure and entire, as part of the churches' treasure; to keep to the fellowship of the saints, not 'forsaking the assembling of ourselves together, but exhorting one another daily'; to do good in an especial manner to the 'household of faith', that is, 'to all in every place who call upon the name of the Lord Jesus, both their Lord and ours'; to own all baptized Christians as our brethren and fellow members; and to comfort and edify one another, as we have ability and opportunity. Thus baptism is an ordinance of admission into the visible church.

A SEAL OF THE COVENANT OF GRACE

It is also a seal of the covenant of grace. This I gather from those words of the institution, baptizing them 'in (or into) the name of the Father, and of the Son, and of the Holy Ghost'.

For the opening of this, I shall endeavour to show what the covenant of grace is; and then (from the words of the institution) how baptism is a seal of this covenant.

WHAT IS THE COVENANT OF GRACE?

A covenant properly signifies a voluntary compact or agreement between distinct persons, touching the disposal of things in their power, to their mutual content and advantage. But when we speak of God's covenanting with men, we must remember that he is the sovereign ruler and owner of mankind, and therefore, that his transactions with us are not mere covenants, as amongst men, between equals, or at least between persons who were antecedently disengaged. No, God is the lawgiver who hath authority 'to save and to destroy' (James 4: 12). But the revelation of his will, which he hath made, for the direction of our duty to him and our expectations from him, is therefore called a covenant, and proposed to us under that form, because infinite goodness would deal with us in a rational way; and thus 'draw us with the cords of a man' (such cords as men are used to be drawn with); and that his righteousness in the ruin of the refusers might be the more magnified.

The same revelation of the will of God concerning man may be considered, therefore, either as a law, backed with promises and threatenings as sanctions, and so there needs not the creature's consent; or as a covenant, and so there must be a restipulation from the creature. Now the sacraments relate to this revelation as a covenant, that is, a promise upon a condition, to which the sacraments are annexed as seals. The promises are of reconciliation, relation, and recompense; the conditions are faith, repentance, and sincere obedience to the whole will of God. This covenant is founded on free grace, and purchased by the blood of Christ. It was revealed, 'at sundry times, and in divers manners' to the Old Testament saints; and now, under the New Testament, may be considered in two ways.

In its internal administration: as savingly closed with by true believers, who join themselves unto the Lord, by a free and hearty consent, which entitles them to the saving benefits of this covenant. And it is not to this that the sacraments are appropriated: for we find Simon Magnus baptized; and multitudes on the left hand of Christ at the great day, who had eaten and drunk in his presence. And the stewards of the mysteries of God would remain under perpetual doubts and uncertainties if they were to go by this rule in applying the seals.

The Lord infallibly 'knows them that are his', but we do not. In this internal administration, the spirit is the seal (Eph. 1: 13).

In its external administration: and so considered, all who profess faith in Christ, and obedience to him, are in the covenant at large, and have a right to the seal. As the church of the Jews; 'with many of whom God was not well pleased; yet to them pertained the adoption, and the glory, and the giving of the law, and the service of God, and the promises' (Rom. 9: 4).

Now the sum and substance of this covenant is, that 'God will be to us a God, and we shall be to him a people' (Heb. 8: 10). This is frequently set down in Scripture as the abridgment of the covenant; which includes all the other promises and conditions. All the privileges of the covenant are summed up in this one, 'that God will be to us a God'; and all the duties of the covenant are summed up in this, 'that we must be to him a people'. And herein it is certainly well ordered and sure; is all our salvation, and should be all our desire.

How Is Baptism a Seal of this Covenant?

Covenanting signs and ceremonies have generally been used by all nations by which contracts have been confirmed and ratified; and those signs are not natural, but instituted. We call this a seal, because with us the usual way of confirming contracts is by sealing; which gives validity to the covenant, and mutual assurance of the sincerity of the covenanters; who do hereby, with the more solemnity, oblige themselves to the performance of the covenant. Now 'God being willing more abundantly to show to the heirs of promise the immutability of his counsel, hath confirmed it, not only with an oath, but with a seal, that by all these immutable things, in which it is impossible for God to lie (or to put a cheat upon his creatures) we might have strong consolation, who have fled for refuge' to the everlasting covenant, 'to lay hold on that hope' as the horns of that altar (Heb. 6: 17–18).

There was a covenanting sign instituted by the Jewish law, which was very significant; in the case of a person's binding himself perpetually to his master, his ear was to be bored with an awl to the door-post, by his master (Exod. 21: 6), by which the master engaged himself to continue his protection and provision, and the servant became obliged to continue his duty and obedience. Thus was the covenant sealed. Baptism is the seal of such a covenant between God and man; an act which obliges us to be his willing servants forever.

God Assures Us

More plainly, when I say that baptism is a seal of the covenant of grace, I mean, that God does, in and by that ordinance, assure us that he is willing 'to be to us a God', according to the tenor of the covenant; a sense of our meanness as creatures, especially of our vileness as sinners, might make us despair of the honour and happiness of such an interest and relation; this ordinance therefore is appointed, not only to convince us that God is reconcilable, but to convey to us all the benefits of reconciliation upon gospel terms. This is the covenant, 'To be a God to thee, and to thy seed after thee' (Gen. 17: 7), and in token thereof, 'you shall be circumcised' (v. 10). And forasmuch as our defilements by sin are the greatest discouragements of our faith in God as our God, to obviate those discouragements, the instituted seal is a significant sign of our cleansing from those defilements.

God Engages Us

God does, in and by that ordinance, engage us to be to him a people. His creating us and preserving us, and all the gracious methods of his providence concerning us, engage us 'to be to him a people'; because 'he made us, and not we ourselves', it follows 'that we are his people' (Ps. 100: 3). But he does by this ordinance lay a stronger and more explicit tie upon us to be his; 'bores our ear to his door-post'; takes us to be 'a people near unto him'; obliges us, not only by the bond of a law, but by the bond of a covenant, to be his. And all little enough; our corrupt hearts are so very treacherous and deceitful, and the enmity of the carnal mind so strong and inveterate. And because our cleansing is a necessary qualification for this relation, we are thus taken 'to be to God a people' by washing; for 'he purifies to himself a peculiar people' (Titus 2: 14). The church must be sanctified and cleansed with the 'washing of water' (Eph. 5: 26). We must first have our 'consciences purged from dead works,' before we can acceptably 'serve the living God' (Heb. 9: 14). God does in this ordinance, as it were, lay hold of us, set apart for himself, and bind us to our duty; that if afterwards we be tempted sacrilegiously to alienate ourselves from him, and to serve under the opposite banner, the abiding obligations of this ordinance may help to keep us steady.

'I will be their God, and they shall be my people,' is the meaning of this service. It is a seal to those articles of agreement, which we find engrossed in the Scriptures, between God and man. An ordinance in which we are marked for God, and receive his image and superscription; marked for his service, marked for his salvation.

Devoted and Dedicated to the Triune God

This being laid down in general, now proceed to open it more particularly, from the institution; 'baptising them in the name of the Father, and of the Son, and of the Holy Ghost'.

That is, by authority from the Father, Son, and Holy Ghost. All the persons of the blessed Trinity concur, as in our creation: 'Let us make man' (Gen. 1: 26), so to our redemption, salvation, and consolation. If we ask the question which Christ put concerning John's baptism, 'The baptism of Jesus, is it from Heaven or of men?' it must be answered, 'It is from Heaven!' Which stamps a very great honour upon the ordinance. Though to a carnal eye it may appear mean and contemptible; yet looking upon it as beautified with the sacred authority of Heaven, it appears truly great: and it is comfortable to those who are called to be 'stewards of the mysteries of God', that they act by an authority which will bear them out.

Invocating, or calling upon, the names of the Father, Son, and Holy Ghost. To do what we do in the name of God, is to sanctify all we do by prayer. So great an action as this, does in an especial manner require that solemnity. It is prayer which fetches down that presence of God with the ordinance, and that blessing of God upon it, which is really the beauty and grace, the life and efficacy, of the ordinance.

There is more in it than this: we are baptized 'into the name of the Father, and of the Son, and of the Holy Ghost'; that is, in token of our believing in God the Father, Son, and Holy Ghost.

It is said that the Israelites were baptized 'into Moses' (1 Cor. 10: 2), which refers to Exodus 14: 31: 'they believed Moses', or in Moses. Faith has in it an assent of the understanding, and a consent of the will; so that to be baptized into the name of the Father, and of the Son, and of the Holy Ghost, is to be baptized into a solemn profession of these two things: our assent to the gospel revelation concerning the Father, Son, and Holy Ghost; and our consent to a covenant relation to these divine persons. God the Father, Son, and Holy Ghost, the three persons in the ever blessed Trinity, are in the New Testament not only made known, but tendered and offered to us. The gospel contains not only a doctrine, but a covenant, and by baptism we are brought into that covenant. The Jews were 'baptized into Moses', that is, were thereby committed to the conduct of Moses: and so 1 Corinthians 1: 13, 15. Paul pleads that he baptized few or none, for this reason, lest they should say that he baptized 'in his own name,' that is, into himself, and his own guidance as their ruler. So that to be 'baptized in the name' is to be solemnly devoted, and dedicated, to 'the Father, Son, and Holy Ghost'.

Renouncing All that Is Contrary to God

Now this dedication to God, this entering into covenant with the whole Trinity, implies a renunciation of everything that is contrary to God. An oath of allegiance to God, as our rightful Sovereign (and such an oath baptism is) necessarily implies an oath of abjuration of all those powers and interests which stand in opposition to, or competition with, his crown and dignity in our souls. The dedication of ourselves to the conduct of God implies an utter disclaiming of the rule of the devil, the world, and the flesh: for what fellowship hath light with darkness, or how can two such masters be served? Hence we are said 'to be buried with Christ by baptism, and planted in the likeness of his death' (Rom. 6: 4–5), which intimates our dying to every lust and sin.

In the early ages of the church, when adult persons who had been trained up under the power of Pagan delusions were baptized Christians, it was required that they should solemnly and expressly renounce that heathenism in which they had been brought up, and disclaim all relation to those gods they had been taught to worship; that none might be admitted who retained any good opinion of their former idolatries and superstitions; and that those who were admitted, when tempted to apostasy, or base compliances, might be deterred by a serious reflection upon so solemn and express a renunciation and a form of renunciation, similar to that of the ancient church, the English liturgy still uses. And even those who have laid aside the form of renunciation, as not countenanced by the precepts or examples of Scripture, allow that the renunciation itself is in effect made, being included in that dedication to God, which enters into the essence of Christian baptism.

SUBJECTION TO SATAN'S RULE. Our dedication to the Father, Son, and Holy Ghost in that ordinance, then, necessarily implies a renouncing of all subjection to Satan's rule. It is throwing off the devil's yoke. The sinful heart is represented in Scripture as Satan's palace, where he resides, where he reigns, where he keeps court, where he keeps garrison. Now our covenanting with God implies a revolt from Satan's jurisdiction. Baptism wrests the keys of the heart out of the hands of the strong man armed, that the possession may be surrendered to him whose right it is. When, by baptism, we enlist ourselves under Christ's banners, we thereby proclaim war with the devil and all his forces.

God in this ordinance seals to us a deliverance from Satan, a rescue out of that house of bondage, that iron furnace, the terrifying and tormenting power of the devil; and we seal to him a compliance with that deliverance, by a steady opposition to his tempting, deceiving power, and a constant disowning of his conduct; keeping ourselves, that we may not be touched by that wicked one, in whom 'the world lieth'.

ALL CONSENT TO FLESHLY LUSTS. The flesh is another enemy against which, in baptism, we declare war. We promise to quit the conduct of that 'carnal mind which is enmity against God' (Rom. 8: 7); engaging to be no longer guided by its dictates, and governed by its laws. The water of baptism is designed for our cleansing from the spots and defilements of the flesh. Hence, the apostle urges our baptism as a pressing motive to persuade us to the mortification of sin (Rom. 5: 2–3). Those who are 'baptized into Christ,' have professedly 'put on Christ'; and it is inconsistent with our putting on Christ, 'to make provision for the flesh to fulfil the lusts therof' (Rom. 13: 14). Being in baptism enrolled among those pilgrims who are journeying towards Canaan, we engage to abstain from, and fight against, those 'fleshly lusts that war against the soul' (1 Pet. 2: 11).

ALL CONFORMITY TO THIS PRESENT WORLD. We disclaim, in baptism, the custom world as our rule, the company of this world as our rule, the company of this world as our people, and the comforts of this world as our portion. Grotius thinks that St. Paul has an especial reference to the baptismal covenant in that caution, 'Be not conformed to this world' (Rom. 12: 2). Being by baptism engaged to conform to the designs and interests of the other world, we must needs be disengaged from a compliance with the counsels and concerns of this world. By this ordinance, we are engaged to swim against the stream of the impieties and follies of the age in which we live. We covenant not to take up with that any good which will satisfy the most of men; not to accept of a portion in this life. We are by Christ delivered from this present evil world, and in baptism we promise never to deliver ourselves up to it again, but 'to stand fast in the liberty wherewith Christ makes us free'.

Thus stands our baptismal renunciation; which is notoriously contradicted by every wilful compliance with the allurements of the flesh, the world, and the devil.

Resigning Ourselves to the Lord

Baptism also implies a resignation of our whole selves to the Lord. This must always accompany that renunciation. 'If thou wilt return, O house of Israel, saith the Lord, return unto me.' Our quitting the rule of sin and Satan, and the world, is not that we may be lawless, but that we may be brought under the yoke of the Lord Jesus Christ. The tyranny is exchanged, not for anarchy, but for rightful sovereignty. It is not enough that we overrun the service of the citizen of the country, but we must submissively return to our Father's house. And this part of the covenant is sealed in this sacrament. In baptism we are not only 'planted in the likeness of Christ's death', but also 'of his resurrection' (Rom. 6: 4–5).

BODY, SOUL, AND SPIRIT. It is a resignation of ourselves, our whole selves; body, soul, and spirit. This is what is given up in baptism (2 Cor. 8: 5: 'They first gave their own selves unto the Lord'). It is not a resignation of our estates only, and relations, but ourselves. The soul, and all its faculties; the body, and all its parts, and powers, must be presented, as a living sacrifice. It is a marriage covenant, in which the parties mutually give themselves to each other; and in such a case, 'if a man would give all the substance of his house for love (that is, instead of it) it would be utterly contemned'.

'I will be for thee, and thou shalt be for me'; that is the covenant (Hos. 3: 3). And therefore, in baptism, the seal is applied to the person, signifying the dedication of the man; as livery and seisin, is the giving of the premises intended to be conveyed. 'Whose I am' is the apostle's acknowledgment (Acts 27: 23).

TO THE LORD. It is a resignation to the Lord. That is the meaning of our being baptized into his name. It is a declaring that we are his, and 'subscribing with our hand to the Lord'. Paul, when he is reproving the Corinthians for saying, 'I am of Paul,' uses this argument, 'Were ye baptized in the name (or rather into the name) of Paul?' (1 Cor. 1: 13), which intimates, that if they had been baptized into his name, they would have been of him. So that to be baptized into the name of God, is to be of God.

Now this resignation or dedication of ourselves to the Lord, is two-fold:

1. In respect of duty. We resign ourselves to God, to be ruled and governed by him; to be commanded by his laws without dispute or contradiction: saying, as Paul (Acts 9: 6), 'Lord, what wilt thou have me to do? Other lords have had dominion, but from henceforth, by thee only will I make mention of thy name' (Isa. 26: 13).
2. In respect of dependence. We resign ourselves to God, to be portioned and made happy by him. When we swear

allegiance to him, we do withal put ourselves under his protection, and profess our expectation of all good from him. Baptism fixes our eyes upon him, as the eyes of a servant upon the hand of his master (Ps. 123: 2), not only for work, but for wages.

This is to yield ourselves to the Lord (2 Chr. 30: 8) to be made holy by him, and to be made happy by him. And it is no more than we are already obliged to, by manifold ties: only in this ordinance, we do more explicitly signify our consent to that, which we were bound to before: and to all the other ties, add an obligation of our own.

IN THE NAME OF THE FATHER

Now, in the form of baptism, all the persons of the blessed Trinity are named; no doubt, first, to confirm the doctrine of the Trinity; which, without controversy, is one of the greatest 'mysteries of godliness'; and, second, to clear the duty; or that we might the better see, and be affected with, our obligations to these sacred persons; and might from thence take direction, both what to do, and what to expect.

We are baptized in (or into) the name of the Father. That is, thereby is sealed our dedication to God the Father; professing to believe that there is a God, and to consent to take him for our God. 'It is avouching the Lord to be our God' (Deut 26: 17). And the consent of the will must be guided by the assent of the understanding. We take God to be that to us which he is, and declare our consent to those moral relations in which he is pleased to stand to us. Now, that which in the creed we profess to believe, in an especial manner, concerning God the Father, is that he is the Creator: this then must, in baptism, be applied and acknowledged concerning ourselves; he is my Creator. We give up ourselves to him as Creator, in all those relations which result from creation.

Our Owner and Lord

More particularly, we give up ourselves to God our Creator, as our absolute owner and Lord; to dispose of us by an absolute sovereignty, and to actuate us by an infinite power. 'He made us, and not we ourselves' (Ps. 100: 3), or as it is in the Hebrew margin, 'and his we are': put them both together and they complete the argument; because he made us, and not we ourselves, therefore we are not our own, but his. There cannot be imagined any sovereignty so despotic, or any property so absolute, as that which arises from creation. He who gave us our being, without any concurrence of ours, may justly call us his own; and may he not do what he will with his own? That little which our parents contributed to our being, only as instruments, produces so great a power, property, and interest, that the law of nations makes children not to be (*sui juris*) at their own command: much more is God our owner, who is the fountain of our being. Now, in baptism we seal our consent to this, and resign ourselves to him, so as no longer to be 'our own' (1 Cor. 6: 19). We receive his mark, his image and superscription, and thereby acknowledge him our Owner.

Our Supreme Governor

As our supreme Governor: morally to rule us, as intellectual free agents, by his revealed law; directing us in, and binding us to, that duty, which as creatures we owe him. We hereby consent, that the Lord should be 'our lawgiver and our judge' (Isa. 33: 22); agreeing to it as fit, that he who gave being, should give law. The language of our baptismal engagement is, 'Thou art my King, O God' (Ps. 44: 4). It is a self surrender to the commanding power of his revealed will.

Our Chief Good

He who made us, is alone able to give perfection to his work, by making us truly happy. This hath special regard to the darling attribute of God, his goodness; the source of all that good which can satisfy the soul's desire. As in baptism we own God for our ruler, so we own him likewise for our benefactor. Christ, speaking of earthly princes, says, 'They that exercise authority are called benefactors' (Luke 22: 25); and they were wont to pride themselves much in the number, compliments, and attendance of their clients, and beneficiaries. Now, to be the Lord's, is to own him for our benefactor, and attend upon him accordingly. 'Whom have I in heaven but thee, and there is none upon earth that I desire besides thee,' (Ps. 73: 25) is the meaning of our baptismal covenant.

Our Highest and Ultimate End

The name of God is often put for his honour and glory, so that being baptized into the name of the Father seals our engagement to direct all our actions to his glory. This follows upon our regard to God the Father as Creator; for if he is the first cause, he must be the last end. If all things are of him, by way of creation, and through him (Rom. 11: 36), by way of providential influence, all things must be to him, in their final tendency and result. In heaven, God is, and will be, all in all (1 Cor. 15: 28); and what is heaven upon earth, but making him our all in all? Now, the consideration of this should engage us to holiness: we are not our own, and therefore may not live as we please: we are God's, and therefore must glorify him, both with our bodies and with our spirits. It may likewise serve for our comfort. When anything troubles us, there is great satisfaction in this, that we are the Lord's. David pleads it in prayer, 'I am thine, save me' (Ps. 119: 94). If we are indeed his, no doubt he will look after his own.

IN THE NAME OF THE SON

We are baptized in (or into) the name of the Son. This seems to have a peculiar emphasis in this administration: and therefore, though the other two are always implied, yet we find this most generally expressed in the New Testament (see Acts 8: 16; 19: 5; Rom. 6: 3; Gal. 3: 27); for into his hands the mediatorial kingdom is in an especial manner put. It is to him, that the name is given above every name, and all judgement is committed. Our religion is called the religion of Christ: the Christian religion. The disciples are from him called Christians (Acts 11: 26). And therefore baptism, the ordinance of admission into that family, of initiation into that religion, is fitly said to be, into the name of Christ. As those who were initiated into the Mosaic dispensation are said to have been baptized into Moses (that is, given up to

God's conduct by the ministry of Moses) so we are baptized into Christ, that is, given up to God in Christ Jesus. That is the grand characteristical mark of the Christian religion, of which baptism is the initiating ordinance. The Jews acknowledge God the Father; and they were more agreed concerning the spirit of the Messiah, than concerning the person of the Messiah, and therefore it was requisite that this should be mainly insisted upon.

Our being baptized into the name of Jesus, doth ratifies and seals two things:

Our Assent to the Truth About Jesus Christ

First, our assent to the truth of all divine revelations concerning him. Baptism is the badge of our profession of the truth 'as it is in Jesus'; not only from Christ, as the spring and Author, but concerning Christ, as the subject matter. In baptism, we set to our seal that God is true in what he hath made known to us concerning him; namely, that Christ was, and is, the eternal Son of God, 'by a generation which none can declare'. This was the summary of the eunuch's faith, upon which he was baptized, 'I believe that Jesus Christ is the Son of God' (Acts 8: 37); a short creed, but the rock on which the church is built. That the Son of God in the fullness of time became man, was made flesh (John 1: 14), was born of a woman, and so became Emmanuel, God with us. That this Jesus was the true Messiah; the Saviour of the world; sanctified and sent for this purpose by the Father; to whom all the prophets bore witness; and in whom the types and predictions of the Old Testament have their full accomplishment. That in pursuance of his undertaking to redeem and save us, after he had lived a holy, useful, and exemplary life, and preached a divine and heavenly doctrine, he suffered death upon the cross as a sacrifice for our sins, and so to bring in an everlasting righteousness. That after he had lain in the grave till the third day, he rose again from the dead by his own power; and having conversed forty days upon earth, and given many infallible proofs of his resurrection to those who were to preach it to the world, he ascended in triumph to heaven; and sat down at the right hand of God: where he ever lives, making intercession for us. That this glorified Jesus is head over all things to the church, that is, its supreme and only Lawgiver and King. And lastly, that a day is coming, when he will appear in the clouds of heaven, to judge the world, and to render to every man according to his works.

This is a summary of the doctrine of Christ, which as Christians we are to believe, and of which our baptism signifies and seals the belief. And it is a sin, and a shame, that many who have been baptized, and are called Christians, know little of these things. They are certainly great things; and we should labour to understand them, and to be rooted and established in the belief of them, and to feel the power of them in our souls. By baptism we were delivered into this form of doctrine (Rom. 6: 17) as into a mould, and should labour, from our hearts, to obey it. Children should betimes be trained in the knowledge of these things; and taught to prefer the superlative excellency of this knowledge of Christ Jesus above any other knowledge whatsoever.

Our Submission to Him in All His Offices

Second, our consent to him in all his appointed offices. Faith is the act of the will, as well as of the understanding. This great doctrine, that 'Jesus Christ came into the world to save sinners' (1 Tim. 1: 15), is not only a faithful saying, to be assented to, but 'worthy of all acceptation,' to be embraced with the greatest affection. Peter said, 'Thou art Christ, the Son of the living God,' (and considering Christ's present state of humiliation, which was a veil to his glory, it was a very great word); there is the assenting act of faith. Thomas said, 'My Lord and my God,' (and it was the triumph of his faith over a prevailing unbelief); there is the consenting act of faith. It is not enough to believe that Christ is 'Lord, and God', but we must take him to be 'our Lord, and our God'. More particularly, in baptism we are sealed, and delivered up to Christ.

AS PROPHET TO TEACH AND INSTRUCT US. He is the great Prophet who was promised to the fathers (Deut. 18: 15), and in the fulness of time, 'he came from God, a teacher' (John 3: 2). He taught a while, in person, and he still teaches by his word and Spirit: he has (if I may so speak) set up a great school, and he calls upon all 'to learn of him'. By baptism we are entered into that school. And (by the way) if parents commonly enter their little children at what school they please, before they are able to choose for themselves, why may they not enter them into Christ's school; who is the teacher of hearts, and can instil his instructions into the soul, earlier than we are aware of? Christ teaches the rudiments (Heb. 5: 12), and those who say that he will not teach little ones, reproach our Master, as if he were the worse for going to heaven; for on earth he invited little children to him (Matt. 19: 14).

Baptism draws us off from all other teachers who stand in opposition to Christ, or in competition with him. Carnal reason, and corrupt understanding, governed by the dictates of a perverse rebellious will, and unsanctified affections, must be disclaimed. Instructions must not be taken from the evil examples of the world, and the prevailing customs of the times. These teachers must be renounced. On the contrary, baptism devotes us to the teaching of Jesus Christ: one who is able to teach us, and as willing as he is able. It places us at wisdom's gates; sets us at the feet of Christ, there to receive his word. And it is the fittest place for us. As baptized Christians, we are the disciples, that is, the scholars, of Christ. 'We call him Master, and we say well, for so he is' (John 13: 13). The proper faculty of the soul, resigned to Christ as our prophet, is the understanding; which must be submitted to the commanding truth of all divine revelations, how mysterious soever. Christ is a master, whose dictates are to be received with implicit faith, without dispute. How happy were it, could we live under the power of this engagement, or behave as Christ's scholars; observant of our Master, attentive to his instructions, affectionate to our school-fellows, concerned for the credit of our school, and still following on to know the Lord.

AS PRIEST TO ATONE FOR US AND SAVE US. He is a Priest forever, and 'such a High Priest as became us' (Heb. 7: 26). Were we but better acquainted with the mysteries of Christ's priestly office, we should see, and seeing admire, the singular propriety and beauty of it. Baptism is our subscription to the mediatorship of the Lord Jesus; it seals our approbation of, and consent to, those methods, which infinite wisdom hath taken to redeem a guilty world by a crucified Saviour. In this ordinance then, we are resigned and given up to Christ:

1. As a Mediator of reconciliation: quitting our confidence in any righteousness of our own, for the satisfaction of divine justice; and enrolling ourselves among the ransomed of the Lord, who profess to owe all their comforts, and all their hopes, to the blood of Jesus, and to receive all, as flowing to them in that stream. In baptism 'we receive the atonement' (Rom. 5: 11), and it is a rich receiving; which makes us unspeakably happy, and without which we should be eternally miserable.

2. As a Mediator of intercession: renouncing other intercessors, and relying on Christ, as our only Advocate with the Father, who appears for us, and pleads for us. We have a cause to be tried, and baptism admits us as Christ's clients, and interests us in his skill and faithfulness, in the management of that great affair.

We thereby also engage to put all our services into his hands, to be perfumed with the incense of his own intercession, and so presented to the Father. In baptism, our names are engraved upon the breastplate of this great High Priest, 'who, as the forerunner, is for us entered'. On this the apostle builds his assurance of the ability of Christ to save unto the uttermost, that 'he ever lives to make intercession' (Heb. 7: 25). And what a source of comfort is this, to all those who sincerely abide by their baptismal covenant, that Christ himself is, and will be, their High Priest; so that all the privileges, which flow from his atonement and intercession, are theirs!

AS KING TO RULE US. 'He is exalted to be a Prince and a Saviour' (Acts 5: 31). 'A Priest upon his throne, and the counsel of peace it between them both' (Zech. 6: 13). Baptism is an oath of allegiance to Christ, as our Saviour Prince. The children of professing parents are born within this allegiance (as our law expresses it), and are therefore to be baptized, as Christ's free-born subjects, and in ratification of their engagements.

In baptism we are put under the power of Christ's government; oblige ourselves to bear faithful and true allegiance to King Jesus, and cordially to adhere to the authority and interests of his kingdom; renouncing all other rule and dominion, and engaging religiously to observe all his laws and injunctions, how contrary soever to our own corrupt wills and affections. In baptism we take the yoke of Christ upon us, and profess ourselves willing, not only in the day of his grace to be made happy by him, but in the day of his power (Ps. 110: 3) to be made holy by him. This is to 'kiss the Son', as it is expressed (Ps. 2: 12), as an expression of cordial and affectionate allegiance.

In baptism we are put under the protection of Christ's government. Where we pay allegiance we expect protection; and shall not here be disappointed, for if the Lord be our 'Judge, our Lawgiver and our King, he will save us' (Isa. 33: 22). Christ's subjects may and must depend upon his love and care, as their guard and defence against the enemies of their souls. In baptism we come under his wings; quitting dependence upon the creature, as a false, deceitful shelter. We appoint to ourselves one head, as the prophet speaks (Hos. 1: 11) that is, own and submit to his headship.

Thus stand the covenant relation between Christ and believers, of which baptism is the seal; which is in short thus; 'My beloved is mine and I am his' (S. of S. 2: 16). Christ doth, in this ordinance, seriously make over himself to us to be ours, on condition we are sincerely his; which we therein profess and oblige ourselves to be.

IN THE NAME OF THE HOLY GHOST

We are baptized in (or into) the name of the Holy Ghost; the third person in the blessed Trinity. When those Ephesians mentioned confessed that they had not so much as heard whether there were an Holy Ghost, it was asked with wonder, 'Unto what then were you baptized?' (Acts 19: 2–3) implying that the believing, consenting acknowledgement of the Holy Ghost is essential to Christian baptism. For herein, as well as in the former particulars, are required both our assent and our consent.

Our Assent to the Truth About the Holy Ghost

Our assent to the truth of the Scripture revelation concerning the Holy Ghost, particularly concerning the divinity of the Holy Ghost, which is more than intimated in this institution; and, concerning his agency, in carrying on the work of our redemption, and completing the undertaking of Christ. That it is the Holy Spirit who indited the Scriptures, which are both the seed and the food of the new creature; so that all the benefits which flow to the church in general, and to believers in particular, from the word (and these are neither few nor small) come originally from the Holy Ghost. And, who works grace, and carries on that work, in the souls of believers; in a free manner, as the wind blows where it listeth, yet according to the election of grace. Of this, in baptism we declare our belief, in opposition to those proud opinions, which by making self all in all, make nothing at all, or next to nothing, of the Spirit. This is a truth perhaps as little thought of as any part of the baptismal profession, though as material as any.

Consent to Stand in a Covenant Relation to the Holy Ghost

AS OUR SANCTIFIER to change our nature, conquer our corruptions, quicken our graces, and make us meet to partake of the inheritance of the saints in light. By baptism we engage to submit to his sanctifying influences and operations, and give up ourselves to him, to be wrought up by him into a meetness for glory. We promise not to quench but to encourage, not to resist but to comply with, his workings; and for this purpose to attend upon those ordinances, which are instituted as means of sanctification, and by which the Spirit ordinarily works; desiring, and designing, to be sanctified by them and waiting upon the Spirit for success.

AS OUR TEACHER. The Spirit is given to teach doctrines to be known and believed, and duties to be known and practised; and our baptismal covenant engages us to receive, and to submit to these teachings. To receive with meekness (the meekness of the understanding, and the meekness of the will) that which the Spirit gives to us. To welcome his remembrances and admonitions; and to receive the teachings of his word, not only in the light of them into our heads, but in the love of them into our hearts.

AS OUR GUIDE to show us the way in which we should go, and to lead us in it. It is the character of all the children of God, that they are led by the Spirit of God (Rom. 8: 14). By baptism we yield up ourselves to that conduct, with David's prayer, 'Thy Spirit is good, lead me into the land of uprightness' (Ps. 143: 10). The Spirit guides out of the way of wickedness, the paths of the destroyer, into the way everlasting: and by baptism we are obliged to follow, humbly, closely, cheerfully, and fully. To walk, not after the flesh, as other Gentiles walk, but after the spirit, is what all are obliged to, who are in Christ Jesus.

AS OUR COMFORTER. He is promised as such (John 14: 16), either our Advocate and Intercessor within us: and as such by baptism we become his clients, and oblige ourselves to take his advice and trust to his management: or our Comforter; and such we receive him; depending upon him for that solid, satisfying comfort, which we have foolishly sought, and may despair ever to find, in the creature. Whatever disquiets us, we are engaged by our baptism to wait upon the Spirit for our comfort, in his own way.

In a word, our Lord Jesus, in this ordinance, does in effect say to us, as he did to the disciples when he breathed on them, 'Receive ye the Holy Ghost' (John 20: 22). And our restipulation is something like the blessed Virgin's submission to the power of the Spirit. 'Behold the servant of the Lord, be it unto me according to thy word' (Luke 1: 38).

And thus I have endeavoured to open the nature of this ordinance; the meaning of this service. And may we not from hence fetch matter of lamentation, that of the many who are baptized, and the many who bring their children to be baptized, there are so few who rightly understand what they do, or what was done to them? And if this be the nature of baptism, however to a carnal eye it may seem a mean thing, yet it is truly great. That which puts a value upon the wax and the seal, is the worth of the inheritance thereby conveyed. Baptism cannot be a little thing, when it is into names so great, as those 'of the Father, and of the Son, and of the Holy Ghost'.

3

THE SUBJECTS OF BAPTISM

Having opened at large the nature of baptism, we come next to inquire, to whom it is to be administered? And we may take some general rules in answer to this question, from what has already been said, in opening the nature and institution of the ordinance. Our Master has directed to baptize all nations; which easily affords this undisputed rule, that difference of nation makes no difference in Christianity. Greek or Jew, Barbarian or Scythian, people of all nations, are alike welcome to Christ upon gospel terms.

In a protestant nation, little needs be said to expose the folly of the church of Rome in administering the ordinance of baptism to things senseless and inanimate; as bells, and oars, and the like. When the apostles are bid to preach the gospel to every creature, it must be restrained to human creatures; the chief of the visible creation.

Baptism, we have found, is an ordinance of Christ's mediatorial kingdom; therefore all who pertain to that kingdom are to be baptized. It is a part of our Magna Carta, which every subject may claim the benefit of, and plead an interest in, unless by any forfeiture he deprive himself of the privilege of it. It belongs not to the internal, but external, administration of this kingdom; it is an ordinance of the visible church, and pertains therefore to those who are visible members of the church.

Baptism is a seal of the covenant of grace; and therefore belongs to those who are in that covenant (at least by profession) and to none other. As for a real and saving covenant interest, we cannot judge of it; it is a secret not belonging to us. In the external administration, we must proceed by a judgment of charity, upon a plausible profession. And according to these rules:

First, all those who seriously profess faith in Christ, and obedience to him, are to be baptized. Be they heathens, 'who have not known God', or Jews or Turks, 'who have not obeyed the gospel of Christ', if they will renounce their delusions, and willingly and deliberately embrace the Christian religion, they are welcome to this ordinance. I say willingly embrace Christianity, for it is a vile abuse of the ordinance, and a contradiction to the constitution of Christ's kingdom, to force people to baptism, and by it to Christianity, by outward violence and compulsion. This was the method the Spaniards took in converting the Indians, of which they boast so much. Christ will have all his subjects 'willing in the day of his power'.

This required profession supposes a competency of knowledge; and consists in a declared consent to the terms of the covenant; in which the judgment can be made only by the outward appearance. The believing consent is in the heart, and that falls not under our cognizance; it is 'with the mouth that confession is made unto salvation' (Rom. 10: 10). In the primitive times, when Christianity was to be planted in a world made up of Jews and heathens, this profession was previously required: though it appears not in what degree of explicitness. Whether every individual of the three thousand baptized (Acts 2: 41) did make a particular confession of his faith, or whether their cheerful submission to the ordinance, upon a public declaration of the nature and obligations of it, sufficed, as an implicit consent, is uncertain. The eunuch's confession was short, 'that Jesus Christ is the Son of God' (Acts 8: 37), which was then 'the present truth'. And perhaps Christianity has gained little, by the lengthening and multiplying of creeds; which, it may justly be feared, have caused more contention than they have cured.

Second, the infants of those who are in covenant with God, and are themselves members of the visible church, are likewise to be baptized. As far as the records of the New Testament go, most were baptized upon the former title: and good reason for it; the Christian church was then in the planting. And hence arises a mistake, like that of supposing that because, upon the first conquest of a kingdom, an actual consent to the prince's sovereignty, by taking the oaths of allegiance, is justly required, as the condition of partaking of the privilege of his protection, therefore it must needs be so, after the government is settled; and that none were to be reckoned his subjects, but those who testified this explicit consent; whereas it is agreed, by the law of all nations, that those who are born of the king's subjects, and in the king's dominions, are within the allegiance of the king, and entitled to the privileges of his subjects.

And here, I profess, I enter upon a very unpleasant part of my province (for I take no delight in opposing), but there is no avoiding it; the truth once delivered to the saints, and entailed on them, and their seed, must be contended for. But because the ground is rough, I promise to tread lightly, and to hasten over it as fast as I can: and the rather, because so much has been said and written, by so many learned and able divines, in defence of infant baptism, which yet remains unanswered, that to be large upon the subject, would be but (*actum agere*) wasted labour. I am asking for the 'good old way', and do not covet new lights.

The people we have occasion to contradict in handling this question, rather assumingly call themselves Baptists, as if there was no baptism, and therefore no Christianity, but amongst them. Call them antipaedobaptists, that is, such as are against infant baptism; or anabaptists, that is, rebaptizers, such as require those who were baptized in infancy to be baptized again; and you call them right.

And as to the persons of this people, I presume not to judge them; yea, I do not doubt that many among them are such as fear God, and are accepted of him. What I myself have seen of Christ among them, I do dearly love and rejoice in; and those who only scruple the baptising of their own children, but do not condemn infant baptism in general as a nullity, and reproach it as a vanity, though I heartily pity their mistake, I would be very backward to censure them: acknowledging, with Mr Flavel, that there are difficulties in this controversy, which may puzzle the minds of well-meaning Christians. But for their way, I must here declare utter dislike of it: and the rather, because in that short experience I have had of the world, I have observed these things concerning it:

It is a very uncharitable way. For whatever they do, I am sure their tenets do unchurch and unchristian more than nineteen parts in twenty of the Christian world; and thus dishonour Christ by narrowing his kingdom.

It is a very unnatural way: cutting children off from being parts of their parents; and prohibiting those to partake of their parents' privileges, who unhappily partake of their corruptions.

It is generally accompanied with (and therefore probably leads to) other errors. For not to go so far as Germany, and reflect upon the anabaptists of Munster, it is too plain, that the greater part of the anabaptists of England, at this day, run into extremes directly opposite to each other, and equally distant from the truth as it is in Jesus. And by the way, methinks those who speak so much of free grace, and the unconditionality of the gospel covenant, should be easily induced to honour free grace by the admission of children under its wings, though incapable of conditioning.

As to the points in question, I shall endeavour with all clearness and brevity to show:

1. What children are to be baptized.
2. What gives them their right to baptism.
3. What proof we have of that right.

WHAT CHILDREN ARE TO BE BAPTIZED?

I answer, not all children promiscuously. If both the parents are out of the visible church, the child is not to be baptized, till it comes to years of understanding:

Yet the children of parents, only one of whom professes faith in Christ and obedience to him, have a right to baptism; the 'unbelieving parent' is so far sanctified by the believing, that the children are 'federally holy' (1 Cor. 7: 14).

Yea though the parents are not actual members of any particular church, yet, as members of the universal visible church, their serious profession of faith entitles their children to baptism; for (as was showed before) baptism seals our admission, not into any particular, but into the universal church.

But in case the parents are excommunicated, it seems to me, that the children's right is thereby, for the present, suspended; supposing that excommunication to be just.

If both the parents are openly profane and scandalous, so that whatever profession they make, their practice doth notoriously give the lie to it; this amounts to the case of those who are excommunicated. Since such cast out themselves, and it is but a mockery to call them Christians, till they repent, and resolve to amend; and it does but harden them in their wickedness, to take their children into the church.

Or finally, if the parents deny the fundamental articles of the Christian religion, or refuse to consent to the covenant of grace, their children are not to be baptized. Those who do not hold the head, have not any title to membership, either for themselves or theirs. In a word, whatever, upon the first disciplining of nations, would have been a bar to a man's own baptism, in the continuation of Christianity, may justly be deemed a bar to the baptism of his children; and nothing else.

What Gives Children a Right to Baptism?

As to what it is that gives children a right to baptism (I mean as the requisite condition of their baptism) I answer, the visible church-membership of one, or both, of their parents; that is, their profession of faith in Christ, and obedience to him.

It is not the profession or promise of any other person or persons for them, which can entitle children to baptism, except in some extraordinary cases. And therefore I think, to that great question, 'Why are children baptized, when, by reason of their tender age, they cannot perform the conditions of the covenant?' the common answer, 'Because they promise them by their sureties', is not at all satisfactory: for unless there be some relation, natural or instituted, between them and their sureties, I see not how the consent of the sureties can either bind or benefit them. And I fear that building the fabric of infant baptism upon so weak a foundation, and erecting a fort so untenable against the adversaries of it, has given them great advantage. By this reasoning, the infants of Jews, Turks, or Pagans, might be baptized, upon the profession of any Christian, though standing in no relation to them: which certainly has no foundation in the word of God. I deny not the antiquity, nor in some cases the expediency, of sponsors. In the primitive times, when temptations to apostasy from the Christian faith were frequent and strong, sureties were generally required; that is, persons of reputation in the church, who did, first, testify that they believed the sincerity of the parents' profession; and that, so far as they were able to judge, they were not likely to apostatize; and, second, engage that in case the parents should die, or apostatize, they would themselves take care of the Christian education of the child. But this custom, laudable enough in its rise, hath sadly degenerated in its continuance; and the children's right to baptism been built so much upon their susception by sponsors, that the parents have been excluded by a law from professing and promising for their own offspring; which doubtless is a great abuse. If the sureties come in only as witnesses, why are they dealt with as the prime agents? If they are looked upon as proprietors of, and undertaking for, the children immediately, I see no ground in Scripture for such a susception, and therefore know not how it can be done in faith. And it is not only depriving parents of their right of dedicating their own children, but it looks too much like releasing them from their obligations to educate them, when the whole care of them is so committed to others: and it is a temptation to neglect their education; while the sureties are bound to take care of that, which they have no opportunity for, and which they are not induced to, by any natural affection. If it be said that they are the parents' deputies (the best which can be made of it), then certainly there should be some word or action appointed, which might, at least, imply such a deputation; and the parents should be permitted, some way or other, to signify their assent and consent to the engagement of the sureties; whereas the canon expressly provides, 'that the parents be not urged to be present': or the sureties should make some mention of the parents; and their transacting not be expressly said to be 'in the name of the child'. At least it should be left to the parent's choice, whether he will make a deputy or not; whereas, on the contrary, the canon enjoins, that 'no parent be admitted to answer as godfather for his own child'.

Having thus taken infant baptism off the wrong foundation, we fix it upon the right, that is, the parents' profession of faith in Christ, and obedience to him, a plausible profession, not contradicted by evident ignorance, or wickedness.

In case of the death, or necessary absence, of the parents, it suffices, that this profession be credibly attested by witnesses, knowing the parents, and known to the church (if the minister and congregation be not otherwise satisfied): and in such a case of necessity, it is very requisite that some person related to the child, or to whom the care of it is committed, should undertake for its Christian education. But if the parents (one or both) be living, it is proper that they should make an express declaration of their belief of the gospel, their consent to the covenant of grace, and their desire to have the child brought into that covenant. This fixes the title upon the right ground, and obliges those who are most fit to be obliged.

This parents most certainly are; because they have the greatest interest in their children. Who so fit to have the disposition of any thing, as the right owner? When the sponsors present a child to God, they give what is not their own—and what thanks have they?

Parents have also the greatest power over their children: a power, during infancy, to choose and to refuse (Num. 30: 3–5). When the sponsors transact in the child's name, they would do well to consider, by what authority they do these things, and who gave them that authority.

And finally, the covenant is, and ever hath been, externally administered to infants in the right of their parents. 'A God to thee, and to thy seed after thee' (Gen. 17: 7), not to thee, and to the seed of a stranger, whom thou canst but pick up, and circumcise, and turn home again. A true domestic owner of a child, who hath power to choose or refuse for him, may perhaps also be admitted to bring that child to baptism; because his interest in, and power over, such a child, is nearly tantamount to that of a parent. As Abraham circumcised all who were born in his house, and bought with his money (Gen. 17: 13, 27).

WHAT PROOF HAVE WE OF THAT RIGHT?

And here, to make some amends for the unpleasantness of disputing, it is no small pleasure to be the infants' advocate; to plead for those who cannot plead for themselves. Our law favours infants, and so doth our gospel.

For clearing what follows, some things are needful to be premised:

1. Consequences from Scripture are good proofs. The Scriptures were written for rational creatures. And is not Scripture rationing the sense and meaning of Scripture? If the premises are plain Scripture truths, and granted, they are unworthy to be disputed with who deny the conclusion.

2. All truths are not alike plain in Scripture. Some things are spoken of more fully, others more sparingly. The Scriptures were written for those who have them, and therefore they speak sparingly of the state of heathens, who have them not. They were written for those who are of ability to use them, and therefore speak sparingly of the state of infants, who are not yet of that ability. And the New Testament speaks less of those things which are more fully spoken of in the Old Testament; and which therefore were well known when the New was written. And infant baptism was not then controverted; for the Jews, to whom the gospel was first sent, understood it well enough.

3. Though the point of infant baptism may seem not so great a point to be contended for, yet the grounds on which it stands, and which they strike at who deny it, are very considerable. And of great moment.

These things premised, I shall mention just a few of the arguments.

BELIEVING PARENTS ARE IN COVENANT WITH GOD

The infants of believing parents are in covenant with God, and therefore have a right to the initiating seal of that covenant. When I say they are in covenant, understand me of the external administration of the covenant of grace, not of that which is internal. To the Jews pertained 'the covenant and the promises' (Rom. 9: 4), and yet with many of them God was not well pleased. Baptism, as was showed before, belongs to the external administration. What I mean is this; the promises of the covenant are provisionally sealed to them, viz. if, as they become capable, they agree to the terms to which they are by their baptism obliged. And what more can be said of the baptism of adults? For the seal of the internal administration to true believers is 'the spirit of promise' (Eph. 1: 13).

The consequence of this argument is seldom denied, viz. that if infants are in covenant, they have a right to the seal. If the crown devolves upon an infant, he hath a right to the ceremony of coronation: and who can forbid water to those who are in the Christian covenant? Yet it does not therefore follow, that these infants have a right to the Lord's supper; because in the two sacraments, though the thing signified be the same, the manner of signification is different. The Lord's supper is an ordinance in which the partaker must be active, but in baptism purely passive (which therefore is still, and in our language, spoken of in the passive voice), as if designed, purposely, for the benefit of infants. Under the Old Testament, infants did partake of circumcision, but not of the Passover.

The antecedent, therefore, is that which especially requires proof, viz. that the children of professing parents are in covenant with God, that is, come under the external administration of the covenant of grace. And I prove it by four steps:

1. It is possible that they may be in covenant.
2. It is probable that they should be in covenant.
3. It is certain that they were in covenant.
4. It is therefore certain that they are in covenant.

It Is Possible That They May Be in Covenant with God

I see no contradiction in the thing itself. The great objection insisted upon is, that they cannot restipulate, or declare their consent to the covenant, as if God's thoughts and ways of mercy were not infinitely above ours; or as if divine grace, which acts by prerogative, could not covenant with those who are not yet able to express their consent. If God made a covenant with the earth (Gen. 9: 13) and instituted a seal of that covenant, surely infants may be *foederati*, though incapable of being *foederantes*: that is, may be happily taken into covenant, though not covenanters.

A right understanding of the nature of the covenant would clear this: viz. that God is the principle agent, and works in us that which he requires of us. 'I will put my laws in their hearts,' so runs the covenant (Heb. 8: 10). Hence it is called a testament as well as a covenant: and if it be disputed, whether it be possible that infants should be taken into covenant, yet I hope it is past dispute, that they may have benefit by a testament.

To me it is very clear, that infants are capable of covenant relations, and of receiving and enjoying covenant privileges and benefits; not only the external, but the internal. Hence we not only read of those who were sanctified from the womb, but are assured that John the Baptist 'was filled with the Holy Ghost, even from his mother's womb' (Luke 1: 15). And indeed, if children are capable of corruption, it would be very hard upon them to say, that they are incapable of sanctification. That would be to give the first Adam a larger power to kill, than the second Adam has to quicken. In a word, none deny the possibility of the salvation of infants, and if it is possible that they may be saved, I am sure it is possible that they may be in covenant with God.

It Is Probable That They Should Be in Covenant with God

Infants are parts of their parents. The very law of nature accounts them so during their infancy, as appears by the concurring law of nations. Hence they are said to be 'in the loins of their parents' (Heb. 7: 10), and in them to act and receive. The propriety of parents in their children is greater than in anything else. Now, in the day when we give up ourselves to the Lord, we lay all that we have at his feet; and pass over all our rights and interests to him; and our children among the rest. God therefore takes it as a notorious invasion of his prerogative, that his people should devote their children to another god; 'Thou hast taken thy sons, and thy daughters, whom thou hast born unto me, to cause them to pass through the fire' (Ezek. 16: 20–1).

All God's other covenants, which he hath made with men, have taken in the seed of the covenantors; which makes it highly probable that the covenant of grace should be so ordered. The covenant of works was made with Adam, not only for himself, but for his posterity; for we all feel the sad effects of his transgression. The covenant which God made with Noah was made with him and his seed after him (Gen. 9: 9), of which we have still the comfortable experience. And the covenant of grace is paralleled with that covenant (Isa. 54: 9).

The covenant of peculiarity made with Israel took in their seed; and therefore, at the solemnity of entering into this covenant, express mention is made of the admission of their little ones (Deut. 29: 11–13). Though they were not capable of actual covenanting, yet they came in the right of their parents. And that covenant, though (taken strictly) no part of the covenant of grace, yet was a remarkable type of it.

The covenant of priesthood made with Phinehas, and the covenant of royalty made with David, included their seed: and Christians are kings and priests unto God.

The God of heaven has, upon all occasions, expressed a particular kindness for little children. Nineveh was spared out of regard to the little children it contained: and we scarcely find, in all the gospel history, such an instance of the tender affection of the Lord Jesus, as in his reception of the 'little ones' who were brought to him; whom he took up in his arms, and blessed (Mark 10: 13–14).

It Is Certain That They Were in Covenant

They were reckoned among those, 'to whom pertained the adoption, and the glory, and the covenants, and the promises' (Rom. 9: 4). It does not very evidently appear in Scripture records how the covenant was administered in the first ages of the world; but then it was administered to families. Family religion was then the face of religion: which puts it beyond reasonable doubt, that children were within the covenant. It is observable, that, in the patriarchal ages, professors were called 'the sons of God' (Gen. 6: 2), supposed to be the posterity of Seth as such. The profession of religion was then entailed upon families: a manifest indication of the covenant right of children, and of the designed method of the administration of the covenant, by propagating a profession.

The first clear manifestation of the covenant of grace is in the transactions between God and Abraham (Gen. 17), and it is very plain that there the seed of the covenanter was taken into covenant. So it runs (v. 7, etc.) 'thee, and thy seed after thee'; and it is repeated with an observable emphasis, 'a God to thee and to thy seed after thee'. To thy seed after thee, for thy sake; as appears (Deut. 4: 37), 'because he loved thy fathers, therefore he chose their seed after them'. Upon Abraham's believing consent to the covenant, all his posterity was graciously admitted into the bonds of the covenant. Ishmael was therefore immediately circumcised as a child of Abraham; and Isaac afterwards: and so all the seed of Abraham according to the flesh, 'to whom pertained the adoption', was circumcised, as the seal of that adoption, and that covenant.

That the covenant with Abraham (Gen. 17) was not a covenant of works, the same with that made with Adam in innocency, is too evident to require proof; and that it was not the covenant of peculiarity, but a pure gospel covenant of grace, will appear, if we consider:

1. That the grand article of this covenant is that which comprehends the whole covenant of grace, and all the riches of that covenant, viz. that 'God will be a God to us'; which doth eminently include all happiness. What can a soul need, or desire more, than a special interest in God? Even the glory and happiness of heaven itself (which is certainly conveyed by no other covenant than the covenant of grace) is thus set forth (Rev. 21: 3).

2. That circumcision, the seal of this covenant, is said to be 'the seal of the righteousness which is by faith' (Rom. 4: 11), which must necessarily be by the covenant of grace.

3. That the blessing of which the Gentiles are made partakers, by being brought into the covenant of grace, is called 'the blessing of Abraham' (Gal. 3: 14), that is, the blessing insured to Abraham and his seed. Those who deny them the blessing of Abraham (for he had it to himself and his seed), as much as in them lies, cut them off from salvation; but it is well that the unbelief of man does not make the righteousness of God of no effect.

4. That the covenant of grace, in the New Testament revelation of it, is expressly distinguished, not from the

covenant made with Abraham (for it was the same with that), but from the covenant which God made with Israel, 'in the day when he took them by the hand to lead them out of Egypt' (Heb. 8: 8–10). Now that was the covenant of peculiarity; the Sinai covenant; which Sinai covenant is, in like manner, manifestly distinguished from the promise made to Abraham, which the law, which came four hundred and thirty years after, could not disannul (Gal. 3: 17; cf. v. 8). Now we build the covenant rights of infants upon the promise made to Abraham, the father of the faithful.

5. If the covenant with Abraham was only the covenant of peculiarity, and circumcision only a seal of the promise of the land of Canaan, how came it that all proselytes, of what nation soever, even the strangers, were to be circumcised; though not being of any of the tribes, they had no part or lot in the land of Canaan? The extending of the seal of circumcision to proselyted strangers, and to their seed, was a plain indication that the New Testament administration of the covenant of grace would reach, not the covenanters only, but their seed. Now, baptism comes in the room of circumcision, as appears by comparing Colossians 2: 11–12, and whatever is objected against children's capacity, of being taken into covenant by baptism, doth very much reflect upon the wisdom of God, in taking them into the same covenant by circumcision.

From all this it appears, that the covenant with Abraham was a covevant of grace; and that the seed of believers were taken into that covenant; and therefore, that the children of professing parents were formerly in covenant with God.

It Is Certain That They Are Still in Covenant

This brings the argument home: and, I think, may be made out without much difficulty.

NO PROOF OF THEIR EJECTION. This follows from what has been said on the former head. If they were in covenant, unless evidence can be produced to prove their ejection, we ought to conclude that they are still in covenant. Our opponents call upon us to prove, by express Scripture, that infants are in covenant: but certainly having proved, even to demonstration, that they were in covenant, it lies upon them to show where and when they were thrown out of covenant; which they were never yet able to evince, no, not by the least footstep of a consequence. It is as clear as the sun at noon-day, that the seed of believers had a right to the initiating seal of the covenant; and how they came to lose that right?

For the clearing of this consequence it is to be considered that the design of the New Testament dispensation was to enlarge, and not to straiten, the manifestations of divine grace; to make the door wider, and not to make it narrower. But if the seed of believers who were taken into covenant, and had a right to the initiating seal under the Old Testament, are now turned out of covenant, and deprived of that right, the times of the law were more full of grace than the times of the gospel; which

> *The design of the New Testament dispensation was to enlarge, and not to straiten, the manifestations of divine grace; to make the door wider, and not to make it narrower.*

is absurd. Can it be imagined that the Gentiles are, in respect of their children, in a worse state than they were under the law? Then if a Gentile was proselyted, and taken into covenant, his seed was taken in with him; and is that privilege denied now? Is the seed of Abraham's faith in a worse condition than the seed of Abraham's flesh?

There needed not any express declaration in the Scriptures concerning this. The not repealing a law is enough to satisfy us of the continuance of it. It was said in the Old Testament revelation of the covenant of grace that God would be 'a God to believers, and their seed'. When or where was this repealed? The gospel being made known to the Jews first, they knew well enough, by the tenor of the covenant with Abraham, that their children were to be taken in. What poor encouragement would it have been for a Jew to turn Christian, if his children, who before were in covenant, and were visible church members, must, upon the father's becoming a Christian, be (*ipso facto*) thrown out, and put to stand upon the same uncomfortable level, and at the same dismal distance from God, as the children of heathens and infidels! A tender father would have said, 'This is very hard, and not agreeable to that comfortable prospect which the prophets, in the name of God, have so often given, of the days of the Messiah, the enlargement of the church, the 'bringing of the sons from far, and the daughters from the ends of the earth', and the owning of the offspring as a seed which the Lord has blessed' (Isa. 61: 9).

It is worth observing that the gospel church is called the 'Israel of God' (Gal. 6: 16), and the gospel covenant is said to be made with the 'house of Israel, and the house of Judah' (Heb. 8: 8), and those who had been 'aliens from the commonwealth of Israel', when effectually called to Christianity, are said to be made nigh (Eph. 2: 12–13). All of which intimates that the same privileges, for substance, which God's Israel had under the Old Testament dispensation, do now pertain to the gospel church. Now one special privilege which the Old Testament Israel had, was that their infant seed was taken into covenant with God: which privilege must certainly remain to the New Testament church, till there appears some evidence of its being cancelled. It is the apostle's inference from a long discourse, 'We are Abraham's seed' (Gal. 3: 29).

NEW TESTAMENT CONFIRMATION. There is not only no evidence in the New Testament, of the repealing and vacating of this privilege, but an abundant evidence of the confirmation and continuation of it, in that remarkable Scripture so often pleaded for infant baptism (Acts 2: 39). For the promise is to you, and to your children. The Jews had brought the blood of Christ upon themselves and their children: Now, said they, what shall we do, who have thus entailed a curse upon our posterity? Why, repent, and you shall have an entailed promise. Peter is there inviting and encouraging the converted Jews to repent, and by baptism, to dedicate themselves to Christ, and so to come under the evangelical dispensation of the covenant of grace. The privileges of that covenant are said to be remission of sins, and the gift of the Holy Ghost; that is, justification and sanctification; pardon of past sins, and grace to go and sin no more; which are the two principal and most inclusive promises of the new covenant. Now this promise is 'to you, and to your children'; which doth as plainly take in the seed of the covenanters, as the covenant

with Abraham did, 'I will be a God to thee, and to thy seed.'
And the Jews, no doubt, understood it so; such a hint being
enough to them who were brought up in the knowledge of the
promise made to the fathers. It was as much as to say, 'For your
encouragement to come into covenant by baptism, know, that
it runs still as it did, "to you, and to your children": not only
your own lives, but your children's too, shall be put into the
lease; so that if they pay the rent, and do the service, they shall
share the benefit of it.'

WHOLE FAMILIES SAVED. I do not see how else to understand
those Scriptures which speak of the salvation of whole families,
upon the believing of the masters of those families, but thus, that
all their children are thereupon brought into covenant, unless
they are of age to refuse, and do enter their dissent; if so, their
blood be upon their own head; but if infants, though they be not
of age to consent, yet not being of age to dissent, their parents
covenanting for them shall be accepted as their act and deed.

'Lydia's heart was opened, and she was baptized and her
household' (Acts 16: 15). The promise of salvation made to the
jailer was, that upon his believing, his house should be saved;
'Believe on the Lord Jesus Christ', do thou believe, and 'thou
shalt be saved,' that is, taken into a covenant of salvation, 'and
thy house' (Acts 16: 31), which, I think, may be explained by
what Christ said to Zaccheus upon his believing (Luke 19: 9):
'This day is salvation come to this house'; that is, the covenant
is externally administered to the whole family; as appears
by the following words, 'forasmuch as he also is the son of
Abraham'. The coming of salvation to his house is grounded
upon his relation to Abraham, and consequently his interest
in Abraham's covenant; 'I will be a God to thee, and thy seed':
which Christ hereby intimates that he came to confirm and ratify,
not to disannul. Apply this to Paul's words to the jailer, and the
sense is plain: Believe in Christ, and salvation shall come to thy
house: forasmuch as the believing jailer also is a son of Abraham.
(See Rom. 4: 11, 12, 16.) It is further observable in this story of
the jailer, that Paul and Silas preached to all that were in his
house probably many of them not of his family (Acts 16: 32);
(perhaps the prisoners); but the expression is altered when the
writer comes to speak of baptising them (v. 33), where it is not

said, that all in his house were baptized, but 'he and all his'; his little ones, no doubt, for the sake of their relation to him; and that straightway upon his believing. What is added in the 34th verse, 'he rejoiced, believing in God with all his house', cannot be seriously objected to this, by any who can read, and will observe the original; which is, 'he having believed in God, rejoiced in (or through, or with) his whole house'. Though, if we allow the believing to be spoken of his whole house, it may only signify that they were all by baptism enrolled amongst visible believers; and so infants are. And we read of the baptizing of whole families, besides those of Lydia and the jailer; and it is hard to imagine that there were no infants in any of them. It is more reasonable to suppose that there were, and that they were taken into covenant with their parents. By all this it is evident that the children of believing parents are in covenant with God, and have a right to baptism, the seal of that covenant.

Why God Takes Children into Covenant with Parents

It will not be amiss, before we proceed to another argument, briefly to enquire into the reasons why God is pleased thus to take children into covenant with their parents.

TO MAGNIFY THE RICHES OF HIS GRACE as diffusive of itself: conveyed, not as in a small vessel, the waters of which will soon be spent, but as in a full stream, which runs with continued supplies. The covenant of grace is a 'river of pleasures' (Ps. 36: 8). Grace is hereby glorified as free and preventing, that is, grace; and here it appears, that the relation between us and God is founded, not on our choice, but his; 'we love him, because he first loved us' (1 John 4: 19). In the providential kingdom, it is mentioned as an especial instance of the divine goodness, that God takes care of the young ones of his creatures (Ps. 147: 9). So is his love manifested into covenant, is an encouraging instance of the goodness of his nature, and his swiftness to show mercy. David lays a peculiar emphasis upon this, in his admiring acknowledgments of God's goodness to him (2 Sam. 7: 19) 'Thou hast spoken concerning thy servant's house, for a great while to come.' Kindness to the seed, for the parent's sake, is therefore called, 'the kindness of God' (2 Sam. 9: 3). When the covenant is so ordered, that the seed of the covenanters is thus established forever, though we should fail in 'singing the mercies of the Lord', yet 'the heavens themselves will praise his wonders' (Ps. 89: 3–4; cf. vs. 1, 5).

THE ANALOGY BETWEEN TWO ADAMS. That the quickening influences of the second Adam may bear some analogy, in the method of communication, to the killing influences of the first Adam. There is a death propagated, and entailed upon our seed, by Adam's breach of the covenant of works; and therefore God would have some kind of life (though not a life of grace, yet a life of privilege) entailed upon our seed likewise, 'by the bringing in of the better hope'; that so, within the visible church, the remedy might be as extensive as the disease. By native corruption, which we are all born in, sin is lodged in the heart; but by their native covenant right, which the seed of believers are all born to, the sin-offering is laid at the door. (I refer to one probable reading of Genesis 4: 7.)

TO ENCOURAGE BELIEVERS. That the hearts of true believers may hereby be comforted and encouraged in reference to their seed. It is a great inducement to come into this covenant, when it is thus entailed upon your children. An estate, in fee, to a man and his heirs, is reckoned of more than twice the value of an estate for life. Though a man cannot be certain that his heir may not abuse or forfeit it, yet it is desirable to leave it to him. This indeed is, in a manner, the only sufficient ground that believers have to build their faith upon, in reference to the salvation of their children dying in infancy; which to one that knows the worth of a soul, is no small thing.

TO BUILD THE CHURCH. 'That he might seek a godly seed' (Mal. 2: 15) (Heb. 'a seed of God'); that his church might be built up in a seed of saints. Thus does God provide for a succession, by a timely taking hold of the rising generation, and marking them for his own, as born within the pale; that the promise may be made good to Christ (Ps. 89: 36): 'His seed shall endure for ever.' 'A seed shall serve him, it shall be accounted to the Lord for a generation.' It is in consideration of the deceitfulness of the human heart (which if left at liberty, is very unapt to choose the good); and to lead the young ones as they spring, by these early cords of love, into the bond of the covenant: that this previous inducement may help to turn the scale of the fluctuating, wavering soul, and so the choice on God's side; which would be much more hazarded if it were left wholly to an adult choice. Infant baptism is intended to pave the way to early piety. The profession of Christianity is a step towards the truth of it; and may prevail to introduce it; as a plea with God to give us his grace, and an argument with ourselves, to receive and submit to it. However, Christ is hereby honoured in the world, and 'his name made great among the nations'. This is one of the fortifications of Christ's kingdom, by which it is secured from the gates of hell; and the design of the powers of darkness, to cut off the line of succession, and wear out the saints, is frustrated. Thus, in times of general corruption, preserve a 'tenth, which shall return, and shall be eaten, even the holy seed' (Isa. 6: 13). During the prevalence of the papal kingdom in the western church, though infant baptism was quite misgrounded, and baptism itself almost lost, in the great corruptions which stained its purity, yet, the preserving of the ashes gave rise to another phoenix. Thus, it is the will of God to preserve the invisible church in the visible, as wheat in the chaff; and as the power of godliness, at the first planting of the church, brought in the form, in restoring the church, brings in the power.

So much for the first argument, which is the main hinge; and the consideration of this will serve for the confirmation of the rest; which I shall but just touch upon.

INFANTS OF BELIEVERS ARE VISIBLE CHURCH MEMBERS

All who ought to be admitted as visible church members, ordinarily ought to be baptized; but the infants of professing parents ought to be admitted as visible church members, and therefore, ordinarily, they ought to be baptized.

That baptism is the door of admission into the visible church, was showed before: 'we are baptized into one body' (1 Cor. 12: 12-13). That then which is to be proved, is that the seed of believers ought to be admitted as visible church members; and this has been so frequently and so fully proved, that a hint or two on this head may suffice.

They Belonged to the Old Testament Church

The seed of believers, by God's gracious appointment, under the Old Testament, were to be admitted as members of the visible church; and that gracious appointment has never yet been repealed; therefore, they are to be admitted as such still. It is true, that the ceremonial institutions, which were but the accidentals of the Jewish church, are abolished (they were a yoke), but it is as true, that the essentials remain; though therefore the particular right of admission be changed, for a special reason, as accidental, it does not therefore follow that infant church membership, which is an essential branch of the constitution, is repealed. If infants be cut off from the body, it is either in judgment or in mercy: not in judgment, for where did they, as infants, commit a forfeiture? Not in mercy, for it can neither be a benefit to them, nor to their parents, nor to the church in general. If then professing parents did formerly bear their children to the Lord, why do they not still?

'Of Such Is the Kindgom of God'

Our Master has expressly told us, that 'of such is the kingdom of God' (Mark 10: 14); that is, the visible church is the kingdom of God among men, and infants belong to that kingdom. A short view of the story will throw some light on the doctrine of infant baptism, and therefore we will turn aside a little to consider it and observe in it:

PARENTS BROUGHT CHILDREN TO CHRIST. The faith of the parents, or other friends, who brought the children to Christ. They brought their children— little children; Luke calls them—infants (the word is used concerning Jesus in the manger). They brought them to Christ, as the great Prophet, to receive his blessing; not, as many others, for the cure of bodily diseases, but for a spiritual blessing. It seems then, that infants are capable of spiritual benefits by Christ: and it is the greatest kindness their parents can do them, to bring them to him by faith and prayer, to receive them. These infants were brought, that Christ might touch them: though infants cannot take hold of Christ, yet that does not hinder, but that he may take hold of them. Paul reduces his interest in Christ to this, 'For which I am apprehended of Christ Jesus' (Phil. 3: 12): and the best of those who have known God, must conclude with a 'rather are known of God'. Infants have need of Christ, and Christ has supplies for infants, and therefore to whom else should they be brought? He has the words of eternal life.

SATAN WANTS TO KEEP CHILDREN FROM CHRIST. The fault of the disciples in rebuking those who brought the children. It is Satan's policy to keep children from Christ; and he does it, sometimes, under very plausible pretences.

It is Satan's policy to keep children from Christ; and he doth it, sometimes, under very plausible pretences.

The disciples thought it a reflection upon their Master, to trouble him with such clients. We must not think it strange, if we meet with rebukes in the way of our duty: carnal reason, and a misguided zeal, prevail, not only to keep many from coming to Christ themselves, but to put them upon rebuking and hindering others; especially at their first dedication.

CHRIST ENCOURAGED THEM TO COME. The favour of Christ to them. He was displeased with his disciples; he took it very heinously, that they should thus misrepresent him to the world as unkind to little ones; and said, 'Suffer the little children to come unto me, and forbid them not.' And the reason added is very considerable, 'for of such is the kingdom of God'; that is, his kingdom of grace, or the church: not only of those who are disposed as children, for then he might have said the same of a lamb, or a dove, and have ordered those to be brought unto him: the word generally signifies not similitude, but identity; nor can any one instance be found where it excludes the person or thing mentioned. 'They that do such things, are worthy of death' (Rom. 1: 32); does not that include the things before mentioned? The argument then from this passage plainly stands thus: the question was, whether infants might be brought to Christ to be blessed by him? By all means, says Christ, for they are members of the church, and therefore I am concerned to look after them: they belong to the fold, and therefore the Shepherd of the sheep will take care of them. And therefore, not only in compliance with the believing desires of the parents, and in compassion to the infants, but to give a rule to his ministers in all generations of the church, 'he took them in his arms, laid his hands upon them, and blessed them'. Thus did he outdo their expectations, and give them more than they could ask or think. It is true he did not baptize them, 'for he baptized none' (John 4: 2); nor was baptism as yet perfectly settled to be the door of admission: but he did that which was tantamount, he invited them to him, encouraged the bringing of them, and signified to his disciples (to whom the keys of the kingdom of God were to be given) that they were members of his kingdom: and accordingly conferred upon them the blessings of that kingdom. And his giving them the thing signified, may sufficiently justify his ministers in giving the sign.

Normal Society Does not Cut Off Children

In other societies, the children of such as are members are commonly looked upon as members. Though a wise man does not beget a wise man, yet a free man begets a free man. The king of England would give those small thanks, who should cut off all the children of the kingdom from being members of the kingdom. Our law calls natural allegiance, due by birth, *alta ligeantia*—'high allegiance', and he that owes it is called, *subditus natus*—'a natural liege subject'. And it is the privilege of the subject, as well as the prerogative of the king, that it should be so. And shall it not be allowed in the visible kingdom of Christ? By the Jewish law, if a servant married and had children, all the children born in the master's house were the master's, and were taken under his protection, and interested in the provision of the family: though they were not as yet capable of doing any service, yet they were part of the master's possession. This law David applies spiritually: 'O Lord, truly I am thy servant; I am thy servant, and the son of thy handmaid' (Ps. 116: 16); born in thy house. And those consult neither the honour of the master, nor the credit of the family, nor the benefit of their children, who, though servants in Christ's family themselves, will not let their children be such.

To deny the church membership of the seed of believers, is to deny privileges to those who once had them, and who have never forfeited them. It is, in effect, to deliver their children to Satan, as members of his visible kingdom; for I know no mean between the kingdom of darkness and the kingdom of light. Give me leave then, as the infants' advocate, to make their complaint in the words of David, 'They have driven me out this day from abiding in the inheritance of the Lord, saying, Go, serve other gods' (1 Sam. 26: 19); and to present their petition for a visible church membership, in the words of the Reubenites and Gadites: 'For fear lest, in time to come, your children might speak unto our children, saying, What have you to do with the Lord God of Israel? Ye have no part in the Lord: so shall your children make our children cease from fearing the Lord' (Josh. 22: 24–5). Therefore, according to the warrant of the written word, we maintain baptism, as a sign of the church membership of our infants; 'that it may be a witness for our generations after us, that they may do the service of the Lord, and might not be cut off from following after him'. For, whatsoever those who are otherwise minded uncharitably suggest, 'the Lord God of gods, the Lord God of gods, he knoweth, and Israel he shall know, that it is not in rebellion, nor transgression against the Lord' (Josh. 22: 22). We desire to express as great a jealousy as they can do for the institutions of Christ, and are as fearful of going a step without a warrant.

Several other scriptural arguments have been undeniably urged, to prove the church membership of infants; but what was said to prove their covenant right, and to show the reasons of it, serve indifferently to this; for the visible church, and the external administration of the covenant, are of equal latitude and extent. Grant me, that infants are of that visible body, or society, to which pertains the adoption, and the glory, and the covenant, etc. in the same sense in which these pertained to the Jews of old, and to their seed; and I desire no more. That is their covenant right, and their church membership, which entitles them to baptism.

INFANTS OF BELIEVERS ARE HOLY

If the infants of believing parents are in some sense holy, they have a right to the ordinance of baptism; but it is certain, that they are in some sense holy, and therefore have a right to be baptized. There is a twofold holiness:

Inherent Holiness

Inherent holiness, or sanctification of the Spirit: and who dares say, that infants are not capable even of this? He that says infants cannot be sanctified, does, in effect, say that they cannot be saved (for without holiness no man can see the Lord); and he that can say this must be a hard hearted father: and if they may be internally sanctified, 'who can forbid water, that those should not be baptized, who have received the Holy Ghost as well as we?' Those who baptize only adults cannot be certain that all they baptize are inherently holy: nay, it appears that many of them are not so.

Federal Holiness

There is also a federal holiness; and this is that which we plead for. It is very true, that inherent holiness is not propagated (we are all 'by nature children of wrath') but that does not hinder the propagation of federal holiness. The children of believers, it is true, are born polluted, but it does not therefore follow that they are not born privileged. David acknowledges the corruption which his mother bore him in, and yet pleads the privilege she bore him to, 'Thy servant, the son of thine handmaid' (Ps. 116: 16); and again, 'Save the son of thy handmaid' (Ps. 86: 16).

To prove this federal holiness, two Scriptures are chiefly insisted upon; 'If the first-fruits be holy, the lump is also holy; and if the root be holy, so are the branches; and if some of the branches were broken off, and thou being a wild olive, were grafted in' (Rom. 11: 16–17). That children are branches of their parents none will deny; that inherent holiness is not communicated to the branches, is certain; it must therefore be meant of a federal holiness; which is explained by being grafted into the good olive tree, that is, the visible church: the fatness of this olive tree is the external privileges of church membership; a fatness which some did partake of, who were then broken off. The other passage is, 'Else were your children unclean, but now are they holy' (1 Cor. 7: 14). Unclean, means upon a level with the seed of the Gentiles; so unclean is used (Acts 10: 28). The children of parents, one or both of whom are believers, are not to be looked upon as thus unclean, but holy; that is, separated and set apart for God; federally holy.

INFANTS OF BELIEVERS ARE DISCIPLES

If the infants of believing parents are disciples, they are to be baptized; but they are disciples, and therefore to be baptized.

They are disciples; for they are intended for learning. If you send little children to school who can learn little or nothing, you do it that they may be ready to be taught, as soon as they are capable. If our Lord Jesus has cast little children out of his school, why does he appoint his ministers to teach them, and express so particular a care to have the lambs fed?

Circumcision was a yoke upon children particularly, yet that is called a yoke upon the necks of the disciples (Acts 15: 1, 10); therefore children are disciples.

They who are so to be received in Christ's name, as that Christ himself is received in them, are to be reckoned the disciples of Christ; but the infants of believers are so to be received. (See Mark 9: 37; Matt. 18: 5; compared with Matt. 10: 42; Luke 9: 48.) They are said to belong to Christ, and must be received as such; as children, they can only be received as creatures, but as the children of professing parents, they may be received in Christ's name; as belonging to Christ, that is, as disciples.

CHRISTIANS MUST DEDICATE THEIR CHILDREN TO GOD

If it is the duty of all Christian parents solemnly to engage, dedicate, and give up their children to God in covenant, whereby those children are obliged to be to God a people, then they ought to do it by baptism, which is the engaging sign; but it is the duty of all Christian parents thus to engage their children to God, and therefore they ought to baptize them.

It is the duty of Christian parents to engage their children to God in covenant. This hath been the practice of God's covenanting people (Deut. 29: 11): 'Your little ones stand here to enter into covenant with the Lord.'

Parents may oblige their children to that, which is good. God, as the spring and fountain of our being, may and does oblige us in a way of sovereignty; and parents, as the natural instruments of our being, are therefore empowered to oblige us in a way of subordinate agency. If not to enlarge the obligation (though 'Jonadab the son of Rechab' (Jer. 35: 18–19) did that, and his seed are commended for their observance of his charge), yet to strengthen and confirm it. The law of God allowed such power to a father as to disannul a vow made by his daughter in his house, though she were come to years of understanding. Much more is it in the power of parents to oblige their children in infancy to that which is plain and undisputed duty. Hannah was accepted in devoting her son to the Lord as a Nazarite from the womb (1 Sam. 1: 11), nor was it ever questioned whether she might do it or not. Whatever was the matter of Jephtha's vow, his daughter never disputed his power over her. And human authorities, that speak of this parental power as consonant to the law of nature, might easily be produced, if it were material. The common law and custom of our nation, as well as of all other civilized nations, does abundantly evince it. It is past dispute, that as far as a child has anything by descent from his father, the father has power to determine the disposal of it, in a lawful way (especially to pay debts), and to bind his child accordingly. We derive our beings by descent from our parents, who may therefore doubtless determine the disposal of them for God, and communicate them to us charged with that great debt of duty which we owe to the sovereign Lord. The case is much strengthened, if the obligation be built upon a contract confessedly in favour of the child, and greatly to his advantage; which is the case here. Such an obligation implying, by way of penalty, in case of an after-refusal, a forfeiture of the privileges so contracted for. Our children are parts of ourselves, more ours than anything we have in the world: not ours to be alienated from God (nothing is so ours), but to be devoted and given up to him. If it be in the power of parents to prejudice their children, by their breach of covenant (for God visits the iniquities of the fathers upon the children), may they not have a power to benefit their children by an adherence to the covenant?

If they may thus oblige their children to that which is good, certainly they ought to do it. When we give up ourselves to God, we ought to give up all that we have to him, to be devoted to him according to its capacity. Those who say, they give themselves to God, but will not give him their children, 'keep back a part of the price'. They ought, especially, to dedicate them, as a testimony of their sincerity in the dedication of themselves, and as a means to induce their children to be his. Those who are in truth the Lord's will lay out all their power and interest for him; and what greater power and interest can there be, than that of parents in, and over, their children?

If this must be done, can it be done in any better way than by baptism; which is instituted to be the mutual engaging sign, and the seal of a covenant between God and man? Under the law, whatever was devoted to God, was to be disposed of, according as it was capable, in such a way as might tend most to the honour of God, and best answer the ends of the dedication. To this purpose is the law (Deut. 27); and though this law be not now in force, the reason of it remains: God is as jealous of his honour as ever. Now the children of believers, notwithstanding their infancy, are capable of receiving the privileges of the covenant (are capable of visible church membership); and therefore are to be dedicated to God by baptism, the seal of the covenant, and the instituted sign of admission into the visible church. And to say that our children are to be dedicated to God, no otherwise than our houses, and estates, and callings, are to be dedicated to him, when really they are capable of a higher dedication, is to wrong both ourselves and our children; and to derogate from the honour of our Master, who would have every thing that is given to him brought as near to him as may be.

Children Should Be Discipled by Baptism

If it be the will and command of the Lord Jesus, that all nations should be discipled by baptism; and children, though a part of all nations, are not excepted, then children are to be discipled by baptism: I say, discipled by baptism, for that is plainly intended by the words of the institution (Matt. 28: 19): 'admit them disciples by baptizing them', as was showed before. The command is to disciple them; baptizing them is the mode of executing that command. As if a general should say, enlist soldiers, giving them my colours (or any like sign); giving them the colours would

Baptism doth not give the title, but recognize it, and complete that church membership which before was imperfect.

be interpreted as enlisting them. So, disciple them, 'baptizing them', does not note two distinct acts, but the body and soul of the same act; as granting land by scaling a deed, or giving livery and seisin. I have said before, that baptism does not give the title, but recognize it, and complete that church membership which before was imperfect.

And all nations are to be so discipled. Hitherto, the nation of the Jews only had been discipled, by circumcision; but now, the partitionwall is taken down, and all nations are to be in like manner discipled, by the New Testament ordinance of initiation; that is, all consenting nations. If any communities or individuals refused, the apostles were to shake off the dust of their feet against them, as having no lot or part in the matter.

And surely infants are a part of nations; and in the discipline of nations, not a dissenting part, but a consenting, by those who are the trustees of their wills. And our Lord has not excepted them. There is not the least word in the commission, or anywhere else in the whole Bible, which implies the exclusion of infants from visible discipleship, when their parents became visible disciples. And, for my part, I dare not except where Christ has not excepted; especially where the exception would tend so much to the dishonour of Christ, the straitening of the church, and the discomfort of the saints, and contradict the clear light of so many other Scriptures. I dare not exclude any, who do not exclude themselves, nor are excluded by those, who have a natural interest in them, and power over them.

In this Magna Carta, therefore, we leave the cause of infants fully vindicated; and are willing to stand or fall by this commission. Many other arguments might have been insisted upon; particularly the doctrine and practice of the primitive church; but this shall suffice.

ANSWERS TO OBJECTIONS

I should next have proceeded to answer the objections of the antipaedobaptists; but that hath been so fully done by others, and in a great measure done in the defence of the foregoing arguments, that I shall be brief in it.

INFANTS HAVE NEITHER UNDERSTANDING NOR FAITH

It is objected that infants are not capable of the ends of baptism, having neither understanding nor faith. To this I answer:

First, that they have as much understanding as the children of the Jews had, who were circumcised, and therein received the seal, both of justification (Rom. 4: 11) and of sanctification (Deut. 30: 6), and baptism is no more.

Second, that there are many ends of baptism of which children are capable, though not of all till they come to some use of reason. Infants are capable of being admitted into Christ's visible kingdom, which is the primary intention of baptism. A lease, or covenant, between a landlord and a tenant, may be of use to a child, though he understands it not; nay though, when he grows up, he may, perhaps, forfeit the benefit of it.

Third, parents may, and must, herein transact for their children; being appointed by nature their agents, and having a power to oblige them in other things, and therefore much more in this, which is not only the duty, but the privilege, of their children. Nor is there any danger, that the guilt of covenant-breaking should lie at the parent's door, in case of the apostasy of the children, because the parents promise not to do the duty themselves, but engage their children to do it; and only oblige themselves to contribute their best endeavours thereunto.

INFANT BAPTISM DOES MORE HARM THAN GOOD

It is objected, that infant baptism does more hurt than good. But certainly, what hurt it does is only through the ignorance or corruption of those who abuse it. Though it may be true, that many carnal people are strengthened in their delusions by their infant baptism, it is well if it be not as true, that many are, in like manner, hardened by being rebaptized; for it is plain, that they are not all saints indeed.

While on the other hand, there are many humble, serious Christians, who can experimentally speak of the benefits of it. Its many practical uses will be shown hereafter. For my own part, I cannot but take this occasion to express my gratitude to God for my infant baptism, not only as it was an early admission into the visible body of Christ, but as it furnished my pious parents with a good argument (and I trust, through grace, a prevailing argument) for an early dedication of my own self to God in my childhood. If God has wrought any good work upon my soul, I desire, with humble thankfulness, to acknowledge the moral influence of my infant baptism upon it.

WE HAVE NO NEW TESTAMENT PRECEDENT

We have no precept (say they) nor precedent, in all the New Testament, for infant baptism.

Though we have already shown considerable footsteps of it in the New Testament, yet, in answer to this objection, we further add that it is sufficient that the essentials of an ordinance be clearly instituted, though the circumstantials, or accidentals, be not. Christ instituted the Lord's supper, but we have neither precept nor precedent for admitting women to it. Our opponents say that the practice of baptising actual believers only, is more agreeable to the practice of Christ and the apostles; I say, that the practice of admitting men only, to the Lord's supper, is more agreeable to the practice of Christ and the apostles; and let the consequences stand or fall together. The substance of the ordinance of baptism is clearly instituted by Christ for the admission of visible church members, and it is left to us to infer the application of it to all those who have a right to visible church membership; which it is undeniably proved that infants have.

Supposing that we cannot show any precept, or precedent, in the New Testament, for baptizing the infant seed of Christians, neither can the anabaptists show one word of precept, or precedent, for baptizing the child of any one Christian at years of discretion, in all the New Testament. I challenge them to produce any one instance of the deferring of the baptism of any believer's child to years of discretion. Now the lawyers have a rule, 'that an estoppel against an estoppel sets the matter at large'. We have no such clear direction, as some may think there should have been, what to do with the seed of believers; and if the dispute be drawn in the New Testament, I know not whither to appeal more properly than to the Old; where we find such abundant evidence of the church membership of the infant seed of believers, and of their title to the ordinance of initiation, while we do not find a word in all the New Testament which deprives them of either (but a great deal in affirmance thereof), that we conclude (blessed be God, abundantly to our satisfaction) that they still remain in full force and virtue.

4

THE NECESSITY AND EFFICACY OF BAPTISM

Having enquired what baptism is, and to whom it is to be administered, our next inquiry must be, what stress is to be laid upon it? And here we have need to walk circumspectly, for fear of mistakes, on the right hand, and on the left. What I have to say on this head shall be reduced to the following questions:

Is Baptism Necessary to Salvation?

In answer to which, we must have recourse to the known distinctions of (*necessitas proecepti*) what is necessary because commanded, and (*necessitas medii*) what is necessary as a mean; and also (*necessitas hypothetica*) conditional necessity, and (*necessitas absoluta*) absolute necessity. And so it seems that baptism is conditionally, a necessary duty; but not, absolutely, a necessary mean. We have adversaries to deal with on both hands; some, who are so far from thinking it a necessary mean, that they deny it to be a necessary duty (so, many of the Socinians); and others, who not only plead for it as a necessary duty, but assert it to be necessary as a means of salvation (so the papists): and the truth seems to be between them.

AS A CONTINUING DUTY

The necessity of water baptism, as a continuing duty, is proved, from the will and command of the Lord Jesus; 'Go and disciple all nations, baptizing them'; which was intended to be a warrant, not only to the apostles, in planting the church, but to all ministers, in all following ages; as the promise annexed abundantly proves, 'Lo, I am with you always, even to the end of the world.' The ordinance of the Lord's supper is expressly said to continue till Christ's coming, that is, till the end of time (I Cor. II: 26), and no reason can be given, why baptism should not run parallel with it, since they are both signs, and seals of the same grace. Nor did the pouring out of the Spirit on the day of Pentecost supersede external ordinances, but rather lead to them; for having received the Holy Ghost, is assigned as the reason why water baptism should not be forbidden to Cornelius and his friends (Acts 10: 47); and though the apostles are bidden to go into all nations and baptize, they went not into any of the nations till after the Spirit was poured out.

Firstly, from the continuance of circumcision in the Old Testament church: which was instituted, not only for the founding of that church, but to be observed 'in their generations' (Gen. 17: 9–10). As therefore circumcision continued a standing ordinance in the Old Testament church till the first coming of Christ, by a parity of reason, baptism, which comes in the room of it, is to continue a standing ordinance in the New Testament church till the second coming of Christ.

Secondly, from the continuance of the end intended in this institution. It was instituted to be the door of admission into the visible church: and without some such door, either all must be shut out, or all must be taken in: either of which would be absurd; for the church is a society distinct from the world, and the God of the church is a God of order, and not of confusion. Though the children of believing parents have, by their birth, a remote church membership, and covenant right, yet it is requisite for the preserving of order in the church, that there should be a solemn recognition of that right, and some visible token of admission. As in the case of converted heathens; though upon their believing, they have a right to the privileges of the covenant before baptism (for baptism does not confer a right, but only recognise it), yet it was the will of Christ that they should be solemnly admitted by baptism, for the honour of the church as a distinct society. Thus in the ordinance of marriage (an ordinance common to the whole world), the mutual declared consent of both parties is the essence of the marriage, yet, for order's sake, all civilized nations have enjoined a solemnity of investiture.

Thirdly, from the continuance of the benefits conferred, and the obligations imposed, by baptism: which are such as pertain, not only to those who are converted from heathenism to Christianity, but to those also who are born of Christian parents. We are all concerned to 'put on Christ', and to have communion with Christ in his death: we all need the 'remission of sins', and the 'sanctification of the Spirit', and 'eternal life'; so that while we are expecting these privileges, and taking upon ourselves these engagements, it is fit that both should be done, in that ordinance, which was appointed to signify and seal both the one and the other. The church must be 'sanctified and cleansed with the washing of water, by the word, till it is presented a glorious church' (Eph. 5: 26–7).

Fourthly, this may be of use to rectify the mistake of some well meaning people, who, having been unhappily defrauded of the privilege of baptism in their infancy, when grown up, do themselves neglect it; thinking it sufficient, that they do that which is intended by baptism, though they do it not in that way. Such would do well to consider what a slight they put upon the law of Christ. It would be thought too harsh, should we, in this, parallel baptism to circumcision, which had so severe a sentence annexed to the law which required it (Gen. 17: 14). 'The uncircumcised man-child' (that is, when he is come to years of discretion) 'whose flesh of his foreskin is not circumcised,' (not only through the neglect of his parents, when he was an infant, but by his own, when grown up) 'that soul shall be cut off from his people; he hath broken my covenant.'

NOT AS A MEAN

Baptism is not simply and absolutely necessary as a mean. This is the popish extreme. But, as in worship, the middle way is the good old way. When we speak of baptism as a mean, and the necessity of it as such, we must distinguish between external and internal means. Internal means are such as have so necessary a connection with the end, as that the end cannot be obtained without them. Such are faith, repentance, and justification; means of salvation absolutely necessary; so that salvation is never without them as the means, nor they without salvation as the end. But external means are not thus connected with the end, but only subservient to it, by God's ordination. Not so, but that the end may sometimes be obtained without them, and they may often miss of the end: and sacraments are such means of salvation. The Council of Trent denounces a curse against those who say that baptism is not absolutely necessary to salvation. But that it is not thus necessary, is fully proved by the following arguments:

God is a free agent in dispensing his grace: 'he begets of his own will', which does not depend upon the will of the parent, so as to be frustrated by his neglecting to baptize his child.

Circumcision, under the Old Testament, was not absolutely necessary to salvation; therefore baptism is not under the New: for then, the condition of Christians would, in this respect, be harder than that of the Jews. God appointed circumcision to be administered on the eighth day, and not before; and certainly it would have been very hard upon children to have deferred it so long, if it had been necessary to salvation. David's child died on the seventh day, consequently uncircumcised; he comforts himself with the hope of its salvation, 'I shall go to him, but he shall not return to me' (2 Sam. 12: 23). Yea, all the children of Israel were forty years together in the wilderness without curcumcision, which it is hard to suppose was damning to those who were born and died during that time. The threatening (Gen. 17: 14) is wilful neglect, and not the involuntary privation.

If baptism were thus absolutely necessary, unbaptized children would perish eternally without any fault of their own; and so the child would bear the personal iniquities of the father: which is contrary to Ezekiel 18: 20.

Our Saviour does plainly put a difference between the necessity of faith, and the necessity of baptism, to salvation: 'He that believeth and is baptized, shall be saved' (Mark 16: 16), but he does not say, 'he that believeth not, and is not baptized shall be damned,' but only, 'he that believeth not shall be damned'; for faith is the internal, baptism but the external, mean.

The infants of believing parents have an interest in the promises of God, which is the thing signified by baptism: and can it be imagined, that they should be shut out of heaven for want of the sign? To suggest such a thing, is not only very uncharitable in itself, but, we think, reflects dishonour upon Christ; the goodness of his nature, the grace of his covenant, and the constitution of his kingdom; and must needs be very uncomfortable to Christian parents. When God hath said that he will be a God to believers, and to their seed, the neglect of man, much less the wise providence of God, shall not make the promise of no effect.

WHAT EFFECT DOES BAPTISM HAVE ON INFANTS?

The anabaptists say it has none at all, and therefore argue, to what purpose is this waste? Their exceptions have been answered before. The papists assert that sacraments confer grace (*ex opere operato*) by virtue of the sacramental action itself: but as to baptism, it is expressly said, that it does not save us, as it is the 'putting away of the filth of the flesh' (which is the sacramental action), but 'the answer of a good conscience' (1 Pet. 3: 21), and there we leave the question. And others, even many protestants, have said, that the sacrament of baptism does as an instrumental, efficient cause, confer, and effect, the grace of actual regeneration; so that the infant baptized is freed, not only from the guilt, but the dominion of sin, and the Spirit of grace is given, as the seed, whence the future acts of grace and holiness, watered by the word, may, in time, spring forth. Thus, the church of England concludes concerning every baptized child, that it is regenerated, and born again. In opposition to which Mr Baxter pleads:

> That baptism was not instituted to be a seal of the absolute promise of the first special grace, 'I will give them a new heart', but to be a seal of the covenant properly so called, wherein God engages himself, conditionally, to be our God, to save us, and we engage ourselves to be his people, to serve him, and so to perform the said condition: and if not to be a seal of the absolute covenant, then not to be an instrument of conveying the grace of that covenant, but a mean of conveying the good promised in the conditional covenant, according to the capacity of the subject: and therefore it seals, to the infants

of believers, the promise of salvation, so as to be a mean of conferring the benefit of salvation upon them, not as a physical, or hyperphysical, instrument, but only as a moral instrument; by sealing, and so conveying, a legal right, which is afterwards improvable, as a mean of working a real change upon the souls of those who have faith, and the use of reason.

What I have to say on this head is, as to the relative influence of baptism, I look upon it to be the door of admission into the visible church: so that all who are duly baptized, are thereby admitted as visible church members, and (to borrow the Hebrew phrase before mentioned) 'gathered under the wings of the Divine Majesty'; and the new covenant being externally administered in the visible church, it is conditionally sealed to all who are baptized (and particularly to the seed of believers) upon the parents' faith: the parents' will being accepted for the child's, and the parents' present consent and dedication laying an obligation upon the child for the future.

This then is the efficacy of baptism; it is putting the child's name into the gospel grant; and thus it is a sealing ordinance, and a binding ordinance. The child's actual faith, and repentance, and obedience, are thereby made (to speak in the lawyers' language) *debita in proesenti, solvenda in futuro*, debts then incurred, to be paid at a future time. And surely this is abundantly sufficient to invite and encourage parents to dedicate their children to God in baptism. For if this be true (as it certainly is), it is not (that *nudum signum*) that empty childish thing which the antipaedobaptists love to call it.

As to the real influence of baptism, we cannot be so clear; nor need we. As far as the parents are concerned, we are sure, that the children are not so regenerated, as not to need good instructions, when they become capable of them, and yet are so regenerated, that if they die in infancy, parents may take comfort from their baptism in reference to their salvation: and as to the children, when they grow up, we are sure, that their baptismal regeneration, without something more, is not sufficient to bring them to heaven: and yet it may be urged (as I said before), in praying to God to give them grace, and in persuading them to submit to it.

5

THE CIRCUMSTANCES OF
THE ADMINISTRATION OF BAPTISM

Baptism, as a sacrament, consists of a sign, and the thing signified by it. Our inquiries now must be about the sign, and the administration of that; in which several things claim a brief consideration.

The Mode

Concerning the manner of administering, or applying water, to the person baptized.

And about this the enemy hath sowed tares; hath raised a great dispute, whether it must necessarily be done by immersion, that is, by dipping the person all over in water: and there are those who make this mode of applying water of the very essence of the ordinance, and, with much bitterness, condemn those who have so much of the spirit of the gospel as not to impose, and make necessary, what Christ has not made so; and who, if water be but solemnly applied, reckon it altogether indifferent, whether it be by infusion, inspersion, or immersion.

THE ARGUMENT FOR IMMERSION

Let us examine a little the strength of their cause, of which they are so confident.

The Word Signifies Only Immersion

They plead that the word signifies only to immerse, or dip into water; and recourse is had to the Greek Lexicons in proof of this; but to little purpose, as the best Lexicons render it, to wash in general, as well as to wash by plunging, or dipping: and we really think, that when Christ saith, baptize, he means no more than wash with water. But, not to trouble ourselves with searching the sense of the word in other Greek authors, we will inquire into the sense of it in the New Testament, and hope our opponents will not refuse to join issue with us in the inquiry.

We read of diverse washings (diverse baptisms; Heb. 9: 10); he instances in the water of purification, verse 13, 'the ashes of an heifer sprinkling the unclean': compare the two, and it appears that that is a true baptism, or washing, which is by sprinkling.

The Pharisees wondered that our Lord 'had not first washed' (Luke 11: 38) (that he was not first baptized); not that he was plunged all over in water, but that he did not wash his hands (cf. Mark 7: 2–3, 5). It seems then, that the washing of the hands may be the baptizing of the man: and why not the washing of the face. Nay, it should seem that the usual way of washing even the hands, among the Jews, was not by dipping them into water, but by having water poured upon them: for Elisha's ministering to Elijah is thus described, 'he poured water upon the hands of Elijah' (2 Kings 3: 11).

Among the superstitious washings or baptisms (as they are called) of the Pharisees (Mark 7: 4), we read of the baptism (that is, washing) of tables, or rather beds, or couches, as the word properly signifies; and was it likely that beds or couches, or even tables, should often be washed by plunging them into water? Surely it was done by sprinkling, or pouring, water upon them.

In Revelation 19: 13 we meet with a garment baptized with blood, that is, stained or tinged with blood; and that by sprinkling, as appears by comparing the parallel passage (Isa. 63: 3): 'Their blood shall be sprinkled upon my garment, and so will I stain all my raiment.' If the word then, so often, or indeed anywhere, signifies washing by sprinkling, or pouring on of water, as it certainly does, the argument for immersion, from the signification of the word, falls to the ground.

Jesus was Immersed

They assert that Jesus Christ, and others in Scripture, were baptized by immersion; and therefore that any other mode of baptizing is not only unlawful, but renders the baptism null and void.

To which we answer, supposing that Christ, and others in Scripture times, were baptized by immersion, yet it does not therefore follow that that mode is still indispensably necessary to the essence of the ordinance. Christ often preached sitting; is it therefore unlawful for ministers to preach standing? But that which is more considerable is, that bathing was very much in use in those times and places, especially among those who were under the ceremonial law; and while this was an ordinary way of washing, to which all persons were accustomed, perhaps it was the fittest to be used in baptism, where washing is the sign. But with us it is far otherwise: bathing is a thing seldom used; and therefore, as in the Lord's supper, not the posture of recumbency, which our Lord used (according to the custom of the country), but our own ordinary table gesture, is the most proper; so in baptism, not dipping, which was then an ordinary way of washing, but sprinkling or pouring water, which is now the usual way of our daily washing, is most proper. For the sign, in both ordinances, is taken from a common action, and the more like it is to that common action, the better and the more instructive.

But, there is no such convincing evidence from Scripture, that Christ and others were baptized by dipping, as (supposing the obligation of the pattern) may justly be required to prove it essential to the ordinance.

As to the baptism of Christ, it is far from certain that it was by immersion. John indeed is said to have baptized in water, but so is Christ said to baptize *en puri*. Does that mean in fire? No, with fire. The preposition *en* frequently signifies (see Rev. 19: 21): *en romphia*—with the sword.

Again, it is urged, that Jesus was baptized into the Jordan. But the preposition (*eis*) often signifies *at*, as well as *in*, or *into*. However, it does not certainly express plunging in the water; they then went bare-legged, and therefore might readily go into the water and be washed, without being dipped all over.

Moreover, Christ is said, after his baptism, to go out of the water (Matt. 3: 16; Mark 1: 10), but it is remarkable, that in both places the original is not *out* of the water, but *from* the water; that is, he came up the ascent from the river: though indeed, had he been only ankle deep, and not plunged, he might have been said to come out of the water.

And once more, John chose a place to baptize in, where there was much water (John 3: 23), but the words are many waters, that is, streams; therefore probably shallow, unfit for plunging: and accordingly travellers find the river Enon only a small brook, which a man may step over.

And as to others, whose baptism we read of, I find none, except the eunuch, of whose immersion there is any apparent probability. Several were baptized in private houses; as Paul, and the jailor, and his family; the latter in the night; and it is very unlikely that he had any conveniency for being dipped there.

Allusions to Immersion

They plead 'Buried with him in baptism' (Rom. 6: 4; and Col. 2: 12) where they fancy an allusion to the ceremony of baptizing by dipping: which I see no necessity for at all. Good wits may from thence illustrate the text, and no harm done: but to force so uncertain an allusion, so far, as to condemn almost all the baptisms of the Christian church, in all ages, is a great wresting of Scripture. Our conformity to Christ lies not in the sign, but in the thing signified. Hypocrites and unbelievers, like Simon Magus, though they be dipped a hundred times, are not buried with Christ by baptism; and true Christians are by faith buried with Christ, though they be not dipped at all; having 'fellowship of his sufferings', and 'being made conformable unto his death' (Phil. 3: 10). 'We are baptized into the death of Christ,' and by baptism 'put on Christ'; but it does not therefore follow that there must needs be, in the external sign, anything that resembles either killing or clothing.

Historical Testimony

The testimony of men is much urged in this case; and I believe that immersion, yea, trine immersion, or plunging the person baptized three times, was commonly used in very early ages; and that, as far as popery prevailed, a great deal of stress was laid upon it: and the church of England, in the rubric of baptism, prescribes dipping, and tolerates sprinkling only in case of bodily weakness: but our recourse is to the law and the testimony.

THE ARGUMENT AGAINST IMMERSION

Let us now see what is to be said against baptism by immersion, or plunging in water.

An Evil Distraction

It unavoidably occasions a very great distraction and discomposure of mind, in the management of a solemn ordinance; and is therefore evil. Putting an adult person, unused to bathing, over head in water, must needs, for the present, unfit him for any thoughts suitable to such a solemnity; and great care is to be taken, that we may 'attend upon the Lord without distraction' (1 Cor. 7: 35).

Dangerous to Health

In many cases, this mode is very perilous to the health, and even life, of the body: and God hath taught us, that he will have 'mercy, and not sacrifice' (Matt. 12: 7).

In so cold a climate as ours, especially to some people, and at some seasons, bathing in cold water would be almost certainly fatal. Ask the best physicians if this be not true.

Immodest

To baptize naked, or next to naked (which is supposed, and generally practised, in immersion) is against the law of modesty; and to do such a thing in public solemn assemblies is so far from being tolerable, that it is abominable, to every chaste soul: and especially to baptize women in this manner. If when veils were commonly used, the woman was to have a veil on her head, to cover her face in the congregation, 'because of the angels' (whether that mean young men, or ministers, or heavenly spirits), I am sure the argument is much stronger, against her appearing almost naked in such a congregation. Is this for 'women to adorn themselves in modest apparel, with shamefacedness, and sobriety?' (1 Tim. 2: 9).

A Little Water Makes the Point

However, I am sure, that to lay such a stress upon the ceremony of dipping, as not only to condemn, but to nullify, and reproach, all those baptismal washings which are performed by pouring on water, is very uncharitable, and dissonant from the spirit of the gospel. 'Bodily exercise profits little' (1 Tim. 4: 8). In sacraments, it is the truth, and not the quantity, of the outward element, that is to be insisted upon. In the Lord's supper, eating a little bread, and drinking a little wine, suffices to exhibit the thing signified; and we need not, nay we should not, fill ourselves with either; and yet it is called a supper (1 Cor. 11: 20). So in the ordinance of baptism, the application of a little water, provided there be water, and a washing with that water, is sufficient to signify spiritual washing. Aaron and his sons were the Lord's priests, though the blood of consecration was only put 'upon the tips of their ears, and on their thumbs, and great toes' (Lev. 8: 24).

THE ARGUMENT FOR SPRINKLING

We shall just hint at what is to be said for the administration of baptismal washing by sprinkling, or pouring, water on the face, or head; which is the more usual mode.

The overthrow of the other mode is, indeed, enough to establish this: washing is the main matter in the sign, which is sufficiently done by sprinkling or pouring water. But I add further, the thing signified by baptism is frequently, in Scripture, set forth by sprinkling or pouring water, but never, that I remember, by dipping or plunging into water. Thus Isaiah 44: 3, 'I will pour water upon him that is thirsty'; and Isaiah 52: 15, 'He shall sprinkle many nations'; a prediction or promise, which many think refers to the ordinance of baptism, and seems to be particularly fulfilled in the commission to 'disciple all nations, by baptising them'. And again, 'I will sprinkle clean water upon you' (Ezek. 36: 25). And particularly, in the improvement of our baptism, we are said to be 'sprinkled from an evil conscience' (Heb. 10: 22). So that which is signified by the laver of regeneration, is the renewing of the Holy Ghost, which he shed on us (Titus 3: 5–6). The blood of Christ is called 'the blood of sprinkling' (Heb. 12: 24). If immersion is so proper, as some conceive, to represent our being buried with Christ (though to me it seems far-fetched), I am sure doth much more plainly represent the sprinkling of the blood, and the pouring forth of the Spirit of Christ upon the soul; and if one Scripture alludes to one manner of washing, and another to another, it intimates to us, that the mode is in itself different, and that Christians are left to choose that, which, upon other accounts, is most convenient and edifying.

On the whole then it appears, that the dust which has been raised about the mode of baptism, is nothing else but a device of Satan, to perplex ignorant, and to delude unstable souls. I shall say but very little.

The Minister

Concerning the persons by whom baptism is to be administered; concluding, that gospel ministers, and they only, have authority to administer this ordinance; for they only are 'the stewards of the mysteries of God'. To them only the commission is given: 'Go ye and disciple all nations, baptizing them, teaching them to observe' (Matt. 28: 19–20). The same persons who are to teach, by office, are to baptize; and 'no man should take this honour to himself, but he that is called of God'.

The Time

I proceed therefore to consider the time when baptism is to be administered. As to adults, who are baptized upon a personal profession, it is plain, that in Scripture times, it was administered presently, and without delay, upon their profession of Christianity: 'the same day there were added (that is, by baptism) three thousand souls' (Acts 2: 41), the same day that they believed. The eunuch was baptized immediately upon his believing (Acts 8: 38), and Paul, as soon as ever he came to himself, and the scales fell from his eyes, 'arose, and was baptized' (Acts 9: 18). And once more, the jailer was baptized, 'he and all his, straightway' (Acts 16: 33).

This was the method the apostles took: but afterwards the church generally required more time; and deferred the baptism of the adult, till they had long been in the state of catechumens, and given ample testimony of their proficiency in knowledge, and of a blameless conversation. The apostolic constitutions appoint three years for the catechumens to be instructed, yet allowing an admission sooner in case of a manifest maturity: but was not in this an excess of strictness, and making the door of the church straiter than Christ and the apostles made it? And certainly, the practice which afterwards prevailed, of restraining the administration of baptism to certain days, and of deferring it to the point of death, from a notion that sin committed after baptism was unpardonable, are to be imputed only to ignorance and superstition.

FOR INFANTS

When is it to be administered to infants? In Cyprian's time (about the middle of the third century), it seems that there was a controversy about the baptising of infants; not whether they ought to be baptized (that had never been disputed), but concerning the time when; whether on the second or third day, or (as circumcision of old) on the eighth day? For the determination of which, Cyprian, with the advice of sixty-six pastors, wrote a synodical letter, to prove, that it was not necessary to defer it till the eighth day, as the mercy and grace of God are not to be denied to new-born children: and in this, says Austin, he did not make a new decree, but preserved the ancient faith of the church.

As to the time of baptizing infants then, the mean is to be kept between two extremes.

No Needless Delay

It should not be causelessly deferred, as if it were a thing indifferent whether it be done or not. It argues a contempt of the ordinance, and a slight regard to our children's covenant right, to delay administration, perhaps because the feast cannot yet be provided, or such and such a fine friend procured to stand gossip. Thus a solemn and important institution of Christ is often made to truckle to mean and inconsiderable respects. Moses's deferring to circumcise his child had like to have cost him dear.

No Superstitious Hurry

On the other hand, it should not be superstitiously hastened and precipitated. There are many, who are most negligent about it while their children are well, who, if they are sick, and likely to die, will be very solicitous to get it done with all speed; and will call up a minister at midnight rather than fail. But where there has not been a culpable delay, that is, where no convenient opportunity has been let slip, if it please God to visit the child with threatening sickness, I see no reason for thus precipitating the ordinance. Baptism is the appointed door into the church militant, which supposes the child likely to live; not into the church triumphant, which supposes the child dying. The administration of baptism is a solemn thing, and ought to be attended with all the natural circumstances of solemnity: and therefore, to hurry the administration, while the child is dying in the arms of the minister, is by no means agreeable. Besides, that this practice is grounded upon a great mistake, viz. that baptism is absolutely necessary to the salvation of the child. Let people be taught, that baptism does not confer, but recognise their children's covenant-right; and that, where there is no wilful neglect, God accepts the will for the deed, and will not lay to the charge of us, or ours, the want of that, which, by his own wise providence we were prevented having in a regular way, and with due solemnity; and they will not be so eager to precipitate the administration.

THE PLACE

It will be proper to say a little concerning the place where baptism is to be administered.

In the first ages of the church, it was usual to baptize anywhere, where there was water, but always (as Dr Cave observes) as near as might be to the place of their public assemblies; for it was seldom done without the presence of the congregation. In process of time, they erected baptisteria (fonts we call them) near the church doors, to signify that baptism is the door of admission into the church.

All that I have to observe upon this head is that it is most fitting and convenient that the ordinance of baptism be administered publicly, in the face of the congregation. And this is the judgment of the best ordered churches, even of those in which baptism is most commonly administered in private; in which it is rather tolerated as a corruption, than countenanced by the constitution. The church of England allows not of private baptism, except in cases of necessity; and even then, appoints the public recognition and ratification of it. The church of Scotland, by a late act of the General Assembly, has strictly forbidden the administration of either of the sacraments in private. And the reformed church in France likewise appoints that baptism should be administered in the presence of the congregation.

And there are good reasons why it should be performed publicly: for it is an act of solemn religious worship, and therefore should be attended with all due circumstances of solemnity; and the more public the more solemn. Huddling it up in a corner is in no way agreeable to the state and grandeur of the ordinance; it should be performed in a 'holy convocation'.

It is the initiating ordinance; the matriculation of visible church members; and therefore ought to be public, that the congregation may be witnesses for the church membership of the person baptized, and against his apostasy. In covenanting with God, as in other contracts, it is good, for the strengthening of the obligation, to have witnesses. Thus Joshua 24: 22, 'You are witnesses gainst yourselves', nay, verse 27, 'this stone shall be a witness to you'.

It is an edifying ordinance. It is of great use to all, to be frequently reminded of their original corruption, and of their baptismal covenant; which is best done by the public administration of this ordinance: and we should consult, not only what makes for peace, but what makes for edification: and therefore ministers ought not to refuse their hearers the benefit they might derive from being spectators of this solemnity. The sacred mysteries of God covet not obscurity, like the profane mysteries of the pagan religion. Truth seeks no corners. Though this institution has not any gaudy attire to recommend it, yet it has so much true native beauty and excellency, that it needs not decline a public administration.

I would not indeed drive this point further than it will fairly go. I do not question but that in many cases, baptism may be administered in private. The jailer was baptized in his own house. And how far ministers should herein comply with the inclinations of their people, I cannot say. Paul preached 'privately to them who were of reputation'; and, perhaps, we may from thence take a direction in this case. Some may be led to public baptism by degrees, who would not be driven to it all at once. I see no reason indeed why any Christians should be ashamed of their profession: it is a culpable bashfulness when we blush to own our covenant relation to God, for ourselves, and for our seed.

The public administration of baptism would be of good use to establish people in the truth concerning it, and would therefore help us to keep our ground against those who oppose it. Many waver about infant baptism, because they were never duly affected by it; as they might have been by the solemn administration of it in public. On all these accounts, I recommend baptizing in public as very convenient, though I would not have it imposed as absolutely necessary.

THE MANNER

I shall just mention the rites and ceremonies attending the administration of baptism: and as to these, Dr Cave well observes, that in the apostolic age baptism was administered with great plainness and simplicity; and the apostles' age was certainly the best and purest age of the church. Strict conformity to the Scripture rule, without the superadded inventions of men, is the true beauty of Christian ordinances.

SANCTIFIED BY WORD AND PRAYER

Everything is sanctified by the word and prayer (1 Tim. 4: 5), and particularly sacraments. The word is our warrant for what we do; and therefore should be read, as our commission, 'Go ye and disciple all nations, baptizing them.' The nature of the ordinance should be opened, and of the covenant of which it is the seal, and care taken to fix a right notion of the institution, and to raise the affections of the congregation.

Prayer must accompany the word: for it is not from any virtue in the administration, or in him who administers, that sacraments become effectual means of salvation, but only by the blessing of Christ; which blessing is to be sought by prayer. Anciently, says Dr Cave, all the formality of baptism was a short prayer, and repeating the words of the institution: and it appears, that for several ages, this baptismal prayer was not any set prescribed form, but, as Justin Martyr says of their other prayers, according to the minister's ability.

This prayer ought to be suited to the ordinance: acknowledging the goodness of God to us in making a new covenant, when the first covenant was so irreparably broken, and in appointing sacraments to be the seals of that covenant, 'that by two immutable things, in which it is impossible for God to lie, we might have strong consolation'; giving his thanks, that the covenant of grace is herein so well ordered, that not only we, but our seed, are taken into it; dedicating the child to God accordingly; begging that he would honour his own ordinance with his presence, and sanctify and bless it to the child; that the washing of the child with water, in the names of the Father, Son, and Holy Ghost, may effectually signify, and seal, his ingrafting into Christ; and that he may thereby partake of the privileges of the new covenant, and be engaged to be the Lord's.

ACCOMPANIED BY THE PARENTS' PROFESSION OF FAITH

For as much as it is the parents' profession of faith in Christ, and obedience to him, that entitles the child to baptism, according to the tenor of the new covenant, it is requisite that at least one of the parents so publicly make that profession, in the presence of the congregation, at the demand of the minister; and likewise declare a desire to have the child brought, by baptism, into the bond of the gospel covenant; and a full purpose and resolution to bring it up (if spared in life) in the nurture and admonition of the Lord; that is, as a Christian. But if the parents are dead, or cannot possibly be present, the minister may doubtless go upon the known profession of the parents, or the proof of it, by the attestation of those who knew them. Only (as was observed before) in this case it is requisite that the children's guardians, or next relations of those who have the care of them, do undertake for their pious and Christian education.

IN THE WORDS OF THE LORD JESUS

Our Master has prescribed the words of dedication, 'I baptize thee in the name of the Father, and of the Son, and of the Holy Ghost': this therefore should be constantly and devoutly pronounced, as the water is applied; and immediately before or after the doing of this, it may not be amiss to declare, that, according to the institution and command of our Lord Jesus Christ, 'I do admit this child as a visible church member.'

After the administration, it is proper that the minister should be a remembrance to the parents of their duty in bringing up their child as a Christian. The people likewise have need, upon such occasions, to be directed in, and excited to, the practical improvement of their own baptism. After which, it is fit to conclude with suitable prayers and praises.

Before we close this chapter, it will be proper just to mention a few appendages to the administration of baptism.

NAMING THE CHILD. And this is a laudable custom, against which I know of no objection. It was borrowed from the Jewish custom of naming children at their circumcision; and as baptism is the enrolment of the person baptized among professing Christians, it is not improper then to fix the name (or *notamen*); though too many ignorant people consider the giving of the name as the main matter; against which they should therefore be cautioned.

GODFATHERS AND GODMOTHERS. And concerning these we have spoken before, and showed how unreasonable and unscriptural a practice it is, to deprive the parents the right of dedicating their own children, to devolve it upon those who have no part or lot in them. Early footsteps indeed there are of this sponsorship in the primitive times, but quite of another nature.

RITES AND CEREMONIES which have been used in the administration of this ordinance.

And in sacraments, where there is appointed something of an outward sign, the inventions of men have been too fruitful of additions: for which they have pleaded a great deal of decency and significancy; while the ordinance itself has been thereby miserably obscured and corrupted. I shall only mention the most considerable of those used very anciently in the church (of those now practised in the church of Rome, see the ritual):

1. A kind of exorcism and insufflation; which signified the expelling of the evil spirit, and the breathing of the good spirit.
2. An unction, or anointing the person baptized upon the breast, and between the shoulders; which they fancied very proper to signify the sanctification of the heart to receive the law of God, and the preparation of the shoulders to bear the yoke of Christ; and that Christians were 'kings and priests unto God'.
3. Dr Cave thinks, that with this unction they used the sign of the cross, made upon the forehead; which they did to show that they were not to be ashamed of the cross of Christ.
4. Trine immersion, or putting the person baptized three times under water, once at the mention of each of the persons of the Trinity, to signify their distinct dedication to each.
5. After a second anointing, when the person was taken out of the water, they put on him a white garment, to signify that 'those who were baptized into Christ, had put on Christ', and were to 'walk with him in white'.

And, besides all these, many countries had particular customs of their own. But setting aside the word, and prayer, and the circumstances of natural decency, I see no need of any of these additions. The spouse of Christ looks most glorious in her native beauty, and needs not the paint and tawdry attire of a harlot. Purity is the true glory of gospel ordinances; and all these appendages, instead of adorning the institutions of Christ, have really deformed and injured them. And those who plead for the continuance of some of these ceremonies, open a door for the admission of the rest. The chrism, or anointing with oil, is as significant, and as ancient, and has as much foundation in Scripture, as the sign of the cross; and if we must be governed so much by the practice of antiquity, while the other is retained, why must this be exploded? Or rather, when this is so decently laid aside, why should the other be so strictly imposed; especially when it is become such a stone of stumbling, and such a rock of offence?

6

THE PRACTICAL IMPROVEMENT
OF OUR OWN BAPTISM

It has been the accursed policy of the great enemy of souls, by raising disputes about Christ's truths and ordinances, to rob the church of the benefit of those truths and ordinances. While the field lies in suit, what should be spent in improving the ground, is thrown away in maintaining the suit, and the land lies fallow. There would not be so much quarrelling about infant baptism, if there were but more care to make that practical improvement of it which is required. It is owing to a carnal heart, that the benefit of it is not obtained, and then the thing itself is disputed. In this circle many a poor soul has been made giddy: infant baptism is questioned, because it is not improved; and then it is not improved, because it is questioned. 'If any man' set himself seriously to 'do his will' in this matter, by diligent and conscientious improvement of his baptism, 'he shall know of the doctrine, whether it be of God, or whether we speak of ourselves' (John 7: 17). We should labour to find, by experience, the moral influence of our baptism, both upon our comfort and our holiness.

When I say we must improve our baptism, I mean, must carry it in everything as a baptized people; and our whole conversation must be under the influence of our baptism. Would you have all our Christian duty in one word, it is, to behave in every respect as those who are baptized; that is, 'to have our conversation as becomes the gospel of Jesus Christ' (Phil. 1: 27).

In opening this, I shall endeavour:

1. To show that it is our great concern to improve our baptism.
2. To give some general rules for the improvement of our baptism.
3. To point out some particular instances in which we should improve our baptism.

LIVE AS BAPTIZED PEOPLE

It is the great concern of those who are by baptism admitted members of the visible church, practically to improve their baptism, and to live accordingly.

In dealing with many people, it is much easier to direct them than to persuade them; to inform them what is to be done, than to prevail with them to do it. And of the many who lie under the baptismal vow, how few are there who are at all sensible of the engagement! As if their baptism were only the giving of them a name. The profane Lucian said, in derision of his baptism, that he got nothing by it but the change of his name: and multitudes there are who get no more.

The improvement of our baptism is very much our concern, if we have any regard to honour, honesty, or interest.

HONOUR YOUR CHRISTIAN NAME

By our baptism, we assume the Christian name; and is it not a shame to profess one thing, and practise another? To own the name, and deny the thing? 'Either change your name, or your manners,' was the reprimand which the great Alexander gave to his namesake, who was a coward. By baptism we engaged ourselves to be the Lord's; and bound ourselves, by the strongest ties imaginable, against all sin, and to all duty; and is it not a shame to say and unsay? The great ones of the earth, whose names are raised a degree or two above their neighbours, stand much upon the punctilios of their honour, and scorn to do anything base, to disparage their families, or forfeit their ensigns of honour, or incur the disgrace of a broken sword, or a reversed escutcheon; and shall not one who professes himself a citizen of the New Jerusalem, have so much of a generous and noble sense of true honour, as to walk worthy of the vocation wherewith he is called, and the dignity to which he is advanced? 'It is not for kings, O Lemuel, it is not for kings to drink wine,' (Prov. 31: 4) was part of the lesson that Solomon's mother taught him. Brutal excesses profane a crown, and defile the horn in the dust: and are not Christians advanced to be kings and priests? It is not then for Christians, who are baptized, it is not for Christians, who wear so honourable a name, to walk as other Gentiles walk. We shame ourselves before God and the world, if we, who by baptism are made members of that family which is 'named of Jesus Christ' (Eph. 3: 14, 15) its illustrious head, do that which is unbecoming to the family.

Be as Good as Your Word

An honest man will be as good as his word. Having sworn, we must perform it; and having given up our names, we must not withdraw them. It is the character of a citizen of Zion, that 'he sweareth to his own hurt, and changeth not'; much less when be sweareth so much to his own good.

Jephthah argues himself into a very hard piece of self-denial from this topic, 'I have opened my mouth unto the Lord, and cannot go back' (Judg. 11: 35); 'How shall we?' (Rom. 6: 2).

God Is Not Mocked

Be not deceived, God is not mocked. He will not be put off with shows and shadows. Baptism not improved, is no baptism, any more than the carcass is the man. Nominal Christianity is but real hypocrisy; the form without the power; the name without the thing. 'He is not a Jew (nor he a Christian) that is one outwardly; neither is that circumcision (nor that baptism) which is outward in the flesh' (Rom. 2: 25, 28–9). The gospel is preached, either 'for a witness to us' (Matt. 24: 14) or (if that witness be not received) 'for a witness against us' (Mark 13: 9); and so our baptism, instead of being a witness to us, if we neglect it, will be a witness against us. In the day of vengeance, Judah and Israel, become uncircumcised in heart, are set abreast with the rest of the uncurcumcised nations (Jer. 9: 25–6). Our baptism, if it be not improved, will be so far from saving us, that it will aggravate our condemnation. It is not 'the putting away the filth of the flesh that saves us,' but 'the answer of a good conscience towards God'; that is, our conformity to our baptismal engagements. In early times, it was usual, in some churches, to lay up the white garment of the baptized, that it might be produced as an evidence against them if they violated or denied that faith which they had owned in baptism.

Baptism is a trust, to which we must be faithful. The profit of baptism is answerable to the profit of circumcision. 'To them were committed the oracles of God' (Rom. 3: 2); we are entrusted with the lively oracles; the sacred laws of the kingdom of heaven; which if we misuse by an unsuitable conversation, we betray a trust.

Baptism is a talent, which must be traded with, and accounted for. It is a price put into the hand to get wisdom; and with this, as with other talents, the charge is, 'Occupy till I come.' By working upon our souls a sense of the obligations we are laid under by our baptism, we put this talent into the bank, and if we were not wanting to ourselves, might receive from it the blessed usury of a great deal of comfort and holiness. I refer to Matthew 25: 27.

Baptism is a privilege, which must be improved. It takes us into the visible church; makes us denizens of that ancient and honourable corporation; and entitles us to its external privileges; 'the adoption, and the glory, and the covenants, and the giving of the law, and the service of God, and the promises' (Rom. 9: 4), privileges capable of a great improvement.

Baptism is a profession, which must be lived up to. By baptism we profess relation to Christ, as scholars to our teacher, servants to our master, soldiers to our captain, subjects to our sovereign;

all which relations call for duty which must be done. The law of nature, and the common sense of mankind, require that we be and do according to our profession; and not profess one thing and practise another.

Baptism is an obligation, which must be performed. It is the seal of a bond. We are in bonds to God; penal bonds, to be the Lord's; which if we break, we expose ourselves to the penalty.

Baptism is an oath, which must be made good. A sacrament is a military oath; an oath of allegiance, to be true and faithful to the Lord Jesus; and having sworn, we must perform it (Ps. 119: 106). An oath is a tie upon conscience: and this is an oath, to which God is not only a witness (as to every oath), but a party principally concerned: for to him are we sworn.

So then, if we do not make use of our baptism, we falsify a trust, we bury a talent, we abuse a privilege, we contradict a profession, we break a sacred bond in sunder, despise an oath, and cast away from us the cords of an everlasting covenant.

How to Improve Our Baptism

I am to give some general rules for the improvement of our baptism.

Recognise That it Cannot Be Annulled

We must rightly apprehend the perpetual obligation of our baptismal covenant. That time does not wear out the strength of it: though it was administered long ago, yet (being a speciality, a bond sealed) it binds us firmly as if we had been baptized but yesterday. God was highly provoked by the breach of a covenant made with the Gibeonites many ages before (2 Sam. 21: 2).

Baptism is an oath of allegiance, from which no power on earth can absolve us. It is a 'perpetual covenant, never to be forgotten' (Jer. 50: 5). God will not forget it, and we must not forget it: the former may comfort us, the latter quicken us. Compare two parallel scriptures, 'Be ye mindful always of his covenant, the word which he commanded to a thousand generations' (1 Chr. 16: 15); borrowed from Psalm 105: 8, but there it is, 'He hath remembered his covenant for ever, the word which he commanded to a thousand generations.' Both put together, speak the perpetuity of the covenant. God remembers it forever, and we must be always mindful of it. It is a covenant of salt (2 Chr. 13: 5), an incorruptible, inviolable covenant, that is not, must not, cannot be disannulled. God is said to remember his covenant, when he brought his first-begotten into the world; it was to perform the oath (Luke 1: 72–3), though that oath was sworn many ages before. So what we do in religion we should do with a regard to our baptismal oath; in remembrance of the holy covenant, and in compliance with the purport and design of it. Upon some special occasions, God remembers his covenant; as when, after a controversy, he returns in ways of mercy (Lev. 26: 42). So upon special occasions, of trouble or temptation, or after we have fallen into sin, we should remember the covenant; which still stands in full force, power, and virtue. The superadding of repeated engagements to the same purpose, at the Lord's table, or upon other occasions, does not supersede, but strengthen and confirm, that first and great engagement; and the design of those renewed covenantings, is to revive the sense of that early bond. God remembers 'the kindness of our youth, and the love of our espousals' (Jer. 2: 2); and we must not forget the covenant of our youth, and the vow of our espousals.

RENEW THE BAPTISMAL COVENANT

It is very good, when we grow up to years of understanding, solemnly to renew our baptismal covenant; and to make that our own act and deed, which our parents, as the trustees of our wills, to act for our good (appointed so by God and nature) then did for us. This will help to make the engagement more sensible, and consequently give it a greater and stronger influence.

This should be done (I think) by a solemn personal profession of assent to the gospel revelation, and consent to the gospel covenant; with a serious promise of a suitable and agreeable conversation: and this to be approved by the minister, or such others as are fit to judge of the seriousness of it. This is to be looked upon as a transition from the state of infant church membership, to that of adult; and as a solemn investiture in the privileges of the adult: which (according to the practice of the primitive church) may not unfitly be done by the imposition of hands. This is what is commonly called confirmation; the revival of which, and its restoration to its original use, Mr Baxter, in his book on that subject, learnedly and convincingly pleads for. The corruptions and abuses of an ordinance are no reasons for its total abolition. But this is one of those things which are much desired, but little practised; for, in the usual administration of confirmation by the bishops, so little is done to answer the intention (and how should it be otherwise, when the confirmation of so many thousands is put into the hands of one man?) that it is too apparent, that the substance is lost in the shadow, and the thing in the name. While every deacon has authority to administer the great ordinance of baptism, and is thought fit to judge of the capable subjects of it, it is a riddle to me, why the subordinate constitution of confirmation should be so strictly appropriated to bishops. The recognition of the baptismal covenant, and the profession of faith, repentance, and a holy life, are fittest to be made in the presence of those to whom the right hand of fellowship is to be given in settled stated communion, or their representatives: and the investiture were most properly received from that pastor, who is to administer other ordinances, and through whose hands those external privileges of adult church membership are to be communicated.

Where this is neglected, or negligently performed by the congregation, it is yet the duty of everyone to do it, as far as possible, for himself in private; in the most solemn manner, as in the presence of God: the more expressly, the better; and it may add some strength to the engagement, to 'Subscribe with the hand unto the Lord' (Isa. 44: 5).

Our law requires, that he who is (*subditus natus*) born within the king's allegiance, and consequently to all intents and purposes the king's subject, shall, when he is of the age of twelve years, take an oath of allegiance, and promise that to which he was bound before, viz. to be true and faithful to the king (Co. Inst i. 68. b. 172. b.), and this oath to be taken among the neighbours in the leet, or in the sheriff's town. I would compare the confirmation I am pleading for to this. It is the solemn profession of that allegiance which was before due to Christ, and an advancement to a higher rank in his kingdom.

The sooner this recognition is made, the better. Youth is quickly capable of impressions; and the more early the impressions are, usually they are the more deep and durable.

RIGHTLY UNDERSTAND BAPTISM

We must rightly understand the nature of the ordinance, and acquaint ourselves with it.

It is a seal of the covenant of grace: we should therefore know the promises and privileges which God seals to us, and the conditions which we seal back to him. How many baptized persons are there, who are altogether strangers to the covenants of promise! Who look upon baptism only as a thing of course; nothing more than the custom of the country! No wonder they do not improve that which they do not understand. Baptism being the badge of our profession, to understand that, is to understand our holy religion; the nature, duties, privileges, and designs of it; to all of which our baptism does some way or other refer. It is sad to consider what ignorance of these reigns, even in the Christian world; and how many are little better than baptized heathens.

The apostle Paul several times presses holiness and sanctification, from the consideration of the design and tendency of our baptism. Let us examine two or three particular passages, and make some improvement of them.

Baptized into Christ's Death

'Know ye not, that so many of us as were baptized into Jesus Christ were baptized into his death?' (Rom. 6: 3). This he urges as a known confessed truth. The nature of our baptism, and the engagement it lays upon us, is a thing of which it is a shame for Christians to be ignorant. As if a soldier should not know the meaning of his being enlisted. We were baptized 'into Jesus Christ' as 'unto Moses' (1 Cor. 10: 2).

But how are we baptized into the death of Jesus Christ? I answer, we may be said to be baptized into Christ's death, upon a threefold account.

BAPTISM IS A PROFESSING ORDINANCE; a sign and token of our Christianity. By and in baptism we profess to believe the death of Christ as a fact. It is one of the main hinges upon which the door of salvation turns, one great article of our creed, that he was crucified and dead. We profess to believe (and it is no small matter to believe it) that he should die. It was not possible that he should be held by the pains of death; how then was it possible that he should be seized, and taken by them? It implies the belief of his incarnation; for if he had not been man, he could not have died. And that he did die; was willing to make his soul an offering for sin. And certainly, that the Lord of life should die for the children of death, the offended Prince for the unnatural rebel, the just for the unjust, is such a mystery, as requires a great faith to receive: which we do in baptism accordingly profess. And there is no need of the sign of the cross in token of that profession; the instituted ordinance is sufficiently expressive of our being baptized into Christ's death, without the invented ceremony.

We profess to depend upon the death of Christ as our righteousness. In baptism we profess our expectation to be saved by the blood of a crucified Jesus; and to hope for heaven, in, and by, that new and living way, which is laid open for us through the veil of his flesh. We entertain the gospel revelation concerning Christ's death, not only as a 'faithful saying', but as 'worthy of all acceptation'. We profess an approbation of, and a complacency in, the method which infinite wisdom took, of saving a guilty world, by the cross of Christ. It was the cross of Christ which was 'to the Jews a stumbling-block, and to the Greeks foolishness' (1 Cor. 1: 23), and therefore an owning of that, is justly made so material a point in Christianity.

BAPTISM IS A RECEIVING ORDINANCE. We are baptized into Christ's death; that is, God does in that ordinance seal, confirm, and make over to us, all the benefits of the death of Christ. All our privileges, both those of our way, and those of our home, are the fruits of his cross; the purchase of his blood; and in baptism are conferred upon us, on the terms of the gospel: so that if we fulfil the condition, we may expect the privileges; pardon of sin, access with boldness to a throne of grace, the gift of the Holy Ghost, and the heavenly inheritance.

BAPTISM IS AN ENGAGING ORDINANCE. We are baptized into Christ's death. That is to say, we are obliged by our baptism to comply with the design of his death; and this in gratitude for the privileges purchased by it. Christ died 'to save us from sin' (Matt. 1: 21), 'to redeem us from all iniquity' (Titus 2: 14) and 'from our vain conversation' (1 Pet. 1: 15); the intention of his death was not only to justify, but to sanctify (Eph. 5: 25–6); now, by baptism, we oblige ourselves to join in with this design of Christ; to set ourselves against that which he died to kill, and that is sin, and to press after that which he died to advance, and that is holiness.

We are obliged to conform to the pattern of his death. Christ's dying for sin was intended to be the pattern of our dying to sin: so the apostle explains it in the following words, 'We are planted together in the likeness' (Rom. 6: 5); it notes not merely a similitude, but a conformity; and that procured, and wrought, by the virtue and efficacy of Christ's death. Hence the mortifying of sin is called, crucifying it (Gal. 5: 24); a slow but a sure death; and we are said to be 'crucified with Christ' (Gal. 2: 20) because of the influence which his death has upon the mortification of sin. Christ rose to die no more, rose and left his grave-clothes behind him; that is the pattern of our living to righteousness, as his death is the pattern of our dying to sin: see both together, 'the power of his resurrection, and the fellowship of his sufferings' (Phil. 3: 10). We should from hence take instruction how to improve our baptism: 'as we have received Christ, so we must walk in him'. We have received Christ crucified, and so we must walk in him: being 'baptized into his death', we must 'bear about with us continually the dying of the Lord Jesus' (2 Cor. 4: 10). If ministers must preach, people must live, as those who know nothing but 'Jesus Christ, and him crucified'. Think for what end Christ died, and you were baptized into his death; and use it as an aggravation of sin, as an answer to temptation, and as an assistant to faith; use it for the crucifying of corruption, for the constraining of you to holiness, and for your comfort in all your sorrows.

Buried with Christ

Again, that of the apostle in the next words, and Colossians 2: 12, are to the same purpose: 'We are buried with him by baptism.' In which, whether there be an allusion to the custom of dipping or plunging, in baptism, is not at all material (if there be, it is but an allusion); the meaning is plainly this: that by our baptism we are obliged to conform to the burial and resurrection of Christ, in our sanctification; dying to sin, and living to righteousness; putting off the old man, and putting on the new man.

INGRAFTED INTO CHRIST. We are by baptism buried with Christ, as baptism signifies and seals our ingrafting into Christ, and our union with him. We are, in Christ our head, buried by baptism, and raised again; he the first-fruits, and we the lump. Our sins are said to have been 'laid upon Christ', and he to have 'borne them in his own body' (1 Pet. 2: 24); so that when he was buried, our sins were put into the same grave, and buried with him. Therefore they are not imputed to us, being dead and buried with Christ. Thus was sin, by Christ's sacrifice, condemned (Rom. 8: 3). But he rose again, not 'in the likeness of sinful flesh'; he did not bear our sins in his glorified body. Now baptism signifies, and seals, our fellowship with Christ, in his sufferings and resurrection; our freedom from the condemning and commanding power of sin. He is our second Adam, the common father, agent, root, and representative of all true believers. Baptism, therefore, being the sign of our union with him, we are said therein to die, and be buried, and rise again, with Christ.

ENGAGED TO BE THE LORD'S. As baptism signifies and seals our engagement to be the Lord's, we are, by our baptismal covenant, obliged to mortify sin, and in baptism receive the promise of the Holy Ghost for that purpose. 'We are buried by baptism'; that is, we are, in profession, and obligation, quite separated and cut off from sin; as those who are not only dead, but buried, are quite parted from the living, and have no more any intercourse, correspondence, or fellowship, with them. We are likewise 'risen again' to another sort of life; a divine and heavenly life. Not as the widow's son and Lazarus were raised, to live just such a life as they lived before; but as Christ was raised, who, though he continued on earth forty days after his resurrection, did not show himself openly, nor converse with this world as he had done; but his life was altogether heavenly, and no more in the world: thus, our baptism, obliging us to die to sin, and live to righteousness; we may be said therein to be buried and risen with Jesus Christ.

A Christian, therefore, who is by baptism buried with Christ, and yet lives in sin, is like a walking ghost; or the frightful motion of a dead body. We should often remember that we are buried, that is, cut off from a life of sin, and risen, that is, entered upon a life of holiness. We should therefore see to it (says the excellent Davenant) that what is done once sacramentally, in baptism, should be always done really, in life.

Put on Christ

I shall only produce one passage more: 'As many of you as have been baptized into Christ, have put on Christ' (Gal. 3: 27). The design of the apostle's discourse there, is to bring them nearer, and bind them faster, to Jesus Christ. The two great rivals to Christ were, the works of sin, and the works of the law: the former, his rival as the Lord their Ruler; the latter, as the Lord their Righteousness. From both these, he is here industriously dissuading them; and he argues from their baptism, 'being baptized into Christ, ye have put on Christ'; ye have done it; that is, you have professed to do it, and consequently are obliged to do it. 'Put on Christ.'

THE RIGHTEOUSNESS OF CHRIST FOR JUSTIFICATION. Put it on, as Jacob put on the garments of his elder brother, when he came for the blessing; as the high priest put on the appointed robes, when he went in to make atonement.

To put on the righteousness of Christ is to consent to it; willing and glad to be saved by that righteousness, which he, by dying, has brought in. This is to 'receive the atonement' (Rom. 5: 11). The garment is already prepared; made up of Christ's merits, dyed with his blood: glorious apparel! It is our consent that puts it on. This is called, 'buying the white raiment' (Rev. 3: 18). Upon our believing submission to the methods of gospel grace, and entertaining that faithful saying as worthy of all acceptation, Jesus Christ is made of God unto us righteousness (1 Cor. 1: 30), and we are made the righteousness of God in him (2 Cor. 5: 21).

To put on the righteousness of Christ is to confide in it. We must be putting it on every day, in all our approaches to God, making mention of Christ's 'righteousness, even of that only' (Ps. 71: 16); abiding by it as our plea; casting anchor there; laying the stress of our souls upon this foundation. The most of men are putting on other things; some righteousness of their own; at best, 'a covering too narrow to wrap themselves in' (Isa. 28: 20); but we who are baptized into Christ, profess to put on Christ; that Sun with which the church is 'clothed' (Rev. 12: 1); that 'best robe' (Luke 15: 22); that 'broidered work' (Ezek. 16: 10).

THE SPIRIT AND GRACE OF CHRIST, FOR SANCTIFICATION. Grace is often compared to clothing. This is that 'fine linen', clean and white (Rev. 19: 8). With this we must be clothed, as the earth with grass and corn; which are not only adherent, but inherent. Thus we must 'put on charity' (Col. 3: 14), 'mercies' (Col. 3: 12), 'humility' (1 Pet. 5: 5), and in general, 'the new man' (Eph. 4: 24); the same with putting on Christ (Rom. 13: 14; cf. v. 13). To put on the grace of Christ, is to get the habit of it planted in our souls, and the acts of it quickened and invigorated: to have grace, and to use grace. To have the disposition, and not to exercise it, is like having clothes lying by us, and not wearing them.

In baptism we have put on Christ; that is, have professed and promised it. Whether the custom of putting a white garment upon the person baptized, was so ancient, as that we may suppose an allusion to that, is not material; I suppose rather, that this custom might, in after ages, take rise from this Scripture.

Christ is here compared to clothing; for clothes are for decency. Sin made us naked, Christ covers our shame (Gen. 3: 7). Again, clothes are for distinction (Rev. 3: 18). Christians are distinguished from other men by their putting on Christ. Hereby it is known what country they belong to; grace is their livery, their badge, their cognizance. Further, clothes are for dignity. And this is honourable clothing; recommends us to God (which no other clothing doth); it is clothing of 'wrought gold' (Ps. 45: 13); in the sight of God of great price. And once more, clothes are for defence. We must put on Christ, not only as attire, but as armour; nothing else will keep us safe from the 'wind and the tempest' (Isa. 32: 2); and 'the fiery darts of the wicked one' (Eph. 6: 16).

Having thus put on Christ in profession, let us do it in truth and sincerity; having begun to put him on, let us be doing it daily more and more; for that is to improve our baptism.

Baptism does not work as a spell, or charm, or by any physical influence; but it acts as a motive, or argument, by moral agency; and we then make use of our baptism, when we improve that argument with ourselves, for our quickening, caution, and encouragement, as there is occasion. That which shakes many in the doctrine of infant baptism, is the uselessness (as they apprehend) of the administration, and the mighty advantages which they fancy in adult baptism. But before they conclude thus, they would do well to answer Dr Ford's proof of this truth, 'That there is much more advantage to be made, in order to sanctification, consolation, and several other ways, of the doctrine and practice of infant baptism, than of that doctrine and practice which limits baptism to personal profession at years of discretion.' And it is to be feared, that the neglect of the improvement of infant baptism hath very much conduced to the opposition that has been made to it.

Baptism is a good motive to be improved by ministers, in preaching to their people. By this we have some hold of them. It is especially to be improved in dealing with young people. We have this to say to them, that being baptized, they are of the fold; lambs of the flock which we are to feed. We have this to say, against their youthful lusts, and for their early piety, that they are baptized, and are thereby laid under special obligations to be the Lord's. This is to be much insisted upon in training up children in the way wherein they should go. It is improvable, in our dealing with them, about their first conversation and return to God, and their after growth and progress in holiness. In treating with souls, we generally find it easier to direct than to persuade, to tell people what they should do than to prevail with them to do it; we have need to choose out words to reason with them: therefore those are poor friends to the success of the word, who rob us of that argument which infant baptism puts into our hands.

Baptism is a good motive to be improved by people in preaching to themselves. The apostle says 'Exhort yourselves' (Heb. 3: 13), reason the case with yourselves, press things upon your own hearts; and, among the rest, we should press upon ourselves the consideration of our infant baptism, and be ever mindful of the covenant, the word which he commanded to a thousand generations.

MAKING GOOD USE OF BAPTISM

To mention some particular instances wherein it is our duty to improve our baptism: and under each, I shall endeavour to urge the consideration of our baptism, especially as administered in infancy.

IN THE FIGHT AGAINST TEMPTATION AND SIN

Baptism, especially infant baptism, is to be improved, as a restraint from all manner of sin. While we are in an ensnaring world, we lie continually exposed to temptation. A malicious spirit lays the plot, and a deceitful heart closes in with it; and thus the poor soul is drawn away and enticed. These temptations are to be opposed, and resisted; all the powers of the soul must be summoned in to the resistance; and the consideration of our baptism, especially our infant baptism, would very much engage us to that resistance, and make it both vigorous and victorious. I say the consideration of our baptism when we are tempted to be proud, or passionate, or intemperate, or unjust, or the like; then to remember that we were baptized, would be of excellent use, to silence and repel the temptation.

Sin Contradicts Our Profession

In baptism, we were solemnly admitted as visible church members, and so took upon us the profession of Christ's holy and excellent religion; by wilful sin we give the lie to that profession, and run counter to it. We then put on Christ; and shall we put on our filthy rags again? Is this to walk as becomes the gospel? Is this to adorn the doctrine of God our Saviour, and to answer that worthy name by which we are called? By baptism, we profess ourselves 'dead to sin'; cut off, and separated, from that life; and 'how then shall we live any longer therein?' (Rom. 6: 2). 'How shall we?' How can we for shame, so far contradict our profession, and walk contrary to the vocation wherewith we are called?

Sin Is a Reproach to Our Family

In baptism, we were admitted into that family which is 'named from Christ' (Eph. 3: 15); its illustrious head; taken to be his servants; nay (because the servant abides not in the house for ever), we have received the 'adoption of sons'; we are enlisted under Christ's banner, and become his soldiers; are entered into his school, and call him Master and Lord; and doth it become those who stand in such relations, to maintain a friendly intercourse with Christ's avowed enemy? How unbecoming is it for those who profess such a friendship for Christ, to have fellowship with the unfruitful works of darkness! 'For what communion is there between Christ and Belial?' 'Holiness becomes God's house' (Ps. 93: 5); and household; his servants, and service: how unbecoming then is unholiness? If, indeed, we had never been put into such relations, it had been another matter: there had been at least not that evil in our sin: but after we have engaged to follow Christ as his servants and soldiers, shall we run our colours, and return to our old master? When we are tempted to sin, let us think we hear Christ saying to us, as to the twelve, 'Will ye also go away?' (John 6: 67); you, my friends, and followers? What thou my son? As Caesar to Brutus. 'Thou, a man mine equal, mine acquaintance?' As the Psalmist (Ps. 55: 13).

Sin Is an Ungrateful Response to Gospel Privileges

Sin is an ill requital of our privileges. They were precious privileges which were sealed to us in baptism; the privileges of the gospel charter, the heavenly corporation; all the inestimable benefits of the covenant of grace; protection from arrests, an interest in the promises, free access to God, and the special tokens of his favour: 'and do we thus requite the Lord?' (Deut. 32: 6). Shall we sin against so much love, preventing love, distinguishing love? Shall we despise such 'riches of grace?' (Rom. 2: 4). The least spark of true generosity would abhor such ingratitude.

Sin Breaches Our Baptismal Engagements

We were then scaled, and bound, to be the Lord's; and shall we be so prodigiously unruly, as to break such sacred bonds in sunder, and cast away such cords of love from us? When a temptation to sin comes, answer it with that of the psalmist, 'Thy vows are upon me, O God!' (Ps. 56: 12); not upon me as a burden, which I am weary of, but upon me as a bond, which I am obliged by. The covenant we were entered into was most reasonable; the engagement just; it was but a confirmation of our former ties: and shall we falsify such engagements? Be not deceived, God is not mocked: therefore vow and pay (Eccles. 5: 4–5).

TO FIGHT THE SOURCE OF CORRUPTION

There is something in baptism, as administered in infancy, the consideration whereof would furnish us with a particular answer to temptation. The argument taken from our baptism, is so far from being less cogent for its infant administration, that it is really more so. Baptism engages us in a quarrel with sin, but infant baptism with the grounds of it, hugely strengthens the engagement.

An Early Quarrel

Infant baptism speaks our engagement in an early quarrel with sin. We were betimes enlisted under Christ's banner; were from the cradle 'buried with him in baptism'; and thereby engaged, that 'sin should not have dominion over us' (Rom. 6: 4, 12). The early date of our covenants should very much strengthen the obligation of them. Shall I love that enemy, and lay it in my bosom, which I did so soon declare war against? When God would stir up himself to show kindness to Israel, he makes mention of his early friendship to them; 'remembers the kindness of their youth' (Jer. 2: 2), his 'love to Israel when a child'. When we would stir up ourselves to strive against sin, we should remember our early quarrel with it, our infant covenants against it. The strongest antipathies are those conceived from infancy; usually not afterwards removable; but taking rise so soon, become rooted in our nature. Such should our antipathy to sin be; and having been so early engaged against it, we should 'early destroy it' (Ps. 101: 8). This is a good argument for children to use against sin; that young as they are, they have long been bound in a bond against sin. We who plead with God 'his loving-kindness of old' (Ps. 25: 6) to us, should plead with ourselves our engagements of old to him. This early engagement against sin should especially curb and cure that vanity, to which childhood and youth are subject. Augustine observes it as a very ill consequence of the careless deferring of children's baptism till they grow up, that in youth the reins were the more let loose.

An Hereditary Quarrel

Infant baptism speaks our engagement in an hereditary quarrel with sin. It is not only a personal quarrel, espoused by ourselves, and no older than our own day, but it is an enmity entailed upon us by our ancestors; a hostility which came to us by descent. When our parents brought us to baptism, they did by us, as Hannibal's father did by him: when be was but a child of nine years old, he made him solemnly swear, with his hand upon the altar, to pursue the Romans with immortal hatred, and to do them all the mischief he could. Which, however justly reckoned inhuman and barbarous, in a quarrel between man and man, is a project truly pious between man and sin: to bequeath a hatred as by legacy. Our godly parents, who found sin such an enemy to themselves, did thereby lay an obligation upon us, to prosecute an eternal war against it, without thought of reconciliation or truce. Let us think then, when we are tempted to sin, was sin my father's enemy as well as my own? Is the quarrel with it of so long a standing, and shall I submit to it? Was the covenant of my ancestors against it, and shall I make a league with it; or ever entertain a good thought of that, which my parents did so much to set me against? Infant baptism implies such a war with sin, as Israel, by divine appointment, was engaged in against Amalek, a war 'from generation to generation' (Exod. 17: 16); and therefore 'no peace with it' (Deut. 25: 19); no pity to be showed it; 'nothing that belongs to it spared' (1 Sam. 15: 3). An hereditary quarrel must needs be inveterate.

A Quarrel with Original Sin

Infant baptism speaks our engagement in a quarrel with original sin; which is the unhappy root and source of all the rest. Baptism at a riper age does indeed bear a testimony against sin, but it gives no particular evidence, as infant baptism does, against original corruption. Baptism tells us, indeed, that we are filthy; but infant baptism tells us that we are polluted from the beginning, 'conceived in sin' (Ps. 51: 5). Baptism in infancy particularly obliges us to lay the axe to the root; that carnal mind, which is enmity against God. It leads us to the spring-head of these polluted streams, and directs as to employ all our care for the drying up of that. Would we see our own faces by nature? They are best seen in the waters of baptism: in them we behold ourselves 'transgressors from the womb' (Isa. 48: 8); and are thereby obliged to employ our forces against that sin that dwells in us; to put off 'the old man, which is corrupt'; to curb the vicious propensity, and 'to crucify the flesh, with its affections and lusts'.

Let us therefore make this use of our baptism, our infant baptism; having in profession put on 'the armour of light, let us put off the works of darkness'. 'My little children, these things write I unto you, that you sin not' (1 John 2: 1).

As a Motivation to Good Works

Baptism, especially infant baptism, is to be improved as an incentive to duty. As we are Christians, we have not only temptations to be resisted, and sins to be avoided, but work to be done; great and necessary work, for God and our souls, and eternity. We were not sent into the world to be idle, or (like leviathan into the deep) to play therein. All the creatures were created to work (as some understand Gen. 2: 3 לַעֲשׂוֹת); much more Christians, who 'are created anew', and that to 'good works' (Eph. 2: 10). We must work the works of him that sent us. Now nothing can more quicken us to that work, than a lively sense of our relation to the Lord Jesus Christ as his servants; 'truly, I am thy servant' (Ps. 116: 16). To maintain that sense, and to excite us in an answerable diligence in our duty, we should frequently consider our baptism; especially our infant baptism.

We Are Christ's Servants

Our baptism was the rite of admission into the relation of servants. In baptism we were taken into our Master's family, and owned as members of it. It was the solemn recognition of our rights, as born in our Master's house. Our Lord Jesus, by that right of investiture, duly administered according to his appointment, did declare, that he took us into the number of his menial servants; and do you think we were taken into the relation for no purpose? Our Master (who was himself so very busy when he took upon him the form of a servant) keeps no servants in his family to be idle; the glorious angels, that attend immediately upon his person, have work to do.

In baptism, we put on our Master's livery: it is the badge of our profession. We have put on Christ; that is, we have done it in profession; are called Christians (a name full both of honour and obligation) from Christ our head. Now, shall we wear our Master's livery, and neglect our Master's work? This livery is our honour; we need not be ashamed of it; let us not, by our slothfulness, be a shame to it.

In baptism we obliged ourselves to do our Master's work. It is a bond upon the soul, a covenant like that of Josiah's: 'to walk after the Lord, and to keep his testimonies' (2 Chr. 34: 31). When we begin to loiter, and spiritual sloth takes off our chariot wheels, let this help to quicken us, that in baptism we took the yoke of Christ upon us, and that we were not yoked to play, but to work.

In baptism we accepted our Master's wages. We had in that ordinance the privileges of the new covenant scaled to us; and we took them as our recompence, and earnests of more. We consented to trust God for a happiness out of sight, as the full reward of all our services, according to the tenor of the new covenant.

Seeing then we have thus signified, and acknowledged, our expectation of 'a kingdom that cannot be moved', shall we not 'serve God with reverence and godly fear'?

He is Our Master

Our baptism, as administered in infancy, does very much strengthen the engagement; and may help to quicken our dullness, and put us forward, when we begin to loiter. Our infant baptism does bespeak our Master to be:

OUR RIGHTFUL MASTER. We are his by the first title, prior to all Satan's claims and presentations; 'truly his servants' (Ps. 116: 16), for we were born in his house. If our engagements to him had been only the result of our own choice, we might have been tempted to think that a recantation would dissolve the obligation; but we are the Lord's by a former dedication: and if afterwards we join ourselves to the citizens of the country, it is our own fault. The first conveyance stands, and cannot be invalidated by a subsequent deed; for there was no clause to reserve a power of revocation.

OUR KIND MASTER. Kind indeed, who would take us into his family, and admit us to the protection, provision, and privileges of his family, when we were incapable of doing him any actual service. Being now grown up, this consideration should quicken us to a double diligence: that we may redeem the time lost when we were children, and make some grateful returns to our generous Master, for the early tokens of his good will. 'When Israel was a child, then I loved him' (Hos. 11: 1); and shall not we then study what we shall render for that love? It was our landlord's kindness then to put our lives into the lease, and we are basely ungrateful if we now refuse to do the services, or are dissatisfied with them.

OUR OLD MASTER. We have been long in his service; from our very infancy: we were born in his service; and shall we now draw back from, or drive on heavily in, his work? Shall we begin to tire now, and lose the things we have obtained? David pleads with God, 'Thou hast taught me from my youth up' (Ps. 71: 17–18); and we should plead it with ourselves. Sober servants love an old service, in which they have been long trained up. Were not our ears bored to the door-post, to serve forever? And shall we fly off from our work now?

OUR FATHER'S MASTER: one whom our fathers served, and recommended to us for a Master. Infant baptism speaks an hereditary relation to God, that comes to us by descent; 'my

God, and my father's God' (Exod. 15: 2). Our fathers found him a good Master, and consigned us over to him, and to his service: shall we then neglect our duty, or be negligent in it? It is Paul's profession: 'So worship I the God of my fathers' (Acts 24: 14). 'Thy own friend, and thy father's friend, forget not'; thy own Master, and thy father's Master, forsake not. The way of religion is the good old way, in which they walked who are gone before us. Idolaters, and evil-doers, are strengthened in their wicked way by this, that it was the way of their fathers. 'We will do as we have done; we and our fathers' (Jer. 44: 17). 'A vain conversation is received by tradition from their fathers' (1 Pet. 1: 18). For which reason it is, that the iniquity of the fathers is visited upon the children. And shall not we be much more confirmed in the ways of God, from the practice and resolution of our fathers; whose covenant was, that not they only, 'but their houses, would serve the Lord'? Though that which is bad is never the better, yet I am sure, that which is good is never the worse, but the more inviting, for its being received from our ancestors. Let us not therefore be weary in well-doing, but always abide, and always abound, in the work of the Lord.

As a Reason to Repent of Sin

Baptism, especially infant baptism, is to be improved by us, as a strong inducement to repent of sin. As we should improve our baptism to prevent our fall; so, when we are fallen, we should improve it to help us up again. Repentance is (as far as possible) the unsaying, and the undoing, of that which we have said and done amiss. It is a retraction. The law of repentance is a remedial law; a plank thrown out after shipwreck: and blessed be God, that the covenant of grace leaves room for repentance: the covenant of works did not.

Baptism Commits Us to Ongoing Repentance

In repentance, we should improve our baptism. And we shall find in it a strong engagement to repent, in our part of the covenant. John's baptism, which made way for Christ's, was 'the baptism of repentance' (Luke 3: 3). The apostles were sent to preach repentance, and to that baptism was annexed; 'Repent, and be baptized' (Acts 2: 38). Our baptism engages us, not only to the first repentance from dead works, but to an after repentance, as there is occasion. Our first washing in the laver of baptism obliges us every day to wash our feet (John 13: 10) from the pollutions we contract. Our covenant was, not to sin; but if we should sin, repent. Impenitency is the most direct falsifying of our baptismal covenant that can be; it is against the prescribed method of cure.

Baptism Speaks of Pardon for the Penitent

We find a sweet encouragement to repent, in God's part of the covenant. In this covenant both parties are engaged, God to us, and we to God. We have obliged ourselves (as in duty bound) to repent; God has been pleased to oblige himself (as in grace and mercy inclined) to forgive upon repentance. So that baptism is a continued seal of our pardon upon repentance: an assurance, that if we be truly sorry for what we have done, and will come and confess it, and do so no more, all shall be well; iniquity shall not be our ruin. 'Repent, and be ye baptized, for the remission of sins' (Acts 2: 38); not for the purchase of remission; that is Christ's work, and was done before, when the 'everlasting righteousness was brought in'; but for the possession and application of it, which are daily needed. 'Let us therefore draw near with boldness, having our hearts sprinkled from an evil conscience, and our bodies washed with pure water' (Heb. 10: 22). Baptismal washing, as it assures us of the pardon of sin upon repentance, purges us from an evil conscience. 'Repent therefore, for the kingdom of heaven is at hand' (Matt. 4: 17); that is, the gospel dispensation, the promise of pardon upon repentance. While the hue and cry is out against the malefactor, he flies, but the proclamation of pardon brings him in. This 'kingdom of God is come nigh unto us'; it was in baptism applied to us in particular, that the encouragement might be past dispute.

Infant Baptism Declares God's Early Kindness

There is much in the consideration of our baptism, as administered in infancy, to strengthen this inducement to repent. Can I do otherwise than melt tears of godly sorrow, when I reflect that I was baptized in infancy!

For if so, then, by sin I have ill requited God's early kindness to me. I have offended my God, and the God of my fathers, who, upon my parents' account, dealt so favourably with me. It is often mentioned, as an aggravation of sin, that it is against the God of our fathers: 'Because they have forsaken the God of their fathers' (2 Chr. 7: 22; 28: 6). God has been kind to my family, to my ancestors before me; how sinful then must my sin needs be, which has put an affront upon such a friend? Besides that I was then taken into covenant with God myself, and owned in a covenant relation. God aggravates the sin of Israel, from the consideration of his early kindness to them (Ezek. 16: 8), especially his early covenant with them. 'Loved when a child, and yet revolting, and dealing treacherously!' (Hos. 11: 1–3). When we were polluted, and exposed, then regarded, pitied, taken up, washed, adorned, taken into covenant, adopted into a good family; and was not that a time of love? Love sealed, love insured, preventing love, unmerited love? What! And yet despise such rich love, spurn at such bowels? 'Do ye thus requite the Lord?' (Deut. 32: 6). 'Is this thy kindness to thy friend?' How should we charge this home upon our souls in our repentance, and blush for our ingratitude! 'Nourished, and brought up, and yet rebelling!' (Isa. 1: 2–3).

By sin I have falsified my early engagements to him. Born in his house, brought up in his family, brought betimes under his law, and yet shaking off the yoke, and bursting the bonds? Did God take me into covenant with himself, when I was a child, and look upon me ever since as a covenanter; and yet, no sooner have I been able to go, than I have gone from him? To speak, than I have spoken to his dishonour? Aggravate sin from this topic; that there hath been in it, not only such base ingratitude, but such horrid perjury. This consideration is especially seasonable, when we are made 'to possess the iniquities of our youth' (Job 13: 26); and are praying with David, 'O remember not those early sins' (Ps. 25: 7). Those who are not baptized till years of discretion, have such considerations to humble them for the sinful vanities of childhood and youth, as they have who were baptized in their infancy. Let this therefore break our hearts for the sins of our youth, that they are violations of our infant covenant; than which how can there be greater disingenuity?

TO SUPPORT OUR FAITH

We are to improve our baptism, especially our infant baptism, as a great support to our faith. Unbelief is the sin that does most easily beset us: there are remainders of it in the best; and it is at the bottom of our many sinful departures from God (Heb. 3: 12). Even those who can say, 'Lord, I believe,' have reason to add, 'help my unbelief' (Mark 9: 24). Now, I say, it would be a special help against unbelief, to consider baptism, especially our infant baptism.

Remember the Covenant of Grace

When we are tempted to distrust God, to question his goodwill, and to think hardly of him, then let us recollect the covenant of grace, and our baptism, the seal thereof.

Consider that by baptism we were admitted into covenant relations. God did then make over himself to us, to be our God; and take us to himself, to be his people; and shall we then ever distrust him? Relation is a great encouragement to dependence. 'My refuge, my fortress, my God', and then follows, 'in him will I trust' (Ps. 91: 2; cf. Ps. 18: 2). As, by baptism, God has hold of us when we depart from him, so, by baptism, we have hold of God when he seems to withdraw from us. It is an excellent support to faith, when we walk in darkness and have no light, that we may stay ourselves upon our God (Isa. 60: 10); ours in covenant; ours, for he has made himself over to us to be our God. Be not dismayed then, for he is your God (Isa. 41: 10). Use this as an anchor of the soul in every storm; and whatever happens, keep hold of your covenant relation to God: even then, when he seems to forsake, yet (as Christ upon the cross) maintain this post against all the assaults of Satan, that he is my God; my God for all this: and happy the people whose God is the Lord.

Consider that by baptism we were interested in the promises of the covenant. To visible church members now, as formerly, pertain the 'covenants, and the promises' (Rom. 9: 4); to which others are strangers (Eph. 2: 12). When the evil heart of unbelief is doubting our immediate interest in the promises, faith may fetch in strength from the remoter interest; 'Although my house be not so with God, yet he hath made with me an everlasting covenant' (2 Sam. 23: 5); and that covenant, 'ordered in all things, and sure'.

In All Generations

There is much to add to the encouragement; and to strengthen this prop, which faith finds in baptism to lean upon. Baptism seals the promise of God's being to me a God, and that is greatly encouraging; but infant baptism increases the encouragement, as it assures me of God's being the God of my fathers, and the God of my infancy.

GOD OF MY FATHERS. Shall I question the kindness of one who is my own friend, and my father's friend? The faithfulness of one, who was in covenant with my fathers, and always true to them? As it is an inducement to me to choose God to be my God, because he was my fathers' God; so having chosen him, it must be very pleasing to reflect upon that hereditary covenant. Nay, when our own interest may be clouded, and eclipsed, it may bring some support and revival to the soul, to think of our fathers' interest. Peter mentions it as a great inducement to his hearers to believe, 'Ye are the children of the covenant which God made with our fathers' (Acts 3: 25). God himself invites us to take hold of this, by fetching his reasons of mercy to his people from the covenant made with their fathers (Lev. 26: 42): 'Then will I remember my covenant with Jacob,' etc. 'The seed of Abraham his friend' (Isa. 41: 8) must not be forsaken, cannot be forgotten. In the great work of our redemption, respect was had 'unto the promise made onto our fathers' (Luke 1: 72–3). Infant baptism, in the parents' right, speaks covenant mercy 'kept for thousands; the word commanded to a thousand generations'; which, if seriously considered, has a great deal in it to encourage faith. The saints have often been kept from sinking by this thought, 'O Lord God of our fathers' (2 Chr. 20: 6); 'Our fathers trusted in thee' (Ps. 22: 4).

GOD OF MY INFANCY. It is a great support to faith, to consider, not only that God is my God, but that he was so betimes. How favourable was he in the admission, to accept of me upon my father's interest! He who took me when I was brought, surely will not cast me off when I come myself, though weak, and trembling, and unworthy. He who called me his own, because I was born in his house, though I was then too little

He who took me when I was brought, surely will not cast me off when I come myself, though weak, and trembling, and unworthy.

to serve him: who then washed me, and clothed me, and entered into covenant with me, surely will not now reject and disown me, though I am still weak, and what I do is next to nothing. Preventing mercies are not only in themselves very obliging, but very encouraging to hope, in reference to further mercy: he who began in ways of love and mercy to me so early, will not now be wanting to me, or backward to do me good. See how David strengthens his faith from hence (Ps. 71: 5, 6) 'Thou art my trust from my youth, by thee have I been holden up from the womb.' Loving-kindnesses, which have been ever of old, must needs be very favourable to faith and hope. God 'remembers the days of old' (Isa. 63: 11), and we should remember those days.

To Encourage Prayer

We should improve our baptism, especially our infant baptism, as a special friend to prayer. God's people are, and should be, a praying people: 'For this shall every one that is godly pray' (Ps. 32: 6). It is a duty to which we are naturally very backward; sinners plead the unprofitableness of it ('What profit shall we have if we pray unto him?'), but sensible souls are convinced, not only of the profit, but of the necessity, of it; not only that there is something to be gained by it, but that really there is no living without it. Prayer is the very breath of the new creature. Now, a due improvement of our baptism would greatly befriend us in this duty.

Baptism Signifies Our Dependence on God

The consideration of our baptism would be of excellent use to bring us to the duty. Baptism did signify and seal our dependence upon God, and our submission to him; both of which are in effect denied, and contradicted, if we live without prayer; either wholly neglect it, or frequently intermit it. 'Restraining prayer' is casting off that fear of God (Job 15: 4) which, in baptism, we assumed. In baptism, we took God for our God: and 'should not a people seek unto their God?' (Isa. 8: 19). Natural light teaches us to attend upon, with our prayers, that Being whom we call and own as a God. Baptism put us into the relation of a people to God; which, while we live in the neglect of prayer, we refuse to stand to, and so forfeit its privileges. When we find our hearts backward to prayer; indifferent whether we pray or not, or degenerating into a lifeless formality, let us quicken them with this: Shall I give the lie to my baptism, and disown dependence upon that God, who then manifested such kindness? and whose I am by so solemn a covenant? David often excites praying graces by similar means; 'Thou art my God, early will I seek thee' (Ps. 63: 1). Baptism is particularly an engagement to family worship: by that, we and ours were taken into covenant with God; therefore, 'we and our households should serve the Lord' (Josh. 24: 15).

It Emboldens Us to Pray

Slavish fear is a great enemy to prayer: takes off our chariot wheels; clips the wings of devotion. Baptism, if duly considered, will be a special remedy against that spirit of bondage, which stands in opposition to the spirit of adoption. It is a seal of our interest in God; and we may from thence, with the greater confidence, call God ours: and it is comfortable coming with an address to one in whom we have such an interest; one who is not ashamed (Heb. 11: 16) of his relation to us; but hath instituted an ordinance for the solemn avowal and recognizance of it. 'Let us therefore come boldly (Heb. 4: 16); 'draw near with a true heart, having our bodies washed' (Heb. 10: 22): Baptism is one special qualification that fits us for a confident approach to God (as circumcision under the law): by that, we were admitted into the relation of children, which should encourage us to improve the relation, by crying, 'Abba, Father' (Gal. 4: 6). We were then enrolled among the seed of Jacob, to whom God never said, 'Seek ye me in vain' (Isa. 45: 19). We were interested in the Mediator, who ever lives to make intercession, for we were baptized into his name. We may plead the promise of the Spirit's assistance, God's acceptance, and an answer of peace; and may we not then come with boldness? In prayer we stand in need of the Father's smiles, the Son's righteousness, and the Spirit's aid; in reference to each of which, we should consider, that we were baptized into the name of the Father, and of the Son, and of the Holy Ghost.

Baptism is especially encouraging in reference to our joint addresses; our approaches to God in the solemn assemblies of his people. Our participation of the privileges of the communion of saints, should encourage us to abound in the duties of that communion. We belong to the praying body; and our spiritual communion with that body in prayers and praises (even with those with whom we cannot maintain a local communion) is very comfortable, when we approach the throne of grace. To think, that that mystical body, into which we were baptized, is attending the same throne of grace, upon the same errands. Let this therefore lift up the hands that hang down, and confirm the feeble knees.

Infant Baptism Drives Away Hard Thoughts of God

But further, the consideration of our baptism, as administered in infancy, will much more befriend prayer; both as an inducement to, and an encouragement in, that duty. Three comfortable inferences may be drawn from it:

GOD IS READY TO RECEIVE THOSE WHO COME TO HIM, and will in no wise cast them out. He who would have little children come to him, infants, such as cannot speak for themselves, surely will not reject and put away those, who, though still very weak, yet do, in some measure, lisp out their desires to him. Infant baptism discovers the goodness of God to be, preventing goodness, unmerited goodness, free in the communication of itself, and not strict in standing upon terms. Hard thoughts of God drive us from, and discourage us in, the duty of prayer; and are no less uncomfortable to ourselves, than they are dishonourable to God. Now, the serious consideration of the favours of our infant baptism, would cause the goodness of God to pass before us; and very much endear our Master, and his service, to us. And this would bring us with cheerfulness, and boldness, to the throne of grace, to ask, and receive, mercy and help.

WE WERE EARLY BROUGHT INTO COVENANT WITH HIM; were betimes received into the number, and entitled to the privileges of children; which is a great enlargement upon us to adhere to God, and a great encouragement to us to hope, that God will not forsake us. It is a good plea in prayer. See how comfortably David pleads it: 'Thou art he that took me out of the womb; (and immediately into covenant) thou didst make me hope (though incapable of the act of hope, didst lay a foundation for hope to build upon) when I was upon my mother's breasts: thou art my God, for I was cast upon thee (by my parents' dedication of me) from the womb; therefore, be not far from me' (Ps. 22: 9–11). He pleads to the same purpose when old (Ps. 71: 5; cf. 17–18) for time doth not wear out the comfort of our infant covenants. How careful was God to get possession of us betimes! And can we find in our hearts now to cast him off! Or can we fear that he should cast us off?

HE WAS OUR FATHERS' GOD. That we may with comfort take hold of, in the darkest seasons. Thus the saints of old used to do (1 Chr. 12: 17; 2 Chr. 6: 15, 16); though they might have said, 'my God', they chose rather to insist upon the covenant relation of their parents. David presses this in his plea for salvation (Ps. 86: 16): Save the son of thy handmaid; born in thy house, therefore obliged to serve thee, and therefore expecting to be saved by thee. We find God often showing kindness, as David to Mephibosheth, for the father's sake; which, perhaps, is therefore called the 'kindness of God' (2 Sam. 9: 7): such kindness as God was used to show, hereditary kindness. Plead then (as Asa with Benbadad) an ancient league between God and thy father; and take encouragement from thence.

Thus may we order our cause before God, and fill our mouths with arguments; not to move God (for he is of one mind, and who can turn him?), but to move ourselves; to strengthen our faith, and to quicken our fervency.

TO ENCOURAGE BROTHERLY LOVE

We should improve our baptism, especially our infant baptism, as a powerful engagement to brotherly love.

This is the 'new commandment'; though an old commandment, enforced by new motives, built upon a new foundation. It is peculiarly the law of Christ's kingdom, the lesson of his school, the livery of his family: an essential branch of our holy and excellent religion. Now there is that in baptism, which should mightily induce us to love one another with a pure heart, fervently: and would (if used aright) eradicate all love-killing principles and practices; and overcome all our feuds and animosities; and readily and powerfully suggest, to all Christians, that necessary caution, 'See that ye fall not out by the way.'

A Uniting Ordinance

The consideration of our baptism would be a great inducement to brotherly love.

ONE BAPTISM. It is the apostle's argument for 'unity of spirit', that there is 'one baptism' (Eph. 4: 3, 5). As there is one faith, so there is one way of professing and owning that faith, viz. baptism; the common door of admission into the visible church. Those who, in lesser things, differ in their apprehensions, and are accordingly subdivided, yet in this agree, that they are baptized into the same great names of the Father, Son, and Holy Ghost. Whatever dividing names we are known by, whether of Paul, or Apollos, or Cephas, whether of Luther, or Calvin, or the Church of England, we were not baptized into those names (the great apostle disowns it: 'Were ye baptized in the name of Paul?' (1 Cor. 1: 13)): no, we were baptized in the name of the Lord Jesus, who hath instituted this ordinance, as a centre of unity to all Christians. The faith professed in baptism is a 'common faith' (Titus 1: 4; that in which all Christians are agreed; abstracted from all controverted opinions of lesser moment), of which, what is commonly called the Apostle's Creed may be considered as a summary. Our Lord Jesus, in baptism, received us, not to 'doubtful disputations'; (Rom. 14: 1); therefore we should so receive one another. All Christians who are duly baptized, however differing in other things, are interested in one and the same covenant, guided by one and the same rule, meet at one and the same throne of grace, are entitled to one and the same inheritance, and all this by one and the same baptism; and should they not then love one another, since the things wherein they agree are so many and so great, while the things wherein they differ are, comparatively, so few, at least, so small? How should this shame us out of our private piques and quarrels, distances and estrangements, that our Lord

> *All Christians who are duly baptized, however differing in other things, are interested in one and the same covenant, guided by one and the same rule, meet at one and the same throne of grace, are entitled to one and the same inheritance, and all this by one and the same baptism; and should they not then love one another...?*

Jesus has not only put up a prayer, but instituted such an ordinance, 'that we all might be one?' (John 17: 21). As for those who enervate the force of this argument, and evade it, by appropriating baptism (like the Donatists of old) to their own way, whatever the monopolizing, excluding principle be, on the one hand or on the other, let not my soul come into their secret, unto their assembly, mine honour, be not then united. To unchurch, unchristianize, unbaptize, all those who are not in everything of our length, is a project so dishonourable to Christ, so destructive to the catholic church, and so directly opposite to the spirit of the gospel, that I cannot mention it without expressing my abhorrence of it. The Lord preserve his church from the mischievous consequences of pride and bigotry.

BAPTIZED INTO ONE BODY. Though baptism does not always produce a real change, yet it does always effect a relative change; so that those who are duly baptized, are thereby admitted as members of the visible church, and therefore stand in a near relation to all the members of it: for 'by one Spirit are we all baptized into one body, whether we be Jews or Gentiles' (1 Cor. 12: 13). By baptism we are all admitted into the family and kingdom of Jesus Christ, and so become related to one another, yea, are adopted to be the children of the same Father. All the saints, both in heaven and earth, make but one family, and

that 'named from Christ' (Eph. 3: 15), the head of it, to whom
they are all united. 'Have we not all one Father?' (Mal. 2: 10);
from whence it follows, 'that all we are brethren' (Matt. 23: 8).
Now relation is a great inducement to love and affection: if
we are brethren, we should love as brethren. No strife, for we
are brethren (Gen. 13: 8). It would be very unnatural for the
children of the same father to fall out, and fight, because they
are not all of the same stature, strength, or complexion. Baptized
Christians are 'members one of another' (Eph. 4: 25); and it is
very unbecoming, if there be not that love and sympathy among
them, which there is between the members of the natural body.
Though the members have not all the same place, strength,
comeliness, and use in the body, yet they love one another, and
have a concern one for another, because it is the same soul which
actuates, and animates, and permeates, every member of the
body; and should it not be so in the mystical body, forasmuch as
we are 'members in particular', and have 'need one of another?'
(1 Cor. 12: 25–7). For though there be a 'diversity of operations,
and gifts, and administrations', yet there is but one Spirit
(1 Cor. 12: 4–6), which actuates all the members. For this reason,
the strong must not despise the weak, nor the weak judge the
strong. This should enlarge and extend our love to all Christians,
however distinguished, dignified, or vilified.

BOUND TO OBEDIENCE. It binds us to obey: and this is the
second great commandment to which we are to yield obedience,
'Thou shalt love thy neighbour as thyself': and this, revived and
confirmed by our Saviour, so often repeated, so much inculcated,
so strongly ratified, and enforced by so many pressing motives
and arguments, that we have precept upon precept, line upon
line, to this purpose. Now our baptism is a bond upon our souls,
'to walk according to this rule'. That which does so richly assure
us of God's love to us, does, no doubt, firmly engage us to love
one another. Envy, hatred, malice, and uncharitableness, are
some of those devilish lusts, which in our baptism we renounced,
and engaged to fight against. Shall we then harbour and embrace
them; or be led, and actuated, and governed by them? It is
the apostle's argument in Colossians 3: 8–10: 'Put off all these,
anger, wrath, malice', seeing you have (at least in profession and
engagement) put off the old man, and put on the new man.

United in Unmerited Love from Infancy

The consideration of our baptism, as administered in infancy, would very much strengthen the inducement to brotherly love.

It is a signal discovery of God's love to us; preventing love, unmerited love. If he loved us when we were infants, and had nothing in us to induce or encourage love, what can we object against loving our brother? The beloved disciple, who had leaned on Jesus' breast, was most loving himself, and did most press love upon others. The more sensible we are of God's love to us, the more will our hearts be drawn out in love to our brethren. All acceptable love in us is but a reflex of God's love to us. Are you to seek for proofs of the love of God to you? As Malachi 1: 2: 'Yet ye say, Wherein hast thou loved us?' Reflect upon your infant baptism, and you will see wherein: that was a time of love indeed; the love of espousals; and should not we then love one another, with a pure heart, fervently?

As it puts us into an early relation to one another. Those relations which take rise with our birth, and into which we are led by nature itself, have usually the greatest influence, and lay the strongest ties upon us. Such is this. We are brethren from our infancy; were born in the same house; and having the same birth right privileges, being interested in the same happiness and hopes, let us not fall out by the way. Especially, considering what was our state when we were put into that relation: we were little children, and therefore, in malice, should be such still (1 Cor. 14: 20). Our infant baptism should teach us to 'receive the kingdom of God as little children' (Mark 10: 15), with all humility and lowliness of mind; which is a temper that would mightily promote our brotherly love. The consideration of our infant baptism would help to make us like little children (Matt. 18: 3), peaceable and loving in all our carriage; plain and open without design, or study of revenge.

Other particulars might be mentioned, wherein our baptism, our infant baptism, may be improved by us, to promote our comfort and holiness, and to build us up in our most holy faith; but these shall suffice.

7

DIRECTIONS TO PARENTS CONCERNING
THE BAPTISM OF THEIR CHILDREN

Next to our own baptism, and the improvement of that, our concern is about our children's baptism; for they are parts of ourselves, and God and nature have constituted us feoffees, in trust for them, to act for their good, in their behalf. And I fear that much of the contempt which infant baptism is brought under with some, is owing to the ignorance, neglect, and mismanagement, which parents are guilty of in that matter; and nothing would be more effectual to revive and preserve the honour of it, than parents' conscientious and serious discharge of their duty with reference to it; for they are the persons concerned, and their carelessness is an error in the first concoction. And therefore 'I write unto you fathers' (1 John 2: 13, 14). The relation of a father, by the consent of nations, as well as by the law of nature, has authority and honour belonging to it. There were several dignities and privileges conferred by the Roman government upon the father of three children. 'Children are a heritage of the Lord': 'Happy is the man that hath his quiver full of them' (Ps. 127: 3, 5). Those who are not quite divested of natural affection, value them accordingly. They are (says

Jacob) 'the children which God hath graciously given thy servant' (Gen. 33: 5). When they are multiplied, they are not to be accounted brothers, but blessings. Obed-Edom had eight sons, 'for the Lord blessed him'. Our duty is to take care of them; especially of their better part. One of the first things we have to do for them, is to dedicate them to God in baptism. And concerning that, we shall endeavour to direct you that are parents:

1. In your preparation for it.
2. In your management of it.
3. In your improvement of it afterwards, in reference to your children.

PREPARING FOR BAPTISM

For the preparation of it, I observe in general, that before this, as before other solemn ordinances, there ought to be due preparation (as much as before the Lord's supper), and yet ordinarily how little is there! The more seldom we have occasion to attend upon the Lord in this service, the more need we have to prepare for it with all seriousness.

UNDERSTAND THE ORDINANCE

Get a right understanding of the ordinance, and of your own concern and interest in it. There are many who bring their children to be baptized, only because it is the fashion of the country, and they would be strangely looked upon if they did not do it; but they know nothing of the meaning of this service. And if we thus offer the blind for sacrifice, is it not evil? Give diligence therefore, clearly and distinctly to understand what you do, and why you do it.

What You Do

You give up your children (which are parts of yourselves) to God. It is a peculiar interest which parents have in their children; founded upon the highest law, and the greatest love; it is undisputed, natural, and unalienable. Know then, that by virtue of this interest, you have a power to dispose of them, for their good, and God's glory. You do therefore accordingly give them up to God; and transfer all your right and title to them, to him, according to the tenor of the covenant. You resign them to God, to be taught, and ruled, and disposed of, and portioned by him; to be made holy and happy by him. You bring them to be laid at the feet of the Lord Jesus.

Understand farther that you do hereby oblige your children; bind them to the Lord; to his word and to his law. As much as in you lies, you lay an obligation upon them, against all sin, and to all duty. Not an original, but an additional, bond. You bind them to a great deal; but to nothing to which they were not bound before. You do in baptism, as when you set your children apprentices; interposing your own authority to oblige them to the duties of the relation, from a sincere regard to their real advantage. And can you think this too much to do for God, who gave his Son, his only-begotten Son, for you? The Father 'sanctified his Son, and sent him into the world'; that is, set him apart for the work of our redemption: and should not we then sanctify our children, and set them apart for God and his glory? Which may afterwards operate, by a moral influence, as an argument with themselves (and all little enough) to fix them to God and duty.

You do hereby oblige yourselves to bring them up accordingly; in the nurture and admonition of the Lord. It is a great charge, which parents take upon themselves, when they bring their children to be baptized; and I fear the reason why so few perform it, is because they do so little understand and consider it. This obligation upon you also, is indeed to no more than you were before bound to, though it does more bind you, and strengthen the natural obligation. Labour to understand this. In dealing with men, you would not put your hand to a bond, without knowing first what it meant, and what you took upon yourselves by it; and will you, in dealing with God, do such a thing rashly and inconsiderately?

Why You Do It

Understand upon what grounds you go, in bringing your children to baptism; else it is not in faith. I have endeavoured, at large, to show what Scripture grounds we go upon in baptizing children: understand them well. In short:

1. You do it in compliance with the tenor of the covenant; which runs, 'to us and to our children', that God will be 'a God to us and to our seed'.
2. You do it, in conformity to the will of God revealed in the Old Testament administration of the covenant; in that which was not ceremonial, viz. the admission of the children of the covenanters into the same covenant with their parents.
3. You do it in obedience to the appointment of Christ; that 'little children should be brought unto him' (Mark 10: 14).
4. You do it in pursuance of your own covenant with God; wherein you gave up yourselves, and all near and dear to you, unto him; your children therefore especially, who are in a manner parts of yourselves.
5. You do it out of a natural affection to your children; which prompts you to do all you can for their good. Labour thus to understand yourselves, and act with reason in what you do.

EXAMINE YOURSELVES

Be serious in examining yourselves, and your own covenant interest in God. What title your children have to the ordinance, they have by descent from you: and there appears no reason to expect that the streams should rise higher than the spring; that you should convey to your children a higher and greater title than you have yourselves. Therefore examine yourselves, whether you be in the faith; for though your profession of faith (in nothing visibly contradicted) be sufficient, so far as the church can decide, to entitle your children to this ordinance, yet God is not to be mocked; he searches the heart, and will not be put off with shows and pretences; he knows where the heart is not right, but unsteady in the covenant. Therefore we should diligently commune with our own hearts in this matter, and take heed of deceiving ourselves. It is a thing in which multitudes are mistaken, and in which a mistake is extremely fatal. Therefore ask, 'Is there not a lie in my right hand?' When we bring our children to be 'ingrafted into Christ', we should inquire, Am I myself ingrafted into him? Am I alive indeed, or have I only a name to live? Take this opportunity of driving the matter to an issue. Such a shaking of the tree, if it be indeed well rooted, will but make it take root the stronger.

RENEW YOUR REPENTANCE

Renew your repentance for the breach of your baptismal engagements. Upon every renewal of our covenant with God, we should penitently reflect upon our violations of it: especially when, in effect, renewing that baptism which is the baptism of repentance. Those whom John baptized confessed their sins; and so should they who bring their children to be baptized. It is well the covenant we are under leaves room for repentance.

PRAY EARNESTLY

Be earnest with God in prayer, for a blessing upon his own ordinance. The blessing of God is all in all to the comfort and benefit of it. Pray that the ordinance may be made effectual to the child, and not be an empty sign. How grace is wrought in the hearts of infants we know not; how should we, when the production of it in the adult is such a mystery? Like the wind, which we cannot tell whence it comes, nor whither it goes: it is like the forming of the bones in the womb of her that is with child. But this we know, that the God of the spirits of all flesh has access to the souls of little infants, and can make them meet for heaven: and from thence we should take encouragement in our prayers for them. God is not tied to means, for he needs them not; but we may, with more confidence, expect his manifestations of himself when we are in the use of the means. Pray then that God would grace his own ordinance with his special presence, and accept the dedication of the child to him. This is a promised mercy, but yet for this God will be sought unto, and 'inquired of by the house of Israel'.

What I say to one, I say to both the parents. The mother must consent to the dedication of the child, as well as the father, though commonly it is the father who makes the profession; and they should both together discourse before of these things, as 'heirs together of the grace of life' (1 Pet. 3: 7). They are generally both contriving about the outside, and the formality of the service: they would do well to help one another in the main matter. The dedication of Samuel (1 Sam. 1: 11) was his mother's act and deed; and David often pleads a relation to God as the son of his handmaid. The mothers, from the conception, should look upon the fruit of their bodies as belonging to God; and, in intention, devote it accordingly. It may minister some comfort and relief to a pious mother, in breeding-sickness, and bearing pains, that they are in order to bring another member into Christ's visible body; and who would not encounter some difficulties to bear a child to the Lord? It was the peculiar honour of Mary, that she was the mother of Christ: and is not some ray of that honour put upon those who are the mothers of Christians? Is it not 'a holy thing which shall be born of thee', and that shall be called a child of God? This, indeed, was said of Christ (Luke 1: 35), but it may, in some sense, be said of Christians. Be not cast down then, or disquieted; 'blessed shall be the fruit of thy body' (Deut. 28: 4). It is the Lord's, and God will look after his own. You should take care accordingly to preserve it, and to keep yourselves pure. Every Christian is a spiritual Nazarite: and if Samson must be a 'Nazarite from the womb', his mother must 'eat no unclean thing' (Judg. 13: 7). Do nothing to destroy, or defile, that temple of God which is in the rearing. Have an eye to this, in your provision for your children, as soon as they come into the world. When the knees prevent them, and the breasts which they suck, say, 'This care I take of them, that they may be given up to the Lord.' Nurse them for him. This would sanctify natural affection, and make those common cares peculiarly pleasing to God, and first abounding to a good account. While you love your children, and take care of them, and provide for them, and nurse them (which those that are able ought to do) only because they are your own offspring, what do you more than others? More than even the brutal creatures? But to do this with an eye to God, to take care of them as born in his house, children of the covenant, who belong to Christ's family; this is to do it 'after a godly sort', and as 'becomes the gospel'. Where special privileges are enjoyed, even in common actions, there ought to be a special regard to those privileges.

DURING BAPTISM

As to the management of the ordinance when it comes, I would direct you as to the externals of it.

FOCUS ON THE PURPOSE OF THE INSTITUTION

Be prudent in ordering the circumstances (so far as they fall within your management) in such a manner, as that the great ends of the institution may be promoted, and not hindered. For time, and place, we gave directions before. In general, consult the solemnity of an ordinance, and let it be managed with an agreeable seriousness. We see too commonly, that inviting and treating the guests is made the main matter at a christening, as they call it. All the care is to please their neighbours, while there is but little thought how to please God in it.

I condemn not the inviting of friends (Christian friends) on such an occasion, provided the ends be right: not to make 'a fair show in the flesh', but that our friends may be witnesses of our covenanting with God for our seed, and may join with us in prayer for a blessing upon the ordinance. When John was circumcised, Elisabeth had her neighbours and cousins with her (Luke 1: 58–9). And this may be a mean to preserve, and increase, that love which there should be amongst neighbours and relatives, and to knit families together.

Nor do I altogether condemn such moderate expressions of rejoicing, as do become Christians, and are consistent with the seriousness of the institution. But how rarely are they so regulated! Abraham made a great feast, not when Isaac was circumcised, but when he was weaned (Gen. 21: 8). How prejudicial such entertainments usually are, not only to the health of the mother, but to the efficacy of the ordinance, is too evident. Meetings of friends upon that occasion, should be to edify, not to ensnare, one another. And yet how often do we see one of the great institutions of the gospel managed much like the idolatrous worship of the golden calf, when, after a piece of blind devotion, 'the people sat down to eat and drink, and rose up to play': thus gratifying that flesh which in baptism we renounce. Fashion is commonly pleaded as an excuse in this case, a poor excuse for a Christian. What is Christianity but a sober singularity? A non-conformity to this present world? We must inquire, what is right not what is fashion; what is the way of Christ, not what is the way of the world.

Particular rules cannot here be given with any certainty, so as to fit all persons, places, and circumstances; only, in general, let not the shadow eat out the substance, nor the beauty of the ordinance be eclipsed by the pomp and gaiety of the feast.

BE SINCERE

As to the frame of your spirits (which is the main matter, and what God especially looks at), take these directions.

Do what you do, uprightly, and sincerely. That good man was much in the right, who professed, 'that he knew no religion but sincerity'. It is the prime condition of the new covenant; and our great privilege, and that wherein the covenant of grace is well ordered, that sincerity is our gospel perfection, 'Walk before me, and be thou perfect' (Gen. 17: 1): that is, upright in the main matter of covenanting with God; sincere in the closing, consenting act, however, in many things, you may come short.

Be upright in dedicating yourselves to God. Mean what you say, when you say you will be the Lord's. It is the comfort of all those who are Israelites indeed, that they are able to say, through grace, that though they have many ways dealt foolishly in the covenant, yet they 'have not dealt falsely in the covenant' (Ps. 44: 17). Take heed of that. Allowed guile in our federal transactions is the radical hypocrisy. Be not deceived, God is not mocked. We may possibly deceive one another, but God is too wise to be imposed upon. If we think to put a cheat upon him, we shall prove in the end to have put the worst cheat upon our own souls. Dread the thought of lying to the God of truth; as they did who only 'flattered him with their tongues, for their heart was not right with him' (Ps. 78: 36–7). Let there be no reserve for any known sin; no exception of any house of Rimmon: such a proviso would be the overthrow and defeasance of the deed.

Be upright in the dedication of your children to God. You say they shall be the Lord's; but are you in good earnest? And do you mean as you say? Do you really intend your children to be taught, and ruled, and disposed of, and provided for, by the Lord Jesus? And this, with a single eye to the will of God as your rule, and the glory of God as your end?

You should examine your own souls, whether you are thus cordial and sincere, or not. He that is not sincere in covenanting for himself, can never be right hearty in covenanting for his children. And who knows what a wrong your hypocrisy may prove to your poor infants?

HAVE FAITH IN CHRIST

Do it in faith; especially faith in the great Mediator. When Hannah came to dedicate her son Samuel to God, she brought a sacrifice (1 Sam. 1: 24–5). Christ is the great sacrifice, in the virtue and value of which we must present ourselves and ours to God.

BE THANKFUL

Do it thankfully. It is our duty, in every thing, to give thanks; especially in such a thing as this, which is so very much to our comfort and advantage.

Bless God for your covenant interest; that God is, and will be, to you a God: and take this occasion to speak of it to his praise. Wonder at his condescending goodness. Whence is this to me, a worthless worm of the earth? So mean, so vile, and yet taken into covenant with God; interested in the Lord of glory; his attributes, his promises! 'Who am I, O Lord God?' (2 Sam. 7: 18). That God should take any notice of me, should show me any token for good, is wonderful, considering how undeserving, how ill-deserving, I am; but that he should communicate his favours in a covenant way, interpose himself for security, make himself a debtor to his own truth, is such a paradox of love, as challenges everlasting wonder and praise. That I should be made a friend and favourite, while so many continue 'aliens and strangers to the covenant of promise!' Be astonished, O heavens, at this! 'Lord, how is it, that thou wilt manifest thyself to us, and not unto the world?' (John 14: 22). A heart to be duly thankful to God for the covenant of grace, is a good evidence of our interest in it. Upon this occasion, take a view of covenant privileges: observe how well ordered and how sure the covenant is; what you have in hope, and what you have in hand, by virtue of it; and let all this draw out your hearts in love and thankfulness. Trace up the streams of all your mercies to the inexhaustible spring; and let this be the burden of every song of praise, 'to perform the mercy promised, and to remember his holy covenant' (Luke 1: 72).

Bless God that the covenant of grace is so ordered, that not you only, but your offspring, are taken into that covenant: that God will be a God, not to you only, but to your seed (Gen. 17: 7), and so entail his kindness, by a covenant commanded to a thousand generations. Thus richly does free grace outdo all expectation. 'I had not thought to see thy face (says dying Jacob to his son Joseph), and lo, God hath showed me also thy seed' (Gen. 48: 11). That God should signify his good will to us, is very wonderful; but lo, 'as if this had been a small matter, he hath spoken concerning his servant's house, for a great while to come: and is this the manner of men, O Lord God?' (2 Sam. 7: 19). Admire the condescension of divine grace herein. Many great men think it beneath them to take notice of children; but our Lord Jesus will have little children brought to him, and by no means forbidden. Mention this to the glory of God's wisdom and goodness, and never forget this instance of his loving-kindness.

Bless God that you have a child to dedicate to him. Much of the mercy of having children lies in this, that we have them to devote to God: not only a seed to be accounted to us, but 'to be accounted to the Lord, for a generation' (Ps. 22: 30); not only to honour us, and to bear up our names, but to honour God, and to bear up his name in the world. What is an estate or office good for, but to glorify God with it, and that we may have something to lay out, and use, for his honour? Bless God, that he has not only given you a child, but that he has invited and encouraged you to give it to him again, and is pleased to accept of it. Be thankful that you have a child admitted, from its birth, into the bosom of the church, and under the wings of the Divine Majesty. How sad were it 'to bring forth children to the murderer' (Hos. 9: 13); but how comfortable to bring forth children to the Saviour! Hannah had been long barren, and it was her great grief; at length God gave her Samuel; but it does not appear that his birth was so much the matter of her praise, as his dedication in the Lord. When she had brought him, in his infancy, to the tabernacle, then it was that she said, 'My soul rejoices in the Lord' (1 Sam. 1: 28; 2: 1). You have more reason to be thankful that you have a child born to inherit the privileges of the covenant, than if you had a child born to inherit the largest estate.

Bless God that you have opportunity, and a heart, thus to dedicate your child to God. That he has given you to see, and claim, and use your privilege; and has appointed his ministers, by baptism, solemnly to invest the children you dedicate to God, in the benefits of the covenant. Bless God that he has erected his tabernacle, and sanctuary, in the midst of us; and has not left himself without witness, nor us without the means of grace and salvation. He has not dealt so with many other nations (they and theirs are afar off); and should not this make us very thankful? Preventing mercies, distinguishing mercies, spiritual mercies, are in a special manner obliging. Rightly understand the nature and intention of the ordinance, and you will say, with wonder and praise, 'This is no other than the house of God, and the gate of heaven: this gate of the Lord, into which the righteous shall enter'(Gen. 28: 17; Ps. 118: 20): enter into it therefore with thanksgiving, and into his courts with praise.

SORROW OVER SIN

Do it sorrowing for the corruption of nature, which needs cleansing. The appointment of infant baptism is an evidence of original sin: if little children were not polluted, they would not need to be washed; and consider, that they derive their pollution from you. 'Who can bring a clean thing out of an unclean?' (Job 14: 4). 'They were shapen in iniquity, and conceived in sin' (Ps. 51: 5). It is so even with the children of pious parents; the natural corruption, not the supernatural grace, is propagated. Methinks this should be a melancholy thought to parents, that while they cannot communicate their graces to their offspring, they cannot but communicate their corruptions. Adam was himself made in the image of God; but when he was fallen, 'he begat a son in his own likeness' (Gen. 5: 3). And the same corrupt likeness is still conveyed. Little children, therefore, need this sacramental regeneration: upon occasion of which you, who are parents, should humbly reflect upon your own corruption, which kindled theirs. It should be matter of grief to you, that your children bear your iniquity; and may blame you for the conveyance of that root of bitterness, which bears so much sin and misery.

REJOICE IN THE COVENANT OF GRACE

Do it, rejoicing in the covenant of grace, which provides cleansing. Thus, at the laying of a stone in the gospel temple, as at the laying of the first stone of Zerubbabel's temple, there is occasion for a mixture of joy and sorrow: and that sorrow for sin is so far from obstructing, that really it befriends, this joy. Your children are polluted, but bless God that there is a 'fountain opened'; not only 'for the house of David', but 'for the inhabitants of Jerusalem' (Zech. 13: 1). Draw water therefore with joy out of these 'wells of salvation'. Rejoice that there is such a covenant, which you can through grace lay any claim to. The expressions of joy, and rejoicing, at the baptism of a child, should be turned into this channel; and should terminate in God, and in the new covenant.

Thus should you bring your children to baptism. And in order thereunto, it is requisite, in general, that you be very serious in it. It certainly is not a thing to be done rashly, and carelessly, but with great concern; and the more it lies out of the way of our usual meditations in other duties, the more need we have to engage all that is within us in this service.

AFTER BAPTISM

I come now to direct you what improvement to make of infant baptism, with reference to your children. If you have not put off humanity, as well as Christianity, and divested yourselves of natural, as well as gracious, affections, you cannot but have a great concern for your children. I desire to adore the wisdom of God, in planting in the hearts of parents such love to their offspring. It is necessary to the preservation, both of the church, and of the world; and is therefore to be encouraged. It is the work of grace to improve, direct, and sanctify, natural affections. Christian parents, therefore, should do more and better than others, in their carriage towards their children.

I undertake not to direct, in general, to all the duties which parents owe to their children; but to instruct them how to improve the baptism of their children; in praying for them; in teaching them; in providing for them; and in parting with them: in all which we should make use of their baptism, for direction, quickening, and encouragement.

PRAY FOR YOUR CHILDREN

Parents should improve the baptism of their children, in praying for them. It is the duty of parents to pray for their children, and to bless them in the name of the Lord. Children's asking their parents' blessing, for aught I see, is a very laudable practice, provided it does not degenerate (as the best duties too often do) into formality. It is good to teach children betimes how to value their interest in the prayers of their pious parents. In praying for children, it is proper sometimes to be particular, as Job for his, 'according to the number of them all' (Job 1: 5).

As to the improvement of their baptism in praying for them, take direction from their baptism, what to beg of God for them; namely, covenant mercies. God's promises are to be the rule of our prayers; we should seek from God, what God has sealed to us. Remember, when you are praying for your children, to mind their spiritual and eternal state, more than their temporal. They were covenant blessings, which Abraham's heart was so much upon, when he prayed 'O that Ishmael might live before thee' (Gen. 17: 18); though God heard him for Isaac. Seek not great things in the world for your children; but be earnest with God to give them knowledge and grace; that good part; the best portion you can desire for them. Help them by your prayers, against their lusts and corruptions. You were accessory to their spiritual distempers, and therefore you should do what you can to get them cured; and what can you do better, than bring them to Christ, the great Physician, in the arms of faith and prayer?

As that poor woman whose daughter was vexed with a devil (Matt. 15: 22).

Take encouragement from their baptism in your prayers for them. Look upon their baptism, and you will see upon what grounds you go in praying for them. You pray for them as in covenant with God, interested in the promises, sealed to be the Lord's; and those are good pleas in prayer, to be used for the confirmation of your faith. Pray that God would treat them as his; tell him, and humbly insist upon it, that they are his; whom you gave to him, and of whom he accepted: and will he not take care of his own? How far the promise of the new heart is sealed in baptism, I do not now inquire; but the sealing of the covenant in general, is a token of God's good will to our seed, as a sufficient handle for faith to take hold on, in praying for our children. I see not how those parents can, with equal confidence, pray for their children, who deny them to be in covenant, and so set them upon even ground with the children of infidels. Isaac and Jacob blessed their children by faith (Heb. 11: 20, 21), and that faith respected the covenant which God had made with them, and with their seed.

Pray that God would treat them as his; tell him, and humbly insist upon it, that they are his; whom you gave to him, and of whom he accepted: and will he not take care of his own?

In praying for children, it is our duty to resign and give them up to God, to be disposed of as he pleases; with a holy resolution quietly to acquiesce in those disposals. Now it is very comfortable thus to give them up in prayer, when we have already given them up in baptism. Having submitted them to such an ordinance, we may, with comfort, submit them to any providence which God shall order for them. With great comfort may you give them up, to one who has already received them, and set his own stamp and superscription upon them. It was said of Augustine, who was so often prayed for by his pious mother Monica, that surely a child of so many prayers could not miscarry. If you be most earnest for spiritual blessings for your children, God will give an answer of peace, some way or other, some time or other. In all your blessings of them (as in the blessing of Jacob) let the 'dew of heaven' (Gen. 27: 28) be put before 'the fatness of earth'; and let the blessings of the 'nether springs' be still postponed to those of the 'upper'.

TEACH THEM

Parents should improve the baptism of their children in teaching them. I take it for granted, that it is the duty of parents to teach their children. The very light of nature dictates this: and many heathens have left, not only good rules to this purpose, but good examples. But it is more clearly enjoined by the Scripture law. And there, the duty of parents is summed up in this (Eph. 6: 4): 'bring them up in the nurture and admonition of the Lord'. Take heed of the devil's nurture, rest not in the world's nurture, but let it be the nurture and admonition of the Lord. It was an Old Testament precept (Prov. 22: 6): 'Train up a child in the way he should go'; and this is equally a duty under the New Testament; and it may still be hoped that he will not afterwards 'depart from it'; but that the well-seasoned vessel will retain the savour of life unto life. The first dispensation of the covenant, to the covenanters and their seed, that we have upon record, was to one who was famous for the religious education of children. 'I know Abraham (says God), that he will command his children and his household after him' (Gen. 18: 19). And this was enjoined to the Jews: 'Thou shalt teach them diligently to thy children' (Deut. 6: 7).

It is very disingenuous, and a perfect mockery, to dedicate your children to God, and then to breed them up for the flesh and for the world, and for the devil (see Ezek. 16: 20).

According to Your Promise

Though this is so great and necessary a duty, yet how sadly it is neglected! Many, who are called Christians, are more solicitous to have their dogs taught, and their horses managed, than they are to have their children educated to the greatest advantage. Remember your dedication of them to God in baptism, as a motive to the utmost diligence in their education. Besides the tie of nature to do them all the good you can, especially to their better part; besides the command of God, which obliges you to it; you have bound yourselves, by a solemn promise, in the presence of God. It was upon these terms that they were baptized; not only your profession of Christianity, but your promise to bring them up in that holy religion; and you break that promise if you neglect to do so. Your children are put out to you to be brought for God. When God graciously gives a child to believing parents, he does, in effect, say to them, as Pharaoh's daughter said to the mother of Moses, 'Take this child, and nurse him for me' (Exod. 2: 9); and if it be, indeed, done for God, 'he will give thee thy wages'. Christian families are the church's nurseries, where the young plants are reared; and parents have, in a special manner, the charge of them; and must be called to account concerning that charge. But what a sad account will many parents have to give of this stewardship another day! Who have not merely buried, but wasted this talent: who have not only neglected to improve their authority, and influence, for the good of their children's soul, but have abused both, to their unspeakable prejudice.

Besides the promise you break, and the trust you falsify, by your neglect of your children's education, consider likewise the intention you frustrate. You do, as much as in you lies, defeat the design of your children's baptism. It was to entitle them to church privileges: and to what purpose is that, if you do not teach them what use to make of those privileges? For want of educating your children aright, then, you receive the grace of God, manifested in their baptism, in vain.

DO NOT DELAY. Begin teaching them betimes. Children are capable of religious impressions sooner than we are commonly aware of; and it is good to season the vessel well at first. Even then, when the understanding is too weak fully to receive, and the memory to retain, truths and notions, the mind, by a prudent, pleasing management, may be formed to that which is good. Endeavour, by a reverend carriage in your religious exercises and your sober deportment on the Lord's day, to possess them with an early apprehension that the worship of God is a serious thing. I think it is good to bring children betimes to the solemn assembly, where there is convenience for it; as soon as they are capable of being kept so quiet as not to give disturbance to others (and with a little care and prudence they will quickly be brought to that), though they are not able to understand what is said and done. My reasons are, that children may hereby be trained up to an observance of religion, and be ready to receive impressions as soon as ever they become capable. And there have been strange instances of the early notice which children

> *I think it is good to bring children betimes to the solemn assem-bly, where there is convenience for it; as soon as they are capable of being kept so quiet as not to give disturbance to others…though they are not able to understand what is said and done.*

have taken of good things. Besides, that the parents do hereby glorify God. And the Hosannas of even little children are not to be considered as a taking of the name of God in vain. Our Lord expressed his approbation of them.

The early dedication of our children to God should excite us to an early care of them. If God's free grace was manifested to them, in such a preventing way, what an inducement should this be to us, to begin with them as soon as ever they are capable. They are therefore taken into the church so young, that (as we say) they may suck in religion with their milk, and, like Timothy, may from their very infancy become acquainted with the 'holy scriptures' (2 Tim. 3: 15).

TAKE PAINS TO TEACH THEM. This is absolutely necessary. 'Thou shalt teach them diligently' (Deut. 4: 9). Whet it upon them (Heb.). In whetting, you turn the thing whetted upon this side, and on that side, and often repeat the strokes. So, in teaching of children, the mind is affected (*non vi, sed sæpe cadendo*) not by the violence, but by the frequency, of the impression. The minds of children, like narrow-necked bottles, must be filled but slowly, drop by drop. The young must be driven with patience, as they can go, to allude to Genesis 33: 14. Special care must be taken to make things plain to them; condescending to their capacities, and lisping to them in their own language; conveying instruction by things sensible, or otherwise affecting;

and making it as much as may be, not a task, or burden, but easy and pleasant. Children are half taught when they are reconciled to instruction.

There is one thing which parents should especially be induced to, by the baptism of their children, and that is, to introduce them early into adult communion; bringing them to own the covenant of their baptism, and to take it upon themselves, by an approved profession of personal faith and repentance, in order to their regular admission to the ordinance of the Lord's supper. The profession of the parents was accepted, when they were infants; but being grown up, they must be called upon to make it their own act and deed. Hereby parents transfer much of their charge to the children themselves; who, becoming capable of acting for themselves, need not be in ward. God has promised to pour out 'his Spirit upon our seed, and his blessing upon our offspring'; and it follows, 'they shall spring as willows by the water courses; and one shall say, I am the Lord's, and another shall call himself by the name of Jacob, and another shall subscribe with his hand unto the Lord, and shall surname himself by the name of Israel' (Isa. 44: 3–5). The blessing promised to our infant seed is in order to hasten them personally to own their relation to God. Many parents, who would think themselves undone if they should not have their children baptized, take no care to bring them to the Lord's supper; as if that were not as necessary a recognition of their adult church membership, as baptism of their infant church membership.

Not that I would have children brought blindfold to confirmation, or the Lord's supper; nor brought by force; no, it must be a reasonable service (thy people shall be willing); but I think that children, when they grow up to a competent understanding, should be first instructed concerning adult communion; the terms of it, the privileges of it, the duty of it, the desirableness of it; should be taught the nature and design of the Lord's supper, and of that covenant of which it is the seal; and then should be persuaded to it, and stirred up to desire it. If they are careless, and unmindful of their souls and eternity, they should be alarmed, and excited to look about them, and concern themselves about so great a salvation. If timorous, and fearful (which is a much better extreme), they should be encouraged and comforted. Parents commonly pretend, as an excuse, that they do not see their children fit for the Lord's supper, or desirous of it, when they do not take pains to make them fit, and do not stir up their desires. I know that the race is not to the swift, nor the battle to the strong: we can but do our duty, and leave the success to the free grace of God; who will be sanctified in all that draw near to him.

Remind Them of Their Baptism

It is to be used as an argument with the children, to receive the instructions that are given them. This will be of use, to open the ear to instruction, and to dispose the heart for learning. You may by this take hold of them, and reason the case with them. Tell them what God promised to them, and what you promised for them; the one to encourage, and the other to engage them, to that which is good. When you are reproving them for sin, and warning them against it, argue from their baptism. Tell them how contradictory lying, and sabbath-breaking, and swearing, and taking God's name in vain are to their profession, and promise, in that ordinance. The sons of nobles are often reminded, that they must do nothing unbecoming to their blood, nothing that would reflect upon their families; and should not the sons of Christians be, in like manner, exhorted not to disparage their Christianity? Remind them of their baptismal dedication and separation, when you are cautioning them to save themselves from an untoward generation; especially in the great turns of life.

PROVIDE FOR THEM

Improve your children's baptism, in providing for them. The light of nature, as well as Scripture precepts, make it your duty to supply them with things needful for them, as God gives you ability. If any man do otherwise, 'he is worse than an infidel' (1 Tim. 5: 8); no better than the unnatural 'ostrich, that leaves its eggs in the earth' (Job 39: 13, 14). Though our main care must be to instruct them, our next must be to make provision for their comfortable subsistence.

We may, from their baptism, take direction in providing for them. Baptism was to them the seal of the covenant of grace. The provision God made for them, in that covenant, was of spiritual blessings in heavenly things: be chiefly solicitous about those things. But that care is not to exclude, but to govern and overrule, your other cares. You must provide callings and employments for them: be directed herein by their baptism: and make that provision which will be most likely to answer and secure the ends of their baptism. As far as you can determine, choose those callings for them, which are best for their souls; most free from temptations, and best subservient to the general calling; in which (according to their place and capacity) they may most glorify God, and be most serviceable to their generation.

If there be a due fitness for the work of the Christian ministry, the consideration of their baptism may be a particular inducement to devote them to that.

In providing estates and portions for them, seek not great things, but good things. Account that to be best for them which will be best in the end, and provide accordingly; food convenient, bread to eat, and raiment to put on, so that they may come at last to their Father's house in peace; and then God will provide.

Parents also should from hence take a caution, to provide for their children by lawful and honest means. There is no need of our sin to bring to the birth God's promises. Those parents do not understand, or do not consider, the baptism of their children, who destroy their own souls to make the children rich. Those who depend upon provision by the covenant, need not take any indirect courses to make that provision. If God be the God of Abraham, and has promised to make him great, Abraham will not reflect upon that covenant, by taking any thing of the king of Sodom, 'lest he should say, I have made Abraham rich' (Gen. 14: 23). Distrust of God, and of his promise, draws many into crooked paths, and puts them upon base and sinful measures, to enrich their children. You went to God for the promise, do not go to the devil for the performance; nor inquire of Baalzebub, the god of Ekron, while there is a God in Israel, who has said that he will be 'a God to you, and to your seed'.

We may take encouragement from their baptism, in providing for them. What can be more encouraging, in this respect, than that God has engaged to provide for them? The seed of the upright shall be blessed (Ps. 112: 2) even with temporal blessings, as far as is for God's glory, and their good. Have an eye to that promise, and plead it with God. Will he not provide for his own, especially those of his own house? If God be to them a God, they have enough. You are in care to lodge what you have for them in good hands; I know not how you can do better, than to lodge it by faith and prayer, in the hands of God.

PREPARE THEM FOR PARTING

Improve your children's baptism, in reference to your parting with them. We live in a parting world, and must provide accordingly. Those who are knit closest together, by love and nature, must expect to be separated. Parents and children are often parting.

In the World

Parents are parting with their children from under their eye, and from under their wing. Sending them abroad for education, or into callings, or in marriage. Concerns which commonly lie much upon the hearts of parents: but so it must be; the young tree must not grow always in the nursery; but at length be transplanted into its proper place in the orchard. And when it comes to that, remember their baptism; and trust them in the arms of covenant love. If they are God's children, wherever they go they are not off their Father's ground, nor out of their Father's house. Though they seem the less yours when they are gone from you, yet they are not less the Lord's; which may be no less a comfort to you, than a caution to them. Are they the Lord's? Then send them nowhere, but where you can in faith desire God to go with them. When they go from under your eye, they do not go from under God's eye; neither the eye of his providence, nor the eye of his observance. When you send them from you, remind them of their baptismal engagements, both to caution and to quicken them. Dismiss them with a covenant blessing; as Isaac sent away Jacob (Gen. 28: 3–5). 'God Almighty bless thee, and give thee the blessing of Abraham.' Tell them and tell yourselves, that 'the Lord watches between you and them, when you are absent the one from the other' (Gen. 31: 49).

Out of the World

Parents and children are parting out of the world. The most solemn partings are those which death makes. Death parts those whom nothing else would part; and particularly, parents and children. You have need to prepare for such parting providences.

WHEN CHILDREN ARE TAKEN BY DEATH, you that are parents may take comfort from your children's baptism. Death observes not the laws of seniority; but often takes the children before the parents.

In such a case, think of their baptism to induce you cheerfully to resign, and give them up to God. When you brought them to be baptized, you devoted them to God; transferred your own interest in them to him; you told him that they should be his, to all intents and purposes, and may he not then do what he will with his own? It is a quieting consideration (I know those who have found it so) that they

> *When you brought them to be baptised, you devoted them to God; transferred your own interest in them to him; you told him that they should be his, to all intents and purposes, and may he not then do what he will with his own?*

are the Lord's, by your own consent. He not only gave them to you, but (which is forever an estoppel to all complaints) you gave them to him again. Make it appear that you did it in sincerity, by your silent submission to the will of God, in removing them from you. Do not say, as David, 'Would God I had died for thee' (2 Sam. 18: 33); but as Job, when he had buried all his children together in the ruins of their elder brother's house, 'Blessed be the name of the Lord' (Job 1: 21). Sense will suggest a great deal, at such a time, that is aggravating: it was a pretty child, very forward and engaging; it may be, an only child, a first born; but let this answer all, that God takes his own. When your children were to be dedicated to God in baptism, forasmuch as they could not do it themselves, you acted as the trustees of their wills; do so when they come to die. As, if you were to die yourselves, you would commit yourselves into the hands of God; so, when your children are dying, who cannot do it for themselves, it lies upon you to do it for them. Say, Father, into thy hands I commend my child's spirit. In baptism you resigned them to be members of the church militant, and surely now you cannot, you will not, gainsay their removal to the church triumphant. It looks like a very contented word of good old Jacob (Gen. 43: 14): 'If I am bereaved of my children, I am bereaved.' He does not say, 'I am undone, I shall never see a good day again'; but, 'I am bereaved, and the will of the Lord be done.'

Think of their baptism to encourage you concerning their eternal happiness. What ground of hope there is concerning the salvation of children of believing parents, who die in infancy, was showed before; take comfort from it on such occasions. They were within the pale of the church; within the verge of the covenant; within reach of that promise, 'I will be a God to thee, and to thy seed.' I ground not the hope of their salvation merely upon the external administration of the ordinance, as if there were no hope concerning those who die unbaptized; but I ground it upon their covenant right to the ordinance. David's child died on the seventh day; it is supposed the seventh day from its birth, and therefore uncircumcised, and yet David comforts himself with the hope of its salvation: 'I shall go to him, but he shall not return to me' (2 Sam. 12: 23). This must needs be very comfortable under such providences. They are taken out of your arms, but are removed to the embraces of a better father. Say not you have lost your child, you have but sent it before you. And it must needs be pleasing to think, that you have a part of yourselves in glory. Who are we, that we should help to people the New Jerusalem? Though your children are early removed from this world, surely there is no harm done, for the time they have lost on earth they have gained in heaven. If therefore it be asked, 'Is it well with thee? Is it well with thy husband? Is it well with the child?' say, as the Shunamite woman did in a like case, 'It is well' (2 Kings 4: 26).

WHEN YOU ARE TAKEN FROM THEM; and perhaps leave them young, and little, and shiftless, undisposed of, unprovided for. This is no uncommon case, and a very melancholy consideration to many a dying father; who is by this, more perhaps than by anything else, made unwilling to die. But let this silence all disquieting cares and fears concerning them, that they are by baptism taken into covenant with God; a God with whom 'the fatherless finds mercy' (Hos. 14: 3). God has expressed a special concern for the fatherless (Ps. 68: 4–5). He who 'rides upon the heavens by his name JAH,' is, and will be, 'a Father of the fatherless'. He has 'taken up, when father and mother have forsaken' (Ps. 27: 10). This God is your God, and the God of your seed; and has encouraged you to 'leave them with him': promising 'to preserve them alive' (Jer. 49: 11). Though you leave many, they are not too many for God to take care of. Though you have little to leave them, let the Lord provide (Jehovah-jireh); there is wealth enough in the promise. Though you have few or no friends to leave them to, God can raise up friends for them. He who can, out of stones, raise up children to Abraham, can and will, out of stones, raise up guardians for those children, rather than they should be deserted. You have never seen the seed of the righteous 'begging bread', forsaken (Ps. 37: 25). Give them your parting blessing in faith; the angel that has delivered you from all evil, will 'bless the lads'; forasmuch as his name is named upon them. They were some of David's last words, and may be a great support and cordial to dying believers; 'Although my house be not so with God (not so as I could wish it), yet he hath made with me an everlasting covenant' (2 Sam. 23: 5).

DIRECTIONS TO THOSE PRESENT
WHEN THE BAPTISM IS ADMINISTERED

Here I take it for granted, that it is most agreeable to the nature and design of the ordinance, that it be administered publicly; not huddled up in a corner, but owned in the face of the congregation (if it may be), the full congregation, that usually meets for other religious exercises; 'in the presence of all his people' (Ps. 116: 18). However, I think it requisite that, except in cases of necessity, there should be a competent number present (such a number as may be called a congregation), that the child may have the benefit of the more prayers, and that others may be benefited by the administration. And therefore, in the close, I would give some directions to the congregation.

BE THERE

Do not turn your backs upon the administration of this ordinance; but be present at it. Think not yourselves unconcerned in it. Though the sacrament be administered only to the child; yet the word and prayer, which accompany the sacrament, you are all interested in, and may reap benefit by, if you have but a heart to it. It is a great contempt of the ordinance, and argues a very low esteem of a divine institution, needlessly to absent ourselves. It is a very ill thing to think meanly of any divine appointment. He said very well, who acknowledged, that the greatest of men are less than the least of the ordinances of Jesus Christ. Besides that it is a contempt of the congregation (as if we thought ourselves too good to bear them company); and 'despising the church of God' (1 Cor. 11: 22) is an affront to God himself.

Act Reverently

Carry yourselves with reverence and seriousness during the administration. It is a very solemn ordinance, and should be attended upon in a solemn manner. That inward awe, which should possess us in divine worship, must put a gravity upon the outward deportment. Whispering, and laughing, and other irreverences of behaviour, at this ordinance, are a provocation to God, an affront to the institution, a disturbance to others, and a bad sign of a vain and carnal mind. And yet how common! Surely in this, as in other duties, God is to be 'worshipped with reverence, and godly fear'; for 'he is greatly to be feared in the assemblies of his saints'. We have need, at this ordinance, to double our guard against such indecencies, because, sometimes, some little accident may happen, in the external administration, which may give occasion to a light and frothy spirit to express itself in such a carriage. But if we remember in whose presence we are, and what is being done, it will be a curb upon us, and keep us serious.

Think Seriously

Apply your minds seriously to observe, and consider that which is the substance, meaning, and end of the ordinance. We are very apt, in positive institutions (*haerere in cortice*) to look no further than the shell, or outside, without penetrating into the substance of the ordinance, or considering what is the 'meaning of the service'. The external signs which should direct us to, many times direct us from, the consideration of the things signified. Therefore lay a charge upon your souls, to consider diligently what is before you. Let not the circumstances of the ordinance (as the manner of washing, or the naming of the child) draw away your thoughts from the substance. Consider it as a seal of the covenant. Your thoughts have a wide field to range in, where (if so disposed) you might furnish them with sweet and profitable matter to work upon.

APPLY IT TO YOURSELF

Make application of that matter to yourselves. Let your thoughts work upon your affections. The case of the baptized infant is a common case: it was once your own, and therefore the business in hand still concerns you. As we should be affected at the burial of our neighbours, because their situation will be, so we should, at the baptism of our neighbours, because it has been, our own. In this therefore, as well as in that, we should lay it to heart. Dionysius Alexandrinus speaks of one of his congregation, who was mightily affected with the questions put to the baptized, and their answers, so that, throwing himself at the minister's feet, he sadly bewailed himself, with many tears (*Euseb. Eccles. Hist.* 1: 8. c. 9).

REFLECT ON YOUR NEED OF CLEANSING

Take this occasion to reflect upon the original corruption of your nature, which needed cleansing.

We have need to be often reminded of this, that we may be daily mourning over it. To an enlightened conscience, it is an aggravation of sin, rather than an extenuation, that it is in our nature. Considering this, as an habitual aversion to the chief good, and an habitual proneness to the greatest evil, the thoughts of it should melt and break our hearts, and keep up an habitual repentance, and self-abhorrence, all our days.

We need to be reminded that we may be daily mortifying it, and keeping it under. Every remembrance of natural corruption should excite our watchfulness and diligence to destroy this root of bitterness. Lay the axe therefore to it: keep a guard against the first motions of sin: get the vicious habit weakened. A sense of the difficulty there is in dealing with such enemies, should not be used as an excuse for our negligence, but rather as a spur to our diligence. Maintain the conflict, and, through the grace of

Jesus Christ, the victory will be sure at last. 'The God of peace shall bruise Satan under your feet shortly.'

THANK GOD FOR YOUR BAPTISM

Take this occasion to acknowledge the mercy of your own infant baptism. In our thanksgiving to God for his mercies, it is very good to begin early. If God remembers, I am sure we have no reason to forget, the kindness of our youth. Not that we loved him, but that he loved us. We should by no means forget his ancient favours, 'When Israel was a child, then I loved him' (Hos. 11: 1). We should be often thinking of God's goodness to us when we were children, especially his spiritual favours, relating to our better part. What is said of God's early kindness to an infant state is very applicable to our infant souls; when we lay exposed and polluted, 'he said unto us, Live; he spread his skirt over us, and sware unto us, and entered into covenant with us, and we became his: then he washed us with water and anointed us with oil, and clothed us with broidered work, and decked us with ornaments' (Ezek. 16: 6-11); and was not the time a time of love? To be often mentioned to the glory of free, preventing grace? Was it he who 'held us up from the womb, and took us (took us into covenant) from our mother's bowels?' Surely then, 'our praise should be continually of him' (Ps. 71: 6).

Bless God for the honour of your infant baptism; that you were added to the visible body of Christ when you were young. To be ranked among the seed of saints, is surely more truly great, and honourable, than to be enrolled in the race of nobles. Ishmael shall beget twelve princes, that is but a small favour; 'my covenant will I establish with Isaac' (Gen. 17: 20-1). Surely herein the covenant of grace, in the external administration of it, was well ordered, and much in our favour, that the lambs are not turned out of the fold. Mention it therefore to the glory of God. Is it not an honour to be admitted into the school, the corporation, the family, of which Christ is the head? Hail! Thou art highly favoured. It is an honour not to be proud of, for we never merited it, but to be thankful for, and lived up to.

Bless God for the opportunity of your baptism. That you were thereby put, as Zacchaeus, into Christ's way; laid at the gate of the temple, ready to receive an alms, and a cure; placed by the poolside, ready to step in, upon the stirring of the waters. If you have not improved this opportunity, it is your own fault; you cannot but own, that it was a favour to have had such a price put into your hands, by which you might have gotten wisdom, if you had not been wanting to yourselves.

REMEMBER YOUR OWN OBLIGATIONS

Take this occasion to remember the obligations of your own infant baptism.

Though you were baptized long since, yet the tie is as strong as if you had been baptized this morning: for as time does not wear out the guilt of our sins, so it does not wear out the obligation of our vows. You know that it was an engagement against all sin, and to all duty; it was a bond upon your souls, to be the Lord's, and to walk and live accordingly. When you see others brought under the same bond, remember that these vows are upon you.

Remember it with a renewed repentance for the breach of your baptismal covenants. Think now, and think with sorrow and shame, in how many things you have violated these engagements (which were so very strong, and yet withal so reasonable): though not in the essentials of the covenant ('by stretching out the hand to a strange god'), yet, in the several articles of the covenant, how wretchedly have we prevaricated! Though in the main we hold to the covenant, and would not disclaim it for all the world, yet in how many instances do we come short! It is well for us, that every transgression in the covenant, does not put us out of covenant: but that there is a door of hope opened; room left for a reconciliation. Repent, therefore, of your manifold transgressions. Aggravate sin by this consideration, that it is ingratitude; that it is perfidiousness: that it is perjury; and reproach yourselves for it.

Remember it with renewed resolution of closer walking for the future. Let the sight of the administration of the ordinance quicken your sense of the vows of God, which are upon you; and confirm your purpose to 'pay that which you have vowed'. We are witnesses against ourselves, if having so solemnly sworn, we do not perform it. They tell us of one in early times, who being present where a child was baptized, and being affected with the solemnity of service, asked, Was I thus baptized? And being told he was, Why then, said he, by the grace of God, I will not do as I have done. It is good to be often engaging ourselves afresh. 'I said, I will take heed to my ways' (Ps. 39: 1); and many a thing we do, because we said, we will do it. Do this therefore, live 'soberly, righteously, and piously, in this world, denying ungodliness, and worldly lusts', because you have said that you will.

PRAY FOR THE CHILD

Join heartily in prayer to God for the child that is baptized. Everything is sanctified by the word and prayer; and particularly this ordinance. It is the minister's work to be the mouth of the congregation in that duty, but it is your business to join. To be where prayer is made, is not praying, if we do not concur in what is said. Pray heartily, that God would receive the child into the embraces of his love; would impress his own image upon it; so as to sanctify it from the womb; and make the ordinance effectual to this end. That which gives prayer its prevalency, is the exercise of grace in prayer. There are two graces to be especially exercised in this prayer:

1. Faith in Christ the head. It is the prayer of faith that is the effectual prayer. Act faith upon the good will of Christ to little children; upon the constitution of the covenant; the promise which is to us and to our children; the encouragement Christ has given us to expect his gracious acceptance: these things we should realise by faith.
2. Love to the mystical body, and to all the members of it; even the little ones, who cannot pray for themselves.

God has expressed a great deal of good will to little children; and we should herein be his followers. Children are therefore publicly presented to God in this ordinance, in the face of the congregation, that they may, the more sensibly, and affectionately, be taken into the compass of our prayers. It is indeed the special duty of parents to pray for their children, but it will be a kindness to them, to help them by your prayers. The best welcome you can give the child, on its admission into the church, is to put up a fervent prayer for it. It is now become one of your 'brethren and companions', for the sake of whom, you must 'pray for the peace of Jerusalem' (Ps. 122: 8). And who knows what influence the effectual fervent prayer of a righteous man, put up in faith, may have upon the good, the spiritual good, of the child. If 'a cup of cold water' given to one of the 'little ones, in the name of a disciple, shall have its reward' (Matt. 10: 42), much more shall a serious believing prayer, put up for one of the little ones, in the name of a disciple, a fellow-disciple, be accepted, and taken kindly. The hearts of Christians are very much knit one to another in love, by their praying one for another. There are many expressions of Christian charity which children are not capable of receiving, but I am sure they are capable of being prayed for, and have need of our prayers. There would then be reason to hope, that the rising generation would be better than this, if we did but pray more and better for it. The children for whom you thus pray at their baptism, may be reaping the benefit of your prayers, when you are dead and gone; however, they will return into your own bosom, for true prayer is never altogether in vain.

Bless God for Another Church Member

Bless God for the addition of another member to the visible church of Christ. It is our duty 'in everything to give thanks'; but the baptism of a child affords special matter for praise.

The Lord is hereby honoured, and his name glorified. It is part of the exaltation of Christ, 'That a seed shall serve him, and shall be accounted for to the Lord a generation.' The further his name goes, the more he is honoured. The preservation of the succession of Christians is, therefore, the propagation of the honour of Christ. The multitude of the people is the glory of the prince. Christ is pleased to reckon himself glorified by the increase of his kingdom. Now that should certainly be matter of rejoicing to us, which any way tends to advance the glory of the Lord Jesus. Additions to his church he places among the achievements of his crown: particularly the addition of little children. Christ had but one day of triumph in all his life, and the glory of that triumph consisted much in the acclamations and Hosannas of the little children (Matt. 21: 15); nay, lest the acceptance should be limited to children who were of age properly to express themselves, it follows in the next verse, 'out of the mouth of babes and sucklings, thou hast perfected praise'; as if it were the top of Christ's praises, that he is in covenant with little children. Mention this therefore to his praise.

There is a precious soul hereby put into the way of salvation: though not necessarily entitled to salvation (that dotesnot follow), yet put into the way; taken into the school of Christ; enrolled amongst those who stand fair for heaven and are entrusted with the means of grace and salvation. This is a great benefit to the child; which we should rejoice in, and bless God for; giving thanks, not only for our own interest in the covenant, and the interest of our seed, but for the interest of our friends, and of their seed. Rejoice that there is one brought into the outward court, whom we are not without hopes of meeting shortly within the veil.

If it be objected, that this child may afterwards prove wicked and vile, not withstanding; may be a scandal to the church, and ruin his own soul; and all this, aggravated by his visible church membership; I answer, it is very true; and that one baptized at a mature age may turn out in like manner; there is no remedy; sacraments do not confer grace (*ex opera operato*) by the mere administration; but till worse appears, we must rejoice, when 'a man is born into the world', when an heir is born into the family; and yet, perhaps, he may prove a burden and a blot to his family, and the curse and the plague of his generation.

The church of God is hereby increased. There is one more brought into the family; and blessed be God, there is room enough in our father's house, and bread enough and to spare. Rejoice that the interest of the church is hereby strengthened. The promise is, that the seed of the saints shall be 'as the stars of heaven'; be thankful for the fulfilling of that promise; that the body of Christ is a growing body; that though the members of the church militant are daily removed by death, yet there are those who are baptized 'in the room of the dead' (1 Cor. 15: 29), to bear up the name of Christ in the world, and to preserve a succession of professing Christians. Thus shall the seed of Christ 'endure for ever, and his throne as the days of heaven' (Ps. 89: 29); and they shall 'fear him as long as the son and moon endure' (Ps. 72: 5); which we should think and speak of, with a great deal of joy and thankfulness. We are not without hopes, that God has great things in store for his church, in the latter days; that there are glorious promises to be fulfilled shortly: in reference to which, it is some encouragement, that there is a seed preserved; that the line is continued; that the entail is not quite cut off; but that a generation is rising, which may enter into that promised Canaan, though our carcasses may fall in the wilderness, for our unbelief and murmuring. And though all are not Israel who are of Israel, though all are not saints indeed who are baptized Christians (would to God they were), yet surely among them there is a remnant, according to the election of grace, which is thus invested in church privileges. And hereby the mystical body is filling up. Which should be matter of joy and praise to us. That the hour hastens on when the number of the elect shall be completed; when 'the bride, the Lamb's wife, shall have made herself ready' (Rev. 19: 7), and 'the marriage of the Lamb shall come' When, though there will be found virgins in profession, with lamps in their hands, who shall be excluded for their folly, yet the chosen remnant of Wisdom's children, the virgins who were so wise as to get oil in their vessels, such as were not only baptized with water but with the Holy Ghost, shall go in to the marriage. Then shall there be a general assembly of the church of the first-born, whose names were written in heaven. The scattered members of the mystical body, that lived in distant places, from one end of heaven to the other, and in distant ages, from the beginning to the end of time, shall all be gathered together to Christ the head, in one pure, unmixed, glorious congregation, and so presented to the Father; and altogether be put in possession of the inheritance of sons. How should the believing prospects of this day raise our thoughts, inflame our joys, and excite our most earnest desires! Even so come, Lord Jesus; come quickly.

Christian Focus Publications
publishes books for all ages

Our mission statement –

STAYING FAITHFUL
In dependence upon God we seek to help make His infallible Word, the Bible, relevant. Our aim is to ensure that the Lord Jesus Christ is presented as the only hope to obtain forgiveness of sin, live a useful life and look forward to heaven with Him.

REACHING OUT
Christ's last command requires us to reach out to our world with His gospel. We seek to help fulfil that by publishing books that point people towards Jesus and help them develop a Christ-like maturity. We aim to equip all levels of readers for life, work, ministry and mission.

Books in our adult range are published in three imprints.
Christian Focus contains popular works including biographies, commentaries, basic doctrine and Christian living. Our children's books are also published in this imprint.
Mentor focuses on books written at a level suitable for Bible College and seminary students, pastors, and other serious readers. The imprint includes commentaries, doctrinal studies, examination of current issues and church history.
Christian Heritage contains classic writings from the past.

Christian Focus Publications, Ltd
Geanies House, Fearn,
Ross-shire, IV20 1TW, Scotland, United Kingdom
info@christianfocus.com

Our titles are available from quality bookstores and
www.christianfocus.com

FREE

4 BOOKS
AND A SURPRISE GIFT!

We would like to take this opportunity to thank you for reading this Mills & Boon® book by offering you the chance to take FOUR more specially selected titles from the Medical Romance™ series absolutely FREE! We're also making this offer to introduce you to the benefits of the Reader Service™ —

★ FREE home delivery
★ FREE monthly Newsletter
★ FREE gifts and competitions
★ Exclusive Reader Service discounts
★ Books available before they're in the shops

Accepting these FREE books and gift places you under no obligation to buy; you may cancel at any time, even after receiving your free shipment. Simply complete your details below and return the entire page to the address below. *You don't even need a stamp!*

YES! Please send me 4 free Medical Romance books and a surprise gift. I understand that unless you hear from me, I will receive 6 superb new titles every month for just £2.49 each, postage and packing free. I am under no obligation to purchase any books and may cancel my subscription at any time. The free books and gift will be mine to keep in any case.

MIZEC

Ms/Mrs/Miss/Mr ....Initials ....
BLOCK CAPITALS PLEASE

Surname ....

Address ....

....

....Postcode ....

Send this whole page to:
UK: FREEPOST CN81, Croydon, CR9 3WZ
EIRE: PO Box 4546, Kilcock, County Kildare (stamp required)

C000051352

WI ...

and lives are on the line!

Irresistible Dr Elliot Mathieson has dated most of the female staff in the hospital—with the exception of his good friend Nurse Jane Halden. And it's Jane he turns to when he discovers he has a daughter! But is he just looking for a temporary nanny, or does he really want a wife?

Join the dedicated team in St Stephen's Accident and Emergency Department, where the pace is hectic, tempers flare and sexual tension is in the air!

Maggie Kingsley lives with her family in a remote cottage in the north of Scotland surrounded by sheep and deer. She is from a family with a strong medical tradition, and has enjoyed a varied career including lecturing and working for a major charity, but writing has always been her first love. When not writing, she combines working for an employment agency with her other interest, interior design.

Recent titles by the same author:

A WIFE FOR DR CUNNINGHAM
JUST GOOD FRIENDS

DR MATHIESON'S DAUGHTER

BY
MAGGIE KINGSLEY

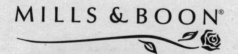

MILLS & BOON®

All the characters in this book have no existence outside the imagination of the author, and have no relation whatsoever to anyone bearing the same name or names. They are not even distantly inspired by any individual known or unknown to the author, and all the incidents are pure invention.

First published in Great Britain 2001
Harlequin Mills & Boon Limited,
Eton House, 18-24 Paradise Road, Richmond, Surrey TW9 1SR

© Maggie Kingsley 2001

ISBN 0 263 82668 6

Set in Times Roman 10½ on 11½ pt.
03-0601-50611

Printed and bound in Spain
by Litografia Rosés, S.A., Barcelona

CHAPTER ONE

ELLIOT MATHIESON gazed blankly at the solicitor for a second, then shook his head. 'I'm sorry, but there has to have been some mistake. I have no daughter.'

The solicitor sifted through the papers on his desk and selected one. 'We have a birth certificate with your name on it, Dr Mathieson—'

'I don't care if you have a hundred birth certificates with my name on them. I have no daughter. No children at all, come to that!'

'Your wife—'

'My *ex*-wife—'

'Was quite adamant in her will that Nicole is yours,' the solicitor declared calmly. 'I can, if you wish, instigate court proceedings to dispute paternity, but...'

It would be a waste of time, Elliot finished for him silently. Whatever else Donna might have been, she hadn't been a fool. She would have known Nicole's paternity could be easily established by means of a simple blood test.

Which meant he had a child. A six-year-old daughter he'd known nothing about until he'd stepped into the solicitor's office this morning, but how?

He and Donna had been divorced for five years. They hadn't even spoken to one another since that disastrous attempt at a reconciliation in Paris almost seven years ago. A reconciliation which had ended in heated words and angry exchanges.

But not at first, he suddenly remembered, his blue eyes darkening with dismay. There'd been no angry words on

5

that first night when they'd gone out to dinner, she'd invited him back to her flat for coffee and somehow they'd ended up in her big double bed.

Oh, hell, but it must have happened then. Nicole must have been conceived then.

'I realise this has come as something of a shock to you, Dr Mathieson,' the solicitor continued, gazing at him not without sympathy, 'but I'm afraid there really wasn't any easy way of breaking the news. If you wish to dispute paternity—'

'Of course I don't,' he interrupted brusquely. 'I accept the child is mine.'

The solicitor smiled with relief. 'Then Nicole will be arriving from Paris tomorrow—'

'Arriving?' Elliot's jaw dropped. 'What do you mean, she'll be arriving?'

'She can hardly remain in France now her mother is dead, Dr Mathieson.'

'What about my wife's sister? Surely she—'

'I'm afraid we haven't even been able to inform Mrs Bouvier of her sister's death. She and her husband are on an archaeological dig in Iran where communications are very poor. And you are the child's father, Dr Mathieson.'

'Yes, but I can't possibly look after a child,' Elliot protested. 'I've recently been promoted to special registrar in St Stephen's A and E department. I work long hours—never know when I'm going to be home—'

'You could employ a nanny or a housekeeper,' the solicitor suggested. 'Or what about boarding school? Many professional people send their children to boarding schools.'

They did, but he'd have to be the biggest louse of all time to send a six-year-old kid who had just lost her mother to a boarding school. A nanny or a housekeeper

might be the answer, but where on earth did you get people like that in twenty-four hours?

'Look, it's not that I don't want Nicole living with me,' he declared, raking his hands through his blond hair in desperation. Like hell it wasn't. 'But I don't know anything about raising a child.'

'Nobody does initially,' the solicitor said bracingly.

Which was all very well for him to say, Elliot thought when he left the solicitor's office some time later, but where did that leave him?

He hadn't even got used to being special registrar at St Stephen's yet, far less the two new members of staff who'd replaced Robert Cunningham and Hannah Blake when they'd got married and left to work for Médecins Sans Frontières. The last thing he needed was a child on top of all his other responsibilities.

Oh, cut the flannel, Elliot, his mind whispered as he strode down the busy London street, heedless of the falling sleet and biting March wind. You wouldn't want this child no matter what the circumstances. You wouldn't want *any* child who reminded you of your marriage to Donna.

'Hey, watch where you're going, mate!' a plump, middle-aged man protested as Elliot collided with him on his way to the entrance to the St Stephen's Accident and Emergency unit.

Watch where he was going? A couple of hours ago Elliot Mathieson had known exactly where he was going, but now...

Now he had a daughter arriving from France tomorrow. Now he was being forced to remember a time in his life he'd tried for the last five years to forget, and he didn't like it. He didn't like it at all.

'I thought Elliot was only going to be away an hour?' Floella Lazear protested, her round face looking distinctly

harassed as she crossed the treatment room. 'What on earth can be keeping him?'

Jane Halden tucked a wayward strand of thick black hair back under her sister's cap and wished she knew. Elliot had told them of his ex-wife's death in a car crash in France, and her London solicitors' urgent request to see him, and she'd assumed—they all had—that he must be a beneficiary in Donna's will, but two hours was an awfully long time for the solicitor to tell him so.

'Maybe his ex-wife's left him a fortune,' Charlie Gordon observed, joining them at the whiteboard. 'She was a successful fashion designer, wasn't she? Maybe she's left him so much money he's handing in his resignation even as we speak.'

'I wish somebody would leave me a fortune,' Floella sighed. 'I'd be off to the travel agent's before you could say enema.'

Charlie laughed. 'What would you do if somebody left you a lot of money, Jane?'

Check into a health farm and lose twelve kilos, she thought. Treat myself to every beautifying facial known to womankind, then throw out all my chain-store clothes and buy designer labels.

'I haven't the faintest idea,' she replied.

'Got everything you want, huh?' The SHO grinned.

'Something like that.' She nodded. And she did. Well, almost everything. She had a job as senior sister in A and E, which she loved, a flat that might be a shoebox but at least it was hers, and if there was no man in her life, well, two out of three wasn't bad. 'How about you, Charlie?' she asked. 'What would you do with a windfall?'

'Send a bottle of champagne and a huge box of chocolates to my girlfriend in Shrewsbury every day to make sure she doesn't forget me.'

'And in six months she'd be a twenty-stone alcoholic, you idiot!' Floella laughed.

A deep blush of embarrassed colour spread across the SHO's face and Jane quickly came to his rescue. 'I think it's a *lovely* idea, Charlie, and your girlfriend's a very lucky girl.'

And she was, too, Jane thought as the SHO hurried away, the colour on his cheeks even darker. They were lucky to have him. Big, bluff, and hearty, Charlie had settled in well into Elliot's old SHO job. It was just a pity the same couldn't be said for their new junior doctor, she thought with a groan as she noticed the man in question bearing down on her. Richard Connery might be bright and enthusiastic, but he was also abrasive and far too self-confident for his own good.

'My patient in 6 has a fractured right arm, Sister Halden,' he declared without preamble. 'Please, arrange for him to go to X-Ray.'

Like he couldn't arrange it himself? she thought as he strode away again before she could reply. No, of course he couldn't. It was obviously too far beneath his dignity to speak to anyone as lowly as a porter so he expected her to drop everything and do it for him.

'And what—pray tell—did his last servant die of?' Floella exclaimed angrily. 'Honestly, Jane—'

'I know, I know,' she interrupted, 'but just leave it right now, Flo, OK?'

'But he has no right to talk to you like that,' the staff nurse protested. 'You're the senior sister in A and E. You've at least six years more medical experience than he has—'

'And if you say I'm old enough to be his mother I'll hit you!' Jane declared, her grey eyes dancing, and a reluctant smile curved Floella's lips.

'Yeah, right. Like you're old Ma Moses. But you know what I mean. It's just not on.'

It wasn't, but working in A and E was difficult enough at the moment, what with Elliot still finding his feet as special registrar and Charlie Gordon learning the ropes as SHO, and the last thing they needed was a full-scale row.

'Try to be patient with him, Flo. I know he can be difficult,' she continued as the staff nurse shook her head, 'but he's only been with us a month, and I'm sure a lot of his abrasiveness is due to him finding the work a lot harder than he imagined.'

'Rubbish!' Floella retorted. 'He just enjoys treating nurses like dirt!'

She didn't need this, not right now, Jane thought as the staff nurse stalked off. Teamwork was important in every department in the hospital, but in A and E it was vital. Without teamwork they couldn't function, but it was going to take time to create a new team, and time, as Floella had just so forcefully revealed, was the one thing they didn't have.

With a sigh she went into cubicle 6 where Richard's patient was still waiting.

'My arm is definitely broken, then?' the elderly man queried, wincing slightly as she helped him into a wheelchair. 'The young lad who saw me earlier said he thought it was, but I wasn't sure whether he was fully qualified to make the diagnosis or not.'

Jane hid a smile. 'Dr Connery's pretty sure your arm's fractured, but to make one hundred per cent sure we're going to send you along to X-Ray. Hey, look on the bright side,' she added encouragingly as his face fell, 'you'll get lots of sympathy from your female admirers.'

'I hope not or my wife will break my other arm,' he observed, his faded brown eyes twinkling. 'Oh, well, I suppose it could have been worse, and at least it's given me

the opportunity to meet a very pretty and charming young lady.'

Jane chuckled. She knew very well that she wasn't pretty, and she supposed that at twenty-eight she wasn't exactly young any more, but that didn't mean it wasn't nice to hear a compliment.

Right now, she could have done with hearing a lot more. It might have cheered her up. In fact, ever since Hannah had married Robert—and it had been a lovely wedding despite the bride's leg being in plaster—she'd been feeling oddly down.

Probably because it's the fourth wedding you've been to in as many months, her mind pointed out, whereas you...

No, she wasn't going to think about her love life. Actually, her completely non-existent love life.

And whose fault is that? Her little voice asked. OK, so Frank was a rat, and you wasted two years of your life believing his protestations of undying love, but what happened after he dumped you? You promptly fell in love with Elliot Mathieson. A man who's had more girlfriends since he got divorced than most other men have had hot dinners. A man who could hurt you a hundred times more than Frank ever did if he found out how you really feel about him.

'Jane, we've got trouble!'

With an effort she turned to see their student nurse gazing at her in dismay. 'What's up, Kelly?'

'We've got that man back in again—the one who thinks his brain's been taken over by aliens. I've phoned Social Services but—'

'They said it's our pigeon,' she finished for her wryly. Social Services always said psychiatric cases were their pigeon unless someone was so bad they had to be sectioned. And Harry's delusions weren't nearly frequent

enough yet to have him compulsorily detained in a psychiatric ward. 'Has Charlie seen him?'

'He's given him a tranquilliser, and he seems pretty quiet at the moment, but you know what happened last time.'

Jane did. Before the tranquilliser could take effect Harry had practically wrecked one of their ECG machines, thinking it was an alien life form. 'OK. I'll sit with him—'

'RTA on the way, Jane!' Floella suddenly called from the end of the treatment room. 'Three casualties, and two look really serious!'

Jane bit her lip. Damn, this would have to happen right now with Mr Mackay, the consultant in charge of A and E, off on his annual break and Elliot not back from the solicitors yet.

'Kelly—'

'Yeah, I know.' The student nurse sighed. 'Make the alien a nice cup of tea, and do my best.'

'Good girl.' Jane nodded, but as she hurried down the treatment room a sigh of relief came from her when Elliot suddenly appeared.

'Now, that's what I call perfect timing,' she said with a smile.

'Perfect timing?'

'We've an RTA on the way,' she explained, 'and I was just wondering how on earth we were going to cope with the casualties.'

'Oh—Right. I see.'

She glanced up at him, her grey eyes concerned. 'Everything OK, Elliot?'

'Great. Fine,' he replied, but he was anything but fine she decided as he walked quickly across to Charlie Gordon.

He looked... Not worried. Elliot never looked worried no matter how dire the situation, but he most definitely

looked preoccupied. Preoccupied and tense, and still quite the handsomest man she'd ever laid eyes on.

In fact, there ought to have been a law against any man being quite so handsome, she thought ruefully. His thick blond hair, deep blue eyes and devastating smile would have been quite potent enough, but when you added a six-foot muscular frame, a pair of shoulders which looked as though they'd been purpose-built for a girl to lean her head against...

It was an unbeatable combination. The kind of combination which turned even the most sensible women into slack-jawed idiots whenever he was around. Herself included, as Jane knew only too well, but she'd always had sense enough not to show it.

Not that it would have made any difference if she had, of course, she realised. Elliot's taste ran to tall, leggy women. Women like Gussie Granton from Paediatrics whose figure would have made a pin-up girl gnash her teeth.

Nobody would ever gnash their teeth over her figure, she thought wistfully, unless it was in complete despair. She was too short, and too fat, and a pair of ordinary grey eyes and stubbornly straight shoulder-length black hair were never going to make up for those deficiencies.

'You have a wonderful sense of humour, Jane,' her mother had told her encouragingly when she was growing up. 'Men like that.'

Yeah, right, Mother. And Frank's admiration for my sense of humour lasted only until a red-haired bimbo with the IQ of a gerbil drifted into his sights, and then he was off.

What on earth was wrong with her today? she wondered crossly as she heard the sound of an ambulance arriving, its siren blaring. All this maudlin self-pity. All right, so she was in love with Elliot Mathieson, and had been ever

since he'd come to St Stephen's two years ago, but he was never going to fall in love with her. She was simply good old Janey and it was high time she accepted that. Time she realised it was only in the movies that the plain, ordinary heroine got the handsome hero, and this wasn't the movies—this was real life.

'OK, what have you got for us?' Elliot asked as the doors of the treatment room banged open and the paramedics appeared with their casualties.

'One adult, plus a seventeen-year-old boy and fifteen-year-old girl. The youngsters suffered the worst damage. They were in the back seat and neither was wearing seat belts.'

Elliot swore under his breath. 'Are they related in any way?'

'The adult's the father. He has a fractured wrist, ankle and minor lacerations.'

'Richard, Kelly—you take the adult—'

'But what about my alien?' the student nurse exclaimed.

'Oh, Lord, he's not back in again, is he?' Elliot groaned. 'Has anyone given him any tranquillisers?'

'I have,' Charlie Gordon said, nodding.

'Then get one of the porters to take him up to Social Services.'

'Elliot, they'll throw a blue fit if we dump him on them!' Jane protested.

'Let them,' he replied grimly. 'It'll give them a chance to see that care in the community means more than simply leaving psychiatric cases to fend for themselves. Charlie, you and Flo take the boy. Jane, I'll need your help with the girl.'

He was going to need his skill a whole lot more, she thought when she helped the paramedic wheel the girl into cubicle 2.

The teenager was a mess. Countless lacerations to her

face and arms, compound fractures to the right and left tibia and fibula which would require the services of both orthopaedics and plastics, but it was her laboured, rasping breathing that was the most worrying. If she wasn't helped—and quickly—not enough oxygen would reach her brain and she'd be in big trouble.

'ET, Jane,' Elliot demanded, though in fact there had been no need for him to ask. She was already holding the correct size of endotracheal tube out to him, and gently he eased it past the girl's vocal cords and down into her trachea. 'IV lines and BP?'

'IV's open and running,' she replied, checking the drip bags containing the saline solution which was providing a temporary substitute for the blood the teenager was losing. 'BP 60 over 40.'

Elliot frowned. Too low, much too low, and the girl's heartbeat was showing an increasingly uneven rhythm.

Quickly he placed his stethoscope on the injured girl's chest. There were no breath sounds on the left side. She must have been thrown against one of the front seats in the crash and her left lung had collapsed, sending blood and air seeping into her chest cavity.

'Chest drain and scalpel?' Jane murmured.

He nodded and swiftly made an incision into the upper right-hand side of the teenager's chest, then carefully inserted a plastic tube directly into her chest cavity. 'BP now?'

'Eighty over sixty,' Jane answered.

Better. Not great, but definitely better. The chest drain had suctioned the excess air and blood out of the girl's chest. She was starting to stabilise at last.

'You'll be wanting six units of O-negative blood, chest, arm and leg X-rays?' Jane asked.

Elliot's eyebrows lifted and he grinned. 'This is getting seriously worrying.'

'Worrying?' she repeated in confusion.

'Your apparent ability to read my mind.'

Just so long as you can't read mine, she thought, and smiled. 'It comes with working with you for two years.'

He was surprised. 'Has it really been that long?'

'Uh-huh.'

He supposed it must have been, but Jane... Well, Jane just always seemed to have been there. Skilled, intuitive, able to instinctively predict whatever he needed whenever he needed it.

But even she couldn't get him out of his current predicament, he thought, watching her as she inserted another IV line to take the O-negative blood they would use until they'd made a cross-match. Nobody could.

If his mother hadn't just left for Canada to stay with his sister Annie for the next three months to help her through what was proving to be a particularly difficult first pregnancy, she would have taken Nicole like a shot—he knew she would. Or if the agencies he'd phoned could have provided him with a nanny or a housekeeper immediately, but none of them could supply anybody until the beginning of April, and that was a month away.

Which meant that not only was he up the creek without a paddle, he was sitting in a leaking boat as well.

How could Donna have done this to him? She'd known the hours he worked, that everything could alter in an instant if a bad accident like this came in. What had she expected him to do with Nicole, then? And what about after school, at weekends?

It probably hadn't even occurred to her, he decided bitterly. Live for today—that had always been Donna's motto. Live for today, and don't think about tomorrow.

Which was what attracted you to her in the first place, his mind pointed out. Her vitality, her lust for life, not to

mention a husky French accent and a face and figure that had done irreparable damage to his libido.

But it hadn't lasted. Within three short years the marriage had been over, leaving him bitter and disillusioned. And now Donna was dead, killed in a car crash. And he had a daughter arriving tomorrow and no earthly idea of how he was going to cope.

'Elliot, are you quite sure you're OK?' Jane said, her gaze fixed on him with concern when the teenager was wheeled out of the treatment room towards the theatre after Radiology had confirmed that the patient did, indeed, have compound fractures, but no other major damage. 'You seem a bit, well, a bit preoccupied this afternoon.'

'Perils of being a new and very inexperienced special reg,' he replied, managing to dredge up a smile. 'Too much to think about.'

She didn't press the point, though he knew she wasn't convinced, and with relief he strode quickly down the treatment room to check on the other casualties. He didn't want to talk about his problem—didn't even want to think about it. All he wanted to do right now was to bury himself in work and forget all about his daughter, and he managed to do just that until late in the afternoon when the sound of children crying caught his attention.

'What on earth's going on in cubicle 8, Flo?' he asked curiously. 'It sounds like somebody's being murdered in there.'

She sighed. 'It's a case of child neglect. Two girls and a boy, aged between one and four. The police brought them in ten minutes ago for a medical assessment before they contact Social Services. Apparently their dad's in jail, their mother is God knows where and a neighbour phoned the police because she hadn't seen them out and about for a week.'

'Medical condition?' Elliot demanded, his professional instincts immediately alert.

'Excellent, considering they've been living in an un-heated flat for the past week, and the oldest child told the police they haven't had anything to eat for two days.' She sighed and shook her head. 'Honestly, some people should never have children.'

People like him, Elliot decided, but it was too late to think about that now, too late to regret that night in the hotel in Paris. 'Who's with them?'

'Jane. Charlie's checked them over, and there's nothing we can do for them except clean them up and give them some food, but...' She shrugged. 'It's better than nothing, isn't it?'

He supposed it was as he strode into the cubicle to find Jane sitting on the trolley, holding the youngest of the three children in her arms while the other two clung to her, wide-eyed and clearly terrified.

'Need any help?' he asked.

She shook her head and smiled, apparently completely oblivious to the overpowering smell of dried urine and faeces emanating from the trio. 'No, thanks. I've sent down to the kitchens for some food, and Kelly's organising a bath for them all.'

'What about clean clothes?' he suggested.

'Flo's phoned her husband and he's bringing some of their twins' old things over.'

There was nothing for him to do here, then, Elliot real-ised, but still he lingered, watching in admiration as Jane managed to eventually coax some smiles from the chil-dren.

She was good with kids. Actually, she was quite amaz-ing with kids. He'd seen her get a response from even the most traumatised of children simply by sitting with them, holding them, murmuring all kinds of nonsense.

And suddenly it hit him. He had the answer to all his problems sitting right in front of him. Jane. Jane would be perfect for Nicole, just perfect.

But would she do it? Would she be prepared to move into his flat to help him out until he could get a nanny or a housekeeper in a month's time?

Of course she would. Jane helped everybody, and it wasn't as though he was asking a lot. Not much, he observed sourly. Just for her to take over your responsibilities, that's all. Nonsense, he wasn't asking her to do that. He wasn't even thinking about himself at all. He was simply thinking about Nicole.

And Jane clearly thought he was, too, when he whisked her into his office and explained what had happened after the police had collected the three abandoned children and taken them off to Social Services.

'Oh, the poor little girl!' she exclaimed, her eyes full of compassion. 'Why on earth didn't Donna tell you about her before?'

He'd wondered about that, too, but all he could think was that she must have been so angry with him when they'd parted that this had been her way of punishing him.

'You're going to have to go very carefully with her,' Jane continued, her forehead creased in thought. 'Not only has she lost her mother, but coming to a strange country, to a man she doesn't know... She's going to need lots of love and attention.'

'But that's the trouble,' he declared. 'How can I give her lots of love and attention when I'm hardly ever going to be there? Janey, you know what our hours are like—'

'We'll all help out,' she said quickly. 'It's a nuisance Mr Mackay being away, but when he gets back I'm sure he'll agree to letting you work days for a while. In the meantime, we could ask Charlie if he'd mind doing most of your night shifts—'

'I don't want Charlie to do my night shifts!' he snapped, then flushed as Jane's eyebrows rose. 'Janey, I've got to be honest with you…'

He paused. How to explain? How to say that it wasn't just a question of the day-to-day complications of taking care of a child that was worrying him, but that he didn't want this girl because she would remind him of a time in his life he preferred to forget. Jane would ask why. She'd ask questions. Questions he didn't want to answer.

Better by far for her to think he was selfish, he decided. Better for her to believe he was the biggest heel of all time than for him to have to reveal the sorry details of his failed marriage.

He took a deep breath. 'Janey, the thing is, kids…they're not really me. I never wanted any—never planned on having any. I'm a loner at heart, you see, always have been.'

Oh, he was something all right, she decided as she stared up at him in utter disbelief. How could he be so unfeeling about a child? And not simply any child. *His* child. *His* daughter.

'So you're getting your mother to look after her, I presume?' she said tightly.

'I can't. She flew out to Canada last Saturday to stay with my sister for the next three months. Annie's been having a really rotten time with her first pregnancy—'

'Then you're hiring a nanny?' Jane asked, her heart going out to his poor little motherless, unwanted child. 'Or are you too damn mean to fork out the money?'

'It's not a question of money!' he exclaimed, his cheeks reddening. 'None of the agencies I contacted could get me anybody until next month, which is why…' He quickly fixed what he hoped was his most appealing smile to his lips. 'Janey, I need you to do me a huge favour. I want

you to come and live with me, to help me look after Nicole.'

'You want me to...' Her mouth fell open, then she shook her head. 'I'm sorry, but I think there must be something wrong with my hearing. I could have sworn you just said you wanted me to come and live with you to look after your daughter.'

'I did—I do. Janey, listen, it makes perfect sense,' he continued as she stared at him, stunned. 'You're a woman—'

'I also like pasta but that doesn't make me Italian,' she protested. 'If you're so desperate for help, why don't you ask Gussie Granton? She's your current girlfriend, according to the hospital grapevine, and as a paediatric sister she's bound to know more about children than I do.' He had the grace at least to look uncomfortable and her grey eyes narrowed. 'You've already asked her, haven't you, and she said no.'

Gussie had. Oh, she'd been wonderfully understanding, her luscious lips curving into an expression of deepest sympathy, but, as she'd pointed out, the demands of her job simply didn't give her the time to take care of a child.

'Janey—'

'So you decided that as your mother couldn't do it, and Gussie wouldn't, muggins here might fit the bill,' she interrupted, her voice harder and colder than he'd ever heard it. 'Well, you can forget it, Elliot. Forget it!'

'But you've *got* to help me,' he cried, coming after her as she made for his office door. 'Surely you can see that I can't do this on my own?'

'You're thirty-two years old, Elliot,' she snapped. 'Get off your butt and try!'

'But you're so good with kids—the very best,' he said, his blue eyes fixed pleadingly on her. 'And I'm not asking

you to do it for ever—just for a month. Until I can get a nanny or a housekeeper. *Please*, Janey.'

She'd heard that wheedling tone in his voice before. It was the one he used on women when he wanted a favour, and it usually worked on her, too, but not today.

'No, Elliot.'

'Look, I'm not asking you to go into purdah for the next month,' he said quickly. 'I have a three-bedroom flat—you can have your friends round whenever you want, go out whenever you want. All I'm asking is for us to dovetail our shifts and personal commitments so at least one of us will be there when Nicole comes home from school.'

'*No*, Elliot.'

'Janey, please. I'm begging you. If you won't do it for me, won't you at least do it for Nicole?'

Blackmail. It was blackmail of the worst possible kind, and anyone who agreed to move in with him under those circumstances needed their head examined. Anyone who had secretly been in love with him for the last two years and agreed to do it needed that head certified.

Tell him it's his problem, not yours, her mind insisted. Tell him to go fly a kite, preferably on the edge of a very high cliff in the middle of a howling gale. OK, so his little girl must be grief-stricken to have lost her mother, but it's *not* your problem.

And she cleared her throat to tell him just that when an image suddenly came into her mind. An image of a little girl with big, frightened eyes. A little girl lost, and alone, and deeply unhappy.

'Just for a month, you said?' she murmured uncertainly.

He nodded, hope, desperation, plain in his eyes.

'You'll have to do your fair share, Elliot,' she declared. 'Nicole is your responsibility, not mine.'

'Oh, absolutely—definitely,' he replied, nodding vigorously.

Only an idiot would agree to this, she thought as she stared up into his handsome face. Only a fool would ever say yes. And yet, before she could stop herself, the words 'All right, then, I'll do it' were out of her mouth.

And as a broad smile lit up his face, and her heart turned over in response, she knew that she wasn't simply an idiot. She was completely and utterly out of her mind.

CHAPTER TWO

'SHE'S arriving this evening, then, on the nine o'clock plane from Paris?' Floella declared as she helped Jane carry a fresh supply of medical dressings out of their small dispensary into the treatment room. 'Poor little soul. Losing her mother like that. My heart goes out to her, it really does.'

And I don't know why MI5 doesn't simply throw in the towel and hand over all its surveillance work to St Stephen's in future, Jane thought ruefully.

How *did* they do it? She'd told nobody about Nicole, and she was pretty sure Elliot hadn't told anybody either, and yet it had taken the staff less than twenty-four hours to discover not only that he had a daughter but what time her plane was arriving as well.

'I bet Gussie's spitting nails about you moving into Elliot's place.' Floella chuckled. 'I hear she's been itching to become his live-in girlfriend.'

'I'm not exactly moving in with him, Flo,' Jane said quickly. 'Simply helping out until he can employ a house-keeper.'

'Oh, I know *that*,' the staff nurse said dismissively. 'We all do.'

Which was another thing that was beginning to seriously annoy her, Jane thought, putting down the boxes of Steri-Strips she was carrying with a bang. The way everyone had instantly assumed there wasn't anything personal about the arrangement.

OK, so there wasn't, but that didn't mean she had to like the idea that nobody thought there might be. She

wasn't *that* plain, and was it really so unlikely that she and Elliot could have become an item? Apparently it was.

'Elliot, we were just talking about your little girl.' Floella beamed as he strode down the treatment room towards them. 'You must be really excited at the prospect of meeting her.'

Jane didn't think he looked even remotely excited, but to his credit he managed to mumble something suitably enthusiastic in reply.

'You must bring her into the hospital one day, so we can all meet her,' the staff nurse continued. 'And, don't forget, if you ever need a babysitter, I'll be only too happy to oblige.'

Elliot smiled and nodded but as Floella bustled away he shook his head wryly. 'You know, this has got to be the worst-kept secret in the hospital.'

'Do you mind everybody knowing about Nicole?' Jane asked.

He shrugged. 'She's a fact of life. Whether I mind or not is immaterial.'

Which sounded very much as though he did mind. As though he'd far rather she didn't exist.

She'd thought—hoped—that since last night he might have had time to see what a great gift he'd been given, how lucky he was, but nothing, it seemed, had changed. He still saw his daughter as a nuisance, an unwelcome intrusion into his life.

'I'd better get back to work,' she said abruptly, but before she could move he suddenly clasped her hands in his.

'Jane, what you're doing for Nicole—for me—I just want to thank you again. It's really good of you to help me out like this, and I do appreciate it.'

Like hell you do, Elliot, she thought sourly, trying very hard not to notice the way her skin was traitorously reacting to the touch of his fingers. You just think you've got

it made. You just think you've managed to offload your responsibilities onto someone else. Well, you're going to find out very quickly that I'm not a complete pushover. You're going to do your full share of taking care of your daughter, or my name isn't Jane Halden.

Determinedly she extricated her hands from his. 'I'd better go—'

'Did you remember to arrange with one of the night staff to start a little earlier tonight so you can come out to the airport with me?' he interrupted.

She nodded, though she still thought Nicole would probably have preferred him to meet her alone.

'I thought we'd take her out to dinner,' he continued. 'A sort of welcome-to-London treat. I know this fabulous restaurant in town which not only does the most amazing lobsters but also the best prawns this side of the Channel.'

He had to be joking. One look at his face told her he wasn't.

'Don't you think fish fingers and chips at home would be a much better idea?' she said quickly.

'Jane, she's French—'

'And she's six years old, Elliot. Look, I wouldn't be at all surprised if she's exhausted and a bit weepy when she arrives,' she continued as he opened his mouth, clearly intending to argue with her, 'so I really do think fish fingers and chips in your flat would suit her much better than dinner out at a fancy restaurant.'

He frowned uncertainly. 'If you say so. I don't think I've got any fish fingers in my freezer but I could easily buy some.'

Frankly she'd have been amazed if he'd had fish fingers in his freezer. *Pâté de foie gras*, quail and partridge eggs for sure, but not fish fingers and chips.

In fact, when she'd dropped off her clothes at his flat this morning her heart had quite sunk when she'd seen

where he lived. Oh, his home was beautiful—all gleaming modern furniture and immaculate white walls—but not by any stretch of the imagination could it have been described as child-friendly. Indeed, its pristine elegance had intimidated her, so who knew what it would do to Nicole?

Flowers might soften the look, she thought suddenly, make it seem more homely, and she'd just opened her mouth to suggest it when two paramedics appeared, their faces taut, grim.

'Twenty-three-year-old mum with bad burns to her face, arms and upper torso. Apparently she was frying some chips for her kids' tea when the pan caught fire. She threw some water on it—'

'And the whole thing went up like a torch,' Elliot groaned as the paramedics wheeled the mother into cubicle 1. 'Didn't she know that oil and water don't mix?'

'Do you want me to page the burns unit?' Jane asked, beckoning to Floella to assist him.

'Please. You'd better alert IC as well. And, Jane…' She turned, her eyebrows raised questioningly. 'Make it fast, eh?'

She nodded. Shock was always the biggest hazard in cases like this. Shock and the danger of infection, and the sooner they could get the young mother stabilised and transferred to specialist care, the better.

And the sooner Richard Connery lost his high-and-mighty attitude the happier she'd be, too, she decided when she put down the phone to see the junior doctor snapping his fingers imperiously at her.

No wonder Floella's temper was close to breaking point, she thought as she walked towards him. Her own was getting pretty wafer-thin as well, and it was getting harder and harder for her to continue believing that Richard's high-handed manner was due to him finding the work in A and E a lot more stressful than he'd expected.

'How can I help you, Doctor?' she asked, determinedly bright as she joined him in cubicle 8.

'Being here considerably earlier would have been a start,' he declared irritably. 'I've been waiting ten minutes for nursing assistance.'

'We're very busy this afternoon, Dr Connery—'

'And I don't have time to listen to excuses,' he interrupted. 'My patient is suffering from acute appendicitis and I need liver, pancreatic and guiac tests to confirm it before I send him up to Theatre.'

It wasn't the only thing he needed, she thought grimly, but she managed to keep her tongue between her teeth and quickly took the samples he wanted.

'Well, is it a ruptured appendix, as I said?' he declared when she returned later with the results.

She cleared her throat awkwardly. 'Could I have a word with you in private Dr Connery?'

'I don't have time for a chat, Sister,' he retorted. 'All I want is a simple answer to a simple question. Is it a ruptured appendix or not?'

Well, he'd asked for it, she thought, and as he'd asked for it he was going to get it. 'I'm afraid it isn't, Dr Connery. Your patient has gallstones.'

'Gallstones?' Richard's normally pale face turned an interesting shade of pink, and he snatched the sheet of papers from her fingers. 'Let me see those results!'

'It can be very easy to confuse the two,' she murmured for the benefit of the young man who was lying on the trolley, glancing from her to Richard with clear concern. 'The symptoms—pain, nausea and sickness—'

'Are you presuming to give me lessons in diagnosis, Sister Halden?' Richard interrupted, his face now almost puce.

Of course I'm not, you big ninny, she thought. I'm simply trying to get you out of a jam. You should never have

told your patient what was wrong with him until you were a hundred per cent sure, and making a diagnosis without having the results of your tests was just plain stupid.

But she didn't say any of that. Instead, she said as calmly as she could, 'Would you like me to make arrangements for your patient to be taken up to Men's Surgical, Dr Connery?'

From his expression Richard looked as though he'd far rather have thrown her under the nearest bus, but he managed to nod.

But he wasn't finished. The minute the young man on the trolley was wheeled out of the treatment room, he rounded on her furiously.

'I do not appreciate being made to look a fool, Sister Halden! That man was *my* patient—in *my* care—and you deliberately undermined his confidence in me!'

'I did no such thing,' she protested. 'I didn't want to give you those results. I asked if I could discuss them with you in private, but you insisted on having them.'

He had, and he knew it. He was also plainly acutely and deeply mortified, and despite her anger she couldn't help feeling a certain sympathy for him.

'Dr Connery…Richard… Look, it's no big deal,' she said gently. 'OK, so your initial diagnosis wasn't correct, but you were sensible enough to order all the necessary tests—'

'I am not a child so stop humouring me!' he interrupted. 'I am the doctor here, Sister Halden, and I suggest you don't forget it!'

He stormed away before she could answer him, but to her dismay her troubles weren't over. As she turned to go back into the cubicle to remove the paper sheet from the examination trolley and replace it with a fresh one, Elliot suddenly appeared and it was clear from his grim face that he'd heard every word.

'Does he always talk to you like that?' he demanded. 'He does—doesn't he?' he continued, seeing the betraying flush of colour on her cheeks. 'Right. It's obviously high time I had a chat with that young man.'

'Oh, Elliot, don't,' she said quickly, dreading the inevitable friction that such a course of action would create. 'He knows he was wrong, but he's very young, still finding his feet—'

'And using them to walk all over you by the sound of it,' he snapped. 'Jane, it's not on. There's such a thing as staff courtesy, not to mention the fact that even a first-year medical student would know never to make a diagnosis before they'd done every test.'

'I know that, but, please, won't you leave it for now?' she begged. 'I'm sure when he's had time to think about it he'll realise he shouldn't have behaved as he did.'

'And if he doesn't?' he demanded. 'If he continues to treat you like this?'

'He won't—I'm sure he won't,' she insisted, and for a second he frowned, then sighed and shook his head.

'You know something, Janey, you're far too soft-hearted for your own good.'

Too damn right I am, she thought, or I'd never have agreed to help you with Nicole, and she would have told him so, too, if she hadn't suddenly noticed he was smiling at her. Smiling the smile that made grown women grow weak at the knees, and her own were none too steady at the moment.

Why in the world had she ever agreed to move in with this man? Her brain must have been out to lunch. Her common sense must have gone with it, too, she realised, feeling an answering smile being irresistibly drawn from her. To live with him. To see him at breakfast. Last thing at night...

Then remember why you agreed to do it, she told herself

sharply. Remember that he's simply using you until he can employ a housekeeper, and that he doesn't give a damn for his daughter.

And if that doesn't bring you down to earth, she thought grimly when the doors of the treatment room swung open and Gussie Granton suddenly appeared, Elliot's current girlfriend certainly should.

'Hello, Gussie,' Elliot said in clear surprise. 'We don't often see you down in A and E. Something I can do for you?'

Gussie wrapped one curl of her long blonde hair round her finger and threw him a provocative glance from under her impossibly thick eyelashes. 'Not in public unfortunately, darling.'

Oh, barf. Barf, barf, and triple barf, Jane thought, deliberately beginning to edge away, but she didn't get far. Gussie placed a beautifully manicured hand on her arm, and subjected her to a smile. A smile which had quite a struggle to make her eyes.

'Don't run off, Jane. At least not until I tell you how very sweet I think you're being to help us out like this. I would have taken care of Nicole in a minute if I could, but being a senior sister in Paediatrics...' She sighed heavily. 'I just don't have any time to myself.'

And I do? Jane thought waspishly. Like being a senior sister in A and E is a dawdle? Like I simply turn up every day, do my eight-hour shift, then go home and put my feet up?

For two pins she'd have liked to tell Gussie where to stick her thanks. Forget the two pins, she decided. She'd do it for free. And right now. 'Gussie—'

'Elliot, darling, it's just occurred to me that you might like some company when you go out to the airport to meet your daughter,' Gussie continued, completely ignoring her.

'I could easily get one of my staff to swop shifts with me—'

'There's no need,' Elliot interrupted. 'Jane's already agreed to come with me.'

'Has she?' Gussie's large brown eyes narrowed slightly, then she smiled again at Jane. And this time her smile most definitely didn't reach her eyes. 'My word, but you are proving to be a little godsend, aren't you?'

Elliot thought she was. In fact, after a sleepless night spent tossing and turning, he was all too aware of how very kind Jane was being, but he wished Gussie hadn't said it—at least not in that particular way. There'd been a very definite edge to her voice. An edge which had made him feel uncomfortable, and if he'd felt like that he was sure Jane did as well.

'Gussie, I'm afraid, can be a bit overbearing at times,' he said the minute the paediatric sister had gone.

'That's one way of putting it,' Jane replied tersely.

He coloured. 'She does mean well, though, even if it doesn't always sound like it.'

Oh, Gussie had made her meaning perfectly clear, Jane thought tightly, walking over to the thirteen-year-old boy and his mother who had come through from the waiting room into cubicle 8.

Hands off—he's mine. That was what she'd said, and there'd been no need. Gussie was welcome to Elliot. In fact, right now the paediatric sister could have had him gift-wrapped with a bow round his neck.

'Your son's had this pain at the top of his chest for the last three days, you said?' Elliot said, once Jane had got the boy and his mother settled.

'At first I thought David had simply pulled a muscle, playing basketball,' the boy's mother replied, twisting her hands together convulsively, 'but when the pain didn't go away—'

'Keen on sport, are you, David?' Elliot asked as Jane helped the boy off with his shirt.

'Only basketball,' he replied. 'The other boys at my school prefer soccer, but basketball... Basketball's the best.'

Gently Elliot pressed on the boy's chest. 'Does it hurt when I do this?'

The boy shook his head. Not musculoskeletal pain, then, Elliot decided, or the pain would have increased under pressure.

'Do you have any other aches and pains anywhere?' he asked, taking his stethoscope out of his pocket and smiling encouragingly at the teenager.

'I don't think so.' David frowned. 'Sometimes I get an odd feeling in my back, but that's all.'

Elliot's ears pricked up. 'Odd in what way?'

'It's hard to explain. It's...it's a sort of ripping feeling. I'm sorry but I can't really describe it.'

He didn't need to. The minute Elliot placed his stethoscope on the boy's chest he heard a distinctive whooshing sound. A sound similar to that he'd heard in much older patients with leaky heart valves. But surely a boy of thirteen was far too young for that?

'Jane, could you get me an ECG reading, please?' he murmured casually.

She nodded.

'So, you play a lot of basketball, do you, David?' he said as Jane deftly applied the sticky electrodes to each of the boy's arms and legs, then across his chest.

'His school thinks he could play professionally when he's older,' his mother replied, clearly torn between maternal pride and concern.

'My height helps a lot,' her son said quickly, shooting his mother the speaking glance all boys used when they

were deeply embarrassed. 'You don't have to jump up so far to reach the basket when you're as tall as me.'

And he was tall—almost as tall as I am, Elliot thought pensively. Rangy, too, with extremely long fingers, and suddenly somewhere in the back of his mind a memory stirred. A memory of something he'd read in a medical journal a long time ago, and he hoped to heaven he was wrong.

'ECG reading normal,' Jane murmured.

'Chest X-ray, please, Sister Halden,' he said, then turned to the boy's mother. 'Has your son always been tall for his age?'

'Not when he was a toddler, but when he hit seven...' She shook her head ruefully. 'It costs me a fortune every time he needs new clothes and shoes. Nothing in any of the ordinary kids' shops fits him, you see.'

Because he wasn't an ordinary boy, Elliot thought sadly, when Radiology had processed David's chest X-rays.

He had Marfan's syndrome, a rare, inherited condition which caused the aorta—the major blood vessel leading from the heart—to become abnormally enlarged, and one of the first indications of the condition was that sufferers were always extremely tall as children with unusually long fingers.

'Historians think Abraham Lincoln might have had Marfan's, don't they?' Jane commented after the boy and his mother had been transferred up to the medical ward where further tests could be performed.

Elliot nodded. 'Thank goodness his mother brought him in when she did. With that enlarged aorta, he could have had a heart attack at any time, but at least now we can give him beta-blockers to control his heart problems, and get him fitted with an orthopaedic corset before his spine starts to become deformed due to the weight of his bones.'

'No more basketball for him, though, I guess,' Jane sighed.

'No. No more basketball,' he answered, and wondered why he should find that thought so deeply depressing.

Oh, he'd always cared about the patients who passed through his hands, had fought tooth and nail to save many of them, but this young boy...

Perhaps it was because he seemed so very young, scarcely more than a child, despite his height. Perhaps it was because all of his dreams to become a world-class basketball player were now lying in the dust.

No, it wasn't that, he realised. It had been the look of total devastation on his mother's face when he'd taken her into one of their private waiting rooms to explain what was wrong.

David's mother would willingly have given everything she possessed to spare her son pain. Would even have given her own life if he could have been cured. That was love. Real love. And he felt none of that for his daughter.

You don't know her yet—haven't even met her—his mind pointed out, and unconsciously he shook his head. It wasn't as simple as that. Even if he'd wanted to be a father—and at the moment he certainly didn't—he didn't know how to be one.

He could do Lover. Oh, he could do a great Lover, provided there was no talk of long-term commitment. He could even do Friend. A sympathetic, willing shoulder for any woman to lean her head on if she needed it, but Father?

There was no way he could do Father—no way—and a wave of panic washed over him.

Panic that didn't get any less when a case of accidental poisoning came in a mere forty minutes before he and Jane were due to leave for the airport.

'We're really cutting it fine,' Jane murmured, seeing his

eye drift to the treatment-room clock while they waited for the results of the blood count and chemistry tests. 'Thank goodness we brought a change of clothes into the hospital just in case.'

He nodded, but he'd hoped to have time to shower, to wash the smell of the hospital off him before he met his daughter, but now it looked as though he'd be phoning the airport to tell them to look after her until they could get there. It was a great start. A really great start.

'Look, why don't the pair of you just go?' Charlie Gordon said. 'It's not like we need either of you here. Flo and I can look after your patient.'

Elliot shook his head. 'It's asking too much—'

'Elliot, I'd bet money that your blood pressure is higher right now than your patient's,' the SHO said with a grin.

'Probably, but—'

'Charlie's right, boss,' Floella chipped in. 'We don't need you here, and it would be awful if your little girl arrived with nobody to meet her.'

She was right, it would. But still he looked across at Jane uncertainly. 'What do you think?'

'Who am I to disagree with the others?' She smiled. 'Come on. Let's go.'

They made the airport with five minutes to spare.

'Relax, Elliot,' Jane said, seeing him scanning the Arrivals board anxiously for information about the 21.00 plane from Paris. 'The plane might land at nine o'clock, but she'll have to collect her luggage first, remember, so try to relax.'

Relax? How could he possibly relax when all his instincts were urging him to run, to leave town, to give no forwarding address? He glanced at his watch, then straightened his tie. 'Do I look all right? I mean, this suit…?'

'You look fine.' Actually, she wished he'd brought a

pair of casual trousers and a sweatshirt to change into at the hospital instead of a suit and tie, but now was hardly the time to tell him so.

'Should I get her some flowers, do you think?' he continued, seeing a man emerging from the florist opposite with an enormous bouquet. 'Girls always like flowers, don't they?'

'Daffodils would be nice…'

'Not roses, then?' he queried. 'You think roses would be too much?'

For sure they would be too much. Roses were for an adult, not a little girl, and she would have told him that if she hadn't suddenly caught a glimpse of his face.

He looked tense. Tense, and taut, and grim.

Surely he couldn't possibly be nervous at the prospect of meeting his daughter? Of course he wasn't. The very idea was ridiculous. He was resentful, yes. Probably even a little bit angry at his ex-wife for doing this to him, but super-confident Elliot nervous about meeting a child? No way. Never. And yet…

Gently she put her hand on his arm. 'Elliot, all she needs is to feel loved and wanted.'

'Loved and wanted.' He nodded, for all the world as though he were ticking off a mental check list of dos and don'ts.

'Just be her father,' she continued, 'and she'll adore you.'

Be her father? He couldn't do it—he knew he couldn't—but a voice over the loudspeaker had announced the arrival of Flight 303 from Paris, and Jane was pushing her way through the crowded concourse, leaving him with no choice but to follow her.

'Do you have a photograph so we'll know what she looks like?' she asked, breaking into his thoughts.

It had never occurred to him to ask if the solicitor had

one! Relax, he told himself, feeling a trickle of sweat run down his back. How many six-year-old kids can be travelling on the plane from Paris? Even if there are dozens she'll have somebody from Donna's French solicitors with her.

She didn't. She was on her own. OK, so one of the air stewardesses was holding her hand, but she was still on her own, and somebody had pinned a label onto her coat for all the world as though she were a parcel to be collected, not a child, not a person.

A surge of quite unexpected anger flooded through him. Anger that was just as quickly replaced by an altogether different emotion as the stewardess led his daughter towards him.

She looked exactly like Donna. The same long auburn hair, the same large dark eyes, the same elfin features. The face that stared uncertainly up at him was the one which had loved and then taunted and mocked him during his marriage, and despite all his best efforts to prevent it he felt himself beginning to withdraw. Knew it was wrong, that she was only a child, but he couldn't stop himself.

And Nicole sensed his withdrawal. He could see it in the clouding of her eyes, and though he managed to swiftly dredge up his brightest smile he knew the damage had been done.

'Elliot....'

Jane's hand was at his back, urging him forward, and he cleared his throat awkwardly.

'Hello, Nicole. I'm...I'm your father.' She gazed up at him without expression and a fresh wave of panic assailed him. What if she didn't speak any English? Donna had been French. She might never have seen any need for her daughter—his daughter, he reminded himself—to learn English.

'Nicole...I'm... *Moi...Je...Je...*' He bit his lip. Oh,

God, but he'd never been any good at languages.
'Nicole… *Moi…votre père?*'

'I know.'

The reply had been barely a whisper.

'And this…' He caught Jane's hand in desperation.
'This is my friend, Jane Halden. We…we're…'

'Flatmates,' Jane said quickly, coming to his rescue.
'Your father and I are flatmates.'

What now? Elliot wondered as the air stewardess disappeared, the loudspeaker announced the arrival of the
21.15 from Berlin and his daughter stared at the floor.
What did he do and say now?

Jane had no such doubts. She simply got down on her
knees, gave the little girl a hug and began talking about
the flight from Paris.

Which is what he should have done, he realised bleakly
as he retrieved Nicole's luggage. But it was too late to
think about that now. Too late for a lot of things.

All he could do was drive them back to his flat and
listen to Jane and Nicole chattering away quite happily
while he sat in silence, feeling as much use as a lamb chop
in a vegetarian restaurant.

Dinner was no better. Nicole ate little, and said less.
Jane—bless her—kept up a steady stream of conversation
while Nicole valiantly attacked her fish fingers, but it was
a relief when his daughter finally pushed her plate away
and asked if she could go to bed.

Jane didn't linger long afterwards. There was plenty she
wanted to say. Things like 'What happened to the famous
Mathieson charm?' And 'Couldn't you at least have *tried*
to make some conversation?' But it would keep.

A lot of things would keep, she decided as she took her
pyjamas out of her suitcase and smiled ruefully as she
looked at them.

Passion-killers. That's what Frank had called the men's

red-and-white-striped pyjamas she liked to wear, and she supposed they were, but she liked them, always had. They were cosy on wintry nights, cool on hot summer evenings, and if they were as sexy as a pair of flannelette knickers then so much the better while she was staying with Elliot.

Not that she had anything to fear on that score, she thought wistfully as she changed into them. She was just Jane. Just good old dependable Jane.

And you should thank your lucky stars you are, her mind declared while she brushed her teeth. How long do Elliot's girlfriends usually last—a month, six weeks? Gussie was doing well at two months. Actually, Gussie was doing incredibly well to have lasted two months.

Sleep, she told herself firmly. Get into bed and get some sleep. And she tried. She really did try, but two o'clock saw her no sleepier than before, and she'd just decided to get up and make herself a cup of tea when she heard it.

The unmistakable sound of a child's muffled sobs in the silence.

She was out of bed in a second, tiptoeing quickly down the corridor so as not to wake Elliot, but her stealth was unnecessary. He was already awake, already heading in the same direction, and he came to a halt with clear relief when he saw her. She stopped too, but it wasn't relief she felt. It was an altogether different emotion.

He only wore boxer shorts to bed. Nothing on top at all. Nothing to disguise the fact that his chest was even broader and more muscular than she'd ever imagined. And the boxer shorts... She swallowed convulsively, and resolutely shifted her gaze to his face and kept it there.

'Nicole's crying,' he said unnecessarily.

'She'll be missing her mother,' she managed to reply. 'Feeling a bit lost.'

'I guess so.'

'I'll leave you to it, then,' she continued, half turning to go.

'Leave me?' he gasped. 'But you can't. I mean, I don't know what to do!'

'Elliot, all she needs is for you to hold her, cuddle her!' she exclaimed, unable to hide her exasperation. 'How hard can that be?'

'Can't you do it?' he begged.

'Elliot—'

'Janey, I told you I wasn't any good with kids. I'll only muck it up if I go in there, say the wrong thing.'

'But—'

'And I have to get some sleep,' he continued in desperation, seeing the shock and disapproval in her face. 'I've got a meeting with Admin tomorrow about next year's budget, and I must have my wits about me.'

For a second she stared at him speechlessly, then she drew herself up to her full five feet one, her grey eyes blazing.

'Go, then!' she snarled. 'Go and get your precious sleep, and I hope you have nightmares. You deserve to, because you sure as hell don't deserve a lovely little girl like Nicole!'

And he didn't, she thought furiously when she went into Nicole's bedroom and gathered the little girl into her arms. He didn't deserve anybody's love.

To think that at the airport she'd been stupid enough to wonder if his apparent callousness might be an act. An act he'd adopted because he was terrified that he wouldn't be able to cope. But it wasn't an act. He was just selfish to the core.

And as she cradled Nicole to her, holding the little girl tightly until she finally fell asleep, she didn't know that Elliot remained outside the bedroom door, listening. Didn't

know that as he stood there, his hands clenched against his sides, his forehead leaning against the door, that he felt not only like the biggest heel of all time but also the world's biggest failure.

CHAPTER THREE

'HEY, Elliot, I know everyone says fatherhood's tough, but don't you think trying to cut your own throat is a bit drastic?' Charlie Gordon grinned.

'Oh, ha, ha, very funny,' Elliot replied, gingerly rubbing his lacerated chin. 'Jane's been using my razor to shave her legs again, and it was blunt as a stone this morning.'

'Don't you just hate it when girls do that?' Charlie laughed. 'I mean, it's bad enough when they hang their wet tights and underwear all over the shower rail—'

'Not to mention all those creams and potions they stack along the bath.' Elliot sighed ruefully. 'Two weeks ago I had a bathroom to call my own, and now—'

'It's become a branch of your local chemist,' Charlie finished for him. 'Still, all that clutter's nice in an odd sort of way. Makes a man's flat seem more homely somehow.'

It did, Elliot acknowledged. Just as he also knew that he could never have got through this last fortnight without Jane, in spite of all her clutter. She was the oil that kept everything running. The cement without which everything would have fallen apart. Without her, Nicole's arrival would have been even more of a nightmare than it actually was.

And it *had* been a nightmare, despite the fact that he'd tried really hard to involve himself in Nicole's life. He'd had to, and it wasn't just because he knew Jane's watchful eyes were constantly on him. It was because he'd felt so guilty about the way he'd reacted when he'd first seen Nicole, the way he'd chickened out of comforting her on that first night, but nothing he'd done had worked.

43

With Jane his daughter was completely at ease, laughing and smiling, but the minute he tried to engage her in conversation all her animation disappeared. Oh, she was polite enough, answering all of his questions, dutifully telling him about her new school, but it had been a duty. A duty she'd got over as quickly as she could.

'Nicole settling in OK at her new school?' Charlie continued as they walked together towards the treatment room.

'Very well, thanks.' Elliot nodded.

And that had been because of Jane, too. He didn't know how she'd managed to do it but somehow she'd contrived to make friends with the mother of one of the girls in Nicole's class, and now invitations were starting to arrive for Nicole to come to tea.

'You must find Jane a great help,' Charlie said as though he'd read his mind.

'Couldn't do without her,' Elliot admitted frankly.

'Nice girl, Jane,' the SHO continued, seeing her coming out of one of the cubicles. 'Lovely smile, too. Sort of lights up her face, if you know what I mean.'

Elliot didn't. To him, Jane was... Well, Jane was just Jane but, judging by Charlie Gordon's admiring gaze, he clearly didn't think so.

Actually, now he came to think of it, the SHO had no business to be thinking *anything* about Jane, Elliot decided irritably. Dammit, the man had a girlfriend in Wales or Norfolk, or some such outlandish place, and if he was planning on fooling around with Jane, breaking her heart...

'Charlie—'

'Good grief, what in the world have you done to your face, Elliot?' Jane asked, smothering a chuckle as she joined them.

'Somebody—*somebody*—has been using my razor to shave their legs again,' he observed.

'Sorry,' she said guiltily. 'I'll try to get to a chemist some time today before I go home.'

'Better buy some plasters while you're about it,' Charlie declared as he headed off towards Reception. 'Those bits of toilet paper he's currently got stuck to his chin aren't exactly going to inspire much confidence in our patients.'

Elliot whipped the forgotten pieces of toilet paper off quickly, but not fast enough. Jane let out a peal of laughter, and as he stared down at her he realised that Charlie was right.

She did have a nice smile. Wide, and full, and generous. She had nice hair, too. Thick and black, it shone like silk when she took it down from its topknot back at his flat after work and brushed it out. And she didn't do anything special with it. Simply washed, then blow-dried it. He knew that because he'd watched her doing it last night when she'd been helping Nicole with her homework.

'S-sorry?' he stammered, suddenly realising from her expectant expression that she must have asked him something. 'What did you just say?'

'I asked—I *asked*—if you remembered that Nicole's going round to her new friend Stephanie's house for tea tonight,' she said tightly. 'But as usual, when it comes to talking about your daughter, you weren't listening!'

He groaned inwardly as Jane whirled angrily round on her heel and strode away. Damn Charlie Gordon. If the SHO hadn't been wittering on about how nice Jane was, and what a terrific smile she had, he would have been paying attention to what she was saying, and not simply gazing at her.

It had taken him three days after the fiasco of Nicole's arrival to get Jane to say anything to him beyond an abrupt 'Yes' or 'No' to any of his questions, and the last thing he wanted was to go through that again.

Swiftly he hurried after her, catching up with her beside

the whiteboard. 'Jane, I'm sorry. I wasn't being uncaring but I was thinking about something else. I was wondering...' Think of something fast, Elliot, he told himself, and make it good. 'I...I was trying to figure out if I could afford another bathroom.'

'Yeah, right,' she said tartly.

'It's true,' he protested, crossing his fingers behind his back. 'One bathroom isn't really sufficient for the three of us, and I was wondering whether the cupboard in the hall could become an extra toilet.'

She gazed at him suspiciously. 'Why do I get the feeling you're spinning me a line?'

'Do I look like the kind of man who would?' he exclaimed, opening his blue eyes very wide.

'Absolutely one hundred per cent,' she replied. 'Elliot, I've known you for two years, seen how you operate, so cut the flannel. Were you *really* thinking about a bathroom?'

He stared at her for a second, then his mouth turned up at the corners. 'Actually, I was thinking what a very nice smile you had.'

Her jaw dropped, then she began to laugh. 'You're impossible, you know that, don't you? Expecting me to swallow a load of old baloney like that—'

'It's true—Scout's honour.'

'Elliot, you were never a Scout,' she protested. 'The kind of man every mother warns her daughter about, but never a Scout. Honestly, sometimes I don't know why I put up with you!'

''Cos you like me?' he suggested, his blue eyes sparkling.

Oh, I do, she thought, laughing and shaking her head. I do, but I just wish you would use some of that charm of yours on your daughter for a change.

To be fair to him, he'd certainly been making more of

an effort, talking to Nicole about her new school, the things she was learning, but he was so stiff with her, so formal. It was obvious that all the little girl wanted was to be loved, and yet Elliot either couldn't, or wouldn't, see it.

'Elliot…'

The rest of what she'd been about to say died in her throat as the treatment-room doors opened, and a young woman stood there, dishevelled, wild-eyed and panic-stricken.

'Please! Please, can somebody help me? My boyfriend. He's out in the car. He has an allergy to almonds, and I think he's dying!'

Elliot reached for an Ambu-bag and was off at a run, with Jane and the young woman not far behind.

'What's his name?' he demanded when they reached the car and he threw open the front passenger door.

'Keith. Keith Fuller,' the young woman sobbed, her face chalk-white with fear. 'We were just leaving to go to work, and—'

'Keith—Keith, can you hear me—do you know where you are?' Elliot asked, lifting the young man's head back from the dashboard.

A slurred, incoherent mumble was his only reply.

With a muttered oath Elliot peeled the sterile cover off the Ambu-bag, took out the long polystyrene tube and skilfully worked it down the young man's throat and into his trachea. Then, just as deftly, he attached the Ambu-bag to the end of the tube and began squeezing it, sending air rushing into Keith's chest.

'Wheelchair?' Jane queried.

Not ideal, but Keith couldn't walk. Giving the Ambu-bag to Jane, Elliot levered the young man into the wheelchair with as much care as was possible under the circum-

stances, and at a run they set off back to the treatment room.

'OK, IV line with adrenaline and corticosteroid,' Elliot ordered the moment the young man had been transferred onto the examination trolley in cubicle 7. 'It looks to me like a full-blown anaphylactic shock.'

It looked that way to Jane, too, as Floella led the weeping girlfriend away. Keith's chest was covered in a mass of deep red welts, his face was red and puffy and his eyes were swollen shut. Somehow he must have eaten almonds without realising it, but the 'how' could wait until later. Right now, they had to concentrate on counteracting the massive amounts of histamine that the young man's body was producing.

'BP?' Elliot demanded, raising the young man's legs to try to improve the flow of blood to his heart and brain.

'Eighty and dropping,' Jane answered, and heard Elliot swear.

The adrenaline and corticosteroid should have acted almost immediately but the young man was still fighting for breath and his circulation was collapsing. He was slowly but surely suffocating.

'Come on, *come on*!' Elliot exclaimed, checking the young man's pulse again. 'You are not going to die on me. I am *not* going to allow you to die on me!'

'BP 85,' Jane announced.

It was up a little, but not enough. Keith's heart was thundering like a train, and if the adrenaline and corticosteroid didn't work soon he'd have a lot more than anaphylactic shock to worry about.

'I want more fluids,' Elliot ordered. 'Up the adrenaline, too, Jane, and get ready in case we have to perform CPR.'

She nodded. If he had a heart attack on top of everything else...

She didn't want to think about the consequences and

determinedly she concentrated on inserting another IV line while keeping her eyes on the BP gauge.

90...95...100. They'd got him!

'That was a close one,' she murmured.

'Too damn close if you ask me.' Elliot grinned. 'Well done.'

'Well done, you, too.' She smiled back, then noticed that Keith had opened his eyes and was staring up at them in confusion. 'How do you feel, Mr Fuller?'

'Terrible,' he croaked, licking his lips gingerly. 'Where am I?'

'St Stephen's Accident and Emergency unit,' Elliot replied, relieved to see that the puffiness around the young man's face was finally beginning to lessen, the welts on his body fading. 'Giving Sister Halden and myself the fright of our lives.'

'Was it almonds again?' the young man asked.

Elliot nodded. 'Any idea how you managed to eat some?'

Keith Fuller hadn't, but his girlfriend supplied the answer. She'd had muesli for breakfast and a tiny fragment of almond must have become lodged in her teeth. When they'd kissed he'd been exposed to the almond and, hey presto, full anaphylactic shock.

'Almost quite literally the kiss of death, in fact,' Elliot observed after the young man had been transferred to IC for observation.

Jane nodded and laughed, but as she did so Elliot suddenly realised that Charlie Gordon had been right about something else, too. Her face *did* light up when she smiled.

Funny how he'd never noticed it before. Neither had he noticed that she had a small dusting of golden freckles on her nose and cheeks. She was quite small, too. Five feet one, he reckoned, and built on generous lines, with wide, curvaceous hips and full, high breasts.

And he knew something that Charlie didn't. She wore plain white cotton bras and briefs. He knew it because he'd seen them draped over the shower rail in the bathroom alongside Nicole's little tights and underwear.

Gussie wore skimpy, transparent bras and briefs. The kind guaranteed to have any red-blooded male wanting nothing more than to tear them straight off her. Jane's underwear was sensible. Sensible, plain white briefs, sensible, plain white bras.

Actually, no. Now he came to think of it, the bras weren't plain. They had tiny little flowers embroidered on them, and some lace on the bits which would cover her breasts. The breasts that were high, and full, and...

And it was obviously time he made a date with Gussie, he decided, feeling a slow crawl of heat edging up the back of his neck. Jane... Well, good grief, she was a very nice girl and everything, but if he was starting to think about her breasts, he definitely needed to make a date with Gussie.

'Something troubling you, Elliot?' Jane asked, her face concerned.

Too damn right there was, he thought, tugging at his collar, but to his relief he was saved from answering.

'I think Richard wants your help,' he said, noticing the junior doctor waving to them from outside cubicle 7. But as she turned to go he put out his hand to stay her for a second. 'Has he come to his senses yet—manners-wise, I mean?'

'Oh, he's been much better lately,' she replied brightly. Actually, he'd taken to virtually totally ignoring her ever since the incident with the gallstones, but frankly she much preferred it to his previous behaviour. 'I think he's finally beginning to settle in at last.'

Elliot hoped he was. Staff friction was bad for morale, and love affairs between members of staff were even

worse, he thought with a deep frown, seeing Charlie beaming at Jane as she passed him.

It's none of your business if Charlie is interested in Jane,
he thought after he'd reassured the woman with a stiff neck
and fever in cubicle 3 that she didn't have meningitis as
she'd feared, but simply a bad cold and a strained shoulder
muscle.

The guy's not married, and Jane's single, so it's none
of your business. And it wasn't, but that didn't mean he
wasn't going to keep his eye on the situation, he decided
as he heard the high-pitched wail of an approaching ambulance. Both eyes if necessary, he told himself as the
doors of the treatment room opened and the paramedics
appeared.

'His name's Vic Imrie, and he's fifty-two,' one of the
paramedics announced as he and his colleague wheeled
their casualty in. 'His son found him collapsed on the floor
by the side of his bed. There were two empty pill bottles
and a half-full bottle of whisky beside him, and the son
thinks he's taken an overdose.'

'Any idea what he's taken?' Elliot asked, beckoning to
Jane and Kelly as the paramedics transferred Mr Imrie
from his stretcher onto the trolley.

'Tetrabenazine and Valium. He's being treated by his
GP for Huntington's chorea. Unfortunately the son doesn't
know how many pills he took, or when. It could be a
couple of hours, maybe more.'

In which case none of the drugs would still be in Mr
Imrie's stomach. They would already be on their way to
the intestines.

'You said his son telephoned you,' Elliot said. 'Is he a
widower, then?'

The paramedic shook his head. 'Apparently, his wife
went to the opening of a new art gallery in town. The
police are trying to contact her, but…'

The condemnation in the paramedic's voice was clear. Any wife who went off to the opening of a new art gallery, leaving a clearly very ill man at home, wasn't up to much.

'Huntington's is an inherited disease, isn't it?' Kelly asked when the paramedics had gone and she was helping Jane to insert a cannula into Vic Imrie's nose to aid his breathing. 'Causing a gradual degeneration of the brain?'

Jane nodded grimly. It was, and the disease was one of the most devastating imaginable. Not only did it cause random, jerky, involuntary movements and grimaces, there were also personality changes as the disease progressed, changes that led to memory loss, and eventually dementia.

And if that wasn't catastrophic enough, symptoms of the disease didn't usually appear until a sufferer was between the ages of 35 and 50, by which time they'd probably already had children. Children who each had a fifty per cent chance of inheriting the disease.

'Mr Imrie—Mr Imrie, can you tell me where you are, and what day of the week it is?' Elliot demanded, putting his head down close to the man's lips, but nothing the man said was even remotely coherent, and he turned to Jane quickly. 'OK, I want a blood sample for a blood-alcohol level, and a toxic screen to find out exactly what he's taken. Just because we've got two empty pill bottles doesn't mean that's all—or even what—he's ingested.'

'An ECG and chest X-ray, too?' she queried as she began removing Vic Imrie's clothing.

'Absolutely.' He nodded.

But they all knew that they couldn't wait for the results of any of these tests. The most important thing at the moment was to prevent the digestion and absorption of as much of the drugs that Mr Imrie had taken as possible, and as most of the pills were probably in the intestine, that meant a stomach pump.

'BP, Jane?'

'One-thirty over ninety.'

A bit high, but normal in the circumstances.

'OK, let's get his stomach emptied,' Elliot said.

It was easier said than done. Mr Imrie might be frail because of his Huntington's chorea, and almost comatose, but he still fought Jane all the way as she pushed the tube up into his nose, then down through his oesophagus and into his stomach.

'Is it in?' Elliot asked when she finally straightened up.

'You bet it is,' she replied.

'ECG?'

She glanced across at the monitor. 'Still normal.'

With the tube in place it was a simple matter to flush Mr Imrie's stomach out with clear water, before passing a slush of charcoal and a cathartic down the tube which would hopefully absorb any remaining medication. A simple job, but a messy and an unpleasant one.

'The results are back from the lab, Elliot,' Kelly announced. 'Tetrabenazine, Valium and whisky.'

He nodded. 'We'll just have to hope we've got most of it out. Jane—'

'He's arrested,' she yelled as the alarm on the ECG monitor suddenly went off. 'V-fib!'

Ventricular fibrillation. Vic Imrie's heart had gone into total chaotic activity, with no co-ordinated pumping action.

Without a word having been said, Jane and Kelly were already beginning to perform cardiopulmonary resuscitation, and swiftly Elliot whacked Vic Imrie in the centre of his chest, hoping to provoke a electrical current across his chest to the heart to induce his heart rhythm back to normal.

It didn't work.

'Defibrillator, Jane!' he demanded.

Quickly she handed the two paddles to him. He set the machine at 200, rubbed the paddles together with electrical

conducting gel to prevent the patient's skin from burning, then called, 'Everybody stand clear!'

Obediently Jane and Kelly stepped back from the trolley, and Elliot placed the paddles on Vic Imrie's chest. A surge of electricity coursed through his body. He convulsed briefly, then lay still.

'Nothing,' Jane reported, glancing at the monitor.

'OK, stand clear again, everybody,' Elliot announced, only to pause with a frown as he heard the sound of angry, raised voices coming from outside the cubicle curtains. 'What the hell's going on out there?'

'Kelly, go and find out,' Jane ordered.

The student nurse nodded but suddenly the curtains round the cubicle were pulled open and a middle-aged woman appeared.

'Don't—oh, please, don't do that!' the woman insisted, tears streaming down her face as Elliot placed the paddles on Vic Imrie's chest and he convulsed again. 'Hasn't he gone through enough already? Hasn't he suffered enough already? Why can't you just leave him alone?'

'Get her out of here,' Elliot ordered as two security guards piled into the cubicle behind the woman.

'But I'm his wife,' she protested as the guards took her firmly by the arms. 'And I don't want you to do that. He wouldn't want you to do that!'

Did Mrs Imrie know what she was saying, what she was suggesting? Elliot wondered, and decided she did. Sufferers of Huntingdon's chorea could live for as long as thirty years after the disease was first diagnosed. Thirty years of physical and mental degeneration. Would *he* want anyone he loved to go through that?

He wouldn't, but it wasn't his decision to make. He was a doctor, trained to do everything in his power to save life, not to end it, and determinedly he motioned to the security guards.

'Take her out.'

Sobbing bitterly, Mrs Imrie allowed the security guards to lead her away, and Elliot upped the charge on the defibrillator to 300. Still there was no change, but when he increased the power to 360 the ECG machine suddenly blipped into life.

'OK, now we're rolling,' he declared. 'Pulse, Jane?'

'Very weak and slow.'

'Right. Give him atropine in the IV line. With luck it should make his heart beat faster.'

It did.

'BP now, Jane?'

'One hundred over sixty.'

That meant they'd stabilised him enough to go up to IC, and normally such a result would have brought beaming smiles of relief from everybody, but not this time.

This time no one said a word as Elliot mechanically replaced the Ambu-bag the paramedics had inserted with an endotracheal tube, and quickly checked Vic Imrie's BP and pulse rate again.

'You did a good job, Elliot,' Jane said as he stood watching the staff from Intensive Care wheeling Vic Imrie away.

'Maybe,' he replied, his voice tired, defeated, 'but the real question is, was it the right one?'

What could she say to him? she wondered, remembering how devastated Mrs Imrie had looked, how much her husband had struggled against the stomach pump. Nothing but the truth.

'I don't know. I honestly don't know. All you can do—all any of us can do—is the job we've been trained for.'

'Even if it's not what the patient wants?' he asked, his eyes bleak. 'Jane, did you get a look at the size of the lids on those pill bottles?'

'The size of the lids?' she echoed in confusion.

'They're tiny, awkward, and the top of a bottle of whisky isn't much bigger. And Vic Imrie has Huntington's chorea.'

Her eyes widened. 'Elliot, do you know what you're suggesting?'

He nodded. 'That he couldn't have opened them himself, not with those tremors in his hands. I think his wife gave them to him with his consent.'

Elliot was saying he thought it was a case of assisted euthanasia. That Vic Imrie had decided he didn't want to go on living any more, and had asked his wife to help him die.

'What are you going to do?' she asked, and he shrugged wearily.

'Nothing. We both know euthanasia's illegal in this country, but do we really want that couple taken to court?'

She didn't. It wouldn't achieve anything. It wouldn't miraculously cure Vic Imrie. OK, so if Mrs Imrie was sent to prison she wouldn't be able to help him to kill himself, but that didn't mean he wouldn't try again. And the next time it could be something infinitely more messy and painful than an overdose.

And Elliot wondered, too. Wondered at the strength of Mrs Imrie's love. A love which had been so great she'd been prepared to help her husband to die even if it meant she was left devastated and guilt-ridden for the rest of her life.

He'd thought he'd loved Donna that much once, he remembered as Jane hurried away to speak to one of their receptionists who had appeared at the treatment-room door, her face grim. In fact, it had been he who had insisted on the church wedding, the white dress, the morning suits, because he'd been so sure it would last for ever.

But it hadn't lasted. Within a year, he and Donna had been arguing, and within two years...

Never again, he'd told himself when the divorce papers had come through. Never again would he ever fall in love, and he'd kept that vow—intended to go on keeping it. To feel the kind of pain Mrs Imrie must have been going through, was still going through… No, he didn't want that. He didn't think he could handle that.

'What is it—what's wrong?' Elliot asked as Jane came running back to him.

'We've got a three-month-old baby girl on the way. She's not breathing and she has no pulse. Sounds like a SIDS.'

Elliot groaned inwardly. He didn't need this. A case of sudden infant death syndrome was bad enough at the best of times, but he really didn't need this right now.

They tried their best. They always did try their best, but Elliot knew the moment he saw the baby that it was hopeless. She was mottled, cool and lifeless, and after forty-five minutes he gave the order to stop trying to resuscitate.

''It's every parent's worst nightmare,' Floella sighed, her eyes full of pity, as Jane gently wrapped the baby in a shawl. 'And it's always the same story. The baby was fine when I put her into her cot. No, she wasn't ill, apart from a slight cold.'

'I just hope somebody finds out what causes it soon,' Jane murmured. 'There have been so many suggestions. Like it's caused by putting a baby to sleep face down, or it's because of prematurity, or cold weather, or the parents smoking in the same room. And yet we still don't know anything for sure other than it's slightly more common in boys than in girls, and more deaths occur in the winter.'

'Look, I'll take the baby down to Pathology,' Floella said quickly, seeing Jane gently stroke the wisps of golden hair on the little girl's head. 'You get off home. Your shift's over—'

'I'll wait for Elliot,' Jane interrupted. 'I've a feeling he might need some company.'

And he did. Never had she seen him look so defeated as when he came out of their private waiting room, having spoken to the baby's parents. Oh, she'd seen him upset when they'd lost a patient they'd fought hard to save, but never had she seen him look so drained, so haggard.

'Want to talk about it?' she asked as they walked together out of the hospital.

For a moment she didn't think he was going to answer, and when he spoke his voice was ragged.

'It's the irony of it, Jane. We saved Vic Imrie, though both he and his wife wanted him to die, but we couldn't save that baby and she had everything to live for. It's the irony—*the irony*!'

What could she say to him? What could anybody say? Nothing that would really help, and gently she linked her arm in his and said through a throat so tight it hurt, 'Let's go home, Elliot.'

And they did, both of them lost in their own private worlds. Both of them hurting, but both equally reluctant for their own private reasons to reach out to one another for comfort.

And there was little comfort for Elliot when they did get home and Nicole returned from her friend's house.

'I don't know what to do with her, Jane,' he sighed the minute his daughter had gone to her room, pleading she wanted an early night. 'No matter what I say, I just don't seem to be getting through to her.'

'It's only been two weeks, Elliot—'

'I try to make conversation with her—I really do try,' he insisted, 'but all I ever get is "Is it OK for me to do this?" and "Is it OK for me to do that?" It's as though she's a guest in my home.'

'Which is probably how she feels right now,' Jane said

gently, as he got to his feet and refilled his wineglass. 'She needs time to feel at home—'

'But she gets on so well with you,' he said, trying and failing to keep the envy out of his voice. 'I've heard the two of you laughing, but with me... Somehow, I just never seem to hit the right note with her. I listen to myself talking to her sometimes, and I sound so false. So pompous, aloof—'

'Could it be because you're trying too hard?' Jane suggested. 'Maybe if you concentrate on simply being her father, on being there when she needs you, you might find it easier.'

He gazed at her silently for a moment, then bit his lip. 'The trouble is, I don't think I can. This afternoon with Vic Imrie—when he went into cardiac arrest—that's what I'm good at, Jane. Medicine. Mending broken limbs, damaged hearts. That's what I can do.'

She put down her glass, bewildered. 'What are you trying to say?'

How much was he prepared to tell her? he wondered, seeing the confusion in her eyes. Was he prepared to tell her the truth about his marriage to Donna? No, he couldn't tell her that, he thought bitterly, could never tell anyone that. He could tell her of his doubts and fears about being able to be a father, but that was all he could tell her.

'But every father feels that way,' she insisted when he'd explained how he felt. 'Nobody is born one. It's something you have to learn, something that comes with practice.'

'Jane...Jane, you don't understand!' he exclaimed, desperately thrusting his hands through his blond hair. 'I'm a wash-out with *all* relationships. The only thing I can handle is a brief love affair with no hard feelings when it ends, but I can't do that with Nicole. I can't flirt with her, or hand her a line. She wants—needs—commitment, and I don't think I can do it.'

'Of course you can,' she protested. 'I've seen you with the kids in A and E—'

'That's medicine again, Jane. I'm treating their injuries, their pain. I'm not living with them, having to relate to them.'

He hadn't used the word 'love', she noticed, but she let that pass. Just as she didn't ask the one question that had been niggling at her ever since Nicole had arrived. Why he'd looked so strange at the airport when he'd first seen his daughter. There was much more to this than a simple fear of not being able to cut it as a father, but for now she didn't ask.

'Look, you're off duty tomorrow afternoon. Why don't you take her somewhere?' she suggested instead. 'The park—the zoo—somewhere like that. I'm sure her teachers would understand if you wanted to pick her up from school early.'

'What good would that do?' he demanded.

She didn't know, but she did know he had to do something. 'I simply wondered if perhaps you both got out of the house into neutral territory, did something different together...'

'I might find it easier.' He nodded, clearly warming to the idea. 'We could make a whole afternoon of it. Go to a café for tea—'

'We?' she interrupted in dismay. That wasn't what she'd intended at all. She'd wanted him to be alone with Nicole, to be forced into talking to her—*really* talking to her. 'Elliot, the whole point of the exercise is to give you and Nicole a chance to get to know one another better.'

'But you'd have to come with me,' he said. 'I couldn't possibly do it on my own.'

'Elliot—'

'Please,' he insisted, his eyes fixed on her. 'Jane, I need your help.'

How often had she heard that? For years, it seemed. Ever since she was small people had always turned to her for help, for her to get them out of a jam, and she was so tired of doing it, so tired of being taken for granted.

But as his deep blue eyes stayed pleadingly on her, she knew she couldn't refuse. It would be good old Jane to the rescue again, and with a deep sigh she said, 'All right, then. I'll come.'

CHAPTER FOUR

'WELL, you could have knocked me down with a feather when Gussie let slip in the canteen that she hadn't been out with Elliot for two weeks.' Floella chuckled, her large brown eyes sparkling as she and Jane stripped the paper sheet off the examination trolley in cubicle 5 and replaced it with a fresh one. 'I mean, *Elliot*? I know he seems to be really keen on being a father to Nicole, but he's the last guy in the world I'd ever have believed would turn celibate!'

'Flo—'

'I wish you'd heard her, Jane,' Floella prattled on. 'To hear Gussie talk, anyone would think you were keeping Elliot chained up in his flat or something!'

'Me?' Jane protested. 'How has him not dating her got anything to do with me?'

'Oh, *I* know it hasn't, and *you* know it hasn't, but you know what Gussie's like. According to her, nobody does anything in this life unless it's for sex or money, so naturally she thinks you've been using your presence in Elliot's flat to roll your eyes at him, and give him that come-hither look.'

Much good it would have done her if she'd tried, Jane thought ruefully. If she'd done any rolling of her eyes at Elliot he would simply have rushed her off to the hospital ophthalmology department to have her eyes tested.

'So it's working out OK, then—you helping Elliot to look after his daughter?' Floella continued as she followed Jane out of the cubicle.

'I think so,' Jane replied. 'We have our ups and downs,

of course.' That was putting it mildly. Last night they'd had a humdinger of a row over Charlie Gordon of all people. Elliot had declared he didn't think the SHO was reliable when it came to personal relationships, she'd told him he was talking through his hat, and... 'Nicole's still having nightmares, but we're hoping they'll lessen once she starts to feel more secure.'

'They should do,' Floella said, 'but these things take time and a lot of patience.'

'I thought it might help if we got her out a bit more,' Jane continued, 'so we're taking her to the zoo this afternoon after work.'

'The zoo?'

'Nicole's never been to one and I thought she might enjoy it.'

'You're going to the zoo with Elliot and Nicole?'

'Yes, I'm going to the zoo with Elliot and Nicole,' Jane declared, beginning to laugh. 'Honestly, Flo, are you taking in anything I'm saying?'

'Oh, I'm taking it in all right,' Floella said dryly. 'I'm just wondering if you are.'

'What on earth does that mean?' Jane asked, bewildered.

'Jane...' Floella bit her lip. 'Jane, has it ever occurred to you that you might be getting rather too fond of Elliot's daughter?'

'Of course I'm fond of her,' Jane protested. 'She's a lovely little girl—'

'And she's not yours. Look, I guess what I'm trying to say is be careful,' Floella continued, her large dark eyes concerned. 'You're only going to be taking care of her for a month. Don't get too involved.'

'I'm not getting involved, I'm just helping.'

'Yeah, right, but just be careful, OK?'

Careful about what? Jane thought angrily as the staff nurse walked away, and she saw Elliot beckoning to her

from cubicle 2. She was only doing what any other half-decent person would have done in the circumstances. It didn't mean she'd forgotten that taking care of Nicole was only a temporary arrangement. It *didn't*.

'Problems, Elliot?' she asked, forcing a smile to her lips as she joined him.

'Not a problem as such,' he replied, his lips quirking. 'What do you know about handcuffs?'

'Handcuffs?' she echoed. 'Not a thing, apart from the fact that the chaps in blue will snap them on you if you get into trouble. Why?'

'I've got one very embarrassed lady in 2. Apparently she and her boyfriend were making mad, passionate love—'

'At eleven o'clock in the morning?'

'Yeah, I know. Some people have all the luck, don't they?' He grinned. 'Anyway, like I said, they were making love, but to add spice to the occasion she was all trussed up in handcuffs, and now she can't get them off.'

'Did she try rubbing butter over her hands and wrists?'

'Is that the voice of experience talking, Sister Halden?' he asked, his blue eyes dancing. 'Because if it is—'

'No, of course it's not,' she protested, blushing furiously to her annoyance. 'I just wondered if perhaps something oily—'

'She's tried butter, Vaseline, hand cream and face cream, but nothing has worked. All that's happened is she's now got pretty deep abrasions to her wrists, abrasions I can't treat until we get the cuffs off her.'

'Looks like a job for the police department, then,' she said, then frowned. 'I wonder if one key fits every pair of handcuffs, or if each set has its own particular key?'

'If they do we could be in for a very long morning,' he said with a sigh. 'OK. Could you phone the local police station for me?'

'Will do.'

'Oh, and, Jane,' he called after her, laughter plain in his voice, 'just remember the next time someone wants to make mad passionate love to you, tell them the handcuffs are out.'

Yeah, right, she thought with a sigh. Considering she had nobody in her life right now to make any kind of love to her, she would have been more than happy to wear handcuffs if a bit of loving had been on offer.

In fact, now she came to think about it, nobody had ever made mad, passionate love to her, with or without handcuffs. Frank's idea of passion had been two minutes of foreplay, followed by a few hefty thrusts which had left her staring up at the ceiling wondering if this was all there was to it.

She'd bet money that the women Elliot made love to didn't think afterwards that they'd have had a lot more fun and considerably more satisfaction if they'd simply eaten an entire carton of ice cream. She'd bet…

No, she wasn't going to bet anything, she told herself firmly after she'd phoned the police station and endured their hoots of laughter and ribald comments. Thinking about sex and Elliot Mathieson at the same time was a bad idea. Thinking about sex *with* Elliot Mathieson was an even worse one, especially as he'd behaved like a perfect gentleman since she'd moved into his flat.

Actually, it was even more demoralising than that, she thought as the doors of the treatment room opened and two paramedics appeared. She didn't think Elliot even realised she was a woman. To him she was simply Jane. Helpful, sexless, good old Jane.

'Gang fight, Sister!' one of the paramedics called. 'Twenty-three years old, no ID, multiple stab wounds to his face, arms and upper and lower torso!'

And losing more and more blood by the second, Jane thought as she raced towards them, and Elliot did, too.

'Boy, but somebody obviously meant business with this guy!' Elliot exclaimed, grimacing as he stared down at the young man's bloodstained face and body. 'OK, we'll need six units of O-negative for starters, an ECG reading and an IV to replace the blood he's lost. Charlie— Where the hell's Charlie?'

'Here, boss,' the SHO replied, arriving in time to help them to push the trolley into one of the cubicles.

'Stick around until we find out what we've got, OK?'

Charlie nodded, but it didn't take them long to discover that what they had was a mess. The knife slashes on the young man's arms and upper torso would heal, but two of the stab wounds had pierced his stomach, and if he managed to survive them he was still going to be left with a face his own mother wouldn't recognise.

'Do you want to retain the cervical collar?' Charlie asked as Jane swiftly cut off the young man's clothes, then attached him to the ECG machine to monitor his heart rhythm.

Elliot shook his head. 'I can't see any sign of any spinal injury, but we need to tube him for sure and it will be easier with the collar off.'

'BP 160 over 95, pulse 140,' Jane declared. 'Heart rate very erratic but no sign of any arrhythmia. Guiac test to check for blood in his stools and a urine analysis?'

'Please,' Elliot replied.

'You should become a doctor, Jane,' Charlie remarked admiringly as Elliot checked the young man's airways to ensure there was nothing in his mouth then deftly inserted an endotracheal tube into his throat. 'Talk about being on the ball. She's terrific, isn't she, Elliot?'

She was, but that didn't mean Elliot had to like Charlie Gordon saying it, or the way Jane's cheeks became pink

from the compliment. The SHO was getting too damn familiar, he decided. In fact, it seemed to him that every time he turned round lately Charlie was talking to Jane, making her laugh.

He'd warned her about him already, but all he'd got back for his pains had been a flea in his ear. A very strident flea in his ear, he remembered ruefully, but that didn't mean he was going to give up. Somebody had to make her see she was much too nice for her own good, too ready to always believe the best in people.

And you'd better get a grip, he told himself as he placed his stethoscope on the young man's chest to ensure the endotracheal tube was in the right place. Anyone would think you were getting interested in Jane yourself, the amount of time you seem to spend speculating on her private life.

Of course he wasn't getting interested, he thought with irritation. All he was trying to do was ensure that a nice girl like her didn't end up being hurt. OK, he admitted that he liked her, admired her, respected her— And what about her breasts? his mind whispered. You noticed her breasts, remember.

Yes, but only because I'm suffering from a massive attack of sexual deprivation right now, he argued back, trying very hard not to notice the breasts in question as Jane leant over to attach another IV line.

'Blood in both urine and stools, Elliot,' she announced. 'Looks like both kidney and liver damage.'

'This guy needs Theatre and fast,' he replied. 'Charlie, could you page them, let them know we've got an urgent one on the way if we can stabilise him?'

'Sure thing,' the SHO replied.

'What do you want to do about his face?' Jane asked as Charlie sped away. 'Will we suture, or leave that to Plastics?'

Elliot glanced critically down at the cut that ran the full length of the young man's cheek from his eye down to his mouth. 'It's a job for Plastics, though not even they will be able to give him back the face he once had.'

'I understand some gangs see scars as a badge of honour,' Jane observed.

'I wouldn't be at all surprised,' Elliot sighed. 'How's his BP doing?'

'BP 120 over 80.' It was still too high, but now that they were pumping in the O-negative blood at least it was coming down and the ECG monitor was showing no worrying irregularities. 'Elliot—'

She didn't get the opportunity to say anything else. The curtains round the cubicle were suddenly thrown open, and to her horror a young man appeared, a knife in his hand, murder plain on his face.

'I'm sorry, sir, but you really shouldn't be in here,' Elliot declared with a calmness that was amazing. 'If you'd like to go through to Reception, fill in one of our forms—'

'I ain't here to fill in any bloody forms,' the young man interrupted. 'I'm here to finish what me and my mates started.'

And he meant it, Jane thought. Without a shadow of a doubt, he meant it. Somehow she had to buy them some time. Time so that either she or Elliot could hit the panic button on the wall behind them to summon the security guards.

'I don't think there's any need for you to finish him off,' she observed, noticing out of the corner of her eye that Elliot was edging slowly round the trolley towards her. 'He's dying as it is.'

'Is that right?' the young man sneered. 'Well, maybe I should just hurry him along and save you a lot of hassle.'

He took a step forward and Jane did, too. 'I'd wear

surgical gloves if you intend going anywhere near him,' she said quickly. 'He's got Aids.'

The young man whitened and stepped back. 'Aids?'

She nodded. Elliot was almost there. Almost close enough to reach the panic button. 'Advanced Aids, according to our special registrar.'

For a second the young man stared at her uncertainly, then his lip curled. 'He ain't got Aids. Me mates and I would have known about it weeks ago if he had.'

'Not necessarily,' she said desperately. 'Do you think he'd want it known—would you, if it were you?'

A mixture of conflicting emotions flashed across the man's face, then he shook his head. 'You're lying to me, you bitch, trying to save that no-good, low-down—'

He let out a strangled, high-pitched cry as a security guard suddenly came from nowhere and grabbed him round the neck, but he wasn't finished yet. Furiously he lashed out with his fist, sending Jane spinning back against the cubicle wall, and with a cry of rage Elliot lunged forward and twisted the young man's arm behind his back. The knife in his hand clattered to the floor, and when a second security guard arrived Elliot all but threw the young man into his arms.

'Jane, Jane, are you all right?' he exclaimed hoarsely, as the young man was dragged away.

'Fine,' she replied, already back in position by their patient. 'His BP's 110 over 80 now. I know it's still a bit high, but could we risk sending him to Theatre with that?'

'Jane—'

'I don't like his colour. I think if we wait too long we could be looking at renal failure here.'

She was right, they could, and quickly he pulled himself together.

'OK, Theatre it is,' he replied, but the minute Floella and Charlie had wheeled their patient out of the treatment

room he snapped off his latex gloves, caught Jane by the shoulders and turned her round to face him, his blue eyes worried and concerned. 'Are you really OK? I mean, really and truly OK?'

'Of course I am,' she protested. 'I'm a bit shaky round the knees...' Actually, now that the man had gone, and she'd no patient to focus on, she felt very shaky, but there was no way she was going to admit it. 'My elbows got a bit of a bang, but apart from that I'm fine.'

He stared at her silently for a moment, then shook his head, and his voice when he spoke was husky, uneven. 'You know, you're quite something, Jane Halden.'

To her dismay her throat constricted and she knew that if he said just one more word she was going to disgrace herself, and embarrass him, by throwing herself onto his chest and bursting into tears. Quickly she forced a smile to her lips.

'Yeah, right, Elliot, and whatever new favour you're wanting, the answer is no.'

A brief answering smile sprang to his lips, and then it was gone.

'You could have been killed!' he exclaimed, his relief giving way to anger. 'Never do that again, do you hear me? *Never*!'

'Do what?' she protested. 'I was simply unlucky enough to get in the way of his fist.'

'Talking to him like that,' he continued as though she hadn't spoken. 'Trying to distract him—'

'It worked, didn't it?' she interrupted.

'That's not the point—'

'Elliot, I don't see why you're making such a fuss,' she said, stripping the blood-soaked paper sheet off the examination trolley and binning it. 'I've been in far greater danger in A and E before, and you never got all macho and protective over me then.'

It was true, he hadn't. Oh, he'd always been worried when one of them had been threatened by a member of the public, feared that it was only a matter of time before somebody got seriously hurt, but he'd reluctantly accepted—as they all had—that it was one of the hazards of the job. And yet now...

Never had he felt such rage before, never had he felt such fear.

Of course you were angry and afraid, he told himself as he watched Jane binning the soiled dressings they had used and saw from the reddening on her elbows that she would be black and blue tomorrow. Dammit, it was Jane who'd been in danger, Jane who'd been slammed into the wall. She's your colleague, your friend, so it's only natural you should feel this way.

And would you have felt the same if it had been Gussie or Floella or Kelly?

Of course he would, he thought firmly, only to suddenly realise it wasn't true. Oh, he would have been concerned about them, angry with the perpetrator, but he wouldn't have felt the overwhelming fear and anger he felt now, and he couldn't understand it. He couldn't understand it at all.

All he knew for certain as he noticed that a policeman had arrived to release the woman in 2 from her handcuffs—handcuffs Elliot hoped he'd use on the young thug who'd attacked Jane—was that he was glad their shift was nearly over. Glad that he'd persuaded Jane to go with Nicole and him to the zoo. After this morning's incident, if she hadn't agreed to come with them he'd have spent the whole afternoon wondering what kind of trouble she was getting into.

At least at the zoo he'd be able to keep an eye on her. At least there he'd be able to relax and enjoy himself.

* * *

He didn't.

Oh, it was a beautiful afternoon, the blue sky shot with the high clouds of early spring, the daffodils starting to die back but the tulips just beginning to open, and everything should have been perfect—but it wasn't.

They took Nicole to see the elephants and the giraffes, and the little girl managed to look dutifully enthusiastic. They took her to watch the penguins and the monkeys being fed, and she laughed at all the right places, but by the middle of the afternoon when Nicole had answered all of Elliot's questions in monosyllables or not at all he was gazing over his daughter's head at Jane in despair.

'Look, why don't you get us all a hot dog from that stand over there?' she suggested. 'I'd love one, and I'm sure Nicole would, too.'

Nicole didn't look as though she cared much one way or another but Elliot made his escape with relief and Jane walked with Nicole towards one of the benches beside the duck pond and sat down.

'It's nice here, isn't it?' she commented.

Nicole nodded noncommittally.

'I'm surprised you've never been to a zoo before,' Jane persisted, extracting a bag of dried bread from her handbag so the girl could feed the ducks. 'I understand there's a very big one in Paris.'

'There is. Mama said she would take me there one day, but…'

The little girl shrugged, and Jane cleared her throat. How was she going to say what she wanted to say tactfully, without it sounding as though she was either begging on Elliot's behalf or trying to blackmail his daughter?

Just say it, a little mental voice insisted, and she did.

'Nicole, I know that sometimes…sometimes your father might appear a bit cool and aloof, but he cares a great deal for you.'

'No, he doesn't,' the little girl replied. 'In fact, he doesn't like me at all.'

'Oh, but he does!' Jane protested, aghast. 'In fact—'

'I like you,' Nicole interrupted, throwing a piece of her bread towards the expectant ducks. 'I think you're nice.'

'Well, thank you,' Jane declared, considerably flustered. 'Nicole, your father—'

'My papa and you—you are lovers?'

'No, of course not!' Jane exclaimed, blushing furiously. 'We're simply friends, that's all. We work together, share a flat...' At least they were sharing one for a month, but she saw no need to tell the child that the arrangement was temporary. 'Nicole, your father loves you—'

'He doesn't. I saw his face when I arrive. He does not want me living with him. I am...' She frowned. 'My friend Stephanie, she uses a word... A pest. That's it. I am a pest to my papa.'

'Nicole—'

'I should have stayed in Paris. I had lots of uncles there. I should have stayed in Paris with one of them.'

Uncles? Elliot had told her his ex-wife had had a sister, a Michelle Bouvier who was an archaeologist, but he'd never mentioned any brothers. 'Nicole, these uncles of yours—'

'They weren't my *real* uncles, of course,' the little girl continued, as though that should have been self-evident. 'They were my mama's boyfriends, but she said it would make things easier if I called them uncle.'

'Did she?' Jane said faintly.

Nicole nodded. 'Some were nice. Some were not so nice, but Mama seemed to like them all.'

All? Good grief, how many had there been?

'Nicole—'

'Two hot dogs, as requested,' Elliot announced brightly, and Jane didn't know whether to feel relieved or sorry that

he'd arrived when he had, and decided that she wished he'd come earlier.

If he'd arrived earlier he would have heard what Nicole had said, and then she wouldn't have to do anything about it. And she didn't want to do anything about it. She wished the girl hadn't told her, wished she'd never suggested coming to the zoo in the first place. If they hadn't come, and Nicole hadn't casually dropped her bombshell, she wouldn't have that knowledge lying on her chest like a lead weight.

And Elliot didn't look any happier than she felt when his daughter took her hot dog and the bag of stale bread over to the duck pond.

'Well, I don't think we can say that this outing is turning out to be any kind of success, do you?' Elliot said ruefully.

'I think Nicole liked the bush-babies—'

'Yes, but we're not exactly talking, are we?' he interrupted. 'I mean, she's over there eating her hot dog, and I'm over here with you.'

She sighed. 'I'm sorry. I thought it was a good idea—'

'I'm not blaming you,' he said quickly. 'I would never blame you.'

You would, if you knew what I know, she thought, staring down at her uneaten hot dog, which suddenly had all the appeal of yesterday's leftovers. If I hadn't said anything to Nicole, I would never have known, and I wish to heaven I didn't.

'Jane.'

'Mmm?'

'You'd feel a lot better if you simply said whatever you've got on your mind, instead of chewing your poor lips to ribbons.'

He'd swung round on the bench to face her, his blue eyes dancing, and she flushed guiltily. 'It's nothing...'

'In a pig's eye is it nothing,' he protested. 'Come on. Spit it out. What have I done wrong now?'

'Nothing. You've done nothing wrong. It's just...'

'Jane, unless you're trying to work up the courage to tell me I have a personal problem my friends are too embarrassed to mention, I think I can handle whatever you want to say,' he declared, a smile tugging at the corners of his mouth. 'Come on, spit it out.'

She didn't want to tell him what Nicole had said. She'd have given anything in the world not to tell him what his daughter had revealed, but he was waiting, and she knew he wouldn't take no for an answer.

'Nicole...when you were getting the hot dogs...she was talking about her mother. She said— Now, Elliot, she could have got this all wrong, completely misunderstood the situation,' she added quickly, seeing the amusement in his face turning to bewilderment, 'but she told me...she said she had lots of uncles in Paris. Uncles who used to come and stay with her mother.'

'She said *what*?'

'Elliot, she's only six,' Jane continued, thankful that Nicole was too happily engaged in jumping off and on the decorative stones that edged the gravel path round the duck pond to hear him. 'She probably didn't understand what she was saying, how we might interpret it—'

'Oh, she knew, all right!' Elliot declared, his voice grim. 'Donna was a tramp when we were married, and she clearly continued being one after we got divorced. I could kill her for exposing Nicole to this. If she were alive, I *would* kill her!'

She gazed at him in complete shock. She'd always assumed that he and Donna had got divorced because, like so many other couples, they'd simply grown apart, but now...

'Do...do you want to talk about it?' she offered, not

knowing whether she really wanted to hear or not but feeling she had to say something.

She didn't think he was going to answer—part of her hoped that he wouldn't—then he leant back against the bench and clenched his hands tightly in his lap. 'I thought Donna was the most incredible, beautiful girl in the world when I met her. I fell madly in love with her, begged her—badgered her—to marry me, and eventually she said yes, and for a year we were happy.'

'And then?' she said softly.

'She got bored. Her job took her all over Europe, from one fashion shoot to the next, and she met a lot of interesting, vibrant people who were a lot more exciting than the husband she'd left at home, slaving away at his boring old hospital. So she slept with a few—just to relieve the boredom, of course, you understand?' he continued, his lip curling. 'Then she slept with a few more, and I found out.'

'Oh, Elliot—'

'Please... Please, don't say you're sorry,' he interrupted, his mouth curving into a sad travesty of a smile. 'Say anything you like but, please, don't say you feel sorry for me.'

So she didn't say it, though she desperately wanted to, and as she gazed at him compassionately a thought came into her mind. A thought that might explain so much. 'Elliot, Nicole... Is she very much like her mother?'

A betraying muscle tightened in his cheek. 'Yes.'

'And does...' She cleared her throat. 'Does that bother you?'

The tendons on his knuckles showed white against the rest of his skin. 'Yes, it bothers me,' he said tightly. 'In fact, if you want the honest truth, it bothers the hell out of me.'

'Because you think if you allow yourself to love Nicole as you loved her mother, she might hurt you, too?'

He kicked one of the pebbles on the gravel path in front of them and sent it ricocheting off the fence opposite. 'Jane, every time I look at her I see Donna. I keep telling myself that she's a child, that I'm not being fair, but… It's sick—*I'm* sick!'

'I'd say you were pretty normal myself,' she said gently. 'Look, how do you think widows or divorced mothers feel if their sons look like a husband they either loved or hated?' she continued as he shook his head. 'It's not easy for them, but they get beyond it, grow to love their sons for themselves.'

'I guess so,' he murmured.

'I *know* so,' she insisted, and his mouth twitched into not quite a smile.

'Bloody-minded, aren't you?'

'Of course I am,' she declared, relieved to see that some of the shadows were lifting from his eyes. 'I'm from Yorkshire, and everyone from Yorkshire's bloody-minded, unlike you soft southerners.'

This time he did laugh. 'Jane, how come a girl like you isn't married or something? I'd have thought some lucky bloke would have snapped you up years ago.'

Her own smile didn't slip for an instant. 'Too choosy, I guess.'

'Stay that way,' he declared, thinking of Charlie. 'Get the very best—you deserve it.'

Maybe she did, but the trouble was that she didn't want the very best, she thought wistfully. She wanted the man sitting next to her. A man who could be thoughtless and stupid and downright blind at times, but still she wanted him.

'And because you're the nicest, kindest person I know,' he continued, 'I want to ask you a huge favour. I want you to stay with me and Nicole until my mother comes back from Canada at the beginning of June.'

Her smile vanished. 'Oh, Elliot—'

'Janey, it's been working really well—the three of us living together. Nicole adores you, and I can go to work, secure in the knowledge that you're there when I can't be.'

'But, Elliot—'

'Janey, I *know* my mother, and I *know* you. The agency could send me anybody, and Nicole's had so much upheaval in her life already, I don't want to put her through more unless I have to.'

Say no, her heart urged as he gazed at her hopefully. Floella was right. You *are* getting too involved. It's bad enough that you're in love with him, but what if you start loving his daughter, too? Get out now before you're in way over your head.

'Elliot, I really don't think this is a good idea—'

'Give me one good reason why not,' he demanded.

She couldn't. At least not one she was prepared to tell him.

'Good, that's settled, then.' He beamed, taking her silence for agreement. 'Now, there's just one other thing I was wondering—'

She never did find out what it was because a sudden sharp cry of pain had her whirling round on the bench to see Nicole lying spread-eagled on the gravel. Jane was on her feet in an instant and running towards her before she realised Elliot was, too, and with difficulty she slowed her pace. Nicole was already sitting up, tears trickling down her cheeks, clearly more frightened than hurt by her fall, and Jane held back deliberately, wondering what he would do.

And at first, to her dismay, he didn't do anything. Oh, he bent over and said something to his daughter, but he didn't *do* anything.

'Pick her up,' she muttered under her breath. 'Elliot,

pick her up, hold her, whisper any nonsense you like, but *pick her up*!'

He couldn't have heard her—there was no way he could have heard her at that distance—but suddenly he did just that, and as he wrapped his arms around his daughter and Nicole clung to him and sobbed into his chest, Jane felt a hard lump in her throat.

It was a step. All right, so perhaps it wasn't a very big one, but at least it was a step.

And as she continued to watch them, her lips curving into a tender smile, she suddenly realised something else. Something that caused the smile on her lips to disappear in an instant.

She'd been wrong when she'd told herself that she should get out now before she grew to love Nicole. It was already too late. She already loved the little girl, and all she could see ahead for herself was heartbreak.

CHAPTER FIVE

'I THINK you're out of your mind.'

'I know, Flo, so you've said,' Jane sighed as they came out of the staffroom and made their way back to A and E. 'Every day since last week.'

'I mean, agreeing to do it for one month was bad enough, but agreeing to do it for three! I think you're crazy.'

'Flo, could you just drop it, please?' Jane pleaded. 'OK, I'm out of my mind. OK, I'm crazy, but it's my life.'

Floella opened her mouth, then closed it again and shook her head. 'Just don't turn round in two months' time and say that I didn't warn you.'

'I won't.'

'And don't expect any sympathy from me when you're sobbing into your coffee because Elliot's whisked his daughter off to live with his mother in Hampshire.'

'Definitely not.' Jane nodded, and a rueful smile appeared on the staff nurse's face as she pushed open the doors of the treatment room and they walked through them together.

'You're too damn soft for your own good, you know.'

Everyone seemed to be telling her that recently, Jane realised as Floella hurried off to speak to Kelly. And everyone was right. But what else could she have done? If she'd walked away, and later discovered that Nicole was desperately unhappy with the housekeeper Elliot had hired, she knew she could never have lived with herself.

And what about you? her little voice demanded. If you can't leave now, how in the world are you going to be

able to cope when Elliot takes Nicole to live with his mother, and you only get to see her occasionally, or maybe not at all?

I'll deal with it, she told herself. Somehow, some way, I'll deal with it.

'Could you give me some help, Sister Halden?'

She turned to see Richard Connery gazing enquiringly at her, and managed to smile. 'What can I do for you?'

'I've a Mr Lawrence in 6 who appears to have fractured his right arm. He's obviously in a great deal of pain, but he's also very frightened, and I thought it might help if he had a nurse standing by while I examined him.'

She nodded, and wished with all her heart that Floella could have heard him. The staff nurse still believed that the only help the junior doctor required was the sharp imprint of her shoe on his backside as she booted him from A and E, but even a week ago it would never have occurred to Richard to consider the mental state of a patient. He was learning, she thought with relief. At long last, he was learning.

And he was certainly right about his patient. The young man in cubicle 2 was obviously terrified. His hands were shaking, there were beads of sweat on his forehead and Jane thought that if he hadn't been sitting down he would have fainted.

'I hear you've been in the wars, Mr Lawrence?' she said with her most encouraging smile.

The young man nodded convulsively. 'I was painting my sitting-room ceiling and fell off the stepladder. Stupid—really stupid.'

And not true, she thought with a slight frown.

Oh, his right forearm was definitely fractured. Not only was it very swollen and tender, it was also hanging at an odd angle, but it was equally obvious that he couldn't possibly have done it when he'd been painting a ceiling.

For a start, his clothes were all wrong. Nobody painted a ceiling while wearing a pair of smart grey trousers and a pale beige sweater, and there wasn't a trace of paint on his clothes or on his hands. Either he was a remarkably neat painter, or he'd washed and changed before coming into A and E, and how anyone could have done that with a fractured arm was beyond her.

'So he didn't do it painting,' Richard said dismissively when she voiced her doubts after he'd given the young man some painkillers and sent him off to X-Ray. 'What difference does it make? His arm's clearly fractured, and surely our job is to treat that, not to question how he did it?'

He was right. It was none of their business how the young man had fractured his arm, but as she walked over to the whiteboard to put an asterisk by Mr Lawrence's name to indicate he hadn't yet been discharged she couldn't deny she would dearly liked to have known.

'You're looking very pensive, Jane,' Charlie remarked, almost bumping into her as he came out of cubicle 6. 'Something bothering you?'

'Curiosity, that's all.' She smiled. 'I'm simply eaten up with curiosity.'

'Well, you know what they say,' he replied. 'Curiosity killed the cat.'

'Yes, but satisfaction brought it back,' she pointed out, her grey eyes sparkling. 'Unfortunately, in this particular case, I don't think I'm going to be satisfied.' Her gaze swept over his blue suit, crisp white shirt and crimson tie. 'You're looking very smart today, Charlie. Going somewhere after work?'

'I'm picking up my girlfriend from the railway station. She's got a whole fortnight off work and she's going to spend it in London with me.'

'Oh, I am pleased for you,' she said, and meant it. The

SHO had been looking a bit down recently, and she knew it was because he was missing his girlfriend.

'Actually, there was something I'd like to ask you,' Charlie continued. 'I don't know London very well yet, and I wondered if you could recommend a nice restaurant I could take her to.'

She frowned. 'Have you a price limit?'

He shook his head and grinned. 'For Barbara, the sky's the limit.'

'Lucky girl.' She laughed. 'In that case, take her to Brambles.'

He took a piece of paper out of his pocket and wrote it down. 'Is it a nice place—I mean *really* nice? You see...' a deep flush of colour appeared on his cheeks '...if all goes well, I'm planning on asking Barbara to marry me.'

'Charlie, I'd marry you myself if you took me to Brambles!'

He roared with laughter, and she did, too, and neither of them noticed Elliot watching them from across the treatment room, his face like thunder.

Charlie Gordon had a nerve. Stringing along some poor girl back in his home town and trying to chat up another. And the annoying thing was that Jane seemed to be responding to him.

Dammit, look at the way she was smiling up at him. He couldn't ever remember a time when she'd smiled at him like that. Oh, she smiled, of course, but now that he came to think of it there always seemed to be an odd mixture of scepticism and wariness in her amusement.

Well, she should have reserved some of that wariness for Charlie Gordon, he thought angrily. She should have kept *all* of it for the SHO, and he was going to tell her so whether she gave him another flea in his ear or not.

But not right now, he realised with frustration as one of

their receptionists escorted a woman and a young boy in a wheelchair into the treatment room.

'The kid's eight years old, and his mother reckons he's drunk,' the receptionist told him under her breath.

'I don't know where he got it from, Doctor,' the child's mother declared, clearly torn between fury and concern. 'We don't have any alcohol in the house. Both my husband and I aren't drinkers, except on rare occasions—birthdays, Christmas, times like that—but as soon as I saw him I knew he was drunk—'

'Your son isn't drunk, Mrs Fraser,' Elliot interrupted. 'Now, if you'd like to go through to one of our private waiting rooms with Staff Nurse Lazear—'

'But I want to stay with him,' Mrs Fraser protested. 'If he's not drunk, what's wrong with him?'

'You'll know as soon as we do,' he said soothingly.

'Yes, but—'

'Mrs Fraser, your son is in the very best of hands,' Jane said reassuringly as Floella began to lead the woman away, 'and there's really nothing you can do here.'

Reluctantly the mother allowed Floella to usher her away, and Jane raised her eyebrows at Elliot questioningly. 'Drugs?'

He shook his head. 'Solvent abuse. Look at the sores around his lips, how flushed he is, and don't you smell something familiar?'

Jane leant down, sniffed, then drew back. 'Cleaning fluid. He's been sniffing cleaning fluid?'

Elliot nodded grimly. 'OK, get me an ECG reading and BP. Solvents can sensitise the heart to the effects of adrenaline and the last thing we want is for him to have a heart attack. Keep him lying on his side, too,' he continued. 'If he's sick, as I suspect he probably shortly will be, he might suffocate on his own vomit.'

The boy's ECG and BP were as normal as they could

be under the circumstances, and there was nothing more they could do for him. What he needed now was constant monitoring, and Intensive Care was the best place for that, but as the boy was wheeled away Jane noticed Elliot's eyes following him.

'Something worrying you?' she asked. 'Something you think we might have missed?'

He sighed and shook his head. 'I was just thinking that they're getting younger and younger, aren't they?'

'I'm afraid so,' she replied.

'I was also thinking that it could be Nicole in a couple of years' time.'

'It won't be,' she said reassuringly. 'She'll have more sense. You'll make sure she has more sense.'

'Maybe,' he murmured with a slightly crooked smile, 'but it's such a dangerous world for kids out there now, Jane. When you and I were young, the biggest thing our parents had to worry about was us being knocked down by a car, but now…'

'You'll take care of her—you're already doing it,' she said firmly.

And he was. OK, so things weren't exactly perfect yet by any means. Nicole was still far too withdrawn, too nervous in his presence, and he still had trouble relaxing with her, but it would come, she knew it would.

'I couldn't have done it without you,' he declared. 'You've been a real godsend, Jane.'

It was what Gussie had said, only considerably more sarcastically, she remembered, and she shook her head as she binned her latex gloves. 'I only did what anyone else would have done in the circumstances.'

'No, you did more,' Elliot insisted, putting out his hand to stop her as she turned to go. 'If you hadn't been there, willing to prop me up, to put up with me and all my hang-

ups and insecurities, I don't know what I would have done.'

There was warmth in his eyes, warmth that made her heart skip a beat, but she managed to reply lightly, 'It's what friends are for, Elliot.'

He smiled, but as he continued to stare down at her the smile slowly disappeared. Disappeared, to be replaced by a look of confusion and puzzlement. Until he was gazing at her as though he'd never actually seen her before, and every alarm bell known to mankind went off in her head.

'I'd better get on,' she said, taking a step back from him. 'We're mobbed as usual out in the waiting room, and it isn't going to get any emptier if we stand around here talking.'

'No, it won't, but, Jane—'

'I think Flo's wanting me,' she lied, and before he could say anything else she wheeled swiftly round on her heel and walked away.

What in the world are you doing? she thought as she strode down the treatment room, all too aware that his eyes were following her. You're in love with the guy. You've been in love with him for the last two years, and now that he seems to be actually realising you're a woman and not simply sexless Jane, you've just run a mile. Have you got rocks in your head, or something? I thought this was what you wanted.

And it was, but it wasn't, she realised. Oh, she wanted him to fall in love with her, of course she did. She wanted him to clasp her in his arms and declare his everlasting love for her. But that was just the problem. Elliot didn't do everlasting. Elliot's idea of everlasting was a couple of months. And was that what she wanted—two months of being loved, followed by a lifetime of loss?

Deliberately she shook her head. She didn't want that.

She couldn't handle that. It was better to keep him at arms' length than to go through that.

And it should be easy for her to do, she told herself as the doors of the treatment room opened and a woman in her early thirties appeared, chalk-white and walking gingerly. She'd spent two years successfully keeping her feelings hidden from him. She could keep on doing it. She had to.

'Elliot, Charlie—I need one of you now!' she called as the woman suddenly crumpled to the floor, clutching her stomach in obvious agony.

It was Elliot who came. Elliot who helped her carry the woman into a cubicle and get her on to the examination trolley.

'I'm sorry…so sorry,' the woman gasped, 'but I think…I think I'm going to be sick!'

Jane got the bowl under her chin in time.

'Better now?' she asked gently, when the woman finally slumped back onto the trolley, ashen and exhausted.

'No, I'm not better,' the woman exclaimed, tears slowly beginning to trickle down her cheeks. 'I'm pregnant—ten weeks pregnant—and I think I'm losing my baby.'

'What's your name?' Elliot asked as Jane swiftly began to strip off the woman's tights and skirt.

'Sally. Sally Thomson. My husband and I have been trying for six years to have a baby, and I can't lose it—*I just can't!*'

'Let's not jump the gun,' Elliot said soothingly. 'Can you tell me where the pain is?'

'Here,' Sally Thompson sobbed, pointing to the lower left side of her stomach. 'I've had a bit of diarrhoea, too, and…and I'm bleeding. It's a miscarriage, isn't it? I'm having a miscarriage.'

'Did you feel the pain before you started to bleed, or

after?' Elliot asked as Jane took the woman's blood pressure.

'I'm sorry?' Sally said, wiping a hand across her tear-stained face.

'The pain you felt. Was it there before you started to bleed or did it begin afterwards?' Elliot repeated.

Sally Thompson frowned in concentration. 'It was painful first.'

Elliot's eyes met Jane's. Not a miscarriage, then. In a miscarriage pain always followed the bleeding. What Sally Thompson was suffering from was infinitely sadder than a miscarriage. She had an ectopic pregnancy. Instead of the fertilised egg implanting itself in her uterus, it was growing in one of her Fallopian tubes, and if it wasn't removed immediately the consequences could be disastrous.

'I'll page Gynae,' Elliot murmured, and was gone in a second.

'Am I losing the baby, Nurse?' Mrs Thompson asked, gripping Jane's hand convulsively.

'I'm afraid so,' she said gently.

There was no point in telling the woman any more. She was devastated enough already, without having to find out the very real possibility that the damage to her Fallopian tube might mean it would be even more difficult for her to conceive again in the future.

'Don't you just wish some days that you'd stayed in bed?' Floella said ruefully when the clock on the treatment-room wall finally showed the end of what had proved to be a very long and weary shift. 'In fact, some days I wish I'd listened to my mother and become a secretary.'

'Yeah, right.' Jane smiled. 'And you'd have been bored out of your skull in three months.'

Floella laughed. 'Probably. It's just...sometimes... Well, you know what I mean.'

Jane did. She loved her job. Could never imagine doing

anything else even when the days were rough, and heart-breaking, but today... Today she would be glad to go home and put her feet up.

But not right away, she realised when she went into the staffroom to collect her coat and bag and found Richard sitting there, looking downright miserable.

Don't ask, she told herself. Just take your bag and go. But she knew that she wouldn't, and with a deep sigh she went over to him and sat down.

'Want to talk about it?'

'It's not your problem.'

Why did people always say that when in reality they desperately wanted somebody to listen? she wondered rue-fully, and with an effort she fixed what she hoped was her most encouraging and sympathetic smile to her lips. 'Don't you think I should be the best judge of that? Come on. Tell me.'

'It's Mr Lawrence.'

'Lawrence?' she echoed. 'I'm sorry, do I know him?'

'He's the guy who told us he'd been painting and fallen off his stepladder.'

'I remember now.' She nodded. 'Was there a problem with his arm—wasn't it fractured after all?'

'Oh, it was fractured all right,' Richard exclaimed bit-terly, 'but the trouble is that the fracture was at least a year old. Well healed but at an angle.'

Jane's heart sank. She knew what was coming, she just knew she did, but she had to ask. 'And Mr Lawrence?'

'Gone. Did a runner as soon as the X-rays were taken. He was a drug addict, wasn't he? I was conned by a drug addict.'

She nodded. 'I'm afraid so.'

'Oh, God, I feel so stupid!' the junior doctor exclaimed. 'Why don't you just tell me I'm an idiot, a prat? I de-serve it!'

She shook her head and smiled. 'Richard, everyone's been outsmarted by a drug addict at least once in their career. Hannah Blake—the junior doctor we had before you—was conned by one as well, so don't think you're the first and you most certainly won't be the last. Druggies are clever. They have to be to get what they want, and I have to say, passing off an old fracture as a new one in order to get some painkillers is pretty smart.'

'Jane…' His cheeks darkened. 'You don't mind if I call you Jane, do you?'

Her smile deepened. 'I've been hoping you would for ages. Every time you called for Sister Halden, it took me a couple of seconds to realise you meant me.'

He didn't smile. Instead, he bit his lip. 'I don't know how you can be so kind. I've been so awful to you—to all the nurses. I never intended to be like that. I don't know why I was—'

'Forget it. It's all water under the bridge now.' He didn't look convinced. He also didn't look any happier, and though she knew it would mean a rush to get home for Nicole on time, she forced herself to say, 'Is there something else bothering you, Richard?'

He stared down at his hands, then up at her again. 'I don't think I've got what it takes to be a doctor.'

'Of course you have,' she protested. 'Look, that drug addict you treated—'

'It's not just him,' he interrupted. 'It's… Jane, I've always wanted to be a doctor. Even when I was at school I wanted to be a doctor, and when I went to med school I decided that A and E was going to be my speciality, but I'm so scared all the time. Scared I'm going to do the wrong thing, scared I'm going to miss something.'

'Richard, everyone feels like that—truly they do,' she said gently, 'and I think you're being way too hard on yourself. How long have you been with us now?'

'Almost two months.'

'Exactly.' She nodded. 'Graduating from med school doesn't mean you're a doctor. It means you've just started out on the long road to becoming one and, believe me, you'll never stop learning.'

'I guess.'

He looked so miserable, and suddenly so very young, that she quickly did a mental review of the contents of Elliot's fridge and made up her mind.

'Look, why don't you come round to the flat tonight for dinner? Sometimes it helps to talk about your fears and worries, rather than letting them fester away inside you. Or perhaps you'd prefer to talk to Elliot about it,' she added hurriedly as he stared at her, open-mouthed.

'Oh, God, no!' he blurted out. 'I'd much rather talk to you. Dr Mathieson... He's...well, he's a bit overpowering, don't you think?'

'Is he?' Jane said in surprise. 'I can't say I've ever found that, but, then, I've known Elliot for more than two years so I guess I've got used to him. So, would you like to drop by tonight? I can offer you chicken curry and a sympathetic ear, if that's any use to you.'

'Are you sure?' Richard said uncertainly. 'I mean, won't Dr Mathieson mind me coming round?'

'Why should he?' she protested. 'Look, I won't tell him why you've come if that's what's bothering you. I'll just say I invited you for dinner.'

'But won't that make it worse?' the junior doctor asked, looking decidedly uncomfortable. 'I mean, won't it be a bit awkward for you, what with...' The colour on his cheeks grew even deeper. He took a deep breath, and got it out in a rush. 'I mean, won't he object, what with you and him living together and everything?'

Jane smiled. 'How long did you say you've been working at St Stephen's now, Richard?'

'Two months.'

'And you still haven't learned that Elliot favours long-legged girls with perfect figures?' She shook her head. 'I think it's time you spent less time worrying about your medical capabilities and more time listening to the hospital grapevine. Elliot and I might be living in the same flat, but we're certainly not living together. I'm there to help look after his little girl.'

'Really?' Richard didn't look convinced.

'Really,' Jane insisted, getting to her feet and reaching for her coat. 'Come round about eight. Nicole will be in bed by then and I can assure you Elliot won't mind a bit.'

But he did. The minute she told him his blond eyebrows snapped together. 'What do you mean, you've asked Richard Connery round for dinner?'

'I thought it would be a kind thing to do,' she replied, closing the oven door and putting on the timer. 'He's new in London, this is his first post and I think he feels a bit lonely.'

'Then let him join one of the hospital clubs,' he retorted, striding into the sitting room and throwing his jacket over the back of one of the chairs. 'He'll be able to meet plenty of people there.'

'That's not very sociable,' she said as she followed him. 'Elliot, I like him—'

'Oh, do you?'

'Yes, I do,' she retorted, beginning to get seriously irritated as he all but glowered at her, 'and when I agreed to move in here with you, one of the conditions was that I could have friends round whenever I wanted to.'

'So Richard's a friend now, is he?' Elliot said tightly. 'He gets invited round to dinner, does he? Jane, much as I don't want to interfere in your private life—'

'My private life?'

'I'd like to point out that Richard's years younger than you are.'

He thought it was a date, she realised. He thought she'd invited Richard round because they'd made a date, and it was on the tip of her tongue to tell him he'd got it all wrong when she suddenly wondered why she should.

Elliot had no right to be standing there, looking all disapproving and suggesting she was cradle-snatching. If she *had* wanted to date Richard Connery it was none of his damn business, and he was just about to find that out.

'Elliot, I'm twenty-eight years old, and Richard is twenty-three,' she declared icily. 'That hardly makes him my toy boy, and as you appear to have acquired such a downer on him, I'll make things easy for you. I'll entertain him in my room. You won't even have to see him.'

'Your room?'

'Yes, my room,' she snapped. 'The one at the end of the corridor, the one with my clothes and books in it.'

'Jane—'

'Unless you have any objections, of course?'

He did. The biggest one being that he knew of only one form of entertainment which took place in a bedroom, and he most certainly didn't like the idea of Richard and Jane indulging in it.

'You can use the sitting room if you like and I'll stay in my study,' he said grudgingly, but Jane wasn't buying any of it.

'Thanks, but, no, thanks,' she said, her voice cold, clipped. 'I wouldn't want to put you to any trouble. My bedroom will do fine.'

And she was as good as her word. The minute the junior doctor arrived she whisked him straight into her room, without even allowing Elliot to say hello, and firmly shut the door, leaving him fuming and frustrated in the hall.

It's all your own fault, he thought. She has a perfect

right to entertain anyone she likes, and you had no right to object.

Yes, but that was before I knew she was going to invite Richard Connery round, a kid who's scarcely out of nappies. Dammit, it would have been bad enough if it had been Charlie, but at least the SHO could string more than two words together.

Stringing words together didn't appear to be a problem for Richard tonight, he realised as he hovered in the hallway, trying without success to hear what all the talking and occasional burst of laughter was about.

Look, at least they *are* still talking, he thought, and not making love. Nobody could continue to talk like that if they were making love. They wouldn't have the breath, for a start.

If he could only find out what they were saying. In the movies people always put a glass against a wall to listen. Quickly he went into the kitchen, picked one up off the draining-board, then put it down again with a bang. This was ridiculous. Jane was entitled to her privacy. He had no right to spy on her. And the glass trick probably wouldn't work anyway.

The sound of a door opening along the corridor had him shooting across to the kitchen window and gazing out into the back garden with apparently rapt interest.

'Oh, I didn't realise you were in here,' Jane said, coming to a stop as she saw him.

Dammit, she looked all flustered and flushed, but at least she was still fully clothed. Clothed in a loose T-shirt and a pair of jeans. Tight jeans. Figure-hugging jeans. Jeans which clung and outlined her full, round bottom, and a top that was just loose enough for a man to slip his hands under if he felt so inclined.

He swallowed hard. 'I was just about to make myself something to eat.'

'I've made a curry for Richard, but there's more than enough for three if you want some,' she offered, taking a bottle of wine out of the fridge.

'Jane, about you and Richard—'

'Oh, I'm sorry,' the junior doctor said, a warm tinge of colour coming to his cheeks as he appeared at the kitchen door. 'I didn't realise you were in here, sir.'

It's my home, Elliot wanted to snap back, and don't call me 'sir'. It makes me sound ancient and decrepit, and I'm neither.

'Do you need any help with the food, Jane?' Richard asked, turning to her before Elliot could say anything.

'I'm fine, thanks. Though if you could take the wine and the glasses through, that would be a big help. Elliot, do you want a plate of this or not?' Jane continued, opening the oven door as Richard disappeared with the wine and the glasses. 'It's chicken curry.'

His favourite, and he was so hungry he could almost taste it.

'I'm not very hungry, thank you,' he said stiffly. 'In fact, I think I might have an early night.'

Jane glanced up at the clock on the wall in surprise. 'At nine o'clock?'

'I really don't think when I choose to go to bed is any of your business,' he retorted, knowing quite well that he was sounding unbelievably petty and childish but completely unable to stop himself.

She shrugged. 'Suit yourself.'

He hovered for an instant, hoping she might try to dissuade him, but to his chagrin she didn't.

'I'll say goodnight, then,' he said coldly. 'And I'd be obliged if you and your *friend* don't make too much noise and wake Nicole.'

And before she could answer he strode out of the

kitchen, down the hall into his bedroom, and only just restrained himself from slamming the door shut.

Elliot didn't restrain himself, however, from pulling off his shoes and throwing them one by one at the bedroom wall.

Damn Richard Connery. He hoped he choked on his chicken curry. He hoped the wine tasted like vinegar, and the junior doctor had an attack of diarrhoea which kept him off work for the rest of the week.

You're jealous!

OK, all right, he was jealous, he admitted it.

And the reason you're jealous is because you're attracted to Jane yourself.

Of course he wasn't, he retorted, only to realise to his dismay that it was true. He didn't know how it had happened, or when, but he did know one thing. It was an attraction that was going to go nowhere. An attraction he firmly intended making sure went nowhere.

When he and Donna had divorced he'd pledged two things. Never to date anyone who worked in his department—it always led to unpleasantness when the relationship ended—and always to date women who knew the score. Women who would shrug their shoulders when he walked away, as he always did.

And Jane was disqualified on both counts.

She didn't know the score. She was too nice, too kind and too gentle to play the kind of games he normally played, and he'd hurt her, he knew he would, and he didn't want to do that.

Which was why he was going to make a date with Gussie for tomorrow night. Gussie knew the score. Gussie could probably have written the rule book. In fact, now he came to think about it, he probably wouldn't be having these disturbing thoughts about Jane in the first place if he

hadn't had to put his social life on hold because he'd been reluctant to ask Gussie round to the flat with Nicole there.

You could have gone round to Gussie's place, his mind pointed out.

OK, so he could, but somehow it hadn't seemed fair to ask Jane to look after Nicole so that he could enjoy Gussie's ample charms.

Well, now he didn't care whether it was fair or not. He was going out with Gussie tomorrow night, or he'd go crazy.

CHAPTER SIX

'NICOLE, Stephanie's mother will be here in five minutes to pick you up and drive you to school, and if you're not ready both you and Stephanie will be late!'

'I know, Jane,' came the shouted reply from the bathroom, 'but I can't find my history book, or my white T-shirt for games!'

'Try the floor behind the sofa in the sitting room for your history book, and your bedroom for your T-shirt!'

For a second there was silence, then the resounding clatter of running feet, followed by the bang of a bedroom door, and Jane winced as she sat down at the kitchen table.

'Overindulged a little on the vino with Richard last night, did we?' Elliot observed, lowering his newspaper to gaze over the top of it at her speculatively, his blue eyes cool.

Actually, she had the mother and father of all headaches this morning, which had a lot more to do with the fact that she hadn't been able to get rid of Richard until two o'clock, but she had absolutely no intention of telling Elliot that.

'Lack of sleep, actually,' she couldn't resist replying, and was gratified to see a flash of anger appear in his blue eyes before he disappeared behind his newspaper again with a furious rustle.

Well, so what if her reply had suggested she'd spent a night of unbridled passion with Richard Connery? she thought waspishly. After Elliot's performance last night—implying she was cradle-snatching, going off to bed in a huff—she was damned if she was going to tell him the

truth. That the only passion which had occurred in her bedroom had been Richard's enthusiastic recounting of his family history dating back to when his great-great-grandfather had been a doctor in Leeds.

'Nicole said she'd like chicken for her dinner tonight,' she observed, quickly slipping a paracetamol into her mouth and swallowing it down with some coffee. 'Would that suit you? If it doesn't I could pick up something else on my way home—'

'Actually, I won't be home for dinner,' Elliot interrupted, lowering his newspaper again, but this time he looked awkward, uncomfortable.

'I thought you had tonight off?' She frowned, then groaned. 'It's not one of those admin meetings again, is it? Honestly, the amount of time they spend discussing budgets—'

'It's not a meeting,' Elliot interrupted. 'I…I've got a date. With Gussie.'

There, it was out. He'd said it, and he waited, half expecting Jane to round on him, to tell him he'd got a nerve, expecting her to look after his daughter while he swanned off with Gussie Granton, but she didn't.

'Oh… Right… I see,' was all she said.

'The thing is, Gussie and I haven't been out for a while,' he said hurriedly as Jane began collecting the dirty breakfast dishes and carrying them over to the sink.

'Elliot, you don't have to explain,' she interrupted, her voice carefully neutral. 'You're going out with Gussie. Fine. End of story.'

And it should have been, he told himself. Dammit, they'd agreed that neither of them would give up their social lives, that as long as one of them was here to look after Nicole they could each go out, but…

'Look, I'll speak to Gussie, tell her something's come

up,' he declared, annoyingly aware that his cheeks were slightly flushed. 'We can go out another time.'

'Don't be silly,' Jane protested, running some water into the sink. 'There's absolutely no need for you to cancel. I hadn't planned on going out tonight anyway.' Chance would have been a fine thing, she added mentally, considering nobody's asked me. 'So it's no problem for me to look after Nicole.'

'And you really don't mind?'

Oh, she minded all right. She minded like hell. 'Of course I don't,' she said brightly, pulling on her washing-up gloves with a snap. 'In fact, I hope you and Gussie have a very pleasant evening.'

Which was exactly what he should have wanted to hear, he realised, but perversely he discovered that he didn't. Was he really such boring company that she couldn't wait to get him out of the house?

Perhaps he was, he thought with dismay, suddenly remembering how Jane always seemed to shoot off to her room the minute Nicole went to bed, saying she had things to do. Gussie didn't seem to find him boring. Anything but. Gussie thought he was witty, and attractive—

'Who's Gussie?'

It was true, Elliot thought as he and Jane turned in unison to see Nicole standing in the kitchen doorway, a frown creasing her forehead. Little pitchers did have big ears.

'She's a friend of mine,' he replied quickly. 'Now, have you got everything you need for school? Your packed lunch, your homework—'

'And you are going out with her, Papa?' Nicole continued, her large, dark eyes on him, her frown deepening. 'On a date?'

Two pairs of eyes were fixed on him now, he noticed. One set accusing, the other apparently indifferent, and to

his annoyance it was the indifferent grey eyes which bothered him the most.

'Well, it's a sort of a date,' he said awkwardly. 'I mean, I'll be having dinner with her.' At Gussie's flat, actually, but there was no way he was going to tell his daughter that. 'Jane will be here to look after you—'

'I think if you are going out to dinner with someone, it should be with Jane,' Nicole interrupted. 'I *like* Jane.'

'And *I* think that sounds like Mrs Massey arriving to pick you up for school,' Elliot declared, clear relief appearing on his face as a car horn sounded in the street outside, but his daughter was having none of it.

'My Aunt Michelle—Mama's sister—gave me a book when I was small called *Gussie's Birthday Party*. Gussie was a big fat elephant. Is she fat, too, this Gussie of yours?'

'No, she is not,' Elliot replied, the colour on his cheeks darkening by the second as he desperately tried to catch Jane's eye, only to discover she seemed to be finding the whole thing highly amusing. 'In fact, she's actually very slim, with blonde hair and...' And this conversation was getting out of hand, he decided. 'I think it's time you went to school, young lady.'

'Yes, but if you want to take someone out to dinner, why don't you take Jane?' Nicole continued. 'She's never been anywhere since I arrived. Why don't you go out with Jane instead of this Gussie person?'

'School, Nicole!'

'Yes, but—'

'School!'

And Nicole went, but it didn't stop her muttering darkly under her breath about fat elephants.

'Honestly, the things kids say!' Floella laughed. 'I remember being in the supermarket once when my twins were

small and this huge woman walks by, and I mean really huge—at least 135 kilos—and my daughter pipes up, "Mummy, is that lady going to have a baby?"'

Jane laughed, too, and if her laughter wasn't quite as hearty as Floella's, thankfully the staff nurse didn't seem to notice.

I'm an idiot, she thought as she watched Elliot crossing the treatment room. I *do* have rocks in my head. To think that only yesterday I was getting myself all in a tizz, thinking he might actually be starting to realise I'm a woman, and what happens? He blithely turns round this morning and tells me he's going out with Gussie.

The plain and simple truth was that Elliot liked women—*all* women. Flirting was as natural to him as breathing, so she'd been right when she'd vowed to keep him at arm's length. She'd been right, so why didn't that knowledge make her feel any better?

'Jane, I wonder if you could give me some help in here, please?' Richard asked, popping his head round the curtains of cubicle 3.

'Jane?' Floella murmured, her eyebrows shooting up to her hairline. '*Jane?* And did mine ears deceive me, or was that also a "please" I just heard?'

'It's a long story, Flo.' Jane couldn't help but chuckle. 'I'll tell you about it some time.'

'You'd better.' The staff nurse grinned, and Jane shook her head and laughed as she walked across to Richard.

'What have you got?' she asked.

'Forty-five-year-old man,' he murmured, deliberately keeping his voice low. 'His wife brought him in because he's been having blinding headaches for the past week. No history of migraine, nor has he had a fall or been involved in a car accident recently. It could just be stress, but...'

Jane nodded. Richard was right to be cautious. A painful headache could be caused by something as simple as a bad

day at the office, but it could also be a warning symptom of a life-threatening ruptured aneurysm in the brain.

'Is there a problem here?' Elliot demanded, joining them without warning, his eyes flicking coldly from Jane to Richard.

Quickly Richard gave him all the information he had, but Elliot knew he was only half listening to him. Try as he might, he couldn't prevent his eyes from drifting back to Jane. She looked so pale this morning, pale and tired and a little depressed. And there were dark shadows under her grey eyes, too, shadows he was positive hadn't been there yesterday or he was sure he would have noticed them.

Richard didn't look at all tired, he thought grimly. He looked bright and alert, as though somebody had recently given his confidence quite a boost. Quite how, Elliot preferred not to contemplate.

'Do you mind if I sit in with you for this patient?' he asked, bringing Richard's explanation to a sudden halt. 'No reflection on your capabilities, of course,' he added smoothly as the junior doctor stared at him in clear dismay, 'but it's part of my job. Checking everything's running smoothly.'

And it was, he told himself as Richard nodded and led the way into the cubicle, looking slightly less confident than he had before, and Jane shot him a puzzled glance. Special registrars were supposed to make sure that the junior doctors on their team were up to scratch, and if his interest was slightly more personal than it should have been, it was nobody's business but his own.

To his chagrin, however, it didn't take him long to discover that not only was Richard Connery quite a personable young man, he was also very good at his job.

He could neither fault the thoroughness of his exami-

nation nor the way he asked his questions. He would have liked to, but he couldn't.

'Would you care to take a look yourself, Dr Mathieson?' Richard asked, turning to him as though he'd read his mind.

Elliot doubted that there was any need, but he took Richard's seat in front of the patient and quickly shone a light into the man's eyes to check whether both of his pupils were equally round and reacted to the light.

'You told Dr Connery you haven't experienced any stiffness in your neck,' he murmured. 'Have you felt any weakness in your arms or legs, or feelings of feverishness, like you're coming down with the flu?'

The man shook his head, only to quite clearly wish he hadn't, and Jane smiled at him sympathetically. The paracetamol she'd taken this morning didn't seem to have helped her headache at all, but at least she knew why she had one. Getting a full eight hours sleep tonight would solve one of the reasons. Doing something about the way she felt about Elliot... Now, that was an entirely different matter altogether.

'Ophthalmoscope, Jane,' Elliot said, interrupting her thoughts, and swiftly she handed him one, only to colour slightly as he shot her a puzzled glance.

And it was no wonder he looked puzzled, she thought, completely mortified. Never had he needed to ask her for anything before. She'd always been able to anticipate his every request, but not this morning. This morning she'd let her mind wander, and it had wandered because she'd been feeling sorry for herself, and it wasn't on. It definitely wasn't on.

Elliot didn't think it was either as he stared through the ophthalmoscope into the back of the middle-aged man's eyes, searching for any signs of increased intracranial pres-

sure which would indicate bleeding or tumour inside the head.

Efficient, on-the-ball Jane daydreaming? Richard had obviously made a big impression last night, and he couldn't for the life of him see why. He was a pleasant enough young man, but he was just a boy, whereas Jane was a woman. A woman with luscious, generous curves. A woman with a shining fall of straight black hair and a sprinkling of golden freckles on her nose. A woman...

Who hadn't even blinked an eye when he'd said he was going out with Gussie tonight, he suddenly remembered. In fact, she'd actually said she hoped he'd have a pleasant evening.

She should have been angry. She should have torn him off a strip. She should...

Have been jealous? Is that what's really bugging you? The realisation that, though you're beginning to find yourself attracted to her, she doesn't even seem to know you're around?

It was, he realised ruefully. God knows, he'd never thought himself a vain man, but to discover that a woman might actually prefer somebody like Richard Connery to him... It was a novel experience, and one he discovered he didn't like at all.

Determinedly he got to his feet, led the way out of the cubicle, then turned to Richard. 'OK, so what do you think we've got?'

The junior doctor took a deep breath. 'I couldn't see any sign of facial drooping, which would indicate he'd had a minor stroke, nor was there any sign of tenderness in his ears, or round his face and head, to suggest an infection.'

'Meningitis?' Elliot suggested, though he knew perfectly well that it wasn't that, but it was worth a try to see if he could catch Richard out. He didn't.

'Definitely not. I suppose it could be a very bad sinus

infection—they can cause severe headaches—but he said he hadn't had a cold recently.'

'Brain tumour?'

Richard frowned. 'I don't *think* it's a tumour, but frankly I've got to admit I don't know what it is, so I'd like to send him for a CAT scan.'

Which would have been exactly what Elliot would have done if the man had been his patient. At a guess he thought it might be temporal arteritis—an inflammation of the large head arteries which, if left untreated, could cause blindness—but, like Richard, his first line of investigation now would be a CAT scan.

'Well, did he pass the test?' Jane asked as she accompanied Elliot down the treatment room, leaving Richard to make the arrangements for his patient.

'The test?' he echoed.

'I presume that's what you were doing,' she observed. 'Seeing if he was up to scratch.'

'He seems a pretty competent doctor,' he declared grudgingly, and to his annoyance Jane laughed.

'Oh, come on, Elliot, you know perfectly well that he's good. OK, so maybe he was a bit high-handed when he first arrived, but he's learned a lot since then. I think he could be a real asset to the department. He's keen, willing to learn, to listen…'

And presumably downright incredible in bed, he wanted to finish for her, but didn't. 'And would that be a personal assessment, or a professional one?' he said tightly instead.

She stared at him, puzzled. 'I don't know what you mean.'

'I *mean* that I hope your friendship with Richard isn't clouding your judgement.'

'Clouding my…' Her dark eyebrows suddenly snapped down, and she looked angrier than he'd ever seen her. 'How long have you and I worked together, Elliot? Oh, I

forgot,' she added as he cleared his throat. 'You don't remember, do you? Well, it's been two years.'

'Jane—'

'Would you say we were friends?'

'I'd like to think so—'

'And do you think I would ignore any situation where I thought you might be making a mistake?'

'No, but—'

'Exactly, so in future stop talking through your hat!'

And before he could reply she was gone, leaving him staring after her, open-mouthed.

'I think you asked for that, Elliot.'

He turned to see Floella gazing up at him, her dark eyes sparkling, and a rueful smile curved his lips. 'You heard?'

'Not everything, but enough. What in the world possessed you to tell Jane she might be behaving unprofessionally?'

For a second he hesitated, then made up his mind. 'Flo, this friendship she has with Richard... Do you think that he and she... I mean, do you think that they...?'

Floella stared at him in total confusion for a second, then burst out laughing. 'Jane and *Richard*? Never in a million years! What in the world put a crazy idea like that into your head?'

The fact that Richard spent hours in her bedroom last night, he thought, but he had no intention of telling Flo that.

'I don't know,' he murmured. 'I just thought... She seems to like him—'

'Elliot, Jane likes *everyone*,' Floella interrupted. 'It's the kind of girl she is. One of the nice ones, if you know what I mean.'

He did know. Just as he also knew that a nice girl would expect faithfulness, commitment. A nice girl would be very badly hurt if someone let her down, and a nice girl

would probably be a lot safer with Richard than she'd ever be with him.

'Flo—'

'RTA for you, Doc!' a paramedic called, as he and his colleague pushed a trolley through the swing doors. 'Fractured tib for sure, slight facial lacerations, and he's drunk.'

'Wonderful,' Elliot sighed, walking quickly towards them. 'Any ID?'

'His name's Jonathan Worrell, and he's a solicitor. The police found his car upside down on its roof and they reckon he skidded and simply lost control. No other vehicles involved, you see.'

'Head, leg and chest X-rays?' Jane asked as she joined them.

Elliot nodded. 'Mr Worrell, can you tell me what your first name is, please—where you work—your address?' A few mumbled, incoherent words was the only reply, and Elliot frowned. 'Was he like this when you picked him up?'

'Not quite so garbled,' one of the paramedics admitted, helping Jane to transfer Mr Worrell onto the examination trolley. 'I expect it's the booze working its way through his system.'

'He doesn't look drunk,' Jane observed when the paramedics had gone and she'd stripped off Mr Worrell's clothing.

'No. No, he doesn't,' Elliot murmured.

'Could it be a stroke?' she suggested, swiftly setting up an IV line and strapping the blood-pressure cuff round the solicitor's arm. 'Or what about drugs?'

'Maybe—maybe not. What have we got on BP and pulse?'

'BP 120 over 80,' she answered as Elliot shone his ophthalmoscope into the solicitor's eyes. 'Pulse rapid and weak.'

Elliot's frown deepened. 'I wonder if it's an extradural haemorrhage. He could have hit his head on the windscreen, fractured his skull and ruptured an artery.'

And if he had, he would be bleeding inside or around his brain, and if it wasn't treated in time Mr Worrell could die.

'Will I page Neurology?' she asked.

'We should, but…'

'But?' Jane prompted.

'It doesn't feel right, Jane. I don't know why, but it doesn't.'

She didn't disagree with him as he pulled his stethoscope out of his pocket and leant over Mr Worrell. She'd seen him have these hunches before, and they had always been right.

'What is it?' she asked, when he suddenly straightened up with a muttered oath, then ran his fingers over the solicitor's face and eyes. 'What's wrong?'

'Stupid, that's what I am!' he exclaimed. 'Stupid, stupid, *stupid*!'

'Elliot—'

'Smell his breath, Jane.'

'You mean, he *is* drunk?'

'No, he's not drunk. Smell his breath!'

She did. 'Oh, Lord, it's sweet, fruity. He's got—'

'Diabetic ketoacidosis. Dry skin and lips, soft eyeballs, slurred speech, looks drunk. He's got diabetic ketoacidosis, and I almost missed it!'

'Soluble insulin and a saline solution through an IV to prevent dehydration?' she said, quickly snapping open the sterilised bags.

'Repeated doses, little and often,' he said, nodding, 'and watch his BP in case he goes into shock.'

He didn't. Slowly but surely the colour began to return

to Mr Worrell's cheeks and gradually his eyes fluttered open.

'You gave us quite a fright there for a minute, sir,' Jane said, smiling down at him.

'W-where am I? W-what happened?' he stammered. 'I was on my way home, and I just seemed to black out.'

'You're in hospital, and you're a very lucky man,' Elliot replied. 'Did you know you were a diabetic?'

'My GP diagnosed it last month—'

'And you're not carrying a medical alert card or any extra insulin.' Elliot shook his head and sighed. 'That's a very dangerous way to live, Mr Worrell.'

It was, but the solicitor had been lucky this time. Lucky it had been Elliot who had been treating him.

'Your hunch was right, then, Elliot,' Jane commented when Mr Worrell was transferred to Theatre to have his fractured tibia set.

'I shouldn't have needed a hunch.' He frowned. 'I should have known.'

'Yeah, right.' Jane laughed. 'Like when someone's brought in to us, having trashed his car, suffered lacerations to his forehead, a compound fractured tibia and a possible fractured skull, your first thought should be diabetic?'

An answering smile was drawn from his lips. 'I guess not.'

'I *know* not, you idiot!' She laughed, and he did, too, but his laughter faded as he watched her walking down the treatment room.

It would be all too easy to fall in love with this woman. All too easy, and all too dangerous. He didn't want to fall in love again. Falling in love brought heartbreak and pain. Oh, it might start out with joy and laughter, but it always ended in disillusionment and bitterness.

Then you should be pleased Jane's not even remotely

interested in you, his mind whispered. You should be relieved it's Richard Connery she wants.

And he *was* relieved, he told himself. OK, so maybe he wasn't pleased that she could prefer a jerk like Richard to him, but it was better that way. Simpler. Safer.

And thank God he was going round to Gussie's flat tonight, because at least for a few hours the one person he wouldn't be able to think about was Jane Halden.

'Darling, I hate to point this out, but do you realise you've done nothing but talk about Jane and Nicole ever since you got here?' Gussie protested, as she handed him a cup of coffee, then sat down beside him on the sofa.

'Have I?' Elliot frowned. 'I'm sorry, Gussie, and I apologise. That dinner was quite superb. In fact, I couldn't tell you the last time I had smoked salmon. The only kind of fish Nicole will eat is fish fingers.'

'Really. Elliot—'

'Actually, she calls them fish thumbs.' He chuckled. 'It's because they're so thick, you see,' he added as Gussie stared at him blankly. 'Thumbs instead of fingers?'

'Oh. Right. Elliot—'

'Jane's trying to get her to eat more vegetables—cutting them into weird and wonderful shapes—but persuading kids to eat vegetables—'

'Must be hell,' Gussie finished for him, sliding along the couch so her breasts brushed against his arm. 'Just as I'm also sure that we could find a whole lot more fun things to do than talk about them.'

He laughed. 'I'm sorry. I'm turning into a right bore when it comes to my daughter, aren't I? It's just that never having had a daughter before... I wish I was as good with her as Jane is. I'm getting better, but Jane always seems to know the right things to say and do.'

'She's quite wonderful, a perfect treasure.' Gussie nod-

ded, running her fingers lightly up his arm and bringing them to rest on his shoulder.

'I really don't know how I'm going to manage when she leaves,' Elliot murmured, a slight frown darkening his eyes. 'I know she can't stay with me for ever...'

'God forbid.' Gussie chuckled throatily. 'For one thing, a *ménage à trois* has never appealed to me.'

His blond eyebrows snapped down. 'There's nothing like that between Jane and me. Jane...she's a very nice girl.'

'A perfect saint, in fact,' Gussie agreed, 'but us sinners do tend to have a lot more fun.'

'Gussie—'

'I thought Nicole was going to stay with your mother when she comes back from Canada?' Gussie continued, nibbling his ear gently with her teeth. 'You did say that, didn't you?'

'I did, but the trouble is I'm going to really miss her when she goes,' he replied, absently rubbing at his ear. 'And she's getting so fond of Jane.'

Gussie forced her lips into a semblance of a smile. 'Darling, if you're so worried about Nicole, would you like me to move in with you when Jane leaves? I'm sure I can organise things at work—' She came to a halt, her brown eyes flashing, as he threw back his head and laughed. 'What's so funny about that?'

Just about everything, Elliot thought. Oh, if he'd wanted someone to take to the special registrar's ball, Gussie would have been perfect, but never could he imagine her pink-cheeked and flushed, her hair scraped back from her face in a ponytail, playing an enthusiastic game of hide-and-seek with Nicole.

'Gussie, you're absolutely wonderful, and I adore you like mad,' he said with a smile, 'but a surrogate mother you're not. Jane—'

'Elliot, if you're going to spend the whole night telling me how marvellous Jane Halden is, I think perhaps you'd better leave!' Gussie snapped, then bit her lip as his eyebrows rose. 'Darling, I'm sorry,' she continued, winding her arms around his neck and pressing her body close to his, 'but a woman has her pride, and she really doesn't want to hear another woman being praised all the time.'

He supposed not. Just as he wished Gussie's perfume wasn't quite so heavy, and that she didn't wear quite so much make-up. Jane didn't wear any make-up. He'd seen her often enough first thing in the morning, her eyes cloudy with sleep, her hair tousled, and then later again at work to know that. Jane...

Abruptly he got to his feet. 'Gussie, I'm sorry, but I have to go.'

'Go?' she gasped. 'But, Elliot, you haven't had your brandy yet, or...' She ran her tongue lightly along her lips. 'Or anything.'

He didn't want the 'anything'. He knew as he left Gussie's flat, mumbling a completely garbled apology which left her staring after him in stunned disbelief, that he didn't want the 'anything' now, or at any time in the future.

'Elliot?'

Well, that made two women he'd managed to stun in the space of an hour, Elliot thought ruefully as he walked into the sitting room, and neither of them appeared to have enjoyed the experience.

'I didn't expect you back so early,' Jane continued. Actually, she hadn't expected him back at all, at least not tonight. 'How's Gussie?'

'Fine. No, don't put that off on my account,' he said quickly as she reached for the television remote control.

'I wasn't really watching it anyway. It's just another of

those mindless American soaps that never seem to get any-where.'

'Has Nicole gone to bed?' he asked, throwing his car keys onto the coffee-table.

'About an hour ago,' she said. Ask him, she told herself. Go on, ask him. You want to know. You know you do. 'Did you have a nice evening?'

'It was OK,' he replied, offhand, dismissive. 'Gussie and I... We don't seem to have a lot in common any more.'

Privately she wondered when they ever had but, then, she'd always supposed they didn't spend much time talk-ing on their dates.

'Did *you* have a good evening?' he asked.

'Oh, quiet, you know. I helped Nicole with her home-work, we played some snakes-and-ladders. She won.'

He smiled. 'I think she cheats.'

She laughed. 'So do I.'

'Have you had supper?'

'About half an hour ago, after my bath. I was just about to go to bed.'

'So I see.'

And he did see as his eyes took in her red and white men's pyjamas, and he found himself wondering why on earth he'd ever thought Gussie's sheer nightdresses sexy.

Jane's pyjamas were sexy. Sexy in the way they re-vealed nothing. Sexy because they hinted at the curves that lay beneath them. Hinted, and tantalised, and simply cried out for a man to investigate them. For him to investigate them.

'Jane, what Nicole said at breakfast about you and I going out together,' he said quickly. 'I was thinking it's actually a very good idea. We could get a babysitter in—Flo's always saying she'd love to—and go out to dinner somewhere.'

'You and me?' she said in obvious surprise.

'Well, I wasn't planning on asking Stephanie's mother.'
He smiled. 'I thought we could try out that new restaurant
in town—the one that's just opened in Flynn Street—'

'Why?'

'Why?' he echoed. The girls he asked out didn't normally ask why. They were usually too busy falling over
themselves to say yes. 'Well, because…because I thought
you might enjoy it.'

Which wasn't exactly the most romantic way to ask a
girl for a date, he thought ruefully, and Jane clearly agreed,
because she shook her head. 'I don't think so, Elliot.'

'But I really would like to take you out to dinner,' he
said desperately. 'You could look on it as a sort of thank
you for all the work you've done with Nicole.'

It had been the wrong thing to say and he knew it immediately. Knew it from the stiffening of her shoulders,
the way her eyes suddenly grew cold.

'I don't consider what I've done with Nicole work,
Elliot,' she said tightly, 'and I certainly don't require dinner as a payment.'

'And I didn't mean it to sound as though it were!' he
exclaimed, cursing himself under his breath. 'What I meant
to say was…'

Hell, he didn't know what he'd meant to say. She was
sitting there in those damn pyjamas of hers, looking so
appealing, so desirable that all he really wanted was to
take her in his arms.

'Look, Jane, you haven't had an evening out since you
moved in.' Oh, that's wonderful, Elliot, he groaned mentally, seeing her bristle even more. Now you've implied
you feel sorry for her. That she's got no social life. What
on earth's wrong with you? You don't usually make such
a mess of asking a girl out, but you sure as heck are making a mess of this. 'I simply thought when Nicole suggested it—'

'That as poor old Jane doesn't get out much maybe she could do with a little treat?' she interrupted acidly. 'That perhaps a little pat on the head might keep her sweet if you need to ask her another favour?'

'No—No!'

'Then why, Elliot? *Why*?'

Because I like you, he thought as she glared at him, her face chalk-white, her eyes glittering with fury. Because I'm growing more and more attracted to you every day, and what I want right now more than anything in the world is to make love to you.

She'd slap his face for sure if he said that. Instead, he forced what he hoped was his most appealing smile to his face. 'Has anyone ever told you you're gorgeous when you're angry?'

She stared at him silently for a full ten seconds, then her lip curled. 'You have, Elliot, most generally when you think your charm and your looks will get you out of a mess. Well, not this time they won't. I won't be patronised—do you hear me? Not now, not ever!'

'Jane—'

'I'm going to bed.'

'But, Jane—'

He was talking to empty air. She'd already swung out of the room, her back ramrod stiff, her head high, and as he heard the sound of her bedroom door slamming shut, he closed his eyes tightly and groaned.

CHAPTER SEVEN

'ELLIOT says there's a two-hour waiting time in Reception now, and X-Ray are warning of at least a one-hour delay in the processing of non-urgent plates,' Kelly reported.

Jane groaned as she leafed through the stack of patient notes the student nurse had brought through from Reception. It was always the same. The minute the schools closed for their Easter break the number of accidents quadrupled. If it wasn't children throwing themselves off walls, or under cars, it was their parents attempting to electrocute themselves with their DIY equipment or driving like maniacs to beat the queues at the tourist attractions.

Thank goodness, Stephanie's mother had agreed to look after Nicole during the day. She wouldn't have been able to relax for a minute otherwise. As it was, if it was up to her, all school holidays would be cancelled. Neither she nor A and E could take the strain.

'Jane, we seem to be running really low on dressings.' Richard frowned, swiftly erasing the name of the last patient he'd seen from the whiteboard. 'Any chance of you nipping along to the dispensary to pick some up?'

'I'll try to arrange—'

'Jane, if you're going to the dispensary, could you pop into Haematology on your way back and see if you can hurry up the results for my patient in 6?' Charlie chipped in.

'Did you just say you're going to Haematology, Jane?' Elliot said as he passed. 'Because if you are, I've got some samples—'

'What am I—the local collection and delivery boy?'

117

Jane snapped before she could stop herself. 'Kelly, go and pick up some dressings, but I want you back a.s.a.p. Charlie, if you're so concerned about your results, lift the telephone. And, Elliot...' Oh, she knew exactly where she'd like to tell him to go, but she was too much of a lady to say it. 'Get a porter to take your samples!'

And before any of them could reply, she strode quickly away, all too aware that the three men were staring in stunned amazement after her.

Well, let them stare, she thought belligerently. Right now she could cheerfully have seen the three of them, and St Stephen's, at the bottom of the Thames.

No, not St Stephen's, she conceded. And not the three of them. Just him. Just Elliot Mathieson.

The nerve of the man. The sheer, unmitigated gall of him. Asking her out like that. Like he was doing her a favour. Like she ought to be grateful. Well, he could stuff his dinner invitation. In fact, she was sorely tempted to go back to the flat tonight, pack her suitcases and leave him and his daughter to get on with it.

No, she wouldn't do that, she realised as she gazed unseeingly, at the clock on the treatment-room wall. No matter how angry she might be with Elliot, she could never do that to Nicole.

She jumped as a white sheet of paper stuck to the end of a ruler suddenly fluttered in front of her nose, and turned to the bearer of it with a frown. 'What's this?'

'A substitute white flag.' Elliot grinned sheepishly. 'Jane, I'm sorry. Charlie and Richard—they're sorry, too,' he added, nodding to where the SHO and junior doctor were standing by the whiteboard, looking decidedly shamefaced. 'We didn't mean to make you feel like an errand boy.'

Yeah, right, she thought sourly. And last night I suppose

you didn't mean to make me feel like a charity case either, but you still did.

'And while we're on the subject of apologising,' he continued quickly as though he'd read her mind, 'you shot out of the house so fast this morning that you didn't give me the chance to set the record straight about last night.'

'Elliot, I think the less said about last night, the better,' she declared.

'Well, I don't!' he snapped, then bit his lip as he noticed that Floella was watching them curiously from the bottom of the treatment room. 'Jane, I really do want to go out with you. Not as a payment, not as a thank you. On a date.'

Boy, but he and Gussie must have had a real humdinger of a row if he was asking her out, she thought waspishly. Well, she had no intention of accepting. She might be a mug and a patsy in many things, but not on this.

'And as I told you last night, Elliot, thanks but, no, thanks,' she said tersely.

She was turning him down? he thought in amazement. She was actually saying no, and meaning it? She couldn't. He wouldn't let her.

Then tell her the truth, his mind urged. Tell her how you feel, why you really want to go out with her.

'Jane…Janey, look, this probably isn't the best time or place for this conversation,' he began awkwardly, 'but I meant what I said. I like you. I like you a lot. I've no idea why I didn't realise it before…'

Probably because you were too busy dating Gussie, she thought bitterly, and before her it had been Marie from Obs and Gynae and Sue from Radiology. Actually, now that she came to think of it, it would have been an awful lot easier to name the girls at St Stephen's that Elliot *hadn't* dated.

'But now I'm asking *you* out, Janey,' he continued. 'Not

because you've been such a great help with Nicole, not because I want to say thank you, but because I truly and honestly do like you very much indeed.'

And she might well have believed him if she hadn't heard him use exactly the same coaxing tone on dozens of women before. Might have been convinced by his earnest expression, the way his lips had curved into one of his lopsided, nerve-tingling smiles, if it hadn't been all too familiar. It had always worked on the women he'd tried it with, and—if she was honest with herself—it was almost working on her, too. Almost, but not quite.

'That's very nice to hear, Elliot,' she declared, 'and I like you as well, but the answer's still no. And now, if you'll excuse me, I have work to do.'

And before he could stop her she'd walked away, leaving him staring helplessly after her.

Where had he gone wrong? It had never failed in the past. A particular smile, a few soft words, and most women had come running. But it hadn't worked this time, and he couldn't for the life of him think why.

'What are you playing at, Elliot?'

He turned quickly to see Floella staring up at him, her normally cheerful face grim, her eyes accusatory.

'I don't know what you mean.'

'Oh, yes, you do,' she said. 'I told Jane to be careful when she agreed to move in with you. Told her she was storing up a whole heap of trouble for herself, but I thought that was because she might get too fond of Nicole.'

'Flo—'

'Elliot, don't mess her around. She's my friend, and if you hurt her—'

'I'd never hurt her, Flo, believe me,' he interrupted indignantly.

'And you don't think persuading her to go out with you, getting her into your bed, and then dumping her will hurt?'

'Flo—'

'And that's what you'll do, Elliot,' she continued. 'It's what you always do, so leave her alone. If you're not serious about her, leave her alone.'

Which was telling him good and proper, he thought ruefully, and Floella was right.

He didn't do commitment. He didn't do fidelity. OK, so maybe he felt an overwhelming attraction for Jane, but the last thing she needed was a man like him in her life, a man who was only comfortable with brief affairs. He'd hurt her, he knew he would, and she didn't need that, didn't deserve it.

He had to start distancing himself from her, and fast. He had to go back to seeing her as good old Janey. For his own sake, as well as for hers. And if that meant standing by and watching her becoming involved with someone like Richard Connery, he decided as he saw the junior doctor say something to her that had made her laugh, so be it.

'Kate Anderson, Doc!' a paramedic exclaimed as he rushed into the treatment room, a heavily pregnant woman on his trolley, and a white-faced man at her side. 'Twenty-two, in labour, and I don't reckon we're going to make the delivery room!'

Elliot didn't reckon she would either when the paramedics had got the woman onto the examination trolley. Her cervix was well dilated, already ten centimetres.

'Jane! Good, you're here,' he said with relief, wincing slightly as Mrs Anderson suddenly grabbed hold of his hand and squeezed hard on it. 'How are you with imminent mums-to-be?'

'Not exactly my speciality, I'm afraid,' she replied ruefully.

'Nor mine,' he replied. 'Has anyone paged the labour ward?'

'Flo was doing it when—'

'Should she be suffering so much?' Mr Anderson interrupted convulsively as his wife let out a scream. 'It doesn't seem right that she should be suffering so much. Can't you give her something—some painkiller?'

'There isn't any point, Mr Anderson,' Elliot said gently. 'By the time it took effect the baby would be here.'

'It's that close?' the young man gulped, and Elliot nodded.

'It's that close.'

'Oh, cripes, oh, God!' Kate Anderson gasped, doubling up as another contraction hit her. 'Nobody ever told me it would hurt this much. John, if you ever come near me again, if you ever even attempt to lay a finger on me—!'

'I can see the baby's head!' her husband exclaimed excitedly. 'I can see the top of its head!'

'I don't care if you can see its head, its shoulders, its entire body!' she yelled. 'I've changed my mind. I don't want to do this any more!'

'I'm afraid it's a bit late for that.' Elliot grinned. 'Breathe, Kate. Huff and pant and breathe like you were taught at the antenatal clinic.'

'But it's not working!' she wailed. 'Those stupid lessons—they're not working!'

'They are—believe me, they are,' Elliot insisted.

Believe me, he'd said, Jane thought as she quickly mopped Kate Anderson's forehead. The young woman believed him, but she couldn't.

He liked her, he'd said, but what did that actually mean? Two or three dates, a few nights of love and then goodbye, Jane, when he got bored or began to feel pressurised?

Could she be happy with that? Right now she could, she realised as she watched him urging the young woman on, smiling at her as only Elliot knew how. Right now she would happily have settled for one night in his arms, but

that was only her hormones reacting. Her head was wiser, her head knew different, and it was her head she was going to listen to.

'It's coming, Kate, it's coming!' he encouraged. 'One more push. Just for me, give one big, huge push!'

And she did, with a cry that was halfway towards a scream, and suddenly the baby was there.

'Is it all right—is my baby all right?' she cried, trying to lever herself upright.

'Perfect, just perfect,' Elliot replied, swiftly cutting the umbilical cord as Jane wiped the mucus from the baby's eyes and mouth and it let out a protesting cry.

'Is it a boy or a girl?' Kate asked, turning eagerly to her husband.

'Yes,' he said, then flushed as he realised what he'd just said. 'It's a... What is it, Nurse?'

'A girl.' Jane laughed. 'You have a lovely baby girl, Mr Anderson.'

And she was beautiful, she thought as she handed her reluctantly to her mother. Perfect in every detail, right down to her tiny toes and fingernails.

And I'm getting broody, she thought as the labour staff arrived to transfer Kate to Theatre to deliver the placenta and repair the small tear she'd sustained during the delivery. I'm twenty-eight years old, soon to be twenty-nine, with no man in my life, and I'm getting broody.

'Wasn't she absolutely gorgeous?' Floella exclaimed, as the baby was whisked away by Sister Strachan of the special care baby unit for monitoring and assessment. 'I told my husband after the twins were born that there'd be no more, but when you see a little scrap like that...'

'You start getting broody.' Charlie Gordon laughed. 'Honestly, you women. Put you within ten yards of a baby—'

'Yeah, right,' Floella interrupted, her dark eyes dancing.

'Like you didn't go a bit misty-eyed yourself. I saw you, so don't try to pretend otherwise. And you weren't any better, Elliot,' she continued as he joined them, 'so don't try to tell me that you were.'

He didn't. He was too busy wishing he'd been present at Nicole's birth. OK, so he and Donna hadn't been on speaking terms, and she would probably have preferred him to be rotting in hell, but he'd seen the look of wonderment on John Anderson's face, the joy, the pride. He'd missed that, hadn't had the chance to experience that.

Maybe the next time, he found himself thinking, only to realise to his horror that his eyes had automatically drifted to Jane, and quickly he wrenched them away.

No, he wasn't going to think that, he must never ever think that. OK, so he expected that Nicole would like a little brother or a sister, but to have one would mean him making a commitment to someone—a long-term commitment—and that was the last thing on his mind.

'Well, if we've all finished admiring little baby Anderson, I suggest we get back to work,' he declared more brusquely than he'd intended. 'There are patients waiting to be seen out in Reception, and their wait isn't going to get any less if we stand around here talking about babies!'

'What in the world's got into him?' Floella demanded as Elliot strode away. 'Good grief, we see enough misery in A and E that it's nice to have a happy ending for once.'

Jane couldn't have agreed with her more as she stared after Elliot with a puzzled frown, but something had obviously got under his skin, and she couldn't for the life of her think what.

'Jane, before you go, I'd like to ask you something,' Charlie said as Floella hurried away, still muttering under her breath.

'Fire away,' she replied, forcing a smile to her lips.

'Barbara and I would like very much to invite you out to dinner with us tonight.'

'To dinner?' she repeated. 'Well, that's very nice of you both, Charlie, and I've certainly never been one to look a gift dinner in the mouth...' Unless it's being offered by Elliot, of course, she amended, but, then, his invitation hadn't been a gift, it had been a payment. 'But why?'

'She said yes, Jane,' he replied, a broad smile lighting up his face. 'I asked her to marry me when we were at Brambles, and she said yes.'

'Oh, congratulations!' she exclaimed. 'I'm so happy for you. Have you told anyone else yet? We must have a party—'

'I'd rather not if you don't mind,' he interrupted. 'Barbara wants to tell her folks first.'

'I understand.' Jane nodded. 'I'm so pleased for you, Charlie, I really am, but what has that got to do with you inviting me to dinner?'

'Well, you suggested the venue—'

'That hardly makes me a matchmaker,' she protested with a chuckle.

'And you've been a very good friend to me since I came to St Stephen's, which is why Barbara and I would like you to come out to dinner with us tonight, just to say thank you.'

He meant it, she could see that he did, and it would certainly get her out of the flat. And tonight she didn't want to be in the flat. Tonight she didn't want to be anywhere near Elliot Mathieson.

'Then I accept the invitation with pleasure, Charlie.' She smiled. 'And thank you very much for asking.'

'Thank *you*.' He smiled back. 'We'll pick you up at eight.'

'You'd better just sound your horn and I'll come out,' she advised. 'It's murder finding anywhere to park, and if

you keep your engine running, I'll just run down and jump in.'

He nodded, then frowned. 'You don't have to square it with Elliot first? I know you have this arrangement whereby there's always one of you home to look after Nicole.'

'No, I don't have to talk to Elliot,' she said firmly. 'He won't mind at all.'

And he'd better not, she thought, or she would want to know the reason why.

Elliot didn't object but his jaw did drop when she came into the sitting room later that evening, one high heel on, the other still in her hand as she scanned the room, clearly looking for something.

'You're going out?' he said faintly.

'Yes, I'm going out,' she replied, homing in on the mantelpiece and retrieving her hairbrush. 'I hope you didn't have anything planned. The invitation was a bit of a last-minute affair—'

'You're going out like that?' he interrupted.

'Like what?' she said, slipping on her other shoe and turning towards him with a slight frown.

He swallowed convulsively. He'd never seen her dressed before. Not dressed to go out. Not wearing a black velvet dress with a fitted waistline and a bodice that sloped off her creamy shoulders, revealing more than a hint of the deep cleft between her breasts.

'Who?' His voice had come out in a slightly strangled squeak and he cleared his throat. 'Who are you going out with?'

'Charlie and—'

'Charlie Gordon?' he exclaimed, sitting bolt upright in his seat. 'You're going out on a date with Charlie Gordon?'

She could have explained—she supposed she ought to have done—but suddenly she was blowed if she would.

It was the stunned expression on his face that riled her. The look that suggested he couldn't quite believe that anybody would actually have asked her out.

'Yes, I'm going out on a date with Charlie Gordon,' she said bluntly. 'What about it?'

'But you can't go out with him!'

Her eyebrows rose as she slipped her hairbrush into her bag. 'Oh, but I can, Elliot. Now, I shouldn't be too late, probably not much after ten—'

'But I've rented a video for tonight,' he protested.

'Then I hope you enjoy it,' she said calmly. 'Like I said, I shouldn't be late. And now I really have to go,' she added as she heard the sound of a car horn tooting in the street outside.

'Jane, you can't do this—you shouldn't,' Elliot exclaimed, coming after her and catching her by the arm. 'Charlie... He's got a girlfriend in Wales or Lancashire—'

'Shrewsbury,' she interrupted without thinking, but he didn't pick her up on that, he was far too worried.

'Exactly.' He nodded. 'He's got a girlfriend, but he's asking you out, too. Don't be a fool, Jane. A man like that will hurt you for sure.'

And you wouldn't? she thought as she stared up at him. Elliot, you would hurt me a hundred times more—you already have—and yet you can't see it.

'I really don't see who I go out with is any of your damn business!' she retorted, pulling free of his arm.

'Janey—'

'And that's another thing,' she interrupted. 'I really, *really* hate it when you call me that. You always call me that when you're wanting a favour, when you're trying to get something out of me, and I don't like it!'

'I didn't realise, I didn't know—'

'Why should you?' she said. 'Why should you know anything at all about me, Elliot?'

And without allowing him to reply, she walked out of the flat and down to the car where Charlie and his fiancée were waiting.

'Everything OK, Jane?' he asked. 'No problems about getting away tonight?'

'Why should there be?' she replied with a brittle smile as she slipped into the back seat. 'I'm so glad you asked me. I'm really, *really* looking forward to this.'

And to her amazement she did enjoy herself. Barbara put her at her ease in a second, the food at the restaurant was superb and if occasionally she found herself thinking about Elliot she quickly trampled on the thought.

'I wish you both every happiness in the world,' she told the couple when the waiter had cleared away their pudding plates and she insisted he bring them a bottle of champagne with their coffees. 'I don't know very much about you, Barbara,' she continued, smiling across at the small red-headed girl, 'but if Charlie loves you then you must be a very nice girl, because he's certainly a very nice man.'

'Hey, any more of that kind of talk and you'll have me blushing,' he protested, then lifted his glass of champagne. 'I'd like to propose a toast.' Obediently Barbara and Jane lifted their glasses, but to Jane's surprise Charlie put his hand over hers. ''You can't drink to yourself, love.'

'Me?' she said in surprise.

'You.' He nodded. 'I want to toast the best A and E sister I know, and also the kindest. May she have long life and happiness.'

'Long life and happiness,' Barbara echoed, and Jane blinked back the tears she could feel welling in her eyes.

The long life she might be lucky enough to achieve, but the happiness... Somehow she doubted it.

'Thanks for a lovely evening,' Jane said when Charlie

had driven her home after he'd first dropped his fiancée off at his flat. 'I still don't think I deserved it, but thank you anyway.'

'I meant what I said, you know,' he said with a smile as she opened the car door. 'I do wish you every happiness.'

'And I think your Barbara's a very lucky woman.' She chuckled, kissing him lightly on the cheek.

'Looks like someone's still up,' he commented, seeing a dim glow through one of the curtains. 'Elliot checking you in, do you reckon?'

'Elliot tackling some paperwork, more like,' she said ruefully.

And most definitely not wanting to be disturbed, she decided as she let herself into the house.

Quickly she slipped off her heels and began tiptoeing along the corridor, but she couldn't have been quiet enough because she'd just passed his study when the door was suddenly thrown open and he stood there, his eyes furious, his face grim.

'Where the hell have you been?'

Her jaw dropped. 'Out to dinner with Charlie, of course.'

'Until this hour?'

She very nearly laughed. He sounded for all the world like an irate father berating his teenage daughter, but he wasn't her father and she most certainly wasn't his daughter.

Deliberately she looked down at her watch then up at him. 'Good grief, is it eleven o'clock already? I really have been painting the town red, haven't I?'

He coloured but his face didn't relax at all. 'You said you'd be back by ten.'

'I thought I would be, but I was having such a very nice time—'

'And you couldn't have phoned to say you'd be late? It never occurred to you that I—we might have been worried, or that Nicole could have been taken ill?'

'What's happened?' she demanded, worry surging through her. 'Nicole—'

'Is perfectly all right, but that's not the point.'

'Then what is?' Jane demanded, her confusion giving way to anger. 'Elliot, this is the first time I've been out in the evening since I moved in with you. Nicole wasn't left on her own—you were here with her—and you have no right to make me feel guilty. Good grief, if I'd wanted to stay out all night I could.'

'And did you?'

'Did I what?' she asked, bewildered.

'Want to stay out all night?'

His eyes were fixed on her, cold, hard, and she felt herself reddening. 'That's none of your business.'

'It is when I have Nicole's moral welfare to consider.'

'When you have her...' Jane took a deep breath and struggled to keep her temper. 'Elliot, I have been out for one evening. I have returned at what—in anybody's book—is a perfectly reasonable hour. I do not see how that in any shape or form makes me some kind of moral degenerate.'

'I didn't say it did,' he replied, his cheeks almost as red as hers now.

'You didn't have to, Elliot, and now—if you'll excuse me—I am going to bed!'

'No, please!' he exclaimed as she whirled round on her heel. 'Jane...Jane, I'm sorry. You have every right to go out whenever and with whoever you choose. I...I have no claim on you, no right to dictate anything. I just... It's just...I can't help worrying about you.'

'Elliot, I'm all grown up in case you hadn't noticed,' she protested.

'I've noticed.'

He was teasing her, of course—she knew he was. But as she looked up at him, fully expecting to see the tell-tale twinkle in his eye, the give-away quirk of his lips, she saw to her amazement that there was none.

And then she saw something else in his eyes. Something that made her breath catch and shudder in her throat.

'Elliot...'

'Jane...'

His voice was low and dark and husky. Slowly, as though in a dream, she saw his hand lift and come towards her, felt it cup her cheek, and she couldn't move. Felt rooted to the spot.

He was going to kiss her. She knew he was, and she stared up at him, wide-eyed, all too aware that her instincts were urging her to run, but she didn't want to run.

Slowly his head came down towards hers. Too slowly, much too slowly, and her hands half rose from her sides to bring him closer, only to fall back instantly as she heard a small voice whisper behind her, 'Papa?'

'N-Nicole!' Elliot stammered. 'What are you doing out of bed? It's late—'

'I heard voices, people shouting...'

'It was the radio,' Jane declared quickly. 'Your father was listening to a play on the radio.'

'I thought it was you, Papa,' Nicole murmured, tears shining in her eyes. 'I thought you were arguing, fighting with Jane—'

'Oh, no, sweetheart, never,' he declared hoarsely, going to her immediately, and lifting her into his arms. 'Jane and I... We're the best of friends, you know that.'

'But I thought—'

'You were dreaming, Nicole,' he insisted, and she buried her face in his shoulder and shook her head.

'I don't like it when people fight. Mama... She used to

fight sometimes with her boyfriends, throwing vases, dishes—'

'Come on, let's get you back into bed,' Jane interrupted, reaching for the little girl, only to see her cling even more tenaciously to her father.

'I want Papa to take me to bed,' she declared. 'Papa, I want you to do it.'

Elliot mouthed an apologetic 'Sorry' over his daughter's head, but Jane shook her head in reply.

It was how it should be. How she'd always hoped it would be. That Elliot and Nicole would finally become father and daughter, and if her throat felt tight, constricted, and she wanted to burst into tears, that was understandable, too.

Elliot turned to carry his daughter back to her bedroom, then paused. 'You'll wait until I get her settled?'

It would have been so easy to say yes. To wait for him, to let what she knew would happen if she did wait simply happen. And if Nicole hadn't arrived when she had she would have gone with him willingly, let him make love to her willingly, but the moment was broken, and the cold light of sanity had returned.

'I don't think that would be a very good idea, do you?' she replied with a crooked smile that tore at his heart.

'Jane—'

'I'm very tired, Elliot. I really would rather just go to bed.'

And he knew, too, that the moment was gone, and didn't argue with her.

It took almost half an hour to get Nicole settled again, and when he came out of her bedroom Jane's room was in darkness.

Wearily he went into the sitting room, poured himself a drink, put a CD on the stereo and sat down and closed his

eyes, only to open them again when he realised what music he'd put on.

Three years ago his sister Annie had given him *The World's Best Love Songs* for his birthday and he'd burst out laughing when he'd unwrapped it. He'd stuffed it at the back of his collection, meaning to give it away to the first bring-and-buy sale that came along, and had promptly forgotten about it. And now he'd accidentally put it on.

But as he listened to the male singer telling of his lost love, of the missed opportunities, and heartbreak, a bitter smile curved his lips. The guy knew what he was talking about, and he did, too, but it wasn't Donna he was thinking of. Donna, whom he'd loved with all the intensity of a bush fire, a bush fire that perhaps inevitably had been bound to burn out, leaving desolation in its wake.

It was Jane. Jane, who had somehow managed to creep her way into his heart without him even realising she was doing it. Jane, whom he knew that he'd fallen in love with, just as surely as he knew that she didn't return his love.

CHAPTER EIGHT

'OK, WHAT have we got in cubicle 4, Flo?'

'Mrs Steel. In London from America on her honeymoon, and she's experiencing excruciating pain when she urinates. Sounds like a bad case of honeymoon cystitis to me, but I'm not a doctor.'

Oh, terrific, Elliot thought wearily. That was all he needed today. After tossing and turning all night, trying desperately hard not to think about sex, what had he been landed with? A case of honeymoon cystitis.

'Is Kelly with her?'

Floella shook her head. 'Jane.'

Even better, he groaned. A case of honeymoon cystitis, and Jane for company. The gods must really have decided to have some fun at his expense this morning.

'I understand you're experiencing pain when you're passing urine, Mrs Steel?' he said as he walked into the cubicle and the tall blonde girl lying on the trolley cautiously levered herself upright.

'And it's not just that it hurts like hell when I go,' the girl replied. 'I'm running backwards and forwards to the john practically every half-hour as well.'

'Any other symptoms?' he asked, quickly taking her pulse. 'Pain in your back or stomach?'

'And how.' She grimaced. 'It feels like someone's sticking red-hot pokers into me.'

'BP, Sister Halden?' he asked, turning to Jane.

'Normal,' she murmured, but she didn't look at him when she said it.

She'd been doing her level best not to look at him all

morning. OK, so at breakfast she could have argued that she was too harassed, trying to get Nicole ready to go off for the day with Stephanie and her mother to indulge in any kind of small talk, but that still didn't explain why she'd left for the hospital before he'd even realised she was gone, or why she'd been avoiding him since they'd started their shift.

He'd made her uncomfortable, he thought sadly. Last night he'd made her angry, and then he'd gone and made her feel uncomfortable, and it had been the last thing he'd wanted. He'd wanted—hoped—she might possibly have fallen in love with him, as he had with her, but she hadn't, and now she was going to be tiptoeing around him, awkward, embarrassed, and it was going to be hell.

'Do you think it's something serious?' Mrs Steel asked, her pale face worried.

Oh, it was serious, all right, Elliot thought, gazing at Jane's carefully lowered head. Falling in love was always serious, and it was devastating if the person you loved didn't love you back.

'I don't think so, Mrs Steel,' he replied, dredging up a smile. 'Could you take a urine sample, Sister Halden, while I take Mrs Steel's temperature?'

'I always think those things aren't nearly so impressive as the good old-fashioned thermometers,' the girl observed as Elliot carefully inserted an electronic probe into her ear canal. 'I love it when in the old black and white movies the doctor shakes his thermometer and puts it in his patient's mouth. It looks real neat.'

'I know what you mean,' Elliot said, smiling, 'but the trouble with the glass thermometers was that sometimes a patient could have drunk something hot or cold before we saw them, which meant the result wasn't very reliable. And if you had a patient with breathing problems it was pretty

unrealistic to expect them to keep their mouths shut while we got an accurate reading.'

'Or you'd end up with a dead patient, huh?' Mrs Steel grinned. 'OK, fair enough, but I still don't think it looks as impressive as the old thermometer.'

It didn't, but it certainly confirmed that Mrs Steel's temperature was higher than it should have been, and the sample Jane had taken also revealed she had a very bad urinary infection.

'Women's urethras are much shorter than men's, which makes it much easier for bacteria to enter,' Elliot explained after he'd told Mrs Steel she had cystitis. 'As you're on your honeymoon, I imagine you're making love more than normal—'

'Sure am.' The girl chuckled.

Lucky you, Elliot thought dryly. He couldn't remember the last time he'd made love, and the trouble was there was only one woman he wanted to make love to, and she wasn't interested. Not interested at all.

'And as you're making love more than usual, and your urethra is close to your vagina, the frequency can lead to bruising,' he continued doggedly, 'and that in turn leads to infection.'

'Hey, that doesn't mean I'm going to have to tell my husband I've gone celibate, does it?' Mrs Steel exclaimed in dismay, and Elliot laughed.

'Of course not. I'll give you some antibiotics to take, and if you can drink as much water as possible to dilute your urine, the pain should ease considerably then disappear.'

'He's *gorgeous*, isn't he?' Mrs Steel commented when Jane escorted her out of the treatment room. 'I mean, if I wasn't married, I could really fall for that guy.'

I've already fallen, Jane thought wistfully as she waved

the girl goodbye. Hook, line and sinker, and much good it's going to do me.

Last night she'd seen desire in his eyes, and if Nicole hadn't arrived when she had…

Part of her wished the little girl hadn't heard them arguing. Part of her—the weak, wimpy part—wished Nicole had simply stayed in her bed.

And then what? her mind whispered. Do you think you would have been happy to have enjoyed just a few short weeks with him, then watched him walk away?

No, she wouldn't have been happy, but Elliot's mother wouldn't be back from Canada for another six weeks. She was going to have to live with him for another six weeks. Six weeks of wanting him. Six weeks of knowing that, though he might want her too, it was only in the way a child would want a new toy. A toy that would be discarded when the novelty wore off.

Forget about the next six weeks, she told herself. What about tonight? Stephanie's mother had taken Nicole with her daughter to visit the Tower of London and Madame Tussaud's, and then they were going to have tea in a café before going on to the cinema.

She and Elliot would be alone together in his flat. Oh, they'd been alone every night once Nicole had gone to bed but she'd always managed to ensure she didn't linger long afterwards, but tonight…

Tonight Nicole wouldn't be home until after ten and she could hardly disappear into her room as soon as they'd had dinner. It would have looked weird. It would have looked as though she was afraid to be alone with him.

And she was.

'A splinter!' Floella exclaimed savagely as she came out of cubicle 8. 'The guy Richard and I have just treated came in because he had a *splinter* in his finger! This is an A and E unit, for God's sake!'

'Flo—'

'And yesterday it was a woman who'd strained a calf muscle while walking her dog. Well, pardon me if I don't consider that to be a life-threatening condition. Haven't these people heard of GPs?'

'I know, but, Flo—'

'No wonder people are having to wait hours in Reception. No wonder—'

'Flo, would you like to go with me to the cinema tonight?' Jane interrupted desperately.

'The cinema?'

'I know it's a bit short notice,' Jane continued as Floella gazed at her in surprise. 'But I haven't been to a movie since I don't know when, and everyone's raving about the new Mel Gibson one—'

'Oh, Jane, I'm sorry, but I can't. It's my husband's birthday today and I thought I'd take him out to dinner as a special treat. What about Friday night? We could go then if you like.'

'Fine…great.' Jane smiled with an effort but the staff nurse wasn't fooled for a second.

'Jane, what's wrong?'

'There's nothing wrong.'

'Don't give me that!' Floella exclaimed. 'Jane, I've known you for six years, and I *know* when something's really worrying you. It's Elliot, isn't it?'

'Of course it's not,' she protested, feeling her cheeks beginning to redden under Floella's steady gaze. 'I don't know what put that idea—'

'Is he hassling you? Coming on to you? Jane, if he is, tell him where to get off. We both know what he's like. Oh, he's a terrific guy—wonderful to work with, and a great friend—but when it comes to women—'

'Flo, I'm not getting involved with Elliot!' Jane exclaimed. 'He's not interested in me. Never has been.'

'He's interested now,' the staff nurse said shrewdly, 'and you're running scared if you're desperately trying to come up with some excuse to get out of his flat for the evening.'

'I'm not—'

'No?' Floella shook her head and sighed. 'Jane, the sooner you leave the better.'

Which was all very well for her to say, Jane thought as the rest of her shift dragged by, but she couldn't just pack her bags and go. What about Nicole? Who would look after her when Elliot worked nights or weekends?

It's not your problem, a little voice at the back of her mind pointed out, and she knew it wasn't, and yet...

All she could hope when the clock on the treatment room wall finally showed her shift was over was that Elliot would soon decide there were plenty more fish in the sea, and start looking for one.

All she could hope even more fervently was that tonight wouldn't turn out to be as big a nightmare as she feared.

But it did.

He watched her all through dinner. Oh, not obviously, not blatantly. The moment she looked up his eyes would skitter away, but they'd been there, she'd felt them, just as she was equally devastatingly conscious of him. Conscious of his hands as he reached for the cruet. Conscious of the taut muscle in his arms as he lifted the casserole from the table and replaced it with their pudding, so that by the time they'd finished their meal her nerves were in shreds.

'I wonder if there's anything interesting on TV tonight?' she said, desperately picking up the TV guide as they walked through to the sitting room.

A football match, a documentary about life in an NHS

A and E department and two American soaps. The soaps were out, as was the documentary. She knew everything that she ever wanted to know about working in an A and E department, but football? Men liked football. Everybody said they did. Everybody said men became so engrossed when they were watching it that they didn't notice anything else.

Everybody was wrong.

'Isn't it a very good match?' she said tentatively, seeing him shift uncomfortably in his seat for what must have been the tenth time in as many minutes.

A rueful smile curved his lips. 'Actually, I'm afraid I don't really like football.'

'You should have said—'

'I thought *you* liked it—'

He began to laugh and she did, too, but then their eyes met. Met, and held, and as she felt her breath catch in her throat she stood up hurriedly.

'W-would you like a cup of coffee—tea?'

'No, thank you.' He'd also got to his feet, and involuntarily she took a step back, only to see his mouth twist into not quite a smile. 'There's no need to be frightened of me, Jane.'

'I'm not frightened,' she managed to reply.

'So I see,' Elliot murmured, his gaze fixed on the telltale leaping of the pulse at her throat. 'Jane, you have nothing to fear from me. Not now, not ever. I...I can't deny that I find you very attractive—more than attractive—but I know you don't feel the same way about me and I would never pressurise you.'

'You find me attractive?' she said faintly.

'Jane...' He stabbed his fingers through his hair. 'Jane, I think you're the most beautiful, desirable woman, I've ever met.'

He didn't mean it. She was sure that he didn't mean it,

and she didn't want him to tease her, couldn't bear for him to tease her like this.

'Please, Elliot—'

'Oh, I know you don't want to hear this, and I never intended telling you—promised myself that I wouldn't— but the way I feel about you… Donna—what I felt for her was a kind of madness, a wild insanity, but for you…'

She tried to swallow, and found that she couldn't. 'Elliot…Elliot, are you saying that you love me?'

For an answer, his hand came up and cupped her cheek, and she stopped breathing.

She could have moved away. Part of her brain was telling her to do just that, but she didn't, couldn't, not when his thumb was gently caressing her skin, sending shock waves of pleasure running through her.

'Elliot…'

It was a last feeble plea, and he ignored it as she'd known he would, putting his arm round her waist, drawing her to him until they were only inches apart. Now is the time to run, the rational part of her brain insisted. Now is the moment to run as fast and as far away from this man as you can.

But she didn't want to listen to the rational part of her brain. She wanted him to kiss her. She wanted to know how it would feel, how he would taste, and it was she who closed those last few precious inches between them, so that they were standing chest to chest, hip to hip.

And Elliot? He'd never felt this way before. Never wanted not simply to make love to a woman but to cherish her, to protect her, to keep her safe. Jane was trembling, but he was trembling as well, not wanting to rush, not wanting to frighten her, but wanting her, wanting her so much.

'Jane…'

She saw the uncertainty that she knew must be in her eyes mirrored in his, and it was that which moved her more than anything he might have said. That unexpected vulnerability which made her throw all caution to the wind and gave her the courage to slide her arms up his shoulders and lock them round his neck.

'I love you, Elliot Mathieson,' she whispered.

She heard his sharp intake of breath, saw the uncertainty in his eyes disappear, to be replaced by one of joy, then he bent his head and kissed her, achingly light, achingly slow.

His body was shaking, trembling under her hands, and she arched up against him, parted her lips, felt the hot touch of his tongue and welcomed it, revelled in it. He shifted against her, drawing her even closer, caressing her back with his hands, and a groan escaped her.

'Jane…' His voice was ragged, hoarse against her hair. 'Jane, I want… You know what I want.'

She did, just as she knew that there was no way in the world she could step back now, and when he took her hand and led her to his bedroom she went with him willingly.

'God, you're so lovely,' he said unsteadily as he gently stripped away her clothes, then his. 'So very, very lovely.'

'Ten-thirty tomorrow morning,' she gasped as his fingers cupped one breast and his mouth closed over its aching, straining peak.

'Ten-thirty…?'

'The ophthalmology department. You need your eyes tested. Maybe glasses—'

'Glasses be damned.' He laughed huskily, turning his attention to her other breast. 'I know beauty when I see it, and you're beautiful.'

And she felt beautiful as he laid her on his bed and caressed her body until she was crying out with need. She

felt beautiful and desirable and everything a woman should be.

'Elliot, please!' she begged, parting her legs beneath him, arching her hips under him, and with a ragged groan he gave up all pretence of control and surged into her, sending her into a glorious freefall.

She heard his cry, deep and harsh and guttural, as he stiffened against her, and then his arms were round her, holding her close as he rolled over onto his back, cradling her against him as though he never wanted to let go.

'Jane…Jane, are you crying?' he said with concern, feeling the wetness of her cheeks against his chest. 'Oh, my love, what's wrong?'

His love. He'd called her *his* love, and she lifted her head to gaze tremulously at him. 'Nothing. I'm just happy, that's all.'

He chuckled, and she felt the vibrations run the length of her body. 'Good, because so am I. In fact, I don't think I've ever been this happy.'

She knew she hadn't, and at this wonderful moment she didn't care what the future might bring. For now this was enough. For now she was in his arms, he was holding her, and it was enough.

So she only sighed slightly when the phone began to ring.

'If it's an emergency at the hospital, I'm going to tell them to get on with it,' Elliot grumbled, reluctantly easing himself out from under her.

'Oh, yeah, right.' She laughed. 'And that I believe, I don't think.'

But her laughter disappeared when she watched him answering the call, saw his face turn suddenly ashen and his knuckles whiten as he clenched the phone.

'What is it, what's wrong?' she demanded when he

banged down the phone and began scrabbling for his clothes.

'There's been an accident. They were crossing the road outside Stephanie's house and Nicole ran ahead and a car hit her.'

'Oh, God, no—is she badly hurt?' Jane cried, reaching for her own clothes.

'Charlie didn't say.'

'Charlie?'

'They've taken her to St Stephen's.'

The journey across London took an eternity. The evening traffic was heavy, every traffic light seemed to be against them and when they finally reached the hospital Elliot simply abandoned his car in the 'No Parking' zone, heedless of the protesting cry of the traffic warden.

'She'll be all right, Elliot, I'm sure she will,' Jane said, running to keep up with him as he strode through the reception area, his face taut, tense. 'We have one of the best A and E units in the city, and if anyone can help her it's Charlie and the rest of the gang.'

He didn't answer her—she doubted whether he'd even really heard her. He had only one goal and as he banged through the treatment room doors, just as Charlie Gordon emerged from a cubicle, the SHO took one look at his face and came hurriedly towards him.

'OK, what's the situation?' Elliot demanded.

'It's really too early to say—'

'Don't hand me that crap, Charlie!' Elliot exclaimed. 'I'm a doctor, remember. Just give me the facts.'

The SHO bit his lip, then nodded. 'OK. It looks like she's sustained compound fractures of both tibias. She has two, possibly three fractured ribs—'

'Lung damage?'

'Her left lung collapsed shortly after she arrived. We

think one of her fractured ribs may have punctured it, and we've tubed her.'

'Glasgow coma scale?'

'Elliot, I really don't see how you knowing it is going to help,' Charlie protested. 'Look, why don't you wait in one of our private waiting rooms—?'

'Scale of consciousness on the Glasgow coma scale, Charlie?' Elliot reiterated, his face grim.

The SHO obviously didn't want to answer. He quite clearly didn't want to answer, but eventually he muttered, 'Two, two, three.'

Jane drew in a shuddering breath. Anything less than eight meant you had very serious injuries indeed. She reached for Elliot's hand and clasped it tightly.

'Does...does she have any head injuries?' she asked, her voice choked.

'I don't know yet,' Charlie replied. 'We've taken X-rays—'

'Where is she—which cubicle?'

'Elliot, I don't think—'

'No, don't,' he retorted. 'Which cubicle is she in?'

Charlie glanced at Jane and she nodded. 'Five. She's in cubicle five, Elliot.'

Elliot brushed quickly past him, but as the SHO made to follow Jane caught hold of his arm. 'Charlie, how...how bad is it?'

'Pretty bad,' he admitted grimly. 'She's lost a hell of a lot of blood, Jane. We're pumping in O-negative while we're waiting for a cross-match, but as fast as we're pumping it in she seems to be losing it.'

'Can I see her?'

'Do you think you should?' Charlie asked, concern plain on his face. 'Jane, she looks pretty bad. I'd rather Elliot hadn't gone in either, but short of knocking him down I didn't think there was any way I could have kept him out.'

'Charlie, I'm a nurse. I see cases like this every day.'

'Maybe you do, but this is different, Jane. This is personal. This is Nicole.'

'I'd still like to see her,' she said firmly, and he shrugged in defeat.

He'd been right. Nicole did look awful. Awful, and tiny, and desperately white, but what really tore at Jane's heart was the way Elliot was standing by the trolley, holding his daughter's hand in his, as though that would somehow keep her with him.

'ECG reading, Flo?' Charlie asked.

'Still fluctuating pretty wildly, I'm afraid,' she replied, tight-lipped.

'Have you inserted a catheter to drain her bladder?' Elliot demanded. 'Emptied her stomach?'

Charlie nodded. 'Elliot, we're doing everything we can.'

Elliot knew that they were and put his hand softly to Nicole's cheek.

He remembered reading somewhere that Britain had one of the worst child fatality statistics in Europe. It had shocked him, but it had been the kind of shock he'd quickly forgotten because it hadn't been personal. It had just been an article. An article you shook your head sadly over, then turned the page.

But he couldn't turn the page on this accident. This was Nicole. His daughter. His child.

A sob welled in his throat. He couldn't lose her. OK, so he hadn't wanted her at first, hadn't wanted to be a father, hadn't wanted any child of Donna's, but if he lost her now…

Please, God, he prayed, don't take her from me. Don't let her die. She's so young, so very young. She has all her life waiting to be lived. If anyone should die, let it be me. Let me be the one who dies, not my daughter. Dear God,

I'll never ask you for anything ever again if you'll just let me keep her.

'Have we got a result back yet on Nicole's blood type?' Charlie demanded, seeing Richard appear at the cubicle curtains.

He nodded. 'It's AB, and on its way now. I've got the chest, leg, and head X-rays here if you want to take a look at them.'

'Elliot?'

Charlie was gazing enquiringly across at him but Elliot's eyes were fixed on Richard as though he didn't quite believe what he'd said.

'AB?' he repeated.

The junior doctor nodded again. 'Do you want to take a look at the X-rays, Elliot?'

He didn't answer. He simply turned back to the trolley, stared down at his daughter, then gently reached out and stroked her bloodstained hair.

'Jane, I think maybe you should take him out,' the SHO muttered. 'Delayed reaction—I've seen it happen before.'

So had she. 'I'll take him to one of the waiting rooms—'

'You'll take me nowhere!' Elliot suddenly exclaimed, swinging round to them. 'Let's take a look at these X-rays.'

Swiftly Richard snapped them up onto the board and hit the light to illuminate them.

Definite compound fractures of both tibias, Jane thought as she stared up at them, and it was three fractured ribs, not two. She could see the one which had punctured Nicole's left lung but luckily the endotracheal tube was in the right place.

'Head X-rays, Richard?' Elliot demanded, a tremor clear in his voice.

The junior doctor removed the first set of X-rays and replaced them with those of Nicole's skull.

'Slight hairline fracture, right side above her ear,' Charlie murmured, peering at the X-rays carefully. 'Anyone see anything else?'

'We'll need a CAT scan to be certain there's no other damage,' Elliot exclaimed. 'What's her CBC?'

'Twenty-five,' Floella replied.

It was getting dangerously close to the level when there wouldn't be enough blood to supply adequate oxygen to Nicole's brain and yet they were constantly pumping in blood.

'She's bleeding in her stomach,' Elliot said flatly.

'Not necessarily—'

'Cut the bull, Charlie,' Elliot exclaimed. 'She's bleeding in her stomach. How's her BP, pulse? Have you stabilised her enough for Theatre?'

Charlie glanced across at Floella.

'Both BP and pulse are still a little low,' she replied, 'but I agree with Elliot. I think we should send her to Theatre.'

She didn't add, Because I think we desperately need their skills, but they all thought it.

Swiftly Floella and Charlie wheeled Nicole out of the treatment room. Elliot and Jane followed them to the operating-theatre door, where one of the theatre staff firmly but kindly ushered them into a small waiting room. They heard the doors of the operating theatre clatter shut.

There was nothing to do now but wait. Wait and pray. Neither of them said very much—Elliot because he seemed to be lost in all his own private misery, and Jane because she didn't want to intrude on it.

What could she say anyway? she wondered. He wouldn't accept any of the platitudes they handed out daily to the relatives of the grievously ill patients they treated. He knew them all too well. Knew them for what they were.

A desperate attempt to give hope when all too often there was none.

Oh, please, don't let her die, Jane prayed. Take anything else from me—I'll willingly give up anything else—but, please, let her be all right, because I don't think either of us will survive if she dies.

It was almost two hours before the door to the waiting room opened and Elliot immediately sprang to his feet when he recognised the paediatric surgical consultant.

'How...how is she?' he said raggedly.

'She'll make it, Elliot.' The consultant smiled. 'Now that we've repaired the damage to her stomach she's not leaking blood any more and her BP and pulse are going up. She's not out of the woods yet by any means, but her heart's strong, and she's a tough little girl.'

'There's no sign of shock, no indication of—?'

'Elliot, she'll be fine. I would stake my professional reputation on it. And before you ask,' the consultant continued, 'we did a CAT scan as well, and there's no sign of any brain damage.'

Elliot let out the breath he'd clearly been holding, then reached out and clasped the consultant's hand. 'Thank you. I know that's a totally inadequate thing to say, but thank you.'

'Hey, it's part and parcel of the St Stephen's service.' He grinned. 'We've transferred her to IC, so if you want to go up to see her one of my nurses will take you.'

Swiftly Jane and Elliot followed the nurse through the labyrinth of corridors towards Intensive Care, but when they reached the door, the nurse paused.

'You're going to see a lot of tubes and paraphernalia,' she said gently. 'It's standard procedure in a case like this so, please, don't get upset. And don't expect her to recognise you. She's been pretty heavily sedated.'

They both nodded, but even though Elliot was a special

registrar, accustomed to dealing daily with life-threatening cases, Jane knew that nothing had prepared him for the sight of his daughter wired and tubed, breathing through a ventilator.

'She's so small, Jane,' he said huskily. 'So very small.'

'And you heard what the consultant said,' she replied firmly. 'She's strong, and she's tough. She'll make it.'

He didn't answer, and she put her arm around his shoulders.

He looked awful, and she couldn't blame him. She'd felt quite sick herself when the nurse had led them into the unit and she'd seen Nicole, but for Elliot it was different. This was his daughter. The child he hadn't even known he'd had until a few weeks ago, and he'd grown to love her, to need her as much as she needed him.

'Elliot, I know she looks horrendous, but most of the damage is superficial,' she continued, willing him to believe her. 'OK, so she's sustained fractures, and it will take time for them and her stomach to heal, but they *will* heal.'

He didn't reply. He simply continued to stare down at his daughter as though he wasn't even seeing her. Shock, her professional mind diagnosed. It affected people in different ways. Some people couldn't stop talking, others retreated into silence.

'Elliot, she *will* be all right,' she repeated, putting her other arm round him and holding him tightly. 'Your daughter will be just fine.'

And this time he managed a crooked, lopsided smile. 'Yes, I know. My...my daughter will be just fine.'

They stayed in Intensive Care for over an hour, even though both the cardiology specialist and the paediatric consultant urged them to go home, to get some sleep. But Elliot wouldn't move, and no one had argued with him.

'Are you coming home now?' Jane asked after he'd

checked yet again with IC's night staff to make sure there was no change in Nicole's condition.

'I thought I might go down to A and E, thank Charlie and the rest of the team—'

'Elliot, they won't expect it,' she protested, 'and you're just about dead on your feet.'

'It won't take me a minute—'

'Then we'll go together—'

'No! I mean, you look completely shattered,' he continued as she gazed at him in surprise. 'I'll get you a taxi, and I won't be long, I promise.'

She debated arguing with him, then gave it up as a lost cause. 'OK, but keep that promise—no sneaking back up again to IC. You heard what the nurses said. Nicole's sleeping soundly, there are no complications, and what you need is sleep.'

He nodded but when he went down to A and E he didn't go into the treatment room but went instead into his own office where a duplicate set of the case notes of all the patients who had been treated that day were stored.

Slowly he sat down at his desk, picked up Nicole's file from the in-tray, and opened it.

The results of all the tests Charlie had ordered were there. The X-rays, the CBC, the blood tests. Each and every one of them was neatly typed now in black and white, and he stared at the words and figures, hoping he might have misheard Richard Connery, but knowing now that he hadn't.

Nicole's blood type was AB. His own was O, and Donna's had been A.

No matter how many times he might reread the notes, hoping that the evidence before him would somehow miraculously change, there was no way it was going to change. Nicole wasn't his daughter. There was no way on earth that the lovely little girl lying upstairs in Intensive Care could possibly be his.

CHAPTER NINE

'CHARLIE, are you trying to tell me you've somehow managed to lose a patient?' Jane demanded.

'Not lost, exactly, no.' The SHO grinned ruefully. 'More sort of temporarily mislaid.'

Jane shook her head. 'I'm sorry, but you're going to have to be a lot more specific than that. This patient you've temporarily mislaid…'

'I sent her off to the toilets over an hour ago to provide me with a urine sample, and I've just realised I haven't seen her since. Look, I've been really snowed under, OK?' he continued as Jane's eyebrows rose. 'There was that bloke with angina, the toddler who'd swallowed a battery—'

'OK, OK. What did she look like?'

'Huge—damn near 120 kilos—and suffering from what I very strongly suspect is a bad case of indigestion.'

'I remember.' She nodded. 'Have you looked in the ladies' loos to check if she's still in there?'

'Jane, I can hardly simply walk into the ladies' toilets—'

'Why not?' she protested. 'Good grief, Charlie, considering you've probably seen more of most women's private anatomies than their own husbands, I'd have thought going into one of their toilets would be a doddle.'

'But that's different,' he murmured uncomfortably. 'Look, couldn't you or one of the other nurses check it out for me?'

And she laughed, and shook her head, but she did.

'Goodness only knows how long the poor woman would have been stuck in that cubicle if Charlie hadn't asked me

about her,' she told Elliot some time later. 'I feel so sorry for her. Jammed between the door and the toilet, far too embarrassed to call for help. She was absolutely mortified.'

'I'll bet,' he replied, his lips twitching. 'And it must have been even worse when you had to call out Maintenance to take the door off its hinges to get her out.'

'Elliot, it's not funny,' Jane chastised, desperately trying to suppress her own instincts to laugh. 'I doubt if she'll ever darken our doors again.'

'Not that particular door for sure,' he observed, his blue eyes dancing. 'According to Maintenance, it's only fit for firewood now.'

She bit down hard on her lip but it didn't help and a peal of laughter came from her.

He laughed, too, and a wave of love and tenderness welled up inside her when she saw it. It was so good to see him laugh. There'd been precious little laughter in his face during these last few weeks.

When Nicole had first been injured Elliot had haunted the IC unit, barely taking time to eat, far less sleep, and even now that she'd been transferred into the children's medical ward he still hadn't relaxed. He still looked as though he carried the worries of the world on his shoulders.

It was inevitable, of course. With Nicole improving daily, and no necessity to worry about her health any more, some form of reaction was bound to kick in. The realisation of how close he'd come to losing his daughter. The knowledge he now possessed of just how very fragile life was, and how easy it could be to lose someone you loved, especially a young, innocent child.

'Nicole was grumbling like mad when I dropped by to visit her this morning,' Jane commented, trying to keep the mood light. 'Apparently, she's decided hospitals are boring.'

He smiled. 'That's a good sign. Once a patient begins to find the hospital boring, it's a sure sign they're on the mend.'

'I know, but the trouble is, she really *does* think hospitals are boring,' Jane said, chuckling,' so I'm afraid it doesn't look as though she's going to be following in her father's footsteps when it comes to choosing a career.'

The smile faded from his eyes. 'She might. She might well follow exactly in her father's footsteps.'

There was a sadness about his face, a wistfulness she didn't understand, and gently she put her hand on his arm.

'Elliot, you do *know* that Nicole is going to be all right, don't you? Everybody's really pleased with her—the surgical reg, the medical reg, orthopaedics. She's made wonderful progress since her accident—'

'I know.'

Did he? Did he *really* know? Somehow she didn't think he did, and she tried again. 'Elliot, if there's something worrying you, something about Nicole—'

'Of course there's not,' he interrupted quickly. 'What on earth gave you that crazy idea?'

And perhaps she would have agreed with him—acknowledged that it was a crazy idea—if she hadn't seen, just for the merest second, a flicker of complete panic appear in his eyes.

But what in the world could Elliot possibly be so worried about? she wondered in confusion as a paramedic appeared with a young girl in a wheelchair, followed by what had to be the girl's white-faced parents. It didn't make any sense. It didn't make any sense at all.

'Her name's Louise,' the paramedic declared, guiding the wheelchair into cubicle 4. 'Eleven years old with what looks to be a fractured right arm and a very bad gash to her face. She was getting off a bus outside her home when she was knocked down by a car.'

'And it's the first time I've ever let her go anywhere on her own,' the girl's mother said tearfully. 'She wanted to go into town, you see, to buy one of those CD things for her birthday. She badgered and badgered me to let her go, and I thought she'd be all right—'

'Kelly, could you take Louise's parents through to one of our private waiting rooms, please?' Elliot interrupted smoothly, beckoning to the student nurse.

'And we made sure she went to all the road safety lessons, Doctor,' the girl's father continued, clutching his wife's hand as though it were a lifeline. 'We're not like some parents, letting her roam the streets to all hours. In fact—'

'Waiting room 2, please, Kelly,' Elliot said, and with obvious reluctance Louise's parents allowed the student nurse to usher them away.

'They panic a lot—my mum and dad,' Louise said, pulling a face the minute they were gone.

Elliot smiled. 'It goes with the job. How do you feel?'

'Sore,' she admitted as Jane carefully cut away her blouse. 'Sore and really, really stupid. I know I should have been watching out for traffic but I wanted to get home to try out my new CD player, and now it's wrecked—trashed. The car went right over it.'

'Better it than you,' Elliot observed, gazing critically at Louise's arm, which was not only very badly swollen but bent at an odd angle. Gently he lifted her hand and felt for her pulse. 'Can you move your fingers for me, please? Good...good. Now, can you feel that?' he added, lightly brushing her hand with his fingers.

'It tickles.' She chuckled.

He was relieved that it did. Her arm might be fractured, but at least the tendons that supplied function to her hand weren't damaged in any way, neither were the blood vessels nor nerves.

'I'm afraid it looks as though you've definitely fractured your arm,' Elliot declared when he'd finished his examination. 'We'll send you along to X-Ray to confirm it—'

'You mean I'm going to have to wear one of those plaster cast things?' the girl protested, only to groan as Elliot nodded. 'But they're *gross*.'

'Perhaps, but think of all the autographs and rude comments you can have written on it.' Jane smiled.

The girl brightened immediately. 'It'll drive my teachers nuts—and my mum and dad. Great.'

'Are you going to suture yourself?' Jane continued, glancing across at Elliot. 'Or would you like me to page Plastics?'

He lifted the girl's chin into the light and surveyed her face with a frown. 'Get Plastics. I've seen what can happen to wounds like this when all the dirt embedded in them isn't removed, and they're much more skilled than I am at dealing with facial cuts.'

'You mean I'm going to be scarred?' Louise exclaimed, tears suddenly welling in her eyes.

'Of course you're not,' Elliot assured her. 'You're going to be fine—just fine. And now I'm going to leave you in Sister Halden's capable hands while I go and put your parents' minds at rest.'

'Tell them I'm OK, will you?' the girl called after him. 'If you don't they'll ground me until I'm thirty!'

Fifty more like, Elliot thought with an inward smile when he went into the waiting room and Louise's parents rose in unison, fear plain on their faces.

'You're absolutely positive there's nothing else wrong with her?' Louise's mother queried when Elliot explained the situation.

'Completely positive.' He nodded. 'Her arm will have to stay in plaster for about six weeks and her face will be sore for quite a while, but apart from that she's fine.'

The mother let out a muffled sob. 'I've told her time and time again to watch what she's doing when she's crossing the road, but the minute she's out of my sight... It's in one ear and straight out the other.'

'Kids, eh, Doctor?' Louise's father exclaimed, trying for a laugh that didn't come off. 'You think you've got it sussed when you get them past the baby stage—that you can finally start to relax—but the minute they learn to walk... Well, I don't have to tell you about it, Doctor. The nurse told us you're a father yourself.'

Yes, he was a father, he thought with a jagged twist of pain as he left the waiting room, or at least he had been until three weeks ago. Until he'd discovered that Nicole wasn't his.

Why had Donna done this to him? She must have realised she wouldn't get away with it. She must have known he would find out eventually, so why had she told him he had a daughter, allowed him to grow to love her, knowing that one day the rug would be pulled out from under his feet?

Had she hated him so much that she'd wanted to get back at him, or was it simply that there'd been so many men in her life that she didn't actually know who Nicole's father was?

'Everything OK, Elliot?' Floella asked curiously as she passed him.

Desperately he swallowed the bitter tears clogging his throat, and nodded. All right? No, nothing was ever going to be 'all right' ever again.

And he'd have to tell Jane, he realised, seeing her coming out of cubicle 7. She'd have to know eventually, but what would she say? Would she insist he must track down this mystery man, that Nicole's real father had the right to be given the opportunity to make contact with her if he wanted?

No!

The word was wrenched from somewhere deep inside him.

The man had no rights. OK, so his sperm had created Nicole, given her life, but he wasn't her father. He hadn't been there for the bad times as well as the good. He hadn't hugged her, and dried her tears, and made sure she went to bed at a reasonable hour whether she wanted to or not.

He wouldn't tell Jane. He wouldn't tell anyone. Nicole was his. He couldn't give her up. He *couldn't*.

'Is Elliot OK?' Floella frowned as Jane joined her by the whiteboard to check on the name and details of her next patient. 'Nicole hasn't had a relapse, has she?'

Jane shook her head. 'She's doing really well. In fact, the medical reg reckons if she keeps on progressing like this we might be able to take her home at the end of next week.'

'Home?' Floella repeated, her eyes fixed on her thoughtfully. 'You consider Elliot's flat your home now, do you?'

A faint tinge of colour crept across Jane's cheeks. 'No, of course I don't—'

'Then why haven't you moved back into your own flat while Nicole is in hospital? I mean, there's no reason for you to be staying there at the moment, is there?'

There wasn't, Jane thought in dismay, and she should have thought of that if she hadn't wanted to set every tongue in the hospital wagging.

'I thought… I mean, Elliot and I decided…' What possible reason could she give that Floella would accept? 'The thing is, Flo—'

'The thing is that you and Elliot are living together,' the staff nurse sighed. 'And I mean *living* together.'

Jane blushed scarlet. 'Flo—'

'Look, I'm not going to blab it all over the hospital if

that's what you're frightened of. All I want to know is, are you happy? Are you sure this is right for you?'

Unconsciously Jane's lips curved into a tender smile. 'Oh, yes. Yes, I'm sure.'

And she was sure. More sure than she'd ever been about anything in her life. Just to look up from the breakfast table and find Elliot's eyes upon her, so warm and unbelievably gentle. Just to have him hold her in his bed at night, not even making love. It was right, so right.

'You've really got it bad, haven't you?' Floella said dryly, watching her. 'Well, all I can say is good luck to you.'

'You mean, you're not going to tell me I'm a fool, that I'll live to regret it?' Jane asked, but to her surprise Floella shook her head.

'You know his track record as well as I do, but if you think it's going to work, that Elliot's ready to settle down now, then, like I said, good luck to you.'

Luck didn't come into it, Jane decided. Elliot loved her. OK, so maybe he hadn't told her that yet, but he did—she just knew that he did—and she loved him, and nothing and no one was ever going to change that.

Not even Elliot himself when he spent the rest of their shift behaving like the original bear with a sore head.

'Boy, but is he a little ray of sunshine today.' Richard grimaced after he'd received the sharp edge of Elliot's tongue for the third time that day. 'Any idea what's wrong?'

'Your guess is as good as mine,' Jane replied, groaning inwardly as she heard the wail in the distance of what sounded like the imminent arrival of more than one ambulance. 'All I know for certain is that any thought we might have had of getting away on time tonight has just flown out the window.'

She was right. There'd been a multiple pile-up on one

of the roads leading into London and every A and E unit in the city had to take its share of the casualties.

'I wouldn't want your job for all the tea in China, Sister,' one of the road traffic policemen said, watching her as she dashed from casualty to casualty, assessing their level of priority.

'I suppose it's one way of keeping fit,' she said with a grin, but she didn't feel much like laughing by the time they'd treated all of the casualties who'd been brought in.

'What was the final count at the finish?' Charlie asked wearily when they finally managed to make their way to the staffroom. 'Three DOAs, five to Theatre with suspected abdominal injuries and four fractures?'

'Three fractures,' Floella corrected him. 'We can't really count that fourth guy.'

Charlie frowned. 'But he was involved in the accident, wasn't he?'

'Only indirectly. The little ghoul was trying to take photographs of the scene when he fell down the embankment.'

'If I'd known that, he could have hopped his way back out again,' Elliot said grimly. 'Lord, but I'm bushed. What's the time?'

'Would you believe it's only half past six?' Jane smiled. 'Some people would consider that a reasonable time to be finishing work.'

'So would I if I hadn't been on duty for twelve hours,' he groaned. 'OK, folks, let's hit the road. I, for one, just want to go home and put my feet up. Are you coming, Jane?'

She nodded, but as he reached for his coat Kelly suddenly let out an apologetic gasp. 'I'm sorry, Elliot, but I've just remembered something. You had a personal phone call earlier this afternoon, but I'm afraid it completely slipped my mind.'

'Tell me about it tomorrow,' he said dismissively, walk-

ing towards the door. 'Phone calls—personal or otherwise—are the least of my priorities at the moment. What I want is a hot bath, a—'

'But it was your sister-in-law.'

He stopped dead, and Jane saw his shoulders stiffen. 'My sister-in-law?'

'Your ex, I suppose I ought to have said.' Kelly smiled. 'Mrs Michelle Bouvier. She wanted to talk to you but you were busy with that young girl who'd fractured her arm.'

'I remember,' he said, and as he turned to face the student nurse Jane saw that his face had gone quite white. 'What did she want ?'

'She said she was in London for a few days and would like to come to see you and Nicole. I told her about Nicole's accident, and what ward she was in—'

'You *told* her what ward Nicole was in?' Elliot exclaimed, his face suddenly taut with fury, his eyes blazing.

'She asked me, and I didn't think it was a secret,' Kelly faltered. 'She said she would probably come in and visit her today around six o'clock. I'm sorry—I didn't think I was doing anything wrong. I mean, she's Nicole's aunt—'

'Of course you didn't do anything wrong,' Jane said soothingly, shooting daggers at Elliot. The student nurse was on the brink of tears and she would have been pretty near the edge herself if Elliot had been glowering at her the way he was glowering at Kelly. 'Mrs Bouvier has a perfect right to know which ward her niece is in.'

'Like hell she has!' Elliot exploded the minute the student nurse hurried away, white-faced and still tearful, and the rest of the staff had followed, throwing puzzled glances at Jane. 'Who the hell does she think she is—swanning back from Peru, or Iran, or wherever she's been, and demanding to see my daughter?'

'Elliot, this is ridiculous,' Jane protested. 'Michelle is Nicole's aunt, so it's only natural she would want to see

her, especially as she's been in an accident. It's called family feeling.'

'Is it?'

'Of course it is! Elliot, this isn't like you,' she continued in confusion, seeing his expression. 'I know Donna hurt you very badly but, no matter what you might think of her, Michelle is the last direct link your daughter has with her mother, and I think you should be encouraging that link, not attempting to put up stupid and irrational barriers against it.'

He could see the disapproval and bewilderment in her eyes, but how to tell her he was frightened? Frightened that Donna might have told Michelle that Nicole wasn't his. Had she come to take her away from him, arguing she had more rights to the child than he did? And she did have more rights. She was Donna's sister, Nicole's aunt. He… He was nothing.

'Elliot…' The disapproval on Jane's face had turned to real concern. 'Elliot, what's wrong?'

It was the irony of the situation, he thought bleakly. The supreme, unutterable irony. He'd never wanted Nicole, would quite happily have palmed her off on Michelle a mere two months ago, but now…

His eyes caught sight of the treatment-room clock. It was a quarter to seven. Michelle would be there, in the medical ward, and swiftly he walked to the staffroom door.

'Where are you going?' Jane demanded.

'You said I ought to see Michelle,' he said grimly. 'Well, that's what I'm going to do!'

He'd liked Michelle the first time they'd met, Elliot remembered. He'd found her entertaining and witty, funny and kind. She hadn't changed a bit, and Nicole clearly liked her a lot, but now he discovered he didn't like her at all.

'Your daughter is quite charming, Elliot,' Michelle said as he and Jane led the way out of the medical ward, leaving Nicole surrounded by all the toys her aunt had brought her from Iran.

His daughter. He let out the breath he'd been holding from the minute he'd stepped into the medical ward, and sent up a silent prayer of thanks. She didn't know. Donna hadn't told her, and she didn't know.

'I confess it gave me quite a start to see how very like Donna she's become,' Michelle continued. 'My husband and I generally spent around six to eight months of every year on archaeological digs, you see,' she continued as Jane gazed at her in surprise, 'so I only ever saw Nicole occasionally, and it's amazing the difference six months can make to a child's appearance.'

'It is,' Jane agreed, heartily wishing Elliot would at least try to contribute to the conversation, instead of making it all too obvious that he wanted to leave. 'I'm sorry about your sister's death—'

'We were never very close,' Michelle interrupted, clearly seeing Jane's embarrassment. 'She had her world, and I had mine.'

'Quite,' Elliot declared tightly. 'And now if you'll excuse us, Michelle—'

'Elliot, I really would like to talk to you about Nicole,' she interrupted. 'Unfortunately I'm only going to be in London for a few days—Raoul is addressing an archaeological seminar in Paris on Thursday—so I wondered if I might come round to your flat later this evening—'

'It's been a long day, and I'm very tired, Michelle.'

'I appreciate that.' She nodded. 'It is not an easy job, being a doctor. In fact, I don't know how you manage to take care of Nicole—'

'I manage.'

The words were clipped, cold, and Michelle coloured.

Jane would have hit him if she'd been in Michelle's shoes.

OK, so his marriage to Donna had ended acrimoniously, but that didn't give him the right to be quite so unbelievably rude to her sister. She'd come with the very best of intentions, and a person would have had to be blind not to have noticed the way her eyes had stayed fixed on her niece throughout her visit, wistful and a little sad.

'Look, why don't you come round to the flat with us now?' she said quickly, and received a look from Elliot that would have killed. 'I'm afraid I can't promise you French cuisine, but it will give you and Elliot the opportunity to talk.'

'Oh, that would be lovely.' Michelle beamed. 'Thank you—thank you very much indeed.'

Jane didn't get any thanks from Elliot when they got back home. In fact, once Michelle was safely installed in the sitting room and Jane had gone into the kitchen to find something for them all to eat, he let fly with a number of comments about interfering women, and people taking too much upon themselves, which were no less effective from being hissed in an acid undertone in case Michelle should hear him.

'Elliot, I don't give a damn whether you're upset by the fact that I invited her or not,' Jane retorted as she slammed some meat into the microwave and took some ice cream out of the freezer. 'She didn't have to come all this way to see Nicole.'

'I don't know why she did.'

'*I* do,' she retorted. 'She came because she's clearly a very nice woman. She came because she wanted to see the only link she has left with her sister, and I'd have thought the very least you could have done was to be pleasant, and polite, and welcoming for one evening!'

She didn't know whether he took her comments to heart

or not. He was certainly less rude over dinner, but it wasn't by any stretch of the imagination a comfortable meal, and when it was finally over Jane got to her feet with relief.

'Why don't you both go through to the sitting room while I make some coffee?' she suggested.

'That would be very nice.' Michelle smiled, but Elliot, Jane noticed, didn't.

In fact, clear panic appeared in his eyes, but there was no way she was going to come to his rescue by suggesting he might like to help her with the coffee. Michelle had said she wanted to talk to him, and he was damn well going to talk to her whether he wanted to or not.

It wasn't the talking that bothered him, Elliot thought grimly when he obediently took Michelle through to the sitting room, it was what his ex-sister-in-law wanted to talk about. Something told him he wasn't going to like it, and it didn't take him long to discover that he'd been right.

'You've done a wonderful job with Nicole,' Michelle declared as soon as she sat down. 'Better than anyone could have expected in the circumstances.'

'I'm glad you think so,' he replied warily, knowing there was a 'but' to come, and there was.

'When the news finally reached me in Iran of Donna's death, I'm afraid it didn't come as any great surprise,' Michelle sighed. 'She always lived life in the fast lane, and a car crash... There was a certain inevitability about it. What did surprise me, however, was hearing she had entrusted Nicole into your care.'

'She is my daughter—'

'A daughter you knew nothing about until two months ago,' Michelle interrupted gently. 'A daughter who must have turned your life upside down.'

'She's made it livelier, certainly,' Elliot admitted, 'and I don't know how I would have managed without Jane—'

'Exactly,' Michelle said. 'You're a doctor, never know-

ing from one day to the next what emergency might come up, which is why Raoul and I have a suggestion to make. We'd like to take Nicole, give her a home.'

'No—no way!'

'Elliot, it makes sense,' Michelle insisted. 'It can't be easy for you, trying to juggle your work with taking care of a child.'

'It wouldn't be easy for you either,' he said. 'You and Raoul spend more than half of each year in the back of beyond. What would you do with Nicole then? Put her in a boarding school? No, Michelle, the answer's no.'

'Of course we wouldn't put her in a boarding school,' she protested. 'We'd take her with us. We could engage a tutor—'

'But—'

'Elliot, we've no children of our own—I can't have any,' Michelle said, her eyes fixed on him, large, pleading. 'We would love her, give her a good home. I know you're her father, but you're a single man, and as a single man you can't possibly give her the love and attention Raoul and I could.'

'Michelle—'

'She needs a mother, Elliot, and you're not asking me to believe that when you first heard of Nicole's existence you didn't wish there was somewhere else she could go rather than to you. Somewhere you knew she'd be loved and well taken care of.'

He had, but that had been then, this was now.

'It is very kind of you to be concerned about my daughter's welfare,' he said tightly as the sitting-room door opened and Jane came in, carrying a tray of coffee and biscuits, 'but there's no need for you to be. Yes, I'm a single man at the moment, but not for much longer.'

'You're getting married?' Michelle said faintly. 'To whom?'

Well, there was only logical answer to that. Only one woman in the world he would ever want to marry. 'To Jane, of course. Jane and I are getting married.'

'I see,' Michelle murmured, disappointment plain in her voice. 'Then I suppose congratulations are in order—to both of you.'

Elliot smiled, and if Jane looked completely stunned he wasn't surprised. He had rather sprung it on her.

'So when's the happy day?' Michelle continued.

'We haven't set a date yet but you can rest assured it will be soon. You were right when you said Nicole needed a mother. She does, and Jane's marvellous with children— the very best, in fact.'

'Is she?' Michelle said.

'Oh, absolutely.' Elliot nodded, then grinned across at Jane who was sitting silently in the corner of the room. 'Nicole adores her. In fact, even if I wanted to marry someone else I think she'd have one or two things to say about it!'

'I see. Well, it sounds like a very sensible arrangement all round,' Michelle said grudgingly.

'Doesn't it?' He beamed.

Michelle didn't stay long after that. She kissed Elliot and Jane on both cheeks, promised to visit them and Nicole when she was next in London and left.

'Thank God, that's over,' Elliot declared with relief, the minute she had gone. 'Let's hope she doesn't visit London very often.'

'Oh, I thought she was very informative,' Jane said evenly. 'In fact, I thought the whole evening was very informative.'

'Really?' he said in surprise. 'In what way?'

'The surprising news that you and I are getting married for a start,' she replied, her voice curiously cold.

A deep wash of colour flashed across his cheeks. 'Jane,

I'm sorry about that. I really should have asked you first, but—'

'You just assumed I'd say yes. You thought, Good old Janey, she always agrees to everything, so why not this, too?'

There wasn't a trace of amusement in her face, not a glimmer of a smile in her grey eyes, and the colour on his cheeks darkened to crimson.

'Of course I didn't think that. I intended to take you somewhere romantic to pop the question, but Michelle was hassling me—'

'She wasn't hassling you, Elliot, she was concerned about Nicole,' she interrupted, her face white, taut. 'Concerned that you might not be able to look after her properly.'

'She had no business to be concerned,' he said irritably. 'I love my daughter—'

'So much that you're prepared to do just about anything for her, including marrying me,' Jane finished for him, her voice breaking slightly.

'*No!*' he protested. 'Dammit, Jane, I want to marry you because I *love* you. You heard what I said to Michelle—'

'Oh, yes, I heard,' she replied, anger giving her strength. 'It would be so sensible to marry me. I'm marvellous with children, and Nicole likes me. You don't want a wife, Elliot. You want a surrogate mother for your daughter and, much as I love her, I think I deserve more from a marriage than that.'

'Jane, you've misunderstood, got hold of the wrong end of the stick—'

'I don't believe you.'

He looked into her face and it was cold and forbidding. Hiding all the pain and heartbreak that she felt.

'Jane—'

'You'd better answer that,' she declared as the phone began to ring. 'It could be important.'

'*This* is important,' he exclaimed. 'Jane, I love you, and I want to marry you.'

'It might be the hospital. Something to do with Nicole.'

He stared at her, indecision plain on his face, then walked quickly over to the phone and lifted it.

'It was one of the night staff,' he informed her when he'd taken the call. 'They need my help.'

'You'd better go, then, hadn't you?' she replied, turning on her heel, only to pause. 'I won't be here when you get back, Elliot. I'll pack my bags while you're away and leave tonight.'

'But you can't go!' he protested. 'What about me—what about Nicole?'

She hardened her heart, though it cost her everything. 'She's not my responsibility, Elliot. She's yours. She's your daughter.'

CHAPTER TEN

'BURNS case, Sister!' a paramedic called as he and his colleague slammed open the doors of the treatment room and wheeled their casualty into the first empty cubicle. 'Injuries to face, upper torso and arms. BP 90 over 70, cardiac output down thirty per cent, and you're never going to believe how the guy got himself in this state!'

'Go on—surprise me,' Jane sighed, beckoning to Floella for help.

'He was filling his lawnmower with petrol and smoking at the same time.'

'He was doing *what*?' Jane gasped in disbelief as she and Floella swiftly began cutting off the young man's charred and burnt clothing.

'I know, I know,' the paramedic said. 'You wouldn't believe how many idiots there are out there in the world, Sister.'

Oh, but she would, she thought sadly as she noticed Elliot striding towards them, and she had just joined their ranks.

No, not joined. She was so stupid she could probably have qualified as a founder member.

Floella had tried to warn her, but had she listened? Oh, no, not her. She'd known better. She'd known different. Just as she'd thought when he'd held her in the darkness of the night and told her she was beautiful, special, that he'd meant he loved her. Just as she'd believed when he'd said he'd never met anybody like her that he'd meant they would have a future together. But all the time he'd simply been thinking about Nicole.

170

And the wretched thing was that she had actually wanted him to grow to love his daughter. Had longed for him to see what a great gift he'd been given. But she couldn't marry him for Nicole. No matter how much she loved the little girl, to know that Elliot only wanted to marry her because of Nicole… No, she couldn't do it. She simply couldn't.

'Haemaccel drip, and lactated Ringer's solution to counteract shock,' Elliot ordered, taking in the situation at a glance.

Swiftly Jane set up the IV lines while Floella inserted a Foley catheter into the young man's bladder to check for signs of the presence of haemoglobin.

'Singed nasal hair indicative of inhalation burns, Elliot,' Floella announced.

'OK, get me a sputum sample, and I want a full colour check on the urine in that catheter. BP and pulse, Jane?' he continued, turning to her.

'Eighty-five over sixty, pulse fast. Respiration becoming very laboured.'

She was already holding out an endotracheal tube to him, but she wasn't looking at him. She hadn't looked him in the eye since the night she'd walked out of his flat almost two weeks ago, and it was driving him crazy.

Anger he could have dealt with, recriminations he thought he could have handled, but being ignored, being shut out of her life, gave him no weapons to fight back with. None at all.

'I want a chest X-ray, Jane,' he declared the minute he'd eased the tube past the young man's vocal cords and down into his trachea.

'Already organised.'

'And the burns unit—'

'I've paged them already.'

Of course she had. Jane was the consummate profes-

sional. Jane was the woman he loved, and he'd messed it up completely.

How could he have been so stupid? Taking it for granted that she must love him as much as he loved her, that she'd want to marry him. Yet he'd told Michelle they were getting married, so arrogant, so sure of himself and so desperate to ensure his ex sister-in-law could stake no claim on Nicole.

No wonder Jane had been angry. No wonder she'd turned him down flat. What woman would accept a proposal of marriage under those circumstances? A woman needed to know she was loved for herself. And he did love her, he thought, feeling his heart contract as he stared across at her white, drawn face. Loved her more than he could ever have believed possible, and yet now she would scarcely give him the time of day.

'Urine in the Foley catheter very dark, Elliot,' Floella reported.

'OK, give him a diuretic with mannitol to counteract it,' he ordered. 'We don't want his kidneys packing in. Not with fifteen per cent burns.'

'BP 90 over 60,' Jane murmured. 'IV's running smoothly, no signs yet of hypovolaemic shock.'

'Keep a check on the ECG reading,' he said. 'And let me know if it changes at all.'

He hadn't needed to give the order. Nothing escaped Jane's attention. Nothing to do with work, that was.

Somehow he had to get her to talk to him. Even more importantly, somehow he had to get her to listen. But how?

The only thing she would discuss with him was work, and even that was in clipped monosyllables. If she wouldn't talk to him, how could he convince her that he wanted to marry her because he loved her and not because he'd wanted a surrogate mother for his daughter?

'BP 95 over 60,' Jane observed. 'I think we could hand over to Burns now.'

She was right, they could.

'Good work, both of you,' Elliot said when the burns unit had ferried their casualty away.

Floella smiled, but for all the reaction Jane gave he might just as well have saved his breath. He gazed at her impotently.

What he wanted to do was stride across the cubicle, grab her by the shoulders and shake her senseless. What he actually did was clear his throat tentatively. 'It must be about time for a coffee-break. Care to join me, Jane?'

'Thank you, but I have requisition forms to fill in,' she replied, her voice even, neutral.

'Couldn't you leave them until later?' he asked, all too aware of the pleading note in his voice and that Floella was glancing thoughtfully from him to Jane and back again but no longer giving a damn. 'I'm sure you could do with a big dose of caffeine first.'

'Like I said, thank you, but I really must get on with the forms,' she replied, and walked away without a backward glance.

He didn't stand a chance, he thought as he stared after her, his eyes tracing the outline of her back, noticing that she had lost weight, that her uniform no longer fitted quite so snugly. Unless he could show her, prove to her, that she could trust him, that he loved her for herself and not simply for what he needed her to be, he didn't stand a chance.

'Why don't you just leave her alone?'

He turned to see Floella glaring up at him, and sighed. 'Flo, you don't understand—'

'Oh, I understand only too well,' she snapped. 'You just couldn't resist it, could you? Jane living in your flat, right

under your nose. You just had to come on to her to see how far you could get.'

'Flo—'

'Well, you've had your fun, broken her heart, and now I want you to leave her alone,' she continued icily. 'If you don't… Well, all I can say is you're going to be sorry. Jane has a lot of friends at St Stephen's who won't take kindly to you messing her around.'

'Dammit, I am *not* messing her around!' Elliot raked his hands through his hair. 'Flo… Flo, I want to marry her. I've asked her to marry me, but she's turned me down flat.'

'You've asked her to… She's turned you down?' Floella gasped. 'But Jane—she loves you. Why in the world would she turn you down?'

His face tightened. 'I made a bit of a mess of my proposal.' That was the biggest understatement of the year, he thought, cringing inwardly as he remembered what he'd said. 'She misunderstood…got completely the wrong idea—'

'But how can you possibly mess up a proposal?' Flo interrupted, bewildered. 'Even an idiot could get that right.'

'Not this idiot, Flo,' he said grimly. 'This idiot really screwed it up, and now she won't even talk to me.'

Or answer any of my phone calls, he thought ruefully, and all the letters he'd sent had been returned unopened. In desperation he'd even gone round to her flat, but she'd shut the door on him, and when he'd point blank refused to go away she'd got one of her neighbours, a big burly guy with tattoos up his arms, who'd told him in no uncertain terms that if he didn't remove himself pretty sharpish his features would shortly be rearranged.

'What am I going to do, Flo?'

'You're asking me for advice?' She shook her head.

'You're the big charmer, Elliot, you figure it out. But figure it out soon. I hate to see Jane unhappy, so beg, plead—do whatever it takes—but sort it out.'

He sighed as he walked into cubicle 3. He would quite happily have begged and pleaded for all he was worth if he'd thought it would have got him anywhere, but he knew that it wouldn't.

He'd blown it. He'd met and fallen in love with the one girl in the world who could have made him happy, and he'd blown it good and proper. There was no way back now, and he was just going to have to live with it.

'I hear on the hospital grapevine that Nicole's being discharged next week,' Charlie commented as Jane binned the soiled swabs they'd used on their last patient, a nervous eighteen-year-old with a bad gash on his foot. 'That's great news.'

'It's wonderful, isn't it?' Jane smiled. 'We—that is, Elliot was hoping she'd be discharged last week, but she had a slight infection at the last minute and they decided to keep her in for just a few more days to be on the safe side.'

Charlie nodded, pulled off his surgical gloves, stared at them awkwardly for a moment, then clearly made up his mind. 'You'll be moving back in with Elliot again, then? I mean, I understand his mother's not due back from Canada for another two weeks.'

Jane closed the disposal unit with a bang. 'No, I won't be moving back in.'

Charlie eyed her sideways. 'But Nicole... Won't she need you there to look after her?'

'Whether she does or doesn't isn't really my concern,' she said, striving to sound dismissive and knowing she was failing quite miserably. 'I have my own life to lead, Charlie, and I can't be Nicole's nanny for ever.'

'Two weeks doesn't sound very much like for ever to me,' he pointed out.

'I have other commitments,' she declared, the redness of her cheeks betraying the lie. 'And I'm sure Elliot can hire a private nurse or a nanny for two weeks.'

'Yes, but—'

'Dammit, Charlie, why does everyone expect good old Janey to ride to the rescue every time?' she flared. 'I'm sick to death of being good old Janey! I want to be selfish, think-about-yourself-for-once Janey!'

The SHO gazed at her uncomfortably. 'And so you should. If anyone deserves some pampering, it's you. But I just thought... Nicole...'

'Charlie, she isn't my responsibility! I helped out for two months. Isn't that enough? Haven't...haven't I given enough?'

Her voice broke on not quite a sob, and Charlie put his hand out to her, his big, hearty face almost as red as hers. 'I'm sorry. I... Look, Jane, I didn't mean to... I wouldn't... I'm really sorry.'

She drew in a shuddering breath. 'I'm sorry, too. Sorry for yelling at you, but...'

'I understand.'

And he did, she thought as she stared up at him. He understood much more than she wanted him to.

'Does Nicole know you won't be there when she gets home?' he asked gently.

Jane shook her head, blinking away the tears that were forming in her eyes. She hadn't stopped visiting Elliot's daughter in Ward 12. She could no more have stopped than fly, but when Nicole had talked excitedly about the things the three of them would do when she got home she'd said nothing. It was cowardly, and she knew it, but she couldn't tell her. It was bad enough knowing she might never see

her again, without having to answer questions she didn't want to answer.

'Jane... You and Elliot. There's no hope that you and he...?'

He didn't have to explain what he meant and she smiled a little tremulously. 'Not a hope in the world, Charlie.'

He sighed. 'That toast I made when Barbara and I took you out to dinner—when I wished you every happiness. It doesn't look much as though it's going to come true, does it?'

'Hey, worse things happen at sea,' she declared with a brightness that moved him more than he could say. 'And now we'd better get on. The waiting room's not getting any emptier while we stand around here chatting.'

It wasn't, Charlie thought as he watched her go, but he wished there was something he could do. It didn't seem fair for him and Barbara to be so happy, while Jane...

He sighed deeply as he saw her disappearing into cubicle 1. It wasn't fair but, then, life, as you very quickly discovered if you worked in A and E, was frequently very unfair.

Elliot didn't think life was particularly fair either when Charlie collared him outside cubicle 8 some time later.

'Charlie, I hardly think a fractured ankle is something requiring my expertise. If you can't see to it yourself—'

'Of course I can deal with it,' the SHO interrupted, 'but the guy says he thinks he knows you.'

Elliot frowned. 'What did you say his name was again?'

'Shaw. Adam Shaw.'

It rang no bells, but obediently Elliot followed Charlie into the cubicle, to be greeted by a wide smile of recognition from the red-haired man in his early thirties sitting awkwardly on the edge of the trolley.

'It *is* the same Elliot Mathieson,' he beamed, 'and looking twice as ugly as you did eight years ago!'

'I'm sorry, but—'

'Rawley Amateur Rugby Club,' Adam Shaw continued helpfully. 'I played prop forward and you were one of the flash boys on the wing. We did a lot of charity matches to raise money for one of the local hospices.'

Elliot grinned. 'I remember now. You borrowed my kit bag at the end of the last season and never gave it back, you thief.'

'Didn't I?' Adam Shaw frowned, then winked up at Charlie. 'Never try to put one over on this bloke. Memory like an elephant—never forgets anything.'

'I'll remember.' The SHO chuckled.

'How's that beautiful wife of yours?' Adam Shaw continued, turning to Elliot again. 'Bonnie, was it?'

The laughter disappeared from Elliot's face. 'Donna. Her name was Donna. We were divorced five years ago, and she was killed in a car crash three months ago.'

'Oh, hell, I'm sorry. I didn't know, never heard on the grapevine. Any family?'

'A daughter.'

'Then at least you have something to remember her by,' Adam replied.

Oh, he did, Elliot thought sadly, but not in the way the whole world would ever imagine.

'Are you married yourself?' he asked, anxious to change the subject.

'Married, and divorced, too, I'm afraid,' Adam replied ruefully. 'Bit of a disaster, actually. Brought it all on myself, of course. Never home, working all the hours God sent, trying to get ahead in my job. And the wife…she felt neglected, found someone else.'

'I'm sorry.'

'It happens. I see my kids occasionally, but it's not the

same. If you don't live with them, become just an occasional visitor, they move on, leave you behind.'

'I guess so,' Elliot murmured.

'Hold on to your kid,' Adam continued. 'Hold on to her, and if there's a girl in your life, hold on to her, too. I've learned the hard way that career, wealth, position, don't amount to anything if you haven't got a family to share it with.'

'He's got a point,' Charlie observed after Elliot had waved Adam goodbye with promises to keep in touch which they both knew would never be kept. 'In fact, it seems to me that you should have everything in your life now that any man could ever want. A lovely daughter, a girl like Jane.'

'Charlie—'

'She *is* a wonderful girl, you know,' the SHO continued doggedly. 'I don't think you could do better.'

'I'm sure you mean well, Charlie,' Elliot declared evenly, 'but my private life isn't really any of your business.'

He began to walk away but the SHO came after him. 'You're right, it isn't any of my business, but it seems to me that a man who's made a girl fall in love with him and then dumped her—'

'I haven't dumped her!'

'A man who's made a girl like Jane fall in love with him, and then dumped her—'

'Charlie, I *haven't* dumped her!'

'Is some kind of louse. I just wanted you to know that,' the SHO declared, 'and to let you know that I, for one, don't like it. I don't like it at all!'

And he swung round on his heel and walked away, leaving Elliot gazing after him, not knowing whether he wanted to laugh or go after the SHO and hit him.

Neither, he decided, as he saw Jane smiling at something

Floella had said, a smile that didn't reach her eyes, a smile that was a little wary and sad. He would do neither.

He would get her back, prove to her that he loved her, refuse to take no for an answer.

And what about Nicole? his mind whispered. Are you going to tell Jane that she's not yours?

One problem at a time, he told himself, noticing from the treatment-room clock that their shift was over. Tackle one problem at a time.

But his first problem was getting out of the door.

'Elliot, could I have a word?' Richard asked, waylaying him.

'Couldn't it wait until tomorrow?' Elliot replied, seeing Floella and Jane walk past him and out into the corridor, clearly making for the staffroom. 'I'm a little busy.'

'If I don't say this now I never will,' the junior doctor said firmly, then took a deep breath. 'Elliot, I know you're my boss, and I'm probably speaking out of turn here, but it's about Jane.'

'Why am I not surprised?' Elliot groaned. 'Go on, then, get it over with,' he continued as the junior doctor coloured. 'Tell me I'm the biggest louse of all time.'

'Well, frankly, I think you are, but that's not what I wanted to say to you,' Richard said determinedly. 'I just wanted to put you straight about something in case...well, in case you'd got hold of the wrong end of the stick. You might remember that I came round to your flat and Jane and I spent the whole evening in her bedroom.'

'Richard, could you please get to the point?' Elliot asked. 'Like I said, I'm in a hurry tonight.' And if I'm not fast, Jane will have left and another opportunity will have slipped through my fingers. 'Say what you want to say, and get it over with.'

To his frustration the junior doctor took another deep breath. 'I wanted you to know that nothing untoward oc-

curred between Jane and me that night. I was feeling a bit down, and Jane volunteered to cheer me up, to listen to my moans and groans.'

'Is that it?' Elliot demanded. 'Is that the end of your revelations?'

Richard flushed scarlet. 'I just thought you should know. I couldn't have lived with myself if it was my fault—my being there that night—you dumped her.'

Elliot opened his mouth, closed it again, struggled with his temper and eventually managed a small, tight smile.

'Thank you for sharing that with me, Richard, and now, if there's nothing else?' The junior doctor shook his head. 'Good. Then I'll bid you a very good night.'

And before the junior doctor could reply Elliot was off and running through the treatment-room doors, down the corridor and into the staffroom.

'Where's the fire?' Jane couldn't help but laugh as he all but fell in the door, red-cheeked and breathless.

'I wanted to talk to you.'

Her laughter died in an instant, and she pulled on her coat and reached for her bag. 'I'm sorry, but anything you want to say to me will have to wait until tomorrow. I'm off duty now, and all I want to do is go home.'

'Jane, it's important—'

'So is the shopping I have to do before I can go home,' she replied, walking to the door.

'Jane, it's about Nicole.' That stopped her in her tracks as he'd known it would.

'What about Nicole? I saw her this afternoon and she seemed fine.'

'She *is* fine,' he reassured her, hating himself for worrying her unnecessarily, but desperate situations called for desperate measures. 'Jane, I need to ask you a favour.'

She stiffened immediately. 'If you're going to ask me

to move back in with you until your mother comes home—'

'No, I'm not going to ask you that,' he interrupted. 'It wouldn't be fair.'

Like it had been really fair of him to allow her to fall in love with him, to let her believe that he loved her, too?

But she didn't say that. Instead, she said, 'What's this favour, then?'

'To talk to you about Nicole. To see if together we can come up with some plausible reason for you not being there when she gets home.'

'Elliot—'

'Jane, she loves you—you know she does—and she's going to be heartbroken if you just disappear out of her life without a word of explanation.'

She stared at him for a long moment. He looked tired, weary, and surely those deep creases on his forehead hadn't been there two weeks ago?

'OK. All right.'

She put down her bag and began taking off her coat, but he shook his head.

'I thought maybe we could talk at the flat. Jane, anyone could walk in while we're talking,' he continued quickly as she opened her mouth, clearly intending to protest. 'And I really think our private lives should remain just that, don't you?'

No need to tell her that all of A and E seemed to know that they had been lovers. No need to reveal that the only thing left private about their relationship was why it had ended.

'Jane, please,' he continued when she said nothing. 'For half an hour, that's all.'

He held his breath as she thought about that, then to his relief she nodded. 'OK. For half an hour.'

*   *   *

It was strange to be back, Jane thought as Elliot ushered her into the sitting room. Strange and familiar at the same time. The seat where she'd always sat in the evening, the coffee-table she and Nicole had played Scrabble on. It had only been two weeks, and yet it felt like a lifetime.

'Would you like a coffee—tea—something stronger?' he asked awkward, eager.

'I don't want to put you to any trouble.'

'It would be no trouble.'

'Coffee, then.' She managed a smile. 'Thank you.'

'I won't be a minute,' he said heartily, too heartily. 'Take a seat, make yourself comfortable.'

She couldn't. There were too many memories associated with this room. Nicole like a little white ghost on that first night. Nicole laughing and giggling as her father tickled her. Michelle Bouvier...

She slipped off her coat, and couldn't prevent a wry smile from curving her lips as she looked around for somewhere to put it. A little over two months ago her heart had sunk when she'd first seen Elliot's home, so pristine, so elegant, so intimidating. Now there were toys on practically every seat, books left lying where they'd been dropped.

'I didn't tidy anything away,' he murmured, clearly reading her thoughts as he came back into the sitting room. 'I thought...if I did that it would be as though I was accepting she was never coming back. I kept the hairbrush you left in the bathroom for the same reason.'

She turned from him quickly, unable to bear the naked plea she could see in his eyes. God knows how much she loved this man, would never love anyone else the way she loved him, but she mustn't let him see it or he'd use it, use her again.

'Nicole... You said you wanted to talk about Nicole.'

'Aren't you going to sit down?' he said softly.

She did. It helped a little. Made her feel less shaky, less vulnerable, more in control.

'About Nicole,' she began firmly, taking the cup of coffee from his outstretched hand. 'I think it would be simpler if we just told her I had to go away on a nursing course.'

He sat down, planted his elbows on his knees and fixed his eyes on her face. 'And when you don't come back after two weeks, what, then?'

'She'll be with your mother in Hampshire.'

'I'm not sending her to my mother,' he said. 'I'm keeping her with me.'

'But how will you manage?' she gasped. 'When you work nights, the weekends?'

'I'll get a nanny—a succession of nannies if need be—but she's staying in London with me.'

He watched her take this in, digest it.

'Then if she's going to be staying with you,' she replied, 'all I can suggest is you tell her I've been looking for a place of my own for a while, and that I've found one.'

'She'll be hurt—upset.'

'Elliot, no one ever said this was going to be easy.'

His eyes caught and held hers. 'It could be, if you'd listen to sense, believe that I love you, and marry me.'

She got to her feet quickly and headed for the door. 'I have to go.'

'Jane, Nicole loves you very much, and I know that you love her—'

'Elliot, don't,' she pleaded, whirling back to him, her eyes large pools of pain and distress. 'Please, don't. What you're doing—it isn't fair. Yes, I love your daughter, and I'm delighted—more than delighted—to see how much you care for her, but I can't marry you simply to give your daughter a mother.'

Can't, not won't. Can't meant there might yet be a

chance for him, that she might love him as much as he loved her.

He took a jagged breath and stepped forward. 'Jane, as God is my witness, I love you. Not as a mother for Nicole—'

'I won't listen to this,' she cried, putting her hands over her ears. 'I won't let you do this to me. It's blackmail! Working on my feelings, knowing how much I care for your daughter!'

He pulled her hands down and held on to them. 'Jane—'

'No! Elliot, your daughter is a wonderful girl, a lovely girl—'

'And she isn't mine.'

She stared at him open-mouthed for a second, then shook her head. 'You're not making any sense. Of course she's yours. Donna—'

'Lied,' he interrupted harshly. 'When Nicole had the accident, and we needed to do all those blood tests… She's Donna's daughter, Jane, but I'm not her father.'

She couldn't take it in, couldn't believe it. 'But why would your wife lie? She must have known paternity could easily be established.'

'I guess she never figured on an accident—the need for blood tests,' he said, his face white, taut. 'She probably hoped Nicole would be all grown up and married before anybody found out.'

'But if you're not Nicole's father, then who…?'

'God alone knows,' he said grimly. 'Perhaps he was some one-night stand whose name she couldn't remember afterwards, or maybe she'd slept with so many men that month she didn't have a clue.'

She shook her head, still dazed, still confused. 'But why would she say she was yours?'

'Perhaps she wanted to do one good thing in her life, knowing that if anything ever happened to her Nicole

would have security.' His mouth twisted bitterly. 'Or perhaps she wasn't that noble, and it was one last joke at my expense, dumping someone else's kid on me.'

She wrenched her hands free from his angrily. 'And is that how you feel? That Nicole was dumped on you?'

'*No*! She's my daughter, Jane. *Mine*. I don't give a damn about blood groups, she's *mine*.'

She stared up at him, frozen, stunned. He was crying. Cool, super-confident Elliot was crying, and she thought it was the most awful, heart-wrenching sound she had ever heard.

And suddenly she was crying, too, as hard as he was. Reaching for him, holding him tightly, trying to contain the sobs that racked his body.

'Why didn't you *tell* me? Oh, Elliot, why did you keep it to yourself? You should have *told* me, let me share it with you, let me help you!'

For a long time he couldn't answer, simply clung to her while she smoothed his hair back from his forehead and kissed him and murmured words that she hoped might give him some comfort, ease some of his pain.

'I didn't tell you because I thought you'd try to persuade me to track down Nicole's real father,' he said shakily at last. 'That you'd say it was the right thing to do.'

'Never!' she protested. 'Elliot, *you* are her father, the man she loves. Her real father could be anybody. Somebody horrible, somebody she would hate.'

'I couldn't give her up, Jane, not now,' he said, his voice cracking. 'Not now that I've grown to love her so much. She is my daughter, and always will be, even though we have no blood connection.'

'I know,' she whispered, holding on to him tightly, hot tears welling in her eyes again, only to feel dismay as he gently eased her away from him. 'Elliot…?'

'I know she will eventually have to be told the truth—

when she's older, a teenager—but I would like—I would very much hope—that we could both be there to tell her together.'

She wanted to say, yes, that she'd be there with him, but she couldn't.

'Elliot, I'm sorry—'

'Jane, even if you won't agree to marry me, even if all you'll ever let me have of you is what I have now—a shoulder to cry on—and not your love, I will still love you. I will *always* love you.'

'My love—you want *my* love?' she said, wanting to believe him, desperately wanting to believe him.

'Jane, I love you for the person you are, not because I want a mother for Nicole,' he said raggedly. 'I love you, and I love Nicole, and I don't want to lose either of you. And if that's selfish then, yes, I'm selfish, but I want both of you for the joy and happiness you've brought into my life.'

The tears in her eyes spilled over and down her cheeks. 'Oh, Elliot—'

'Jane, I love you so much that I'm trusting you with my future happiness. What I've just told you—you could use that knowledge, go to Michelle, tell her the truth, and that would mean I'd lose both of you. I'm putting all my future happiness in your hands.'

And he was, she realised, and it gave her the courage to say what she did.

'Elliot Mathieson, I have loved you since the first moment I set eyes on you.'

'You have?' he said, hope and uncertainty plain in his eyes.

She nodded.

'Then you'll marry me?' he said eagerly. 'You're saying, yes?'

'I'm saying yes, Elliot. I'm saying yes because I love you, and I love Nicole, and no matter what the future brings, we're in this together.'

MILLS & BOON®

Makes any time special™

Mills & Boon publish 29 new titles every month. Select from...

Modern Romance™   Tender Romance™

Sensual Romance™

Medical Romance™   Historical Romance™

MAT2

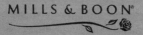